HIGH TIMES
GREATEST HITS
TWENTY YEARS OF SMOKE IN YOUR FACE
FROM THE EDITORS OF HIGH TIMES

St. Martin's Press New York

In the last big score (1974-1994) the war on marijuana, although lost from the first puff of smoke, has claimed over seven million victims arrested and imprisoned.

This book is dedicated to them.

And to the newest casualties who are still being arrested at the rate of two every minute for growing and smoking the same flowers that can bring some measure of relief to the millions of people who need but cannot get medical marijuana.

Printed in the U.S.A.

HIGH TIMES GREATEST HITS. Copyright © 1994 by Trans-High Corporation.
All rights reserved. No part of this book may be
reproduced or transmitted in any form or by any
means, electronic or mechanical, including
photocopying, without permission in writing from
the publisher except in the case of brief quotations
embodied in critical articles or reviews.
For information, address St. Martin's Press, 175 Fifth Avenue,
New York, N.Y. 10010.

Editor: Steven Hager
Art Director: Frank Max
Managing Editor: Alison Jones
Copy Editor: Gabe Kirchheimer
Photo Editor: Malcolm MacKinnon
Part 6 edited by Peter Gorman
Part 7 edited by Steve Bloom
Cover photograph by Andre Grossmann
"The Fabulous Furry Freak Brothers and the
Mysterious Visitor," (page 45) courtesy
Fabulous Furry Freak Brothers by
Gilbert Shelton, © Rip Off Press, Inc.
20th Anniversary Hemp 100 (color section)
compiled by John Holmstrom, art by Flick Ford

Library of Congress Cataloging-in-Publication Data

High times greatest hits / the editors of High times.
    p.   cm.
ISBN 0-312-11134-7
1. Popular culture—United States.   2. Drugs.   3. Drug abuse-
United States.   4. United States—Social life and customs—1971—
I. High times.
E169.12.H53   1994
306.4'0973—dc20   94-424
                                                             CIP

First edition: May 1994
10   9   8   7   6   5   4

INTRODUCTION
by Steven Hager

In its early years, HIGH TIMES' biggest threat to survival was keeping pace with its own runaway success. Then, after the death of founder Tom Forçade in 1978, the magazine was racked by internal power struggles, and foundered through several changes in identity. But by the late 1980s, governmental harassment proved to be HIGH TIMES' greatest threat.

Throughout the past two decades, however, the magazine has had one important asset on its side: the truth about cannabis. Unfairly branded as a noxious weed with no beneficial uses, cannabis is, in fact, the most valuable and useful crop known to man, an important source of fiber, fuel, food and medicine. Although HIGH TIMES has carefully documented these facts for twenty years, the national media has always chosen to ignore us. I hope this changes, and someday HIGH TIMES gets the credit it deserves.

In the past five years, HIGH TIMES has become the most politically active magazine in America. After publishing the industrial and environmental benefits of cannabis, the magazine went on the road to college campuses across the Midwest, spreading its message about hemp. That effort ignited what has become the most vital protest movement of the '90s.

The articles presented here were chosen to illuminate several sagas: First of all, Tom Forçade, the most overlooked influence on the counterculture, finally gets his due; Second, the hidden history of marijuana, the government's disinformation campaign against it, the changes in cultivation techniques, and the growing awareness of its many uses are all well-documented here; Third, the struggles within the legalization movement and the fall and rise of smoke-ins across America are told for the first time. Most of all, however, it is the story of the most notorious magazine in the world, a magazine that offended and provoked the most powerful forces in the land, and yet managed to survive two decades of repression with its values intact.

FOREWORD

by Thomas (Gary Goodson) "King" Forçade

The general public (us) has no idea who really owns, controls and manages *Time* magazine, the *Washington Post*, *The New York Times*, the three monopolistic TV networks, Random House, Simon & Shuster and so on. Many fine people work for the straight media, but as A.J. Leibling said, freedom of the press belongs to those who own one.

We own one, and that is an important point. After all, it was the media that made marijuana illegal! Their pot scare campaigns created the temporary popular support that made it politically expedient to outlaw marijuana.

Trans-High Corporation (THC—the parent company of HIGH TIMES) was started to bring new consciousness projects into reality, particularly projects within the media. As we stated some time ago, we have no particular interest in manufacturing rolling papers or hash pipes, or starting HIGH TIMES key clubs. We are mainly interested in opening up communication, providing access to information.

One of the first THC projects was HIGH TIMES magazine. It was a coldly conceived concept, there was nothing accidental about it, and we definitely expected it to succeed, eventually. Instead, it took off like a rocket, right from the beginning, and our main problem has been holding on. Holding on—to our personal identities, to our editorial independence, to our corporate independence, to reality, to our rapport and unique communication with our readers, to our sanity. Coping with the staggering business/financial/organizational problems caused by our rapid growth. Finding honest, competent, creative people to be the staff. And retaining our perspective amidst a barrage of publicity—all of it strangely favorable.

To outsiders, the HIGH TIMES "success story" appears to be a typical capitalist trip, with one or more individuals on top raking in tons of money to be used for buying Lamborghini sports cars, McIntosh stereos, penthouses, Peruvian flake, and sexual companionship that resembles the people in the cigarette ads as closely as possible. While we assure you that we at HIGH TIMES fully appreciate the value of hedonism (learned in part from that pioneering personal researcher in the field, Hugh M. Hefner), the fact is that THC is owned by a nonprofit trust fund and the staff makes very modest salaries indeed. Should we make any excess profits, they will be given to organizations concerned with social, cultural, political and economic change. We'd like to own McIntosh stereos, but other things are more important to us. Like putting out the best magazine imaginable. A magazine that has always been far more than a "dope" magazine. Lately, as you have seen, we have been broadening our editorial scope even more. It is obvious that our readers want to hear about a broad range of contemporary and historical subjects. We have no desire to be limited to being the magazine of substances that people put in their mouth.

Making money is not enough for us. Money and political "power" (often a goal in publishing) strike us as irrelevant. We are faced with a future that needs help. We know that as far as the future is concerned, we are playing for keeps. Our goal is to go all the way, whatever that may bring.

Lines, #15, November 1976

CONTENTS

PART 1

Thomas King Forçade
LIVING AND DYING THE GREAT ADVENTURE

by Albert Goldman

OUR FOUNDER IN 1970.

November 16, 1978: A cold, gloomy day. A small boyish-looking man is lying on a rumpled bed in a loft in Greenwich Village. He's restless, depressed, obsessed with paranoid fears. The day before at the office, he scored a handful of ludes. They didn't cool him out. Now he wants to lapse into unconsciousness.

He asks his wife to bring him a Tuinal. "Try to sleep," she urges. "If you can't get to sleep in twenty minutes, I'll bring you a pill." "What time is it now?" he asks. "Twenty to one," she answers. "You'll hear from me in twenty minutes," he warns. Then, fully clothed in an old paisley shirt and blue jeans, he burrows under the covers.

Twenty minutes later, his wife is talking with a friend in an adjoining room. Suddenly, she hears a popping sound. It isn't a backfire. It sounds like it came from the bedroom. She opens the door and looks inside. Nothing appears amiss.

Her husband is still lying in bed, only he has moved over to her side. Then she notices a small round hole in his left temple and a pearl-handled .22 at his side. What rivets her attention is his hands. They are suspended before his chest, like a puppy begging. Instinctively, she reaches forward to still their trembling.

Thus was extinguished the most brilliant and fascinating mind ignited by the youth revolt of the '60s—Thomas King Forçade. Most people have never heard of Tom Forçade; yet he should have been world-renowned as a counterculture guru and drug culture mastermind. Even if you confine your attention to his most notable achievement, the founding of HIGH TIMES, the journal of drug hedonism, humor and adventure, Forçade should rate as one of the most innovative and resourceful figures in current-day journalism. His counterparts in an earlier generation, Hugh Hefner and Bob Guccione, are famous for having pulled the covers off sex in the mass media. Forçade pulled the covers off drugs in precisely the same manner. He took as many risks, made as many millions and sparked as many violent reactions as his famous rivals at comparable moments in their careers. Yet, when he blew out his brains at age 33, the media barely noticed his demise. *The New York Times,* which every year commemorates scores of obscure doctors, professors, actors and businessmen, could not bring itself to print an obituary of Tom Forçade.

The basic reason for this neglect is the fact that Forçade avoided publicity as relentlessly as most men seek it. Like a junior version of Howard Hughes, he spent his life in dreary holes and corners, cutting deals, giving orders and engaging in the sort of outlaw enterprises that can put you in prison for many years. Forçade had a lot to hide. He was a hippie Robin Hood who gave the money he made breaking the law to those whom the law would have broken. A complex and splintered personality, a man whose behavior was sometimes distorted by spells of madness, he was not the sort of person who permits anyone to comprehend him fully. At most, after years of intimacy, you might qualify for a few glimpses of the face behind the mask.

My knowledge of Forçade commenced with an incident that was emblematic of his personality, combining as it did his love of persiflage and role-playing with his even greater passion for instructing the world in the mysteries of drugs and the moral and political issues that the drug controversy brings to focus. The time was the spring of 1975. I—an innocent in the ways of weed—had just received an assignment to write a piece on the New York drug underground. Having read in an early issue of HIGH TIMES a fascinating interview with a professional dope taster—a man who claimed that he was sent by drug syndicates to the growing areas to ascertain the quality of the crop—I determined to meet this mysterious figure and pick his brain. After prolonged negotiations, during which I learned that my authority went by the name of "Mike, the Marijuana Maven," I experienced at last the thrill of seeing the Exigente of the drug world walk into my living room.

At first glance the Maven looked like a wasted, blinking hippie scientist with a pale mushroom face and eroding hairline. He was engrossed in conversation as he stepped through the door, and he was engrossed in conversation many hours later when he exited. Never at any moment in that long evening did he stop talking. Nor were any of these words addressed especially to me. They came out of his mouth as they might have emerged from the speaker of a radio, low-keyed, perfectly phrased, and totally oblivious of whether they were being heard or ignored.

The only demand the Maven made was that my "researcher," Chic Eder (a tough, smart professional criminal recently released from prison), keep the speaker supplied throughout the night with an endless series of joints. The drugs were extracted from a zippered pill case containing a row of glass vials, each of which was filled with a different kind of exotic and costly marijuana. What was most remarkable was not the quantity of the drug that was rolled up and placed submissively in the Maven's hand but the fact that he virtually never took a drag. Joint after joint of Colombian, Oaxacan, Thai and Maui grass went up in smoke in the grasp of that small stained hand because the motor that powered the Maven's mouth never stalled long enough to allow him to put the butt between his lips.

I was spellbound by this performance not just because it filled my mind with vast amounts of unimaginable drug lore but because the Maven's rap emerged in a fascinating spiral of dialectic. Up and up a line of thought would climb, like the smoke from his smoldering joint; then, inevitably, at a certain point, like the coil in the smoke stream, the drift of the thought would reverse itself and start down in the opposite direction. After each of these elaborate mental somersaults, the Maven would pause for a moment and a sly, dissociative giggle would emerge from the side of his frozen face. Then, his eyes would blink, blink, blink, like a computer receiving a fresh set of signals, and he would be off again.

The next morning, when I lifted my woozy head off the pillow and switched on my tape recorder, I half-expected to find that my impression of this drug-saturated evening was highly distorted and that the Maven's wondrous rap, like fairy gold, had faded into hippie bullshit. The moment I heard that low, murmurous voice steadily paying out its endless line, I knew there had been no mirage. The Maven talked like a book. He had left me with pages upon pages of highly quotable material.

As I got deeper into the dope game, I soon came to realize that there was no such thing in this world as a professional dope taster. This was just one of those whimsical shucks that Forçade liked to strap on fools like me—a college professor for 20 years—or the kids who read HIGH TIMES as if it were the Bible of Hell. It wasn't all that long until I was informed that Mike, the Marijuana Maven, was really Tom Forçade, a shadowy figure with a long and fabulous past. Some people told me that he was a sinister government agent. Others that he was a heroic radical. What most intrigued me was the rumor that he was an audacious drug dealer and smuggler.

Finding out anything about Forçade was difficult. Even his connection with HIGH TIMES was kept very quiet. His name never appeared on the masthead. His appearances at the office were sporadic and broken by long absences. Once my first article on the drug world appeared—especially after it elicited a movie offer from Elliott Kastner—Forçade shifted in his attitude towards me, dropping his mask and offering to finance my first trip to Colombia, where I planned to go to the source of the golden stream that was pouring into America in the year 1976. It was at this moment that I got my first real insight into the way Forçade had created America's first journal of illicit drugs.

HIGH TIMES was conceived and produced in the same spirit as that in which a group of undergraduates would put together a college humor magazine. Though there were numerous writers, editors, art directors, eventually as many as 70 people working in the office, the whole enterprise, from the us-against-them editorials to the startlingly explicit articles on how to smuggle drugs to the lovingly fondled imagery of World War II airplanes, fast speedboats and S/M Punk Rock geariness, was the spiritual emanation of Tom Forçade. Ed Dwyer, the magazine's first editor and one of its two most important in-house writers, recalled recently how the key pieces were produced. "Tom would come over to my place about eleven in the evening with Bob [Singer, the other house writer] in tow. Then he'd proceed to expound. What he said generally left us either dazed or laughing. He never gave us any timetable. He just expected that at some point his ideas would be crystallized. He allowed us to improvise and cop our own styles. 'Ventriloquize' is a good word for the way he operated."

Though the magazine was concocted like a comedy show with a half-stoned cast, the soundness of its basic concept made it an overnight success. For by the mid-'70s, dope was no longer a fad or a problem. Dope was a world. There were millions of drug users, who had patterned themselves into a vast underground society that had its own myths and folklore, social etiquette and pecking order, songs and language, heroes and humor. There were scores of drugs, each with its special mystique. There was a rapidly developing industry that manufactured an endless array of drug paraphernalia, ranging from simple rolling papers to sophisticated electric stills that could convert a hemp doormat into a jigger of hash oil that would blow your noggin to the moon. There was a mountain of undigested botanical, chemical and medical information. There were great stretches of history demanding exploration, underground classics crying for publication and a whole network of interconnections—between drugs and sex, drugs and health, drugs and religion—about which people were eager to learn.

Most interesting of all, there was a labyrinthine underground of drug dealers and drug smugglers who journeyed to marvelously exotic places—to the Himalayan countries of Nepal, Bhutan and Tibet; to the jungles and deserts of South America; to the Arab kingdoms of the Middle East; to the war zones of the Far East—to bring back drugs for America. The scams and stratagems of these colorful characters comprised an endless novel of crime, foreign intrigue and high adventure. And all this heady stuff was just lying there waiting to be released through the stopped-up channels of the mass media, which still persisted in treating drugs simply as a social disease or a criminal racket.

From a business standpoint Forçade knew his magazine would click because the kids would gobble it up and the paraphernalia merchants would pour money into it, having no other advertising outlets. Eventually, the magazine would attract the record companies and all the other industries that compete for the youth dollar. Starting the magazine on a $20,000 shoestring, Forçade would see the circulation double with every issue for years, until at its peak, in 1978, HIGH TIMES was read by four million people a month, grossed five million dollars a year and had been acclaimed as the "publishing success story of the seventies."

The same shrewdness exemplified by the concept and the financing was evinced in the design and packaging of the product. Instead of aping the butcher-paper drabness of *Rolling Stone* or the hapless scribbling of the underground press, Forçade produced a slick knockoff of the paramount magazine formula of recent times: the *Playboy-Penthouse* sex mag. His reasoning was flawless.

Dope was the sex of the '70s: a universal pleasure fighting for full acceptance. From the intellectual standpoint, it was a large and confused subject clamoring for scientific clarification. From the literary standpoint, it was a world of inexhaustible sensory and intellectual experience seeking expression in words and images. That being the case, why shouldn't the formula that worked for pussy work for pot?

Only one important difference separated HIGH TIMES from its famous models, *Playboy* and *Penthouse*. Advocating the liberalization of the sex code meant at most modifying the manners and morals of American society. Advocating the liberalization of the drug code meant abolishing some of the most punitive statutes of American law. Meantime, it meant *breaking* that law. Though HIGH TIMES never advocated any criminal act—god forbid!—it did not stop with the mere description of drug usage. From an early point in the magazine's history and with increasing attention to detail as years went by, HIGH TIMES provided very precise and valuable instruction in the secret art of smuggling dope. Lengthy interviews with veteran smugglers, illustrated guides to the "Ten Best Smuggling Planes" or the "Ten Best Smuggling Boats" and technical discussions of how to make radio transmissions to South America in code were typical features of the magazine. In a country where vast numbers of people have the means and the desire to play the smuggling game but are inhibited simply by lack of the requisite knowledge and experience, these articles were bound to make the gap between thinking and doing much smaller. What's more, they were certain to provoke the authorities to take measures to turn off this frothing fountain of forbidden knowledge.

The most determined effort to get HIGH TIMES and Forçade occurred in the years 1976 and 1977. I became aware that something serious had gone wrong as soon as I returned from Colombia, in January 1976. I discovered, to my chagrin, that Forçade had vanished and the deal we had made to publish a one-shot magazine containing my adventures had been unilaterally abrogated. Naturally, I sought by every means to discover what had happened to my erstwhile publisher. Eventually, by piecing together accounts gathered from Forçade's partners in and outside the dope game, I was able to picture very clearly the sequence of events.

The whole story commenced on the night of January 25, 1976. That Sunday evening, Forçade was cruising down Fifth Avenue with a lady dope dealer. Full of tea and happiness, he passed the building where he lived: the Fifth Avenue Hotel, a big, seedy old establishment near Washington Square. Glancing up at the windows of his apartment, which he had left in total darkness, he was startled to see that all the lights were burning. Stopping to look more carefully, he could see silhouetted in the bright panes strangely costumed people. In a flash, Forçade jumped out of the car and darted up the service stairs to scope out the scene. What he saw sent his brain spinning. His rooms were swarming with firemen and police officers.

Evidently a pipe had burst and someone had called the fire department. In tracing the leak, the firemen had opened the apartment's main closet. Stacked inside were a lot of foul-smelling suitcases, which, when opened, revealed a stash of 200 pounds of high-quality marijuana. In the State of New York, with its recently enacted Rockefeller drug laws, 200 pounds of weed could get you a long stretch in prison. What was alarming Forçade, however, was not just the threat of a dope bust. In the apartment were all his personal and business papers. These documents proved conclusively that though he had no public connection with HIGH TIMES, he was the magazine's sole owner. If the authorities wanted to put the country's first journal of drug use out of business, these papers would make the task much easier.

Most men caught in such a trap would have run for their lives or their lawyers. Not Forçade. Dashing down to the street, he ducked into a phone booth and called up Chic Eder, who had once been a burglar. Late that night, when the police had padlocked the apartment and left the premises, Tom and Chic

slipped up to the floor armed with a 20-pound sledgehammer, one of Forçade's favorite tools. Four heavy shots with the hammer and the door flew off its hinges.

Forçade dashed into his kitchen, tore the stove away from the wall and thrust his hand up the ventilation pipe. He pulled out a small satchel and threw it at Chic. "Grab it and run!" he barked. Then, he added, with characteristic humor: "I'll hold them off!"

Chic ran down the stairs, tore out of the building and whipped around the corner, where he paused to draw breath. In a dark doorway, he cracked the satchel and examined its contents with a practiced eye. It contained about 100,000 dollars in wads of 100s neatly bound with thick rubber bands. Forçade had saved his stash. Meantime, he was upstairs busily collecting his business papers and his passport.

Later that night, while Tom and Chic were driving through the city's streets, Forçade nodded towards the satchel lying between them on the front seat. Nonchalantly, he said: "Help yourself!"

"That's chump change!" rasped Chic in his toughest gangster voice.

"What do you want then?" asked Tom, genuinely puzzled.

"I want *in!*"

"In what?"

"In the *game!*"

Tom responded with a supercilious giggle, but from that time on, Chic was in.

Forçade's next move was to the Barbary Coast of the American drug trade, the southwest coast of Florida, near Naples. Here he gathered his gang and started communicating by shortwave radio with Colombian mother-ships. These expendable old tramp steamers would sail parallel to the coast of Florida far out in international waters rendezvousing with first one, then another American smuggling party, until their supplies of weed, coke and bogus-Quaaludes were exhausted— or the ships were captured by the Coast Guard. After repeatedly failing to work out a deal with the Colombians, Forçade changed his strategy.

On the night of March 15, near the Remuda Ranch, southeast of Naples, Forçade supervised the unloading of a 44-foot sailboat that had been crammed with nine tons of Colombian weed. It was a "guerrilla" operation: no dock, no pay-off to the cops, in short, no protection. It was also a clumsy operation because it took 24 hours to unload the sailer with a 29-foot Thunderbird, obliging Chic Eder on the first night to stay aboard the sailboat stuffed with over 6,000 pounds of pungent weed. During that night, a Coast Guard patrol boat shone its searchlight on the sailboat and commanded the vessel to switch on its running lights. "Aye aye, sir," snapped the quick-witted Chic—and the Coast Guard sailed away looking for smugglers.

The following night, the off-loading was finally completed. The last two trucks had just pulled away from the shore when they were challenged by a uniformed wildlife officer in a patrol car. One of the rules of clandestine operations is that in the event of discovery one party must draw off the enemy in the wrong direction while the rest of the group completes its mission and makes good its escape. Forçade was driving a camper filled with 2,800 pounds of weed. A veteran hot-rodder, he floorboarded his four-wheel-drive and took off at 65 miles an hour along the Tamiami Trail.

As the wildlife officer reported next day in the local press, he gave chase, but he could never pull abreast of the truck because the driver kept steering a dizzying serpentine pattern. In the cab of the truck with Forçade were Chic Eder and Tom's 20-year-old sidekick. This kid started to come apart the minute he felt the heat. Now as they approached Everglades City, they looked up ahead and spotted the flickering lights of a police blockade. (The wildlife officer had radioed for assistance.) At that moment, it looked like the game was over for Tom Forçade. Actually, the best was yet to come.

Shouting at his men to hold tight, Forçade drove the truck off the highway and into the Everglades. The moment they bogged down, the men threw open their doors and took off on foot. Instantly, they were up to their knees in muck and slime. Next thing they knew, they were beset by hundreds of mosquitoes and a plague of seed ticks, jiggers and swamp vermin. The local cops had no desire to follow the smugglers to their doom. The police figured it would be an easy matter to surround the fugitives and wait them out. Soon a helicopter was thut-thut-thutting overhead. Periodically, the police would shout through bullhorns: "You better come out! We've got you surrounded!"

For nearly 24 hours, Forçade scurried around in the swamp seeking a way to escape. He was chilled and exhausted, hungry and thirsty. Never once, though, did he lose his nerve. Wearing a white dress shirt and an orange jacket, clothes for the office not the field, he kept joking, "Just another chapter in The Great Adventure." Forçade's young companion was made of weaker stuff. He finally walked out on the road and gave himself up, providing the police with a lengthy deposition that was forwarded to New York and joined with the information on the Fifth Avenue Hotel bust. Forçade and Chic held out until the second night. Then, they made an audacious move.

Observing that the police avoided the mosquitoes by remaining in their squad cars with the windows shut tight, they decided to crawl past the cars that were guarding the best way out of the area. Moving just a few inches at a time, they crawled through a whole covey of cop cars, wondering why there were so many parked in this particular spot. Later they learned that they had slithered through the parking lot of a sheriff's substation.

Getting past the cops was just the first step in getting away. The next was crossing a bridge that was in full view of the police. Forçade started out by swinging hand over hand from the edge of the bridge. Halfway across, he felt his arms going numb. With a desperate effort he hoisted himself to the roadbed and crawled the rest of the way.

Now it was a comparatively simple task to hike 10 miles until they found a motel; call up the gang, who had given them up for lost; settle into the back of a car driven by two of the women in the gang; and, finally, receive the congratulations of

everyone at the stash pad in Miami, where Tom presided with grim good humor—and a mosquito-riddled face like a huge tomato—over the division of the spoils. Next time I saw Forçade he told me that he had just made a million dollars.

Over the next couple of years, as I learned more and more of Forçade's history, I came to recognize that this mild-mannered, highly intellectual little guy was actually one with the heroes of the Wild West. Though Tom appeared to people in New York like a novocaine-faced weirdo who had dropped from outer space, he was actually a man with deep regional roots, a son of the pioneers.

His native state was Arizona, a barren and thinly inhabited region when his mother's family entered it in 1881, at the end of a cattle drive from Colorado. The family stopped first in the town of Tucson; but, finding there was not sufficient water to husband their herds, they moved down near the Mexican border, settling in the tiny sulfur-springs hamlet of Wilcox. There they built an adobe house with walls two feet thick; and there they remained, as generation after generation was born and reared in the same house.

Forçade's mother married a brilliant young engineer named Kenneth Forçade Goodson, who was a specialist in heavy construction. Goodson worked for many years building military installations for the Defense Department. Tom Forçade—whose real name was Gary Goodson—was reared in a succession of military bases in faraway places, like Okinawa, Alaska and Greenland. This military milieu had a profound effect upon the development of both his personality and his imagination.

The military influence explained Forçade's fascination with weapons (one of his prize possessions was his Thompson submachine gun) and his alarming tendency to draw on anyone who crossed him. Likewise it shaped his whole conception of a smuggling operation, which he described in HIGH TIMES as: "like a military operation with overtones of religious fervor." Even the trademark of Forçade's Trans-High Corporation (THC, ya dig, man?) betrayed this obsession. Any other hippie entrepreneur would have chosen an emblem like the seven-leafed marijuana frond. Not Forçade. He stamped everything he touched, from glossy ads to clunky belt buckles, from chunky ashtrays to blazoned t-shirts, with the image of the most glamorous fighter plane of World War II, the twin-tailboomed P-38.

The influence of Forçade's father was apparent in his son's mania for driving souped-up cars and for flying airplanes; for the father had been a flyer and he met his death while driving a fast car. This sudden death of an adored father, which occurred when Forçade was 11, was the decisive stroke in the shaping of the boy's character. Not long afterwards, Forçade began to have trouble at school and to display symptoms of depression, an affliction that dogged him all the rest of his life and led eventually to his death.

Forçade was always a good student, so it is not surprising to learn that he got through the four-year program for a bachelor's degree in business administration in just two-and-a-half years at the University of Utah. More characteristic were his adventures as the school's most notorious hot-rodder. One of his fellow students, Therese Coe, composed a recollection of Forçade after his death that brings back the young man known as "Junior Goodson." "His pad," she wrote, "was lined with hulking black auto engine parts in various stages of custom greasiness. The black forties buggy he drove sported fat racing tires, a blast-furnace engine and a rear end four feet off the ground. Around midnight he would take us up the winding four-lane highway on the western slope of the Wasatch Mountain. Then as he floored the short and shot down the twisting road, he would shimmy the steering wheel violently.... Another of his games was to take us out to the Utah-Nevada border and then outrun the local cops for a hundred miles across the Bonneville Salt Flats."

Tom married his college sweetheart only to soon divorce her. Then as the hippie lifestyle began to crystallize, he founded a commune near Tucson and published his first magazine, a dim little booklet titled *Orpheus* (singer of songs, teller of truths, martyr at the hands of the maenads) that relied on stuff reprinted from the underground press. At this point, he had his first brush with the law, a bust for acid. Not wanting to taint his family name with scandal, he changed his name from Goodson (how ironic!) to Forçade, which rhymes with "arcade." As his new middle name, he adopted the title "King."

In the late '60s, Forçade came to New York in a battered old school bus emblazoned with psychedelic symbols. In 1967, he organized with John Wilcock (of the *East Village Other*) the Underground Press Syndicate (UPS), a useful device for pooling and exchanging all the information gathered by the hundreds of underground newspapers that were springing up at the time. Characteristically, Forçade financed the new business by persuading Bell & Howell to underwrite the venture in exchange for the rights to copy all the papers on microfilm and sell the film to university libraries. This was an early example of what became Forçade's great goal in later years: "making the system work against itself."

At this point in the history of the counterculture, everything suddenly assumed a political coloring. Forçade plunged head over heels into the alphabet soup of the Movement and became an activist and a radical. He raised funds for the cause by shaking down the promoters of rock concerts. His most characteristic efforts, however, were in the genre titled "guerrilla theater"—or just plain disruption. Working in this idiom, Forçade turned up in May 1970 before the President's Commission on Obscenity and Pornography dressed in full clerical costume: black suit, reversed collar, black slouch hat. After denouncing the commission, he slammed a custard pie into the face of Professor Otto N. Larsen of the University of Washington.

In August of the same year, he performed one of his most legendary exploits, a caper about which he published a paperback book, by disrupting a Warner Brothers movie project that entailed herding a caravan of hippies (including Wavy Gravy and the Hog Farm) across America and towards the Isle of Wight Rock Festival. Forçade emerged from a cloud of dust five miles outside Boulder driving a Cadillac limousine painted olive drab and emblazoned on each side with a big white Army star. Atop the car was a haranguing platform rigged with two powerful Missile Man speakers. Inside, the vehicle was loaded with all the devices of disruption from smoke bombs to skyrockets. Forçade himself was costumed as the head of the Free Rangers (a branch of the White Panthers), a classic frontiersman in laced leather tunic, floppy leather sombrero, shoulder-length hair and a skull-and-crossbones button proclaiming "The American Revolution."

When Forçade's efforts to radicalize the caravan failed, he called to his aide David Peel, the New York street musician, whose album, *The Pope Smokes Dope,* was produced by John Lennon—and instantly banned everywhere in the world. Peel and his crew of veteran Lower East Side street tummlers accomplished swiftly what Tom's highly intellectualized rap could not. They provoked the camp boss to whip out a knife. (Peel had looked at the guy's Indian swastikas and screamed, "I'm Jewish and you're Hitler for Warner Brothers!") At the critical moment, with the camp boss standing over Peel wielding his knife, Tom leaped on his back and wrestled him to the ground. The great aim had been achieved. The "Caravan of Love" had been shown up as a Caravan of Hate. When the film, *Medicine Ball Caravan,* was released, everybody pronounced the fight the best part.

Jerry Rubin remarked that he never viewed Forçade as a political activist but rather as an outlaw and a drug dealer, a "rogue genius." This strikes me as the root of the matter; for when you examine Forçade's political pranks carefully, you sometimes discover that they had a hidden underside of adventurism or criminality. For example, in later years, Forçade confessed to Ed Dwyer that a Warner Brothers' publicity hireling had actually commissioned Tom to disrupt the Medicine Ball Caravan, thus guaranteeing some violent on-camera action. A high-ranking former official of the company told me that he strongly suspected that Forçade's real interest in the project was as a cover for moving loads of weed across the country. (Using a movie production company as a disguise for a smuggling operation was later to become standard practice in the dope world.) One thing certain about Tom Forçade: for all his obvious idealism and Robin Hood generosity, he was not a man with a fixed moral center. Idealism and opportunism ran like wet colors back and forth across his bizarre life history in a manner that will make it very difficult for any future biographer to determine how to weigh his actions.

Personal passions were also a very big factor in Forçade's political career. In fact, his debacle as a political activist was produced in the most direct manner by personal animosities and non-political motives. The final spin began with a bitter battle over Abbie Hoffman's *Steal This Book,* in which Forçade claimed certain rights. After a "people's court" rendered a verdict in Hoffman's favor, Forçade brought suit against Hoffman in civil court, an action that was regarded in the Movement as a serious breach of counterculture ethics. Subsequently, Forçade broke with the Yippie leadership over the issue of whether to disrupt the Democratic presidential convention in Miami. Forçade organized his own group, the Zippies (motto: "Put the zip back into YIP"), who ran wild during this silly season.

At the height of the madness, Abbie Hoffman and Jerry Rubin accused Forçade of acting as if he were an agent provocateur of the federal government. They instanced his bringing suit against Hoffman and his inflammatory speeches against the Yippie leadership. When the story ran in Jack Anderson's column, Forçade's reputation as a radical was ruined. At the same time, the girl he loved, Gabrielle Schang, fell in love with Ed Sanders of the Yippies and defected from the Zippies.

The final blow came when Forçade returned to New York and was busted by the FBI on a charge of possessing a fire bomb. Forçade, always the supreme put-on artist, told the feds that his brothers and sisters, the Weathermen, would soon break him out of jail. The feds, highly alarmed, posted two shotgun-toting guards before Forçade's cell.

When the dust settled and Forçade had been cleared—as he always was—of criminal charges, the erstwhile guerrilla theater virtuoso revealed himself as a profoundly embittered man. He felt betrayed and he declared that Miami had been the "Movement's Waterloo." Surrounding himself with a handful of trusted comrades, he returned to the world where he had always felt most at home, the dope-running and dealing scene, deep underground.

Forçade's headquarters in this period was a safe house—across the street from the old Women's Detention Center on Greenwich Avenue—called "Bobby's." (The fictitious name on the apartment lease was "Robert" So-and-So.) The protocol of a visit to Bobby's was very strict, very elaborate and highly characteristic of Tom's paranoid and fantastical imagination, fueled by James Bond movies.

When you arrived, you were greeted by Forçade's "valet," who presented the visitor with a two-page, single-spaced set of house rules. Every detail of doing business at the house was anticipated and defined: where to park, how to call, what passwords to employ, how to leave, etc. There were even punishments specified for each infraction of the rules.

Once inside the pad, you found a grungy decor redolent of both the flophouse and the suburban ranch house. One side of the room was piled from floor to ceiling with cheap suitcases stuffed with weed. The other side was furnished with a living-room bar spotlighted with high-intensity lamps for examining the goods. Forçade's private accommodations comprised just two items: a Navaho blanket, in which he slept on the floor; and a portable electric log fireplace, before whose dependable glow this acid cowboy would smoke his last joint and nod out at dawn.

Subsequently, Forçade established at 714 Broadway a "smokeasy," a unique institution of the time, which offered dealers a place to sample wares, talk prices, cut deals and conduct all the business appropriate to the trade. Tom's smokeasy looked like a rock rehearsal studio. Huge speakers dominated the front room; proceeding to the rear, you went down a corridor lined with cubicles, in which the merchandise was examined and deals made. The back room was a warehouse. The most characteristic feature of such operations was the "menu," a sometimes fancifully decorated card on which were listed all the products currently available and their prices, *viz.* "Thai Stick, $25 per. Indian Hash, $10 gram. Colombian Gold, $5 bag, $50 oz." We'll never see those prices again.

Even when Forçade made a lot of money in the smuggling game, he never lived in style. Anhedonistic in sensibility, he cared nothing for other men's pleasures. His idea of dining out was a couple of tacos and a glass of milk. His notion of a party was a big tank of nitrous oxide and a plentiful supply of penny balloons. Though he quipped, "I never met a drug I didn't like," he had no heavy habits. Once somebody gave him a handsomely carved opium pipe. Forçade lectured us learnedly on the ritual and ecstasy of opium. Then he displayed a few little amber wafers of the drug. Just as we prepared ourselves for the great experience, Tom discovered that the pipe was broken. That ended our pipe dream. As for women, Forçade generally had an attractive girl who was primarily a comrade in arms. Cindy Ornstein, for example, was a sexy little blonde from Philadelphia who used to go around in Brownie costumes. In Miami, she led the Zippie women just as Forçade led the men. Usually, though, Forçade went to bed with his clothes on. His wardrobe ran to polyester shirts and black nylon socks.

What did get Forçade off in the smuggling game—or any game—was *power,* particularly the power of the unmoved mover, the invisible godlike presence who sits behind the scenes, like one of those master criminals in a James Bond movie, manipulating the complicated technology of modern crime and the tricky interpersonal relationships that spawn about the throne. Just before his death, Forçade ventriloquized an account of his early smuggling adventures through a fake interview conducted by "Leslie Morrison" (Forçade's favorite nom de plume) with "A Smuggling Ace." After recounting in his typical deadpan style a history of crime that commenced in high school, when he would drive over the Mexican border with his wheel wells stuffed with grass, and then escalated steadily until, in his mid-20s, he was conducting dangerous aerial operations, Forçade the ace finally got around to characterizing his type, the smuggling "kingpin." "The bigger you are," he remarked, "the less known you are. You're the mirror image of a successful public figure, like a novelist, a rock star, sports figure. You get addicted to having that much control over and effect upon people."

The mixture of self-effacement and megalomania in this description provides the precise formula for Tom Forçade. He did see himself as a "kingpin," but he knew his strength lay in denying the normal appetite for fame. His ultimate strength, therefore, was the power of self-control. Unfortunately, this stern discipline developed a masochistic edge. Once, when Forçade removed his shirt, I was astonished to see that he had pierced both his nipples with gold rings.

Though Forçade's exercise of power over himself was

implicitly cruel, his exercise of this same power over others was generally benign. He was a loyal and helpful friend, a faithful comrade, a fair employer, a benefactor of countless good causes and a patron of the counterculture in its most authentic and advanced forms. There were times, however, when he lost control and began to behave like a mad monarch. The most prolonged and bizarre of these seizures occurred when Forçade returned to New York in November 1976, after living for seven months underground.

Pitching camp in a cavelike loft across the street from the offices of HIGH TIMES on East 27th Street, he resumed control over every aspect of the magazine, from the editorials to the cover art, from the distribution strategy to the placement of ads on the page. After a couple months of this activity, one day he called up Paul Tornetta, the general manager, and started issuing insane commands. "I want you to fire everyone," he began, "except yourself and Stan [Place, circulation director]. Collect all the money from people who owe us money. Sell all the furniture and typewriters. We're closing down the magazine." Tornetta replied: "I can't do that, Tom. If you want to fire everyone, you do it."

Ten minutes later Forçade stalked into the office, downed out on Valiums and acting like the Frankenstein monster. Seizing the switchboard, he tore it off the wall and hurled it at the operator. Then he went from office to office uttering in slow motion the same robotlike formula: "You are terminated.... You are terminated.... You are terminated."

Next day, after a wild night of phone calls, crash meetings and frantic skull busting, Andy Kowl, the magazine's publisher, arrived at Forçade's loft with a couple other executives to offer to buy the business for a half-million dollars. Kowl recalls that they found Forçade lying on a sofa with his spindly little legs sticking out of a ratty bathrobe. All he would say is: "I can't sell the magazine. I'm not in my right mind." Kowl, assuming this was just sales resistance, made an impassioned pitch. "Look, man," he pleaded, "you and I started this thing together, we went through a lot, you made me a lot of promises..." Before he could get the next phrase out of his mouth, Tom held up his hand to stop him. "I made you a lot of promises?" echoed Forçade. "I'm breakin' promises?" Kowl replied automatically, "Yeah!"

At that moment there was one of those chilling pauses that would occur when Tom was in his moods. Turning in slow motion on the sofa, like a sinister candy cane, Forçade said to his sidekick: "Gimme my piece." As everyone froze in terror, the aide flipped his boss a massive .45. Kowl stares at Forçade in horror. A downed-out psycho with a gun in his hand! He figures he's a dead man. Forçade is staring just as intently at Kowl, his hard, keen eyes starting to come through the drug haze. Suddenly, Forçade hands Kowl the gun, saying in his best Boris Karloff baritone: "If I broke all those promises—kill me!" Paul Tornetta reaches over and grabs the weapon. The negotiations conclude with Forçade still in possession of his magazine.

The meaning of this strange episode was understood by R-- R-------, the writer of the "'R.' Dope Connoisseur" page in

HIGH TIMES and one of the few highly perceptive people in the Forçade circle. R---- explained: "Tom wanted to jolt the staff back into his frame of reference: make them realize that it was all a whim of his and not a business where everybody fights for power and watches out for his own career. I think if he had killed the magazine, he might not have killed himself."

Even if Forçade had a rational motive for blowing up HIGH TIMES, it would be hard to find one for certain other episodes in this same period. Even with regard to his favorite cause, NORML, the National Organization for the Reform of Marijuana Laws, Forçade could not resist his impulse to do the impermissible. It should be understood that Tom Forçade regarded marijuana almost as a sacred substance. It was the emblem of all his most cherished values: freedom, thought, humor. Unlike a real criminal, Forçade would have gladly sacrificed all the millions he made in the dope game if he could have gotten this precious substance legalized. Once, for example, he left 10,000 dollars in cash on the desk of the director of NORML. The money was accompanied by a note that read: "From a smuggler." The gesture was carefully calculated: it got NORML a lot of publicity; it invited other players to follow suit. Subsequently, at the NORML convention in the winter of 1975, Forçade took a rare public bow as NORML's biggest contributor, superseding in that role Hugh Hefner. Yet when Forçade decided the following spring to attend an important NORML party at the posh Park Avenue apartment of Mrs. —, he behaved like a boor.

Like Little Caesar, he made a late entrance surrounded by his entourage. Then, as if impelled by some instinct for the perverse, he made off in the opposite direction from that in which the party was being held. Wandering into the elegant dining room, he lit the tapers in the silver candelabra and then sprawled in a chair with his feet up on the polished wood table. He was just lighting a joint when the mistress of the house walked in and started screaming with outrage. Staring at her with half-closed eyes, Tom sneered: "Go fuck yourself!" At that moment the butler—a dead ringer for Sammy Davis, Jr.— appeared and started rousting Forçade. Touching the "Kingpin," the "Ace," was a dangerous act. Instantly, he exploded in rage. First he took a swing at the startled flunky; then he started throwing everything that came to hand. Fifteen minutes after his arrival at the big NORML party, NORML's leading contributor was hustled, kicking and cursing, out the door.

Forçade's bouts of depression were cyclical in nature. They came on when the days grew short and gloomy in the early winter. They would pass in the early spring, the slow motion of depression gradually quickening to the fast-forward speed of Forçade's manic phase. Vital to his recovery were the ministrations of his closest friend and aide, Jack Coombs. Jack figured so largely in the last years of Forçade's life that no picture of Tom could be complete without an answering shot of his soul mate. The key to this pair's great love for one another was their opposite but complementary characters.

Forçade was a desiccated and jaded little mastermind,

totally devoid of social grace. When he was depressed, his affectless gaze, laconic responses and attitude of you're-talking-and-I'm-listening-so-whatha-hell-else-do-you-want? could chill you to the bone or drive you into a murderous rage. Jack was very tall, strong and physically adroit, with a smiling, charming, obliging manner. Jack would welcome you at the door and usher you into the presence; Forçade would be lying back on some dirty cushions on the floor, talking his face off and listening to reggae playing at ear-damaging volume from a pair of ominous-looking old movie-house speakers. Jack would offer you a drink or see that you got a toke on the joint that Forçade was neglecting while he rapped.

Forçade, for his part, treated Jack like a proud and doting parent. He was especially fond of rattling off all of Jack's licenses and credentials: "He's got a radio operator's license, both FAA and marine radio telephone; a first-class ham license; marine sea captain's license; expert in computers, super technically oriented, ya dig?" Jack was a digital virtuoso and Tom was the brains of the outfit. They were made for each other.

On a deeper level, Jack was the human antidote to his friend's emotional illness. When Forçade would get into bed, curl up in the fetal position and withdraw from the world, Jack would hold him in his arms and coax him out of his gloom. Jack was Forçade's lithium. Even after Tom married Gabrielle Schang, the girl he had been courting intermittently for nearly six years, Jack continued to play a vital role in his friend's life, often joining the newly married couple for outings or evenings at home.

Gabrielle recalls: "Tom and Jack spoke at least once a day on the phone. Tom had total trust in Jack. They loved each other. They were always laying plans and sharing dreams. One big dream was to buy a plane. Tom would walk around with a copy of Trade-a-Plane under his arm. Once in a while they would call about a particular plane. 'My god!' I'd think, 'they're really going to fly!'" As always, Jack had fallen in with his friend's designs. The digital virtuoso qualified himself to operate multi-engine aircraft in a remarkably short time. Gabrielle quipped that Jack's hasty education in aviation was a "crash course."

In the spring of 1978, the two pals decided that the time was ripe for another chapter in The Great Adventure. The plan was that Jack and another, more experienced pilot would fly down to Colombia in a two-engine plane, pick up a load of grass and fly it back to the States, where they would drop it by parachute onto an isolated spot in Florida. After the load had come to ground, a recovery crew would secure the stuff and run it to a stash pad in Atlanta.

Tom and Jack being such romantics, it would never do for them to adopt a method that didn't allow for comradeship. Their plan had to be a scheme that after they brought it off would allow them to kick back on many subsequent nights in New York and say, "Hey, man, we did it *together,* didn't we?"

Hence it was decided that when the smuggling plane reached the vicinity of the drop site, Tom would meet it in another professionally piloted plane and lead it in over the spot. This aerial rendezvous was a wholly unnecessary complication because smuggling planes have no trouble reaching their destinations through normal navigational procedures and the ground crews can signal them at the last minute by radio or by flashing lights. A further complication was introduced by Tom's financial partner in this move, a flamboyant character named Tom Sullivan, a raw-boned, redneck lad from Tampa, who subsequently achieved celebrity at Studio 54, where he was called Cowboy because of his penchant for dressing in costly Western gear.

On the night of the flight, Sullivan was stationed in the lavish two-story penthouse of the Peachtree Plaza in Atlanta, a 40-story tower of black glass. High on heroin, he was wild with the anticipation of a big killing because on this same night a shrimpboat loaded with weed was scheduled to dock in Louisiana. The Cowboy liked to think of himself as the hero of a reckless adventure movie with a rock'n'roll soundtrack; in fact, he eventually made a movie about himself titled *Cocaine Cowboys,* starring Jack Palance and Andy Warhol. Tonight, the movie would carry "the poor little cracker boy from the boonies" to unparalleled heights of glamour and adventure.

At one in the afternoon, Sullivan had received a reassuring call from his Colombian connection, who reported that the plane had taken off 25 minutes earlier. At the last minute, Sullivan's lieutenant, a soft Southern boy named Joe, who lived with Sullivan's sister, had decided to deadhead home aboard the plane. Sullivan gave a whoop of joy because that meant that by midnight, he and his closest buddy would be sitting in this lavish pad out of their minds on drugs, toasting each other with champagne, while awaiting the call that would tell them that they had brought in a whole shipload of marijuana. Nobody in the history of the dope game had ever played or won such a great doubleheader.

At midnight, the phone rang. The Cowboy caught it before the second ring. "Hello!" he cried with a startled inflection that said, "Tell me quick what's happenin'."

"It's bad news," said the heavy rural voice of a member of the offloading crew. "They come in right, but when we tole 'em to git down, they got down so low they musta hit a tree. The plane crashed. We jist got back. We hung theah three hours—thass how cool it wuz! They wasn't a man exscaped. They's all dead."

The disaster was Forçade's fault.

Two hundred miles down course, the smuggling plane radioed that all was well and gave an ETA. When Forçade made visual contact with the blue-and-white Queen Air, he turned around and started leading it in over the ground. As the two planes maneuvered, Forçade kept urging the dope plane to get lower. "Get lower, man, get lower!" he barked into the mike as he skimmed along about 200 feet above the tree level. Suddenly, he heard an explosion and saw a blaze of light all around him.

Banking sharply, he stared down at the ground. There he saw the image that was to haunt him till the day he died. Jack's plane was going up in a ball of flames. Forçade circled as low as he dared over the burning plane, straining to see figures crawling out of the wreckage. As the plane, a flying incendiary bomb stuffed with hay and high-test gas, exploded, it was obvious that there were no survivors. Finally, Forçade had no choice but to fly back to his base and land.

When he got home the next day, he told Gabrielle: "We won't be getting any more calls from Jack." Then he burst into tears. Soon, he got control of himself and started the search that occupied him for many months. Though there was no hope of survivors, he wouldn't relinquish his belief that Jack had escaped and was lying up somewhere in a hospital, too sick to make contact. Tom hired private investigators and attorneys to work on the case. He held painful meetings with Jack's family. When he told me the story, I did an impermissible thing. I told him that he was a suicidal psychotic and, like all intellectuals, a fuck-up in the real world. He tolerated my outburst, remarking simply, "It wasn't any different than any other time."

Having abandoned smuggling for the time being, Forçade threw all his energy into entrepreneurial activities. He opened the first bookstore in SoHo, naming it after the dispatch the Weathermen released after their bomb factory blew up, New Morning. Forçade was also preparing to buy a restaurant, a bank and a Concorde airliner. (The plane took several years to build; by the time his was finished, he figured to have found a buyer.) He bought a pioneer dope movie, *The Polk County Pot Plane;* and he bankrolled for $400,000 the greatest of all rock documentaries, *D.O.A.,* the cinematic record of the Sex Pistols' American tour. (Once again Tom was up against Warner Brothers, who sought unsuccessfully to stop his film crews from ripping off the concerts with their cameras and mikes.) All this activity was characteristic of Forçade when his mood was elevated and his ever-restless spirit began to assert itself.

When the days started growing short, however, Forçade began to droop. Ed Dwyer recalls: "He would call up twelve at night, obviously luded. He would start talking old stuff, the kind of thing we had talked about when I first met him in 1969. Like getting a Sikorsky amphibian and relocating the magazine to Nassau—as if he were Howard Hughes.... I would walk in the office in the morning and he would be sitting there pink-eyed as if he had been crying all night. I'd say, 'You look like shit.' He'd say, 'I feel like shit.' "

One of Forçade's problems was that he wasn't recognized as a kingpin by anybody outside of his circle. When he went out to Hollywood to sell his dope movie, the studio people refused to take him seriously. Every conversation ended with them asking him how to get some good coke. When he threw a big celebrity party in a restaurant on West Broadway, Andy Warhol ignored Forçade. He was beginning to suffer from the Gatsby syndrome.

About a week before he died, Tom told me that many people become sick with paranoia before they die, instancing Lenny Bruce and Howard Hughes. "I refuse to become sick with paranoia ever again," he vowed. Then, three days before he committed suicide, we had another conversation. His whole mood had changed. He was depressed, compulsively talkative, full of fears. He said he was afraid an informer was giving him up to the DEA. After his death, I learned that he had confided

to other intimates other fears of a similar nature. His lawyer, Michael Kennedy, recalled that Tom had told him that he feared assassination by Larry Flynt, whose organization was distributing HIGH TIMES. Tom's reasoning was highly characteristic of a paranoid.

Though Flynt's distribution had greatly improved sales of HIGH TIMES, Tom feared that Flynt might conspire with the magazine's printer—to whom Tom was always in debt—to take away the magazine. To protect himself against this threat, Tom had amassed a lot of secret information on Flynt. When he read that two Flynt executives had been shot in a parking lot, he suddenly began to fear he would be next. Clearly, at the end, Tom saw himself menaced on every side.

Tom's marriage must have also contributed to his depression because, though it had its good moments, it appeared to be a struggle of antagonistic wills. If Tom said, "Let's drive," Gabrielle would say, "No, I want to walk." They had so many disagreements that sometimes it appeared that they had gotten together simply in order to prove that marriage entailed no responsibility to give up even the most trivial whims of the unattached individual. Nor could Gabrielle, who had no connection with the world of drug dealing and smuggling, ever share in Tom's principal passion. By committing suicide while she was in the next room, Tom got in the last and cruelest lick.

Finally, there was Tom's grief over Jack's death. It was no coincidence that Tom killed himself just a couple of days before he was supposed to join Jack's parents in a memorial service. To those who speculated so frantically over the cause of Tom's death, I would say as one who has spent years trying to reconstruct his life that there was no single cause for his impulsive act of self-murder. It was an act produced by the coincidence of many distinct causes.

Whatever the reasons for Tom's death, the event was emblematic of the final failure of adaptation by the hippies to the alien climate of the '70s. Tom had made the most of the two strategies that promised most for the survival of the counterculture in the new decade. He had made the system work against itself, and he had become an outlaw hero of the drug culture. But beating the system meant immersing yourself in what you most despised, while stepping outside the system to play Robin Hood could finally mean seeing your closest friend incinerated in a ball of flames. Either way the exhilarating sense of triumph was soon lost in the dreary aftermath. Nor was there any other solution to the problem in the terms posed.

To a man in the grip of paranoia, death can become a personified adversary. A demon to be confronted in a final shootout. Better die like a desperado with a gun in your hand than go down to defeat inch by inch. Tom died like a soldier. He didn't flinch, he didn't fail. His hand was steady, his aim was true. He died without a cry or even a complaint. He was alone, wounded, cut off from his comrade. But he was in supreme command of himself. Such have been the deaths of many men who cared less for life than they did for living The Great Adventure.

PART 2
THE EARLY YEARS OF WILD SUCCESS
1974-1978

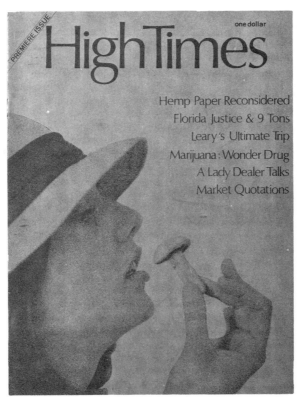

THE FIRST ISSUE.

EARLY ENGRAVING OF A HEMP PAPERMILL.

THE GRASS MARKET

The grass market, like any other, works on a supply and demand basis, and more or less establishes its own price structure. Quality smoke is in demand today more and more; connoisseurs are going beyond inferior domestic and low-grade imports. Most people now place Colombian at the top, with Jamaican and Mexican placing two and three, respectively. This, however, does not mean that super weed is not sometimes produced in those two areas.

Forum, #1, Summer 1974

A KENTUCKY HEMP BREAK, USED FOR REDUCING THE HEMP STALKS TO USEABLE FIBER.

HEMP PAPER RECONSIDERED
by Jack Frazier

Hemp (cannabis sativa) was one of the first crops to be planted by the early American colonists. Their knowledge and use of the plant, however, started much earlier. The ships which they sailed from Europe were rigged with hemp rope and hemp or flax sailcloth. Many wore hempen britches and coarse clothing from hemp fabric. And in all probability their land grants, sailing orders, and maps were inscribed on hemp/flax paper made from discarded cordage and rags.

The word paper comes from the Latin word papyrus, but the paper our ancestors knew was a substance totally different from both ancient papyrus and modern woodpulp. It was a mixture of flax and hemp, or a composition made from one of the substances. This was true for the first 1750 years of paper making, until a little over a 100 years ago, when a new synthetic paper was developed from chemically treated woodpulp.

According to a generally accepted tradition, the first paper was made by the Chinese in the first century A.D. The inventor was Ts'ai Lun, from the province of Hunan, north of Canton. The oldest documents written on paper and found by archeologists are in the British Museum. They are Buddhist texts from the 2nd and 3rd Centuries A.D. These and other manuscript rolls, some with Sanskrit characters, have been analyzed by Dr. Weiner of Vienna. His study showed that they were a mixture of bark and old rags, principally hemp.

After keeping the art to themselves for 500 years, Chinese papermaking spread to Japan and Korea in the east, and to Persia and Arabia in the west. It reached Korea in 600 A.D. and Baghdad in 793 A.D. Four hundred years went by before Europeans picked up papermaking from the Arabs. The first western paper mill was built in Spain in 1150 A.D. by the Moors; the second was built in Italy in 1276. The art of papermaking finally reached England in 1494.

Some scholars attribute the illiteracy and "flat world" science of Western Europe to the late development of papermaking and book printing. No doubt this is true, but by the 16th century hemp had become such an integral part of European culture some were wondering how they could possibly function without it. Francois Rabelais (1490-1553) devoted eight pages to the mighty hemp plant in his classic *The Histories of Gargantua and Pantagruel*: "Without it, how could water be drawn from the well? What would scribes, copiests, secretaries, and writers do without it? Would not official documents and rent rolls disappear? Would not the noble art of printing perish?"

William Thompson points out, in his provocative book *At The Edge Of History*, that "industry runs on paper as much as on coal, and if English mercantile society had no means of producing and controlling the vast amounts of information commerce generates, the Industrial Revolution would never have happened."

Hemp and flax had to compete with tobacco from the very first days of colonial agriculture. The tobacco smoking craze was sweeping Europe at the same time the early colonists were trying to establish an economic base. Tobacco, because it was less bulky in proportion to its value, proved to be the most renumerative crop the colonists could grow. Some of the colonial families actually came close to starvation due to their dependency on tobacco and their failure to grow grain, vegetable and fiber crops. The fact that tobacco was inedible, unwearable, unrecyclable, and soil-depleting made it even more of a curse.

To counteract the tendency of the colonists to be one-crop oriented, the Parliament of England and the colonial governments placed bounties on hemp and flax to encourage their production. The bounties were paid all during the 1600's and even during the pre-revolutionary period, primarily as a means to encourage fiber production for British shipping. In 1762, Virginia not only rewarded those who grew hemp, but also imposed penalties upon those who did not produce it.

The colonists were never able to grow enough flax and hemp for British shipping needs, but by 1690 a sufficient supply was produced to take care of the home market. Once this surplus had been created, one of the first manufacturing industries to be established was papermaking.

By the early 1700's, both the flax and hemp industries were thriving and more papermills were built. One of the people instrumental in getting these mills in operation was Benjamin Franklin.

Remember, many colonists were refugees from state and church controlled monarchies, where freedom of the press was unheard of. Their foresight in starting paper mills and presses was rewarded later when the Revolutionary war with England broke out. The colonists were able to aid their cause immensely because they had a healthy people's press. As a result, the works of revolutionaries like Thomas Paine could be read by most of the literate population.

THE FIRST RECYCLED PAPER

In a very real sense, papermaking in New England was made possible by the widespread use of hemp and flax clothing and the availability of discarded underwear, dresses, britches, shirts, rope and sailcloth. Paper in those days was made from 100% recycled material. Flax, hemp, and later cotton was turned into canvas; then, after it was threadbare and no longer serviceable, it was recycled into paper. This was our only source of paper for the first two hundred years of our history. Our forefathers and foremothers were much too thrifty to throw anything away.

George Washington, our first president, was both a hemp farmer and a patron of the early paper industry. Washington also recorded his hemp farming exploits in his diary. His entries in the spring and summer of 1765 should be of interest to the hemp farmers of today:

May 12-13, 1765: "Sowed Hemp at Muddy hole by swamp."

August 7, 1765: "Began to separate the male from the female. Rather, too late."

Most hemp historians have assumed that Washington was trying to raise a superior marijuana crop by separating the male and female before pollination had taken place. This may be true. Another possibility is that he was trying to harvest the male plants while they were still tender and would make good linen, since both hemp and flax can be used for linen manufacture if they are harvested at the right time and prepared properly.

Thomas Jefferson too was an early disciple of hemp culture. A 1811 entry in Jefferson's Garden Book reveals the special attention hemp received: "An acre of the best ground for hemp, is to be selected, & sown in hemp & to be kept for a permanent hemp patch."

WOODPULP PAPER AND WASTE

After the Civil War, the sulfite woodpulp process began to replace hemp paper. This process made woodpulp useable for many grades of paper, and by 1900 all newspapers and most books and magazines were printed

A LADY DEALER SPEAKS

I was at an apartment uptown on the west side and was tying up a deal for fifteen pounds of Jamaican. I had just put the money in my shoulder bag when the door was shoved in by a pneumatic hammer. It seems that the cops had these guys figured for major dealers. They took the guys out to the squad car, but kept me behind.... The oldest detective started calling me honey and putting his hand on my shoulder...I guess it's lonely at the barracks or something.... I took off my blouse and let them feel my breasts for a few minutes.... I blew all three of them and let the older one eat me. It was horribly degrading.... They let me walk away from the place.... No one knows what happened to the rest of the weed. *Recollections of a Lady Dealer, #1, Summer 1974*

HEMP SEED REMNANTS FOUND IN THIS FIFTH CENTURY B.C. SCYTHIAN COPPER CENSER SUGGEST HEMP SMOKING WAS KNOWN BY THE SCYTHIANS OF ANCIENT TIMES.

"All these years I was admiring Senator Abel's unwavering attention span; now it turns out he's just been stoned all the time."

SENATE TO CONFRONT LEGALIZATION OF POT

The United States Senate has finally moved to confront the marijuana decriminalization question head on, but some Senate members continue a rear-guard reactionary action.

Senators Jacob Javits (R-NY) and Harold Hughes (D-Iowa), both former members of the President's Marijuana Commission, have announced that serious discussion on the prospects of decriminalizing private marijuana usage by adults will be held before Hughes's Subcommittee on Alcoholism and Narcotics.

This is the first time in its history that hearings on marijuana have been held in the Senate and witnesses are being contacted who will testify "pro" and "con" on removing federal penalties for most marijuana offenses.

Javits and Hughes are co-sponsoring a bill, introduced in the last session of the Senate, that specifies that persons 18 and older may not be criminally prosecuted under federal law for possessing, exchanging or smoking small quantities of marijuana. Their bill is based on the recommendations of the National Marijuana Commission.

Meanwhile, the Senate Internal Security Subcommittee, headed by Senator James Eastland, claims that cannabis consumption was up 300% in 1973 from the previous year. According to Eastland's figures, American consumers smoked some 5 billion joints in 1973, or some 20 joints for every man, woman and child in the country.

Eastland blames this rise on the New Left, the academic community and Dr. Timothy Leary. The ISS claims evidence linking Communist agents to the smuggling of marijuana and hashish.

News, #1, Summer 1974

on woodpulp paper. The new, cheap, throwaway paper fit in perfectly with a growing, dynamic, disposable economy. The era of the "wastemakers" had arrived.

But while cheap woodpulp was a blessing to newspapers, it was a curse to book publishers and libraries. Books began to deteriorate at an alarming rate after the introduction of woodpulp paper. A Library of Congress study found that "while the paper in volumes three or four hundred years old is still strong...ninety-seven percent of the books of non-fiction printed between 1900 and 1939 will be useable for less than fifty years."

But hemp is scarce and costly and is rarely used alone. The highest qualities of India paper, however, consist mainly of hemp. The resistance to tearing and folding of papers made from simple cellulose is due in part to the length of the fibres. Of all the fibres mentioned hemp is the longest, and therefore the strongest. Bible makers and printers of paper money have always known this, so they use hemp whenever possible.

1916—HEMP RECONSIDERED

After cotton replaced flax and hemp as the major fibre crop, and woodpulp replaced rag paper, both of these once essential crops began to decline. Some rag paper continued to be made for "important" uses such as paper money, Bibles, and cigarette papers, but for books and newspapers it had become too expensive.

It was in the early 1900's, during World War I, when the federal government first became concerned about the rapidly dwindling timber supply, and started shopping around for alternate sources of paper. The Department of Agriculture was asked to solve the problem. In 1916, Lyster Dewey, Botanist in charge of Fibre-Plant Investigations, and Jason Merrill, Paper-Plant Chemist, published Department of Agriculture Bulletin No. 404. It was a research project to determine the feasibility of using Hemp Hurds As Paper Making Material.

Dewey and Merrill came to some startling conclusions about both hemp and our timber supply: "There seems to be little doubt that the present wood supply can not withstand indefinitely the demands placed upon it, and with increasing scarcity economy in the use of wood will become imperative. This effect is already apparent in many wood using industries.... Our forests are being cut three times as fast as they grow.... In view of these conditions it is advisable to investigate the paper-making value of the more promising plant materials before a critical situation arises." Now, fifty years later, the "critical situation" is here.

Dewey and Merrill made several batches of paper, using different processing methods; then they ran strength tests, finish and folding tests, and cost analysis comparisons between woodpulp paper and hemp-hurds paper. Not surprisingly, they found the "general character and tests of these papers correspond very closely with No. 1 machine finish paper, according to the specifications of the United States Government Printing Office...."

They found that to grow hemp for fibre and paper made far more ecological sense than using the same land for woodpulp production. "The most important point derived from this calculation is in regard to areas required for a sustained supply which are in the ratio of 4 to 1"— in favor of hemp. "Every tract of 10,000 acres which is devoted to hemp raising year by year is equivalent to a sustained pulp-producing capacity of 40,500 acres of average pulpwood lands."

At the time this study was done, the authors were confident hemp would continue to be grown in these United States. They concluded that "without a doubt, hemp will continue to be one of the staple agricultural crops of the United States. The wholesale destruction of the supply by fire, as frequently happens in the case of wood, is precluded by the very nature of the hemp raising industry. Since only one year's growth can be harvested annually the supply is not endangered by the pernicious practice of overcropping, which has contributed so much to the present high and increasing cost of pulp wood. The permanency of the supply of hemp seems assured."

Dewey and Merrill were not alone in that belief. As late as 1938 there were people working to revive the sagging hemp industry. The February, 1938, issue of *Popular Mechanics* featured an article on hemp, with the heading: "New Billion Dollar Crop." The reason for excitement was the invention of a new machine. The article began, "American farmers are promised a new cash crop with an annual value of several hundred million dollars, all because a machine has been invented which solves a problem more than 6,000 years old....

"The machine which makes this possible is designed for removing the fibre-bearing cortex from the rest of the stalk, making hemp fibre available for use without prohibitive amount of human labor...."

At last, a solution to the labor problem, but one year too late. The Marijuana Tax Act had gone into effect on October 1st, 1937, four months before the *Popular Mechanics* article appeared.

Popular Mechanics concluded their article with this statement: "If federal regulations can be drawn to protect the public without preventing the legitimate culture of hemp, this new crop can add immeasurably to American agriculture and industry." It was probably the last honest statement made about hemp in the 30s. From that point on, all the establishment newspapers and periodicals, including *Popular Mechanics*, limited their coverage to the "marijuana menace."

In the 40s, Fate intervened on the side of hemp for a brief period. The Japanese bombed Pearl Harbor and invaded the Philippines, cutting off the supply of manilla rope and twine, on which our government was depending as a hemp substitute to protect the youth of the country from the dread "marijuana menace." The health of the youth had to be forgotten temporarily, while the farmers of Iowa, Nebraska, Minnesota and other midwestern states rushed into the fields wih their tractors to plant hemp.

Their law-breaking was aided by the federal government. The Department of Agriculture provided seeds, fertilizer, machines, and planting instructions for those who had forgotten how to farm the vile weed. Although they were a little rusty, not having raised hemp for four years, the hard-working farmers did their best and produced 62,000 tons in 1943. As they say back home, that's a lot of grass!

The bumper crops of the 40s show how effective the federal government can be at stimulating hemp raising when it suits their political purposes. Without any change in the law or an act of Congress, the Department of Agriculture was able to get a crash program in high gear almost immediately. Willing farmers were located, seed was found, and a hemp planting manual was rushed into print.

Known as the *Farmers Bulletin No. 1935*, the planting manual is both a historical curiosity and a valuable source of useful information. It was reprinted in 1952, when someone in Washington got worried that the Chinese might invade the Philippines, while our troops were tied down in Korea, and cut off our manilla rope supply as the Japanese had done in 1941. Now that the paper shortage has hit and another crisis is

LYSTER DEWEY'S 1916 REPORT ON HEMP.

NIXON CALLS FOR HARSH NEW LAWS

Apparently conscious of his badly tarnished image, President Nixon included a tough new stance on drug traffickers in a recent special address to Congress. He cited a study by the Drug Enforcement Agency which reported average sentences for convicted pushers down from 73 months to 54 months. He also noted that federal studies show "more than a quarter of those who are convicted never serve a single day behind bars."

The President's new penalties would require minimum federal sentences of not less than 3 years for a first offense, with a maximum 15 years. Sentences for second offenses would not be less than 10 years or more than 30 years.

Apparently ignoring the recommendations of his own Marijuana Commission, Nixon's proposals would also increase the maximum penalty for trafficking in non-narcotic drugs, including marijuana, from the present 5 years for a first offense to 10 years.

News, #1, Summer 1974

THE FIRST THMQ
NEW YORK-PHILADELPHIA-BOSTON-BALTIMORE-WASHINGTON DC

Mexican commercial $15-30/oz...$130-200/lb. depending on quantity...Colombia connoisseur $45-90/oz...$400-900/lb...lavendar Thai sticks $100-175/oz...$700-2500/lb...Mushrooms $350/lb.
Trans-High Market Quotations, #1, Summer 1974

"R." INTERVIEWS TOM FORÇADE

Millions of people smoke grass for pleasure and many consider themselves cannabis connoisseurs. But our interviewee smokes pot for money. He is a professional dope taster, as essential to the modern marijuana industry as the wine or cheese taster is to the epicurean economy of Europe. This interview was conducted for HIGH TIMES by "R.," a noted dope critic and writer who is published regularly in New York City magazines and newspapers.
#4, Spring 1975

at hand, a third printing of *Farmers Bulletin No. 1935* would seem to be in order.

THE FUTURE OF HEMP PAPER

At first glance, the possibility of hemp paper making a comeback may seem pretty remote. However, when we consider the alternatives: a rapidly diminishing timber supply, clearcutting in our national forests, ecological disasters from lost watersheds and oxygen resources, deteriorating books in libraries, and escalating woodpulp paper prices—the repeal of anti-hemp legislation and a crash program to raise hemp and flax may be our best, if not only way out.

Actually, the repeal of the senseless anti-hemp laws and the restoration of the hemp industry may not be far off. As most of you probably know, the Consumers Union has recommended legalization and various state legislatures have legalization bills under consideration. According to a recent story in *Harper's Magazine*, Iowa is moving rapidly in that direction, and the next marijuana initiative in California is sure to succeed. The optimists are saying anti-hemp laws will be overturned in 1974 or '75. The pessimists say 1977—or later. I think it will be during the next Democratic administration.

While reading the comments of book publishers, binders, and printers, one gets the impression they'd like nothing better than to see the return of paper made from hemp. Librarians, most of all who must watch their cheap woodpulp books deteriorate and fall apart, would welcome the return of durable hemp/flax paper. The Library of Congress, in a recent report on paper-making says: "To preserve man's recorded ideas for future generations, paper manufacturers, book publishers, librarians and archivists must not only understand the magnitude of the problem, but also its urgency and must join forces to stop it."

I would add one more name to the list of people who must "join forces" to solve the paper problem—the hemp farmers.

For more information about hemp paper, contact: Solar Age Press, Box 610, Peterstown, WV 24963.

INTERVIEW WITH A DOPE TASTER

HIGH TIMES: How did you get into this unique profession?
Dope Taster: I was a dealer, starting out in high school with ounces and dime bags to my friends. I did it for about five years until I worked my way up to a brownstone in Brooklyn Heights. Then I lost all my money. I realized my real talent was not in dealing, but in tasting dope. I could never keep track of money. I couldn't judge people either. The one thing I could judge was dope.
HIGH TIMES: What led you to believe you had this talent?
Dope Taster: My friends who were dealers kept bringing dope to me to get my opinion. But I would never tell them whether to buy or not, and I still don't. I only articulate what it is that's unique about each dope. Ultimately, the dealers must decide whether to buy. I just give my opinion, in the most accurate and descriptive terms possible. I gather together and try to develop a vocabulary of pot and use it creatively to describe the effects of the weed.
HIGH TIMES: As I understand it, your reaction to a dope can do a lot to determine its market price. Just as a book critic's or a movie critic's

reaction is often a pretty good indication of saleability, in your position as a dope critic representing a syndicate your opinion may affect the price by $30 or $40 per pound, which may be hundreds of thousands of dollars overall. Right?

Dope Taster: Right. But it wasn't that way in the beginning. I had trouble establishing my credibility. Credibility is everything in this business. But now, I'd say that if I reject a dope, that dope probably won't be seen next year, and if I accept it, it will be in a lot of places. Our syndicate, my people that I work for, aren't...the biggest, but they may be the steadiest.

HIGH TIMES: You're filling a need, then.

Dope Taster: There are trendsetters in any industry. I'd say a lot of the other syndicates look to us for what to do.

HIGH TIMES: Your job is to scout out the fields, right? You go back in the mountains and find fields to buy. What have you found that became a hit on the dope hit parade?

Dope Taster: Well, for the East, Oaxacan was one of my early hits. Most of the Oaxacan weight that came in a few years ago was from what I chose. And then there was *punta roja*.

HIGH TIMES: Explain what *punta roja* is.

Dope Taster: *Punta roja* is Spanish for red point. It means that there are tiny red fibers in the buds. Now, to the average person it doesn't look red. But to someone who looks at dope all day long, day in and day out, night after night, very slight differences in coloration tell a lot. In the case of *punta roja*, it is apparently a sub-species of cannabis *sativa* that is extremely potent. It comes from the Llano area in Colombia, around Santa Marta. Another hit I had was the Jamaican from Blue Mountain.

HIGH TIMES: I remember that. It had a slightly metallic taste.

Dope Taster: From the iron in the soil down there. Now the Oaxacan has a minty taste and is also spicy. It tingles the taste buds.

HIGH TIMES: Sounds great.

Dope Taster: The minty taste allows the throat to stay open, which means you draw more smoke into your lungs without coughing it out.

HIGH TIMES: Like mentholated tobacco.

Dope Taster: It has that flavor, but naturally. There is a difference between mint and menthol, you know.

HIGH TIMES: Would you describe Oaxacan as an airy high?

Dope Taster: It's quite airy considering its power. Something from Culiacan has that airiness, but not the power.

HIGH TIMES: Explain where Culiacan is.

Dope Taster: Culiacan is in Mexico, north of Oaxaca, which is one of the southern-most provinces of Mexico. The intense sunlight there accounts for the strength, and it's also at a high altitude.

HIGH TIMES: Does altitude have anything to do with the high?

Dope Taster: Definitely. People who I consider my predecessors as dope critics have commented on it. I recall Mezz Mezzrow in his book *Living the Blues* commenting about the incredible gold pot grown in the mountains of Mexico. Even then, in the '30s, the high altitude stuff sold for more in Harlem.

HIGH TIMES: What's your professional reaction to this stuff here?

Dope Taster: This is Santa Marta gold. Excellent intellectual high. Very creative. If you look at the buds here, you see that the seeds are dark, but the bud is blond.

HIGH TIMES: What does that mean?

Dope Taster: It means that it is mature weed, fully developed, with a full complement of pollen, resin, and THC isomers. Very sophisticated high,

THE SECOND ISSUE.

"Coffee, tea, or grass?"

CANNABIS CRYONICS

Keep your smoke cool and it will keep you higher longer. According to the Journal of the American Medical Association, THC, the active ingredient in marijuana, decomposes over time. Dope kept refrigerated in the AMA study retained its full potency for over two years, while unfrozen weed lost at least one-sixth of its potency.
News, #1, Summer 1974

CONNECT CELEBS WITH CANNABIS CRIMES

BUDDY RICH.

AP/WIDE WORLD

On May 3, 1974, drummer Buddy Rich was fined $75 for possession of marijuana and ordered to forfeit $750 bail in Hobart, Tasmania.

James Miller, a member of the rock group War, has been arrested in Los Angeles for possession of marijuana and cocaine. Mayor Gail Anglada of Millstone, NJ, has been charged with growing marijuana in the peaceful Garden State village. She and her husband pleaded innocent to the charges, which entail a maximum sentence of five years in prison and a $15,000 fine.

HighWitness News, #2, Fall 1974

MOM'S MARIJUANA BUST

I just finished reading your second issue of HIGH TIMES and was entertained. But in the HighWitness News section I found an error. You have stated that Mayor Gail Anglada of Millstone, NJ, was busted. You also state that the charge which she pleaded innocent to was subject to a maximum sentence of 5 years and/or $5000 fine. This is incorrect. The charges were reduced to disorderly conduct. Also, her husband was arrested. I can guarantee the above info to be correct. You see, they're my parents.

Elton Anglada Jr., Millstone NJ

Letters, #3, Winter 1975

SONS OF FORD

AP/WIDE WORLD

Michael Ford, son of President Gerald Ford, recently admitted to Women's Wear Daily that he had smoked grass. His brother, Jack, admitted nothing, but both favor easing of marijuana laws. Steven Ford said he has never smoked grass, but that it wasn't for lack of chances to do so.

HighWitness News, #3, Winter 1975

but not particularly psychedelic like the best Mexicans.

HIGH TIMES: So you look at the seeds.

Dope Taster: Certainly. The seed is the heart of the matter, quite truly. You see how this seed has the chiaroscuro quality of a Rembrandt painting?

HIGH TIMES: Frankly, I never looked at it that way.

Dope Taster: Look! It has a delicate marbled pattern. And it's shiny. That's a good sign. I always look at the seeds first. They give a good idea of the quality. Usually. Of course, the only real test is smoking it.

HIGH TIMES: How do you preserve a critical detachment when you're high?

Dope Taster: I don't even try. I immerse myself into the flow of energy, the feeling that comes from the weed. I speak spontaneously from it.

HIGH TIMES: I've noticed that the most successful dealers usually have catchy phrases to describe the highs of their various pots.

Dope Taster: The language of dope criticism, yes.

HIGH TIMES: The dope speaks through you and you become its PR man, in a way.

Dope Taster: In a way, but I'm not a PR man for anybody or anything.

HIGH TIMES: It's more sophisticated, you mean?

Dope Taster: Not exactly sophisticated. You have to have a sophisticated sense, but also a sense of the masses. I compare it to Duke Ellington.

HIGH TIMES: So you have to appreciate fine nuances, but also know what the Furry Freak Brothers are going to like.

Dope Taster: Exactly. Of course, everyone does it. Everyone is their own dope taster, but I get paid for it so I begin to take it much more seriously. I feel a tremendous responsibility. If I fuck up, I may fuck up America.

HIGH TIMES: How do you extrapolate how pot is going to taste in Chicago when you're smoking it down in the field?

Dope Taster: Well, it's infinitely more powerful and more tasty down there, but you can tell. Bad weed tastes worse when it is fresh, and good weed tastes better.

HIGH TIMES: Explain that again.

Dope Taster: Any negative properties of the weed are greatly amplified when it's fresh, so it's easy to pick up on.

HIGH TIMES: What is an example of some bad grass?

Dope Taster: Bad grass? What is bad grass?

HIGH TIMES: Stuff you wouldn't recommend.

Dope Taster: Well, I never smoked a pot I didn't like, you know. I've smoked the humblest window-grown Kansas City weed and gotten off, and I would again. I never turn down any dope. I'm not a snob.

HIGH TIMES: What are the criteria for good reefer, though?

Dope Taster: Good taste is important. Of course, there are many different tastes, but some are more popular than others. And strength, obviously. But strength isn't everything. Lowland Colombian knocks you out, but it does not get you high. In other words, the narcoticizing effect overwhelms the psychoactive effect. Smell, or bouquet, is important. And appearance. Cosmetics are more and more important in this business.

HIGH TIMES: What's the best grass for fucking?

Dope Taster: It depends on what kind of a fuck you want. This grass would be good for an intellectual fuck.

HIGH TIMES: An intellectual fuck?

Dope Taster: Yes. Something like a mind-body communion, you know. I hate to hedge, but all grass is good for fucking. I mean, Jamaican is good for fucking.

HIGH TIMES: Why is that?

Dope Taster: It's very stimulating. It apparently has tetrahydro-cannabinol isomers that stimulate the pleasure centers of the body. Remember, all pot is not alike. The government studies that are being done are all totally invalid, because they fail to take this into account. THC typically occurs in nature in over 200 isomer forms. It's a very sophisticated molecule, one of the most sophisticated in organic chemistry. Each isomer has different subtle effects, and these isomers are present in varying proportions in different pot. These various permutations and combinations create vastly different highs. Do you understand?

HIGH TIMES: Yes. Getting back to this grass for a second, I notice that some of the buds have flecks of green. What does that mean?

Dope Taster: Well, this plant was probably picked a little early. Some of it was still alive, and therefore packed with chlorophyll, which makes it green. Chlorophyll is a source of harshness in grass. Now, greenness is not always bad. Hawaiian is green. Thai weed is green sometimes. But it's something to keep an eye on. You see, I have to say this in a properly qualified manner, because to make cavalier remarks in my position could be dangerous. Sometimes there are hundreds of thousands of dollars riding on deals, and that's no joke.

HIGH TIMES: There must be some tense moments in your profession when you're between two big syndicates, and you have to guess the various wholesale and retail values down the line.

Dope Taster: It's true. I have to know what I'm talking about and be able to explain it, sometimes in several languages.

HIGH TIMES: What languages?

Dope Taster: I speak Spanish, French and Arabic.

HIGH TIMES: Has anyone ever seriously challenged your judgment?

Dope Taster: There was one occasion. We were in the hotel in Bogota. A considerable sample, about 25 pounds, had been brought to us from a warehouse in Medellin. I smoked it and was not impressed. I leaned more toward another weed that we were considering, a very spicy, hashy gold thing. At that point, we were trying to choose from several warehouse loads. This one thing didn't even pass the initial test and we weren't willing to go down and even check it out further.

HIGH TIMES: You say warehouse load. How many pounds or tons in a warehouse load?

Dope Taster: Well, a warehouse could contain any amount, of course, but in this particular scene a warehouse usually contains one field and one field as they grow them in Colombia weighs in at around 5,000 to 10,000 pounds. Some less, some more. To get back to the story, the fellow who brought us the 25 pounds and I were in direct conflict about the relative qualities of the two dopes. His people, some rather nasty Spanish gentlemen with guns, were backing him up. Considerable trouble had been invested on both sides for us to be in the room, so the outcome of the issue was a serious matter. I suggested we roll up 25 joints of each of the two dopes. I then smoked his stuff, and he smoked mine, or at least the stuff I thought was better. Well, on about the eleventh joint, this guy just slid under the table; he just melted into the floor. He went with the flow. He became the flow, as it were. He flew. My stuff just cut through his brain like it was butter.

HIGH TIMES: Could you suggest some tips to the average person who is looking for good pot. What to look for?

Dope Taster: Naturally, I can't counsel to commit an illegal act. From a botanical point of view, however, I could make a few comments about cannabis sativa. The first thing is to understand that you have to get down

PRUNES, POT AND MONKEYS

Long-term marijuana use may affect human social behavior, according to a two-year study by Dr. Ethelda N. Sasenrath at the University of California, Davis, Primate Research Center. The investigator fed a group of macaque monkeys the equivalent of 20 joints a day for two years in the form of THC-spiked, iced raisin cookies and prunes.

She said the amount of marijuana was not as important to the study as its prolonged, daily use. After a month, she reported, the monkeys showed intoxication. "They were alternately restless and sleepy...there was a reduction in all social interaction...after two months the monkeys developed a tolerance to the drugged cookies and prunes.... After six to eight months, the females in the group grew so aggresive that they bit and hit a number of undrugged, control animals, and were subservient only to the alpha male, the group leader."

Dr. Sassenrath postulates that after months of daily marijuana use the monkeys' personalities were altered. She said she could find no evidence that regular marijuana use changed the monkeys physiologically or altered their sex drive.

Health, #6, October/November 1975

SITUATION NORML

Most people who have heard about NORML really don't know much about it. From their ads they look to be a well-meaning, liberalish organization that sells knick-knacks sporting its logo to raise funds, and they run ads in expensive magazines like Playboy. As a result, it's almost natural to assume that NORML is a pack of well-heeled opportunists who intend to cash in on the inevitable legalization of marijuana. Nothing could be further from the truth—or more dangerous to believe.

NORML is chronically broke. Its costly ad campaigns in Playboy and HIGH TIMES use space donated by the publishers. The staff at the national and local levels live from hand to mouth. National Director Keith Stroup, for example, earns only $13,500 a year to support his family and lives in the Washington NORML office. Stroup is a highly qualified attorney who could be earning an incomparably higher income, but he has turned down many lucrative dope cases because he felt they would interfere with his work at NORML. He has recently filed for personal bankruptcy.

Lines, #8, March 1976

THE FITZ-HUGH LUDLOW MEMORIAL LIBRARY

BY CLAY GEERDES

In 1857, a New England School Teacher named Fitz-Hugh Ludlow purchased six-pence worth of pure cannabis tincture and began experimenting with its effects and pleasures. The result was his essay "The Apocalypse of Hasheesh" and, later, *The Hasheesh Eater*, the first discussions of dope usage in American literature. For over a century these and other invaluable reflections on psychoactive substances have been ignored. But no longer. In 1970 a trio of rare book collectors (Robert Barker, William Daley, Michael Horowitz) in San Francisco decided to pool their resources and gather the world's most complete collection of the literature of drug usage.

Fitz-Hugh Ludlow Library, Spring 1975

THE MOST PROFITABLE HOBBY

If there are 20,000,000 regular marijuana smokers, and each smokes just one modest ounce of boo per month, that means a weekly consumption of over 160,000 pounds of pot! Analyzing a typical distribution pattern, this means that over 200,000 people are employed full-time just in dealing marijuana, not to mention an approximate 800,000 others earning a partial income. ("America's most profitable part-time hobby" as one sage put it.) Further clampdowns on pot traffic could throw the U.S. into an economic tailspin that only declaring war on Saudi Arabia or legalizing cocaine could pull us out of. Unless, of course, some nut decides to get us out of the Second Depression by declaring "war" on dope, thus on ourselves.

Flash, #3, Winter 1975

really close and look at it, like a couple of inches away from your eye, in a good strong light. Look at the color—gold, green, red, brown, silver, and the relative proportions of those colors. Look at the seeds, of course. Is it leaves or buds? Is it in good condition or is it falling apart? Is it fresh or dry? Does it have a weird smell or appearance? How is it packaged? Bricked? Pressed? Loose? What is the proportion of buds?

HIGH TIMES: Are buds over-rated?

Dope Taster: Yes. But there's a reason. If the buyer can see intact buds he or she knows that it definitely came from the top part of the plant, whereas if it's powder, it could be bottom leaf. You know, it's prestige. The bottom part of the plant is associated with the lower middle class. Someone upwardly mobile aspires to the top of the plant.

HIGH TIMES: Can you identify a pot by sight?

Dope Taster: Oh yes. I can look at any pot and tell you what province it came from. In some cases, I can tell the valley it came from. Because I've usually been there.

HIGH TIMES: Did you ever have a grass that became a bigger hit than you thought justified?

Dope Taster: At first I considered Hawaiian a foolish fantasy, but it became a bestseller in 1973. I didn't think Hawaii could grow enough grass to be significant in the commercial market. Also, I thought the green color wasn't marketable to a green-conscious America. But I went on taste and high, and committed my people very heavily financially to backing a few fields there. It turned out well. They sold it on the wholesale level for about $500 a pound and it retailed on up to $1500. Very fine stuff. They had financed it from the seedlings.

HIGH TIMES: What made it so good?

Dope Taster: One reason was the hypnotic intensity of it. Hawaiian is an extremely dramatic pot. The intensity was so great that few people could finish a joint, because they were so stoned they forgot they had a joint in their hand. The joint would go out and the people would sit transfixed by the sheer power of the stuff.

HIGH TIMES: How would you compare it to wacky weed?

Dope Taster: Hawaiian is high grass, lots of top end. Mental. Wacky weed is total. It makes you laugh, it makes everything absurd, it reduces your body to jelly. Wacky weed is not anti-intellectual, but it's not exactly cerebral either. Sort of reminds me of Quaaludes.

HIGH TIMES: I understand you're the person who gave wacky weed its name.

Dope Taster: When you're stoned, it becomes difficult to remember just who said what at a particular time in a particular room. There was a time and a room. Someone said wacky weed. I don't remember who. But the hardest part of dope criticism is developing the new vocabulary, an almost technological vocabulary. One thing about wacky weed, it's not for everyone. It shouldn't be given to people who aren't used to getting high a lot. I've seen people literally go into cardiac arrest. I hate to say that because it sounds bad, but it's true. Like they thought they had smoked pot before, but they just didn't know. That would never happen with Thai weed, by the way. Wacky weed is physical stuff.

HIGH TIMES: How does a dope earn the title wacky weed?

Dope Taster: To me, wacky weed is not just ultra-powerful dope. It's a special kind of Colombian that comes from certain parts of Colombia. It's pot that has produced so much resin that it has stifled itself and died—that's why it's black sometimes. The opium poppy does the same thing. It requires a purposeful overstimulation of resin production until the plant can't get air or sunlight. It drowns in its own oil, and then is carefully manicured and pressed in a hydraulic press.

HIGH TIMES: Is it true that there's counterfeit wacky weed around?

Dope Taster: It's true. You spread some hash oil over some good weed, press it in a hydraulic press, and come up with something that looks and smokes like wack. That's one thing I wouldn't smoke. Because it's synthetic. The delicate, volatile isomers are lost entirely. The most delicate ones are lost before dope ever even gets to America, but this process leaves you with only the crudest and most powerful knockout isomers, and it's a crude high. Forget it.

HIGH TIMES: What do you think of hash oil?

Dope Taster: Hash oil is another story. Good hash oil, like cherry red Lebanese or honey oil, is a great high. Although it loses many isomers, others are intensified. It's a different drug than pot, but it's still a fine drug. The worst oil, poorly refined and made from garbage to begin with, has a taste and high somewhat similar to...

HIGH TIMES: Iodine?

Dope Taster: Exactly. Crude oil has a lot of delta 3, 7, and 9. Those are the stultifying ones which suppress areas of the brain so others can become active; they are not the ones that stimulate. In other words, they stop old games, but they do not start new ones. The volatile, fragile top-end isomers are the creative ones that start new games, so to speak.

HIGH TIMES: Do you feel that pot has some evangelical purpose?

Dope Taster: In the Bible, they talk about how Moses was given the Ten Commandments through a burning bush. In the allegorical language of the Bible, that may have meant he was smoking weed. There are early versions of the Old Testament which have numerous references to wisdom weed, which is probably marijuana. I think marijuana just may be the plant substance humankind needs to achieve wisdom as a race. Maybe not. It's not for everyone, but widespread use of it seems to cool out a lot of macho tendencies in people. I certainly don't think the Bible is talking about smoking tobacco, although there are strains of tobacco that have psychedelic properties. Indian strains and South American strains like Kinnikinik, which will definitely send you tripping if you don't throw up first. Very harsh. That's why they were smoked through a long pipe in order to cool them down.

HIGH TIMES: What can you tell us about this year's pot market in terms of tastes and trends?

Dope Taster: I don't want to talk about this season until it's over. A lot of different people's money is still tied up in it.

HIGH TIMES: Let's talk about last year's market.

Dope Taster: Let's not talk about last year's market because last season was a tragedy for us.

HIGH TIMES: If you were being executed and were offered a last joint, what grass would you choose?

Dope Taster: You know, I've often thought about that as I was lighting up in some of the situations I've been in. Are you sure that I couldn't have two joints instead of one?

HIGH TIMES: Okay, two joints then.

Dope Taster: Thanks. You see, I'd rather smoke half of two than all of one. In many ways, this is a difficult question because if I were to die I would want the dope that would exalt me. That would probably be Thai weed. Half of a Thai joint to get me going, to give me the momentum to get off the ground and climbing. For the other half-joint, I think I'd go for top Mexican, for its astral ability to flow with the experience of dying, you know, the understanding and acceptance that comes with psychedelic consciousness.

JFK'S DEALER

"Early one evening I received a phone call at my apartment in Georgetown. It was one of Jack's most trusted press liasons, who informed me the President was planning a short vacation. He was taking his boat out with family and friends, and I was asked if I could provide him with the memos I had drawn up in accordance with our conversation two weeks earlier. Could I have everything ready by ten o'clock that night? I knew exactly what was meant by the call, because the President hadn't asked me to draw up any memos. By ten I had prepared a manila folder fill of blank paper. Inside was an ounce of fresh Panamanian."

I Was JFK's Dealer, #2, Fall 1974

SENATOR EASTLAND ON POT ZOMBIES

Introducing a report of subcommittee hearings on marijuana, Sen. James D. Eastland, chairman of the Internal Security Subcommittee, warned that the unchecked spread of marijuana use may cause many problems.

"If the cannabis epidemic continues to spread at the rate of the post-Berkeley period (since 1965)," Eastland raved, "we may find ourselves saddled with a large population of semi-zombies—of young people acutely afflicted by the amotivational syndrome." Eastland said that American society could be "largely taken over by a marijuana culture—a culture motivated by a desire to escape from reality and by a consuming lust for self-gratification, and lacking any higher moral guidance."

HighWitness News, #3, Winter 1975

MEXICAN
REVOLUTIONARY
EMILIANO ZAPATA.

POT, PEASANTS & PANCHO VILLA

by Robert Lemmo

On March 17, 1914, a year after Pancho Villa slipped across the border after hiding out in Texas as a disgraced fugitive, his 5,000 enthusiastic soldiers disembarked from their railroad fleet 70 miles north of Torreon, the only remaining obstacle to Villa's triumphant march to Mexico City. With the sympathy and support of the United States government and the Mexican people, Villa had amassed 28 pieces of field artillery, a score of machine guns, and eight railroad trains, including two construction trains and a press train for foreign journalists. Poised on the brink of their greatest triumph, the Villistas were only missing one thing: General Pancho Villa. He had left the train about 500 miles north to be best man at the wedding of an old friend. Villa finally showed up three days later, bedraggled, besodden, and red-eyed from lack of sleep. At the arrival of the Chief, the Villistas stormed the town, killed 7,000 men, lost 1,000, and toppled the government of Mexico.

A folksong was written to celebrate his victory at Torreon:
Well done, Pancho Villa
His heart did not waver;
He took the strongest fort
On the hill at Torreon.

One thing always gives me laughter,
Pancho Villa the morning after,
Ay, there go the Carranzistras...
Who comes here? The Villistas.

Chorus:
La Cucaracha, la cucaracha
Ya no puede caminar;
Porque no tiene, porque no tiene,
Marihuana que fumar.

(The cockroach, the cockroach
Can no longer walk;
Because he hasn't, because he hasn't,
Marijuana to smoke.)

Though Pancho Villa's military career is well documented, the personal history of the great man is almost unknown to the public. His legends are recorded mainly in the oral tradition of Mexico, passing from father to son in the form of corridos, the Mexican folk songs. Since most of the revolutionaries of Villa's army could not read or write, the songs of the people tell the story: Not only was Villa a great fighter, he also knew how to party.

There were four battle hymns of the Mexican Revolution: Adelita, La Cucaracha, Marcha Zacatescas, and Valentina. Two deal with Villa. Adelita, a mournful love song, was inspired by a tragic alliance between Villa and an inspiringly beautiful soldier-girl in his army. But it was La Cucaracha that served as Villa's theme song, swelling to over 100 verses chronicling all his victories, hardships, and debaucheries in ten years of revolution.

Verse after verse of La Cucaracha speaks lovingly and intimately of marijuana, which was virtually the official refreshment of the Mexican Revolution. As such, it marked the first time in modern warfare that an entire war was fought stoned. About half of Villa's army was comprised of long-haired Indians (primarily Yaquis) who used marijuana as casually and regularly as we might use salt. Haldeen Braddy, a Villa biographer, states that at Torreon, "The Yaquis grew fanatical. High on marijuana, they fought like demonic spirits. They stormed the entrenchments. They ground out yards and still got nowhere. Then they staggered about here and there confused."

After getting devoutly zonked for the battle of Agua Prieta, according to Braddy, "The intrepid Indians acted like wild men completely out of their heads from inhaling marijuana. Immediately the Indians rose to a crouch and headed for the barbed wire. The marijuana gave them superhuman strength. So frenzied were they with the drug that some of them succeeded in breaking the wire with their hands."

As for the rest of Villa's troops—Mexicans, Spaniards, Negroes, Caucasians, and all combinations thereof, marijuana was a staple in their revolutionary diet. Likewise, many stayed high on potent mixes of mescal and sotol, native forms of psychedelic whiskey distilled from desert cacti. Villa himself was probably the greatest debaucher and carouser of them all. That's why they made him the leader, according to some accounts. Revolutionary author Marin Luiz Guzman, describing his first meeting with Villa, remembered entering a smoke-filled shed, where he spied the notorious leader in a dimly lit corner. Villa lay in bed, covered by a blanket, fully dressed in hat, coat, and cartridge belts. The Chief was giggling and talking excitedly to his two companeros, also fully clad and on the bed. As Guzman was introduced, "Villa listened to him unblinkingly. His mouth was open and there were traces on his face of the mechanical smile that seemed to start at the end of his teeth."

Pancho Villa was a truly popular revolutionary leader, one of the common people, a peon responsible for some of the most brilliant and successful military operations ever fought; this done under adverse conditions, with untrained, ragtag troops, while simultaneously throwing some of the biggest parties ever seen in Mexico before or since. In fact whether fortune waxed or waned on the Villistas, they maintained a steady choogle on the road of revolution. The siege of Agua Prieta, says Braddy, resembled something of a weary modern rock festival: "The women nursed their crying babies and cooked frijoles; the moon-bosomed girls made promiscuous love; the peons swigged their sotol...long haired Indians, some of whom smoked marijuana at night and danced wildly about their campfires." Constantly low on supplies, the followers of Pancho were never low on the basic inspiration for their actions.

Born Doroteo Arango in 1878 of Indian and Spanish ancestry, Villa began life as a simple peasant. Villa began his career as an outlaw, bandit and enemy of the ruling class suddenly and early. When he was sixteen, his young sister Mariana was raped by the son of the owner of the hacienda on which Villa's family worked. Villa immediately grabbed the family pistol, killed the man, and then took to the hills. A corrido describes his flight:

In the wilderness untrammeled,
In the highest mountain crags,
I'll hide myself,
Where none will know I was guilty,
For my love of thee,
For such a crime.

"Well, how about if I do a study correlating marijuana use with dandruff?...bad breath?...lint?"

LATEST POT SCARE DISMISSED

Another marijuana health scare was unveiled recently by a Columbia University College of Physicians & Surgeons researcher. Dr. Gabriel Nahas and his team claim to have found a direct link between long-term marijuana smoking and inhibited production of white blood cells.

According to Nahas's paper, which appeared in *Science* Magazine, Feb. 1, 1974, the constant doper is more susceptible to communicable diseases. The paper suggested a reconsideration of the Shafer Commission's call for decriminalization of grass. It also calls on the medical profession to oppose any easing of marijuana penalties.

Keith Stroup of NORML (National Organization for the Reform of Marijuana Laws) charged that Nahas was a biased observer. For example, Nahas's recently published book *Marijuana: Deceptive Weed* claims a connection between marijuana and mental illness, even suicide, and contained such witty generalizations as "There's no such thing as a little marijuana."

Dr. Norman Zinberg in the *Journal of Contemporary Drug Problems* compared Nahas's attitude with the film *Reefer Madness*. Dr. Lester Grinspoon in the *New England Journal of Medicine* called *Weed* "The most biased account of cannabis since 1938." Grinspoon, the author of *Marijuana Reconsidered*, and a Harvard professor, accused Nahas of "pharmacological McCarthyism, which compels him to use half truths, innuendo, and unverifiable assertions...."
Health, #1, Summer 1974

POT JEWELRY LEGAL

The DEA has announced that "pot jewelry" is now the only marijuana sold legally across the counter. In the last several years, key chains, chokers, belt buckles and pendants containing marijuana leaves have become a popular holiday gift. The announcement comes after inquiries from manufacturers of the costume baubles that feature pot encased in a solid resin base, or a laminate plastic chunk. The agency has decided that marijuana so preserved is "effectively destroyed."
Law, #4, Spring 1975

PAUL KIRCHNER

Never prosecuted for the killing, Villa soon gathered about him a band of similar outlaws and began a career of banditry unparalleled in Mexican history, which is rich in colorful criminals. Unlike other banditos, Villa would slaughter a rich hacienda's cattle herd, then give an old peasant farmer 1,000 pesos to keep his tiny spread. In a land where a mere 17 families owned one-fifth of all Mexico, Villa quickly became a folk hero among the poor farmers.

Though he was a cold-blooded killer in battle, the young Villa was a smoldering Latin in love. The buckskin-clad nomad caught many a lady's fancy. If not, Villa was more than willing to commit rape. The only documented instance of Villa abandoning a seduction occurred in the El Dorado Bar in Juarez. Eyeing an attrative young barmaid, Villa threw her a provocative look, then rubbed his fist on his face, which at that time and place meant something like, "Let's get going." She seemed complacent until he revealed his identity, whereupon she answered tartly, "Senor, you should remember that Villa has the charm of a gentleman, and does not pass the time in small, dark bars. He lives in the sun, fights clean battles, and makes short work of little men like you."

Usually, however, Villa got the girl. One night in Chihuahua City, Villa was getting high and wenching in a fancy cantina. One of Villa's men was eyeing a Federalista's girl. The Federalista made his resentment clear, but Villa's lieutenant persisted with crude courting gestures. The Federalista drew his gun and shot the lieutenant in the mouth. Before the dead man even toppled, Villa fired from under his arm and drilled the Federalista neatly through the head. Instantly Villa dragged the girl away and made ferocious (by all accounts) love to her.

For all his dope, booze, and philandering, Pancho Villa was a firm believer in marriage. In fact, he had at least four "legal" wives, and was happy to marry any young senorita for the night, if that's what it took. It is said that when Villa married his second wife, the first wife was convinced to serve breakfast in bed to the honeymoon couple. But he loved his first wife, Luz Corral, most, and for all his days.

Villa pursued a colorful career as a bandit, but had no ambitions as a revolutionary until 1909. In that year, his little daughter died. Villa's wife sent messengers to him with the news, but they were detained and mistreated by Don Luis Terrazas, governor of the state of Chihuahua and one of the wealthiest cattlemen in the entire world. (It is reported that a Chicago slaughterer once wired Terrazas asking him if he could possibly supply a million head of cattle and Terrazas wired back: "What color?") When Villa eventually learned of the daughter's death and Terrazas's mistreatment of the messengers, he immediately assembled a huge band and raided Terrazas's territory. In a raging bloodlust, Villa utterly devastated the property, and killed hundreds. Without even intending to, Villa took over the land, destroyed the state government, and won the idolatry of the peons as never before. The peons saw Villa as an hombre who could transform bitter dissatisfaction into successful revolution.

At first, Pancho Villa joined the revolution for profit. There were many revolutionary movements in Mexico at the time, and often the line between a revolutionary and a bandit was narrow indeed. Villa was delighted to loot, plunder and kill with impunity as a captain in the Revolutionary Army. Why not? But upon meeting the acknowledged leader of the Revolution, Francesco Madero, Villa became a changed man. Madero was a small, black-bearded, hollow-eyed vegetarian. His

ANDREW WEIL

"Some plants remain relatively independent of man while others get very involved. Marijuana for one has been involved with us for so long, thousands of years, following campsites and settlements and the like, that there's no information about what it was like in prehistory. It appears that some plants make some kind of evolutionary decision to become involved with our trip. Marijuana is very involved."

Interview with Andrew Weil by Peter Fremont, #5, August/September 1975

intense idealism and devotion to land reform for the people touched Villa's heart, and though he little understood the details, he committed himself to Madero and the Revolution. For all his erratic fits of temper, Villa was constant in his devotion to Madero.

Villa did not fare too well as a revolutionary. Once he was sentenced to be hanged, another time to be shot, but each time a reprieve from Madero saved his life at the last possible moment. Villa languished in jail in Mexico City for four months. On Mexican Independence Day, Villa escaped and fled to El Paso, where he soon assembled a new army, by carrier pigeon, in Chihuahua City. After a bloody battle, Juarez was captured. The untutored Villa administered the city himself, and during his one-year rule he legalized gambling and prostitution, paved the streets, raised the salaries of the teachers, rebuilt the hospitals, maintained the railroads, and happily levied tribute from the gringos. As for dope, it was not only legal, but practically free. A whole armload of marijuana could be had for a few pesos. Villa bided time, using the opportunity to purchase huge supplies of equipment and guns from the U.S. and making friends with General "Black Jack" Pershing.

During the Juarez period, Villa lived high, wide and handsome. Using gold treasures he had buried in chests throughout Mexico, he outfitted his army and bought his wife a deluxe Hudson and himself a Cadillac.

Villa was now at his peak. He controlled most of northern Mexico. Parties were thrown almost nightly, and farmers labored hard harvesting enough mescal, sotol, and marijuana to keep Villa's hedonistic troops supplied. After the climactic battle at Torreon, Madero was installed as President, and Villa was a national hero as Madero's finest general. Villa was happy, and as a Christmas present, he returned the government of Chihuahua City to the people. In return, the soldiers of the town presented Villa with a medal. But Villa had been stoned all night on a potent breed of high mountain marijuana which had just been harvested (1913 was a vintage year, according to Mexicanos, and that in itself may have provided the additional impetus to push the revolution over the top). According to radical writer John Reed, who witnessed the formal ceremony, Villa arrived in an old khaki uniform, with several buttons missing, his hair in disarray. Reed wrote:

"He entered the aisle between the rigid lines of soldiers, walking a little pigeon-toed, in the fashion of a horseman, hands in his trouser pockets. Finally, pulling his moustache and looking very uncomfortable, he moved toward a gilded throne, with lions-paw arms, raised on a dais under a canopy of crimson velvet. He shook the arms violently to test the throne's dependability, then sat down. There followed six speeches extolling Villa's bravery on the field. Through it all Villa slouched on the throne, his mouth hanging open, his shrewd eyes playing around the room. Once or twice he yawned, but for the most part seemed to be speculating with some intense interior amusement, like a small boy in church.... Finally, with an impressive gesture, an Artillery officer stepped forward with a small cardboard box. The officers applauded, the crowds cheered, the band burst into a triumphant march."

Villa put out both hands eagerly.... He could hardly wait to open the box and see what was inside.... He held up the medal, scratched his head, and, in a reverent silence, said clearly, "This is a hell of a little thing to give a man for all that heroism you are talking about."

Pancho Villa did not spend all his time wandering about as a stoned buffoon. Tragedy stalked him everywhere, even in pleasure. Around this

The deranged mind behind

DOPE RIDER belongs to Paul Kirchner, a spaghetti Western addict from New York. Paul has

done illustrations for both *Screw* and *The New York Times*, but says, "HIGH TIMES is the only suitable outlet for me to communicate how the world actually works." Paul did his location research for *Dope Rider* by hitchhiking to California several times while he was in high school, and his favorite artist is Sergio Leone.
Closers, #12, August 1976

TETRAHYDROCANNIBINOL (THC),
the psychoactive ingredient in marijuana and hashish, may retard the spread of cancer, medical researchers at the College of Virginia in Richmond recently reported. Doctor Richard Carchman supervised a group of pharmacologists who treated cancer-ridden rodents with injections of THC. The THC apparently "slowed the growth of lung tumors, a mammary tumor and a virus-induced leukemia" and thus "significantly prolonged the lives of the animals afflicted with the illness." The Virginia researchers also found that smoking marijuana may relieve the depression of cancer patients.
Health, #3, Winter 1975

WACKY CAKE

BY ALLEGRA LOOMIS

1/3 cup oil
1/4 lid marijuana
Saute grass in oil for about 30 minutes, strain, and let cool.
Sift together into one small baking dish (6" x 9"):
1 1/2 cups flour
1 cup sugar
1/2 tsp. baking soda
1/2 tsp. salt
3 tbs. cocoa (unsweetened)
Dig three holes in mixture. Into one hole add 1/3 cup strained oil; into one hole add 1 tbs. white vinegar; and into last hole add 1 tsp. vanilla. Pour one cup water over entire mixture, stir carefully with fork until blended. Bake at 350 degrees for 30-35 minutes. Sift powdered sugar over top while still warm and serve (best when warm).
An hour later, you're *sanpaku* again.
Cuisine, #2, Fall 1974

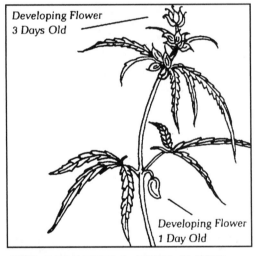

Developing Flower
3 Days Old

Developing Flower
1 Day Old

SEPARATING THE BOYS FROM THE GIRLS

Q: The sinsemilla article in your July issue had some beautiful photos of the stars of the show, the virgin female plants. At least one shot of a male with flowers would have been a good idea, like the author described in the text. It would help your readers recognize the pollen producers in time to uproot them.
Audrey Hepplewhite, Shenandoah, PA
A: The male flowers can be recognized in the early stages of development by the tiny flowerets dangling from the opened calyx (see ill.). When the flowerets open, pollen is dispersed by the wind from protruding yellow stamens.
Forum, #13, September 1976

time, he became involved with the beautiful Adelita. Their romance became the symbol of the tragedy and poetry of the Revolution. Adelita was dark, olive, tall and ravishingly attractive—just Villa's type. At twenty, this country goddess was already betrothed to the blonde Portillo, one of Villa's loyal friends. But she couldn't resist one last fling, particularly with the lusty revolutionary leader. At one banquet, Adelita rose and made a speech in honor of Villa, casting hot eyes on him. She ended her accolade with the hope that Villa would become president of Mexico. Pancho later talked alone with her in the courtyard in hot, hungry kisses, while the band played La Cantela, a song from the Bajio region of Michoacan:

I find myself a prisoner in cunning.
I find myself imprisoned by a woman
As long as I live in this world and don't die,
Never in my life will I love again.

We took for granted that we were trash
Along came the whirlwind and took us up,
And while high up in the air we flew,
The same winds blew us apart.

Suddenly, Portillo, Adelita's betrothed, stepped into the garden and beheld Villa and Adelita. He paused, torn between fury and despair; then, with a hopeless gesture, he pushed his gun into his mouth and thunderously blew off the top of his head.

Villa, ignorant of Adelita's engagement, sat petrified with surprise. He had loved and trusted Portillo. Learning the truth, he shook Adelita roughly, and commanded his men to take her where he would never see her again. Villa built a special tomb for Portillo and even buried a pair of his best boots with the man as an expression of grief. His sorrow would be sung about by the rebel minstrels after battle had been retired, when, as Braddy describes, "the Villistas attended their wounds, patched their saddles—and wet their whistles. Sotol irrigated parched throats, burning away the shock of recent defeat. In the dark night, marihuana cigarettes spurted tiny red tongues of fire and crackled a little as the flames ate into the haylike weed."

The incident continued to bother Villa, and no amount of getting high or military success could erase it. One night about a year later, he became so despondent that he sought out the leading songwriter of the Revolution, Ochoa, and requested something new to soothe his nerves. Ochoa then sang the mournful verses of "Adelita":

Adelita is the name of the young one
Who I love and cannot forget.
In the world I have a rose
And, with time, I shall pluck her.

If Adelita should go with another
If Adelita should leave me all alone,
I would follow in a boat made of thunder
I found follow in a train made of bone.

On and on Ochoa sang, through ten more stanzas. Villa stumbled away and bowed his kinky head in tears. Adelita was to grow to over a hundred verses after Villa's second tragic encounter with the girl. Early in 1913, Villa organized an elite force known as the Dorados (Golden Ones). There were three squadrons, each of 100 horsemen, superbly mounted and armed. Although the rest of Villa's army traveled with women and children in tow, the Dorados were unencumbered with camp followers and could strike swiftly.

One afternoon, during a bloody carnage, Villa observed a youthful Dorado with a yellow scarf in the thick of battle. He was enraged; he had ordered his elite Dorados to stay out of this particular fight. After the battle, he saw the Dorado sprawled on the sand, his yellow scarf stained bloody red. Turning over the corpse, he discovered it to be the girl Adelita.

Villa's fortunes began to decline after this. His old enemy Carranza came into power, backed by the United States, and Villa fought a desperate battle to regain the Republic. In retribution for U.S. support of the Carranza dictatorship, he raided Columbus, New Mexico. General "Black Jack" Pershing and his troops were sent on a punitive mission. Pershing, an old friend, always managed to be a few days behind Villa and battle was never joined, but it created pressure. Villa's Yaqui Indians smoked marijuana and drank more and more sotol to keep their wounded moving. Supposedly in hot pursuit, Pershing's men were furiously learning the secrets of romantic Mexico. Tamales and tequila, warm women and long marijuana cigarettes under the Chihuahua moon were much more appealing than battle with a drifting band of wild-eyed Villistas. The Americans pursued town after town, composing troopers' songs about Pancho, quaffing Mexican beer, lusting after young prostitutes and being taught the delights of exotic Mexican weeds. Theirs was not the staunch cavalry duty glorified by Gary Cooper and John Wayne.

Early in June, 1919, Villa occupied the northern town of Guadalupe, and prepared to attack Juarez. His new army consisted of a motley band of misfits, and they drank Guadalupe dry before mounting their assualt on Juarez sometime before dawn on June 15. Riding crazily into the midst of the city, yelling and screaming profanities, firing wildly and overwhelming the terrified Carranzistas, Villa conquered Juarez for the third and final time. By daybreak, the frustrations of the past months erupted into a memorable party that engulfed the whole city. Tequila, cheap perfume, young girls, soldiers, the smell of marijuana, and the sounds of fist fights filled the night. It was, by all accounts, the longest and most exuberant fiesta of the revolution. The staunchest of carousers were still staggering along the boulevards in a stupor, bawling out corridas, when the Carranzistas counterattacked the next morning.

Bleary-eyed and exhausted from lack of sleep, the Villistas were in no condition to fight. The Carranzistas easily overpowered Villa's disorganized pack of revelers.

Thus the revolution ended as it had begun—a drunken, stoned, ferocious brawl. This was to be Villa's swan song, as his foes adopted the modern techniques and hardware developed in the war in Europe. Villa fled the battlefields and hid in the mountains. Shortly after, Carranza was assassinated, and a new phalanx of generals took his place. They looked more kindly on the old war horse and allowed him to retire to a large ranch, where he tried to live quietly. But too many atrocities had been committed, too many wives courted, too many political intrigues still brewed, and on Friday, July 20, 1923, as General Villa motored out of Parral in his Dodge automobile, accompanied by several bodyguards, a pumpkinseed vendor, standing beside the road, shouted, "Viva Villa!" The general slowed his car and lifted his hand in obliging salute. A

THE POTENT MAJORITY

The U.S. government is growing concerned over the possibility that the giant domestic marijuana plants, which grow wild through the Midwest, may become extremely potent as the years go by. The Department of Health, Education, and Welfare has found, through a series of studies, what many smokers have long known: the wild plants contain almost no THC and are virtually useless for getting high.

However, the HEW also found that of the wild plants, the high THC-producing strains are dominant, that is, when they are cross-pollinated with low THC plants, high THC pot is the inevitable result. The government has found that successive marijuana crops in Mississippi have been growing stronger by the year, and it is worried that the same thing will happen to the wild weeds in the Midwest.
HighWitness News, #3, Winter 1975

THE INDOOR OUTDOOR HIGHEST QUALITY MARIJUANA GROWER'S GUIDE

by Mel Frank and Ed Rosenthal (Level Press, San Francisco, $2.95) This is the season generally associated with harvesting crops, legal as well as illegal; and if your crop turned out to be as dismal a failure as mine, you are ready for some good advice for the next attempt. Advice for growing healthy marijuana is common, advice cultivated from scientific research isn't. That is why *The Indoor Outdoor Highest Quality Marijuana Grower's Guide* is probably what you have been looking for.

Ed Rosenthal has compiled an authoritative and easy to use manual on growing cannabis. Most of the book deals with indoor growing, making this autumn as worthwhile a time as any to bone up on raising your own stash of homegrown. Rosenthal and Frank combine uncomplicated terminology with explicit illustrations to turn even the most colorless thumb green. Not only does the book describe the most functional methods of utilizing growing space in even the smallest apartment for a continuous supply of pot, but it makes avalable products from Clearlight Growing System.
Books, #2, Fall 1974

"THE ANSWER TO THE PROBLEM IS SIMPLE—GET RID OF DRUGS, PUSHERS AND USERS. PERIOD."
—Harry Jacob Anslinger, 1892-1975

HARRY JACOB ANSLINGER,

zealous mastermind of international antidope legislation and America's number two lawman for over 30 years, finally died in Hollidaysburg, Pennsylvania, on November 14, 1975. Anslinger was 83.

As commissioner of the Bureau of Narcotics, Anslinger was singlehandedly responsible for outlawing marijuana and writing the tough dope laws of today. He created the federal system of drug enforcement and administered it from 1930 to 1962.

In 1937, Anslinger wrote his definitive study on the "evils" of marijuana. First published in *The American Magazine*, "Marijuana: Assassin of Youth" had immeasurable impact, resulting in generations of fear and intolerance on the part of parents, teachers, police, clergy and other traditional guardians of youth's developing consciousness. Within a year of its publication, the United States Congress banned marijuana with the passage of the Marijuana Tax Act.
Marijuana: Assassin of Youth, #8, March 1976

MARIJUANA AIDS CANCER PATIENTS

New research indicates that marijuana is effective for alleviating the vomiting and nausea that plague thousands of cancer patients undergoing chemotherapy, and should be used as a treatment for such side effects.

In a report published by researchers at the Sidney Farber Cancer Center, a branch of the Harvard Medical School, there was at least a 50 percent reduction in vomiting and nausea in 12 of 15 cases involving marijuana drug treatments. Five patients suffered no nausea at all. There was no decrease in vomiting or nausea in 14 control cases on whom a placebo was used.

Patients in the study received delta-9 THC, the active ingredient in marijuana and the one responsible for pot's euphoric effect.
Health, #8, March 1976

volley of machine-gun fire clattered down on the car's occupants, and all but one fell dead. Villa's body was torn by sixteen bullets. One bodyguard, a conspirator, escaped and was never seen again.

A corrido, La Muenerte, memorialized him:

> *Though you may not like it, I repeat*
> *In these plain and honest words,*
> *That young roosters like Pancho Villa*
> *Are not born every day.*

On Villa's grave, a single marijuana plant grew tall and straight, a lonely reminder of the cockroach who could not walk without marijuana.

MARIJUANA: ASSASSIN OF YOUTH
by Harry Anslinger

The sprawled body of a young girl lay crushed on the sidewalk the other day after a plunge from the fifth story of a Chicago apartment house. Everyone called it suicide, but actually it was murder. The killer was a narcotic known to America as marijuana, and to history as hashish. It is a narcotic used in the form of cigarettes, comparatively new to the United States and as dangerous as a coiled rattlesnake.

How many murders, suicides, robberies, criminal assaults, holdups, burglaries, and deeds of maniacal insanity it causes each year, especially among the young, can be only conjectured. The sweeping march of its addiction has been so insidious that, in numerous communities, it thrives almost unmolested, largely because of official ignorance of its effects.

Here indeed is the unknown quantity among narcotics. No one can predict its effect. No one knows, when he places a marijuana cigarette to his lips, whether he will become a joyous reveler in a musical heaven, a mad insensate, a calm philosopher, or a murderer.

That youth has been selected by the peddlers of this poison as an especially fertile field makes it a problem of serious concern to every man and woman in America.

There was the young girl, for instance, who leaped to her death. Her story is typical. Some time before, this girl, like others of her age who attend our high schools, had heard the whispering of a secret which has gone the rounds of American youth. It promised a new thrill, the smoking of a type of cigarette which contained a "real kick." According to the whispers, this cigarette could accomplish wonderful reactions and with no harmful aftereffects. So the adventurous girl and a group of her friends gathered in an apartment, thrilled with the idea of doing "something different" in which there was "no harm." Then a friend produced a few cigarettes of the loosely rolled "homemade" type. They were passed from one to another of the young people, each taking a few puffs.

The results were weird. Some of the party went into paroxysms of laughter; every remark, no matter how silly, seemed excruciatingly funny. Others of mediocre musical ability became almost expert; the piano dinned constantly. Still others found themselves discussing weighty problems of youth with remarkable clarity. As one youngster expressed it, he "could see through stone walls." The girl danced without fatigue, and the night of unexplainable exhilaration seemed to stretch out as though it were a year long. Time, conscience, or consequences became too trivial for consideration.

Other parties followed, in which inhibitions vanished, conventional barriers departed, all at the command of this strange cigarette with its ropy, resinous odor. Finally there came a gathering at a time when the girl was behind in her studies and greatly worried. With every puff of the smoke the feeling of despondency lessened. Everything was going to be all right—at last. The girl was "floating" now, a term given to marijuana intoxication. Suddenly, in the midst of her laughter and dancing, she thought of her school problems. Instantly they were solved. Without hesitancy she walked to a window and leaped to her death. Thus can marijuana "solve" one's difficulties.

The cigarettes may have been sold by a hot tamale vendor or by a street peddler, or in a dance hall or over a lunch counter, or even from sources much nearer to the customer. The police of a Midwestern city recently accused a school janitor of having conspired with four other men, not only to peddle cigarettes to children, but even to furnish apartments where smoking parties might be held.

A Chicago mother, watching her daughter die as an indirect result of marijuana addiction, told officers that at least 50 of the girl's young friends were slaves to the narcotic. This means 50 unpredictables. They may cease its use; that is not so difficult as with some narcotics. They may continue addiction until they deteriorate mentally and become insane. Or they may turn to violent forms of crime, to suicide or to murder. Marijuana gives few warnings of what it intends to do to the human brain.

The menace of marijuana addiction is comparatively new to America. In 1931, the marijuana file of the United States Narcotic Bureau was less than two inches thick, while today the reports crowd many large cabinets. Marijuana is a weed of the Indian hemp family, known in Asia as Cannabis Indica and in America as Cannabis Sativa. Almost everyone who has spent much time in rural communities has seen it, for it is cultivated in practically every state. Growing plants by the thousands were destroyed by law-enforcement officers last year in Texas, New York, New Jersey, Mississippi, Michigan, Maryland, Louisiana, Illinois, and the attack on the weed is only beginning. It was an unprovoked crime some years ago which brought the first realization that the age-old drug had gained a foothold in America. An entire family was murdered by a youthful addict in Florida. When officers arrived at the home they found the youth staggering about in a human slaughterhouse. With an ax he had killed his father, his mother, two brothers, and a sister. He seemed to be in a daze.

"I've had a terrible dream," he said. "People tried to hack off my arms!"

"Who were they?" an officer asked.

"I don't know. Maybe one was my uncle. They slashed me with knives and I saw blood dripping from an ax."

He had no recollection of having committed the multiple crime. The officers knew him ordinarily as a sane, rather quiet young man; now he was pitifully crazed. They sought the reason. The boy said he had been in the habit of smoking something which youthful friends

FINLATOR ON ANSLINGER

"Before Harry Anslinger came along, the public didn't know anything about marijuana and they didn't care. They just believed what people told them.

Particularly, the Mexican-Americans were using it, and we thought that was bad for a number of reasons. Racial bias was one of them. The last Harris poll showed seventy percent still against legalization. But when asked how they felt about the new Oregon law, where marijuana is treated like a parking ticket, thirty-six percent favored it with forty-nine percent opposed. So you can see the trend. Decriminalization is coming soon."

Interview with John Finlator, former Deputy Director of the Bureau of Narcotics and Dangerous Drugs (BNDD), #2, 1974

ANSLINGER'S BID FOR CELLULOID STARDOM

To the Ends of the Earth (1947) was Harry Anslinger's bid for celluloid stardom, one skirmish in the lengthy rivalry between the great narc and J. Edgar Hoover, the great commie hunter. But where Hoover got Jimmy Stewart for *The FBI Story*, Anslinger's Hollywood friends slipped him Dick Powell, ferret-faced former Busby Berkeley song-and-dance man, looking slightly constipated as a tough T-man. And so dope ran a poor second to communism as America's number one Fear. Anslinger's grasping ambition and racism propel the film forward, but the great killjoy's mug appears only briefly at the beginning, where he is pictured at a treaty signing on "Long Island, home of the United Nations."
Movies, #4, Spring 1975

THE RISING COST OF GETTING HIGH

In Mazatlan, a pound of primo tops wholesales for $25. In Tucson, it changes hands for $175. In Boston, the same weed costs $250; in all, a 1,000 percent markup from the producer's price and a rise of 50 to 100 percent above the top prices of five years ago. This is no exception, but the rule—and signs point to worsening dope-dollar inflation in the years to come.

What causes dope inflation? A recent article in *The New York Times*—they quoted us, so they must know—credited the price rise to the growing purchasing power of those people who, a decade ago, began to get high in high school or college. Today, thousands of these smokers are affluent doctors, lawyers and professionals in every profitable field. Experienced connoisseurs, they can and will pay top dollar for high-quality weed. Even younger consumers are prepared to pay for the status of high-priced dope.
Lines, #10, June 1976

called "muggles:" a childish name for marijuana.

Since that tragedy there has been a race between the spread of marijuana and its suppression. Unhappily, so far, marijuana has won by many lengths. The years 1935 and 1936 saw its most rapid growth in traffic. But at least we now know what we are facing. We know its history, its effects, and its potential victims. Perhaps with the spread of this knowledge the public may be aroused sufficiently to conquer the menace. Every parent owes it to his children to tell them of the terrible effects of marijuana to offset the enticing "private information" which these youths may have received. There must be constant enforcement and equally constant education against this enemy, which has a record of murder and terror running through the centuries.

The weed was known to the ancient Greeks and it is mentioned in Homer's Odyssey. Homer wrote that it made men forget their homes and turned them into swine. Ancient Egyptians used it. In the year 1090, there was founded in Persia the religious and military order of the Assassins, whose history is one of cruelty, barbarity, and murder, and for good reason. The members were confirmed users of hashish, or marijuana, and it is from the Arabic "hashshashin" that we have the English word "assassin." Even the term "running amok" relates to the drug, for the expression has been used to describe natives of the Malay Peninsula who, under the influence of hashish, engage in violent and bloody deeds.

Marijuana was introduced into the United States from Mexico, and swept across America with incredible speed.

It began with the whispering of vendors in the Southwest that marijuana would perform miracles for those who smoked it, giving them a feeling of physical strength and mental power, stimulation of the imagination, the ability to be "the life of the party." The peddlers preached also of the weed's capabilities as a "love potion." Youth, always adventurous, began to look into these claims and found some of them true, not knowing that this was only half the story. They were not told that addicts may often develop a delirious rage during which they are temporarily and violently insane; that this insanity may take the form of a desire for self-destruction or a persecution complex to be satisfied only by the commission of some heinous crime.

It would be well for law-enforcement officers everywhere to search for marijuana behind cases of criminal and sex assault. During the last year a young male addict was hanged in Baltimore for criminal assault on a ten-year-old girl. His defense was that he was temporarily insane from smoking marijuana. In Alamosa, Colorado, a degenerate brutally attacked a young girl while under the influence of the drug. In Chicago, two marijuana-smoking boys murdered a policeman.

In at least two dozen other comparatively recent cases of murder or degenerate sex attacks, many of them committed by youths, marijuana proved to be a contributing cause. Perhaps you remember the young desperado in Michigan who, a few months ago, caused a reign of terror by his career of burglaries and holdups, finally to be sent to prison for life after kidnapping a Michigan state policeman, killing him, then handcuffing him to the post of a rural mailbox. This young bandit was a marijuana fiend.

A 16-year-old boy was arrested in California for burglary. Under the influence of marijuana he had stolen a revolver and was on the way to stage a holdup when apprehended. Then there was the 19-year-old addict in Columbus, Ohio, who, when police responded to a disturbance complaint, opened fire upon an officer, wounding him three times, and was himself killed by the returning fire of the police. In Ohio a gang of seven young men, all less than 20 years old, had been caught after a series of 38 holdups. An officer asked them where they got their incentive.

"We only work when we're high on tea," one explained.

"On what?"

"On tea. Oh, there are lots of names for it. Some people call it 'mu' or 'muggles' or 'Mary Weaver' or 'moocah' or 'weed' or 'reefers'—there's a million names for it."

"All of which mean marijuana ?"

"Sure. Us kids got on to it in high school three or four years ago; there must have been 25 or 30 of us who started smoking it. The stuff was cheaper then; you could buy a whole tobacco tin of it for 50 cents. Now these peddlers will charge you all they can get, depending on how shaky you are. Usually though, it's two cigarettes for a quarter."

This boy's casual procurement of the drug was typical of conditions in many cities in America. He told of buying the cigarettes in dance halls, from the owners of small hamburger joints, from peddlers who appeared near high schools at dismissal time. Then there were the "booth joints" or Bar-B-Q stands, where one might obtain a cigarette and a sandwich for a quarter, and there were the shabby apartments of women who provided not only the cigarettes but rooms in which girls and boys might smoke them.

"But after you get the habit," the boy added, "you don't bother much about finding a place to smoke. I've seen as many as three or four high-school kids jam into a telephone booth and take a few drags."

The officer questioned him about the gang's crimes: "Remember that filling station attendant you robbed—how you threatened to beat his brains out?"

The youth thought hard. "I've got a sort of hazy recollection," he answered. "I'm not trying to say I wasn't there, you understand. The trouble is, with all my gang, we can't remember exactly what we've done or said. When you get to 'floating,' it's hard to keep track of things." "If I had killed somebody on one of those jobs, I'd never have known it," explained one youth. "Sometimes it was over before I realized that I'd even been out of my room."

Therein lies much of the cruelty of marijuana, especially in its attack upon youth. The young, immature brain is a thing of impulses, upon which the "unknown quantity" of the drug acts as an almost overpowering stimulant. There are numerous cases on record like that of an Atlanta boy who robbed his father's safe of thousands of dollars in jewelry and cash. Of high-school age, this boy apparently had been headed for an honest, successful career. Gradually, however, his father noticed a change in him. Spells of shakiness and nervousness would be succeeded by periods when the boy would assume a grandiose manner and engage in excessive, senseless laughter, extravagant conversation, and wildly impulsive actions. When these actions finally resulted in robbery the father went at his son's problem in earnest and found the cause of it—a marijuana peddler who catered to school children. The peddler was arrested.

It is this useless destruction of youth which is so heartbreaking to all of us who labor in the field of narcotic suppression. No one can predict what may happen after the smoking of the weed. I am reminded of a Los

ANSLINGER'S LAST INTERVIEW

As he explains in this interview, Anslinger never really believed that Prohibition could work, but he did his job zealously because it was there. Finally in 1961, Anslinger's persistant labors paid off. The Single Convention on Narcotic Drugs created an international commitment to unilateral war on dope. The worst part of the Single Convention is that it places federal drug laws beyond the reach of American voters and their elected representatives. . .the U.S. government is bound by law to honor any international treaty; the treaty may not be altered or discontinued without the consent of every party to the treaty. With the Single Convention in effect, Harry Anslinger's work was done. He retired to Hollidaysburg, Pennsylvania.

HIGH TIMES: Having enforced laws against both alcohol and drugs, how do you feel about the dangers of strong drink?

Anslinger: I can tell you about alcohol. After all, it doesn't have the prolonged effect marijuana has. Now, there's where the danger is.

HT: Haven't most comparative studies found that alcohol is more destructive than marijuana?

A: I'm talking about the man who will use one marijuana cigarette and go out and drive a car and knock things over. A fellow with one or two drinks, it will wear off in a couple of hours.

HT: One marijuana cigarette wears off a lot quicker than eight or ten drinks, which is the more usual alcohol ration in cases of drunken driving.

A: Marijuana, that stuff'll stay with you for about six hours. You're not going to get away from it and you don't have that immediate effect.

HT: Most experts today feel that marijuana is harmless.

A: It has been condemned as a dangerous drug by the American Medical Association, by the World Health Organization and also by the United Nations Commission of Narcotic Drugs.

HT: On the other hand, it's been pronounced harmless by the Board of Trustees of the American Medical Association in 1973, the National Institute of Drug Abuse in 1975, the congressionally sponsored Brown Commission law enforcement study of 1972 and the Canadian Commission of Inquiry into the Non-Medical Use of Drugs in 1971.

The Man Who Turned Off the World by Peter Biasucci, #21, May 1977

MARIJUANA AND VIOLENT CRIME

A government study on the relationship between marijuana and violent crime—marijuana seems to disincline folks to violent crime—has been suppressed by the National Institute of Mental Health.

The study, conducted in Jamaica two years ago by Dr. Vera Rubin of New York, found that pot smokers are much less prone to aggressive behavior than alcohol drinkers.

Dr. Rubin's study, which cost taxpayers $158,000, has been repressed because of "politics," an NIMH offical stated.
Health, #4, Spring 1975

MARIJUANA ARRESTS

1965	18,815
1966	31,119
1967	61,843
1968	95,870
1969	118,903
1970	188,682
1971	225,828
1972	292,179
1973	420,700
1974	445,600

Source: FBI Uniform Crime Reports
HighWitness News, #8, March 1976

Angeles case in which a boy of 17 killed a policeman. They had been great friends. Patrolling his beat, the officer often stopped to talk to the young fellow, to advise him. But one day the boy surged toward the patrolman with a gun in his hand; there was a blaze of yellowish flame, and the officer fell dead.

"Why did you kill him?" the youth was asked.

"I don't know," he sobbed. "He was good to me. I was high on reefers. Suddenly I decided to shoot him."

In a small Ohio town, a few months ago, a 15-year-old boy was found wandering the streets, mentally deranged by marijuana. Officers learned that he had obtained the dope at a garage.

"Are any other school kids getting cigarettes there?" he was asked. "Sure. I know fifteen or twenty, maybe more. I'm only counting my friends." The garage was raided. Three men were arrested and 18 pounds of marijuana seized.

"We'd been figuring on quitting the racket," one of the dopesters told the arresting officer. "These kids had us scared. After we'd gotten 'em on the weed, it looked like easy money for awhile. Then they kept wanting more and more of it, and if we didn't have it for 'em, they'd get tough. Along toward the last, we were scared that one of 'em would get high and kill us all. There wasn't any fun in it."

Not long ago a 15-year-old girl ran away from her home in Muskegon, Michigan, to be arrested later in company with five young men in a Detroit marijuana den. A man and his wife ran the place. How many children had smoked there will never be known. There were 60 cigarettes on hand, enough fodder for 60 murders.

A newspaper in St. Louis reported after an investigation this year that it had discovered marijuana "dens," all frequented by children of high-school age. The same sort of story came from Missouri, Ohio, Louisiana, Colorado—in fact, from coast to coast.

In Birmingham, Alabama, a hot tamale salesman had pushed his cart about town for five years, and for a large part of that time he had been peddling marijuana cigarettes to students of a downtown high school. His stock of the weed, he said, came from Texas and consisted when he was captured, of enough marijuana to manufacture hundreds of cigarettes.

In New Orleans, of 437 persons of varying ages arrested for a wide range of crimes, 125 were addicts. Of 37 murderers, 17 used marijuana, and of 193 convicted thieves, 34 were "on the weed." One of the first places in which marijuana found a ready welcome was in a closely congested section of New York. Among those who first introduced it there were musicians, who had brought the habit northward with the surge of "hot" music demanding players of exceptional ability especially in improvisation. Along the Mexican border and in seaport cities it had been known for some time that the musician who desired to get the "hottest" effects from his playing often turned to marijuana for aid.

One reason was that marijuana had a strangely exhilarating effect upon the musical sensibilities (Indian hemp has long been used as a component of "singing seed" for canary birds). Another reason was that strange quality of marijuana which makes a rubber band out of time, stretching it to unbelievable lengths. The musician who uses "reefers" finds that the musical beat seemingly comes to him quite slowly, thus allowing him to interpolate any number of improvised notes with comparative ease. While under the influence of marijuana, he does not realize that he is tapping the keys with a furious speed impossible for one in a normal state of mind; marijuana has stretched out the time of the music until a dozen notes may be crowded into the space normally occupied by one. Or, to quote a young musician arrested by Kansas City officers as a "muggles smoker":

"Of course I use it—I've got to. I can't play any more without it, and I know a hundred other musicians who are in the same fix. You see, when I'm 'floating' I *own* my saxophone. I mean I can do anything with it. The notes seem to dance out of it—no effort at all. I don't have to worry about reading the music—I'm music-crazy. Where do I get the stuff? In almost any low-class dance hall or night spot in the United States."

Soon a song was written about the drug. Perhaps you remember:
Have you seen that funny reefer man?
He says he swam to China;
Any time he takes a notion,
He can walk across the ocean.

It sounded funny. Dancing girls and boys pondered about "reefers" and learned through the whispers of other boys and girls that these cigarettes could make one accomplish the impossible. Sadly enough, they can—in the imagination. The boy who plans a holdup, the youth who seizes a gun and prepares for a murder, the girl who decides suddenly to elope with a boy she did not even know a few hours ago, does so with the confident belief that this is a thoroughly logical action without the slightest possibility of disastrous consequences. Command a person "high" on "mu" or "muggles" or "Mary Jane" to crawl on the floor and bark like a dog, and he will do it without a thought of the idiocy of the action. Everything, no matter how insane, becomes plausible. The underworld calls marijuana "that stuff that makes you able to jump off the tops of skyscrapers."

Reports from various sections of the country indicate that the control and sale of marijuana has not yet passed into the hands of the big gangster syndicates. The supply is so vast and grows in so many places that gangsters perhaps have found it difficult to dominate the sources. A big, hardy weed, with serrated, swordlike leaves topped by bunchy small blooms supported upon a thick, stringy stalk, marijuana has been discovered in almost every state. New York police uprooted hundreds of plants growing in a vacant lot in Brooklyn. In New York State alone last year 200 tons of the growing weed were destroyed. Acres of it have been found in various communities. Patches have been revealed in backyards, behind signboards, in gardens. In many places in the West it grows wild. Wandering dopesters gather the tops from along the right of way of railroads.

An evidence of how large the traffic may be came to light last year near LaFitte, Louisiana. Neighbors of an Italian family had become alarmed by wild stories told by the children of the family. They, it seemed, had suddenly become millionaires. They talked of owning inconceivable amounts of money, of automobiles they did not possess, of living in a palatial home. At last their absurd lies were reported to the police, who discovered that their parents were allowing them to smoke something that came from the tops of tall plants which their father grew on his farm. There was a raid, in which more than 500,000 marijuana plants were destroyed. This discovery led next day to another raid on a farm at Bourg, Louisiana. Here a crop of some 2,000 plants was found to be growing between rows of vegetables. The eight persons arrested confessed that their main source of income from this crop was in sales to boys and girls of high-school age.

G. GORDON LIDDY
THE MAN WHO FIXED THE 1969 DOPE SHORTAGE

AP/WIDE WORLD

The newly installed Nixon regime, eager to consolidate its shaky power with more law-and-order, decided to crack down on dope in a dramatic way. The chief of the Bureau of Narcotics and Dangerous Drugs (BNDD) at the time was John Ingersoll, a colorless bureaucrat ill-disposed to Nixon's extreme measures. An outside hit man was called for, someone willing to do a dirty job with enthusiasm. G. Gordon Liddy was the man.

The most ambitious attempt ever mounted by the American government to choke off the flow of marijuana from Mexico began on September 21, 1969.

Administered by Liddy on location in Mexico City, Operation Intercept made intensive checks of every vehicle crossing the border...as detailed in Lawrence A. Gooberman's sociological study *Operation Intercept: The Multiple Consequences of Public Policy*, the shortage of marijuana caused many young drug users to switch to hard drugs.
G. Gordon Liddy's Killer Narc Squad
by Pam Lloyd, #5, August/September 1975

HIGH TIMES IS GROWING

Compulsive enumerators will notice that HIGH TIMES has grown from 84 to 116 pages, of which about 35 are advertising. Still, HIGH TIMES has about 30 percent ads, well below the 40 percent-and-up ratio of other publications. More ads mean we can expand the magazine.

Why does HIGH TIMES have so many ads? We can't say for sure. It might be that the prevalence of potheadedness has spawned a cottage industry of craftspeople and small paraphernalia manufacturers who see HIGH TIMES as their big break, their chance to reach the public with an idea whose time has come.

Businesswise, if you're waiting for HIGH TIMES rolling papers, HIGH TIMES hash pipes, HIGH TIMES massage oil, HIGH TIMES clubs, etc., forget it, because there probably aren't going to be any. HIGH TIMES is into information and entertainment, not empires.

One of the nice things about this magazine is that we've received approximately 30,000 letters since we started and only five have been negative. Thanks.
Closers, #6, October/November 1975

Centerfold — Nepalese Temple Balls and Hash Fingers

High Times

August '76

$1.50

Daredevil Doperunners

The Case for Valium

Pulque, Booze of Brujos

The Story of O

Poppy Time in Laos

Comix: Dope Ride

Leather, Sex and Mushrooms

Interview: Harvard's Dr. Norman Zinberg

RYAN O'NEAL BUSTED

Actor Ryan O'Neal gained the dubious distinction of being one of the first people to be arrested under California's new dope laws. O'Neal was arrested at his home in Beverly Glen, California, after police acting on an informant's tip searched his home and allegedly found five ounces of marijuana. Police did not name the informant. O'Neal, who gained fame in the television series *Peyton Place* and the movies *Love Story* and *Paper Moon*, is free on $500 bail.
HighWitness News, #9, May 1976

GLENN O'BRIEN

"Even my fan club is a secret society," claims rock star Glenn O'Brien, lead singer for the somewhat secretive band, Konelrad, and author of this month's investigative speculation about Masonic influence on 200 years of American history. The editor of Andy Warhol's *Interview* magazine for three years and a veteran of *Rolling Stone* and *Oui*, O'Brien has now given up editing for rock'n'roll. Before he vanishes into the limelight, though, O'Brien will give one clue to his disappearance soon when HIGH TIMES publishes his conclusive guess that all of Western Civilization itself is a secret society. Stay tuned.
Closers, #11, July 1976

With possibilities for such tremendous crops, grown secretly, gangdom has been hampered in its efforts to corner the profits of what has now become an enormous business. It is to be hoped that the menace of marijuana can be wiped out before it falls into the vicious protectorate of powerful members of the underworld.

But to crush this traffic we must first squarely face the facts. Unfortunately, while every state except one has laws to cope with the traffic, the powerful right arm which could support these states has been all but impotent. I refer to the United States government. There has been no national law against the growing, the sale, or the possession of marijuana.

As this is written a bill to give the federal government control over marijuana has been introduced in Congress by Representative Robert L. Doughton of North Carolina, Chairman of the House Ways and Means Committee. It has the backing of Secretary of the Treasury Morgenthau, who has under his supervision the various agencies of the United States Treasury Department, including the Bureau of Narcotics, through which Uncle Sam fights the dope evil. It is a revenue bill, modeled after other narcotic laws which make use of the taxing power to bring about regulation and control.

The passage of such a law, however, should not be the signal for the public to lean back, fold its hands, and decide that all danger is over. America now faces a condition in which a new, although ancient, narcotic has come to live next door to us, a narcotic that does not have to be smuggled into the country. This means a job of unceasing watchfulness by every police department and by every public spirited civic organization. It calls for campaigns of education in every school, so that children will not be deceived by the wiles of peddlers, but will know of the insanity, the disgrace, the horror which marijuana can bring to its victim. And, above all, every citizen should keep constantly before him the real picture of the "reefer man"—not some funny fellow who, should he take the notion, could walk across the ocean, but—

In Los Angeles, California, a youth was walking along a downtown street after inhaling a marijuana cigarette. For many addicts, merely a portion of a "reefer" is enough to induce intoxication. Suddenly, for no reason, he decided that someone had threatened to kill him and that his life was in danger. Wildly he looked about him. The only person in sight was an aged bootblack. Drug-crazed nerve centers conjured the innocent old shoeshiner into a destroying monster. Mad with fright, the addict hurried to his room and got a gun. He killed the old man, and then, later, babbled his grief over what had been wanton, uncontrolled murder.

"I thought someone was after me," he said. "That's the only reason I did it. I had never seen the old fellow before. Something just told me to kill him!"

PISS, LEATHER AND WESTERN CIVILIZATION
by Glenn O'Brien

This is a story about perverts and how they got that way. As it happens, some of my best friends are. The Anvil Bar is down on the corner of 14th and West Streets in the heart of Manhattan's meat district. During the day butchers and truckers drink beer there and watch the go-go girls dance.

The girls pull down their G-strings and snatch up dollar bills from big, bloody fists. At night the trucks still roll in filled with carcasses, and the Anvil is still hopping. Macho men in denim, flannel shirts and leather jackets swagger into the bar, big keyrings swinging from their belts. But they're there for a different kind of show. These men aren't truckers, though they could be taken for truckers. Almost, but not quite, sweetheart.

In fact, these are the infamous leather boys, denizens of the gay S & M subculture. By day they may be stockbrokers, window dressers, artists, you name it—but by night they are leather. You've caught rumors of them in *Vogue* magazine (which didn't write up the Anvil for its go-go girls), you might have noticed a certain style in the pages of *After Dark* or you might have wondered about that new store in your neighborhood that sells handcuffs and Crisco T-shirts. These fags are no drag queens. These are male impersonators; no swishes need apply. They take it tough and dirty. The show they come to see at the Anvil features boys hanging from chains by the balls, from hooks by the asshole, men humping men and fist fucking—which in case you're not aware of the latest craze, is one man performing a high colonic on another, an arm up the ass to the elbow. That's entertainment!

The Anvil was busted a few weeks before this writing. A couple of New York's Finest swore they actually saw this fist feat performed. No doubt they were undercover (if they were in uniform, going undercover would involve removing their badges and putting their handcuffs on their belts). Can you imagine what they told the boys down at the station house? Anyway, the Anvil is still open for business, so you can see for yourself if you can pass muster at the door. But sorry, it's been closed to ladies ever since Lee Radziwill was reported drinking ringside there in *Women's Wear Daily*. Even Fran Lebowitz, who "covers the Waterfront" for *Andy Warhol's Interview*, couldn't get into the place on the arm of John Waters, director of *Pink Flamingos*, and she was wearing denim!

But who can blame the cops and the beautiful people for wanting to crash a party like the Anvil. There's so little excitement in show business and the arts these days, a fist-fucking show is bound to be a deeply felt performance. And it's not just the Anvil that's on the forefront of decadent culture. The many other leather, western attire and specialty bars in this S & M neighborhood create a unique culture center of the world. Look out, Cleveland!

It's all there under the West Side Highway, an elevated road up the Hudson that's been closed down since it started to fall apart dangerously a few years ago. The iron skeleton roadway is itself a symbol of decadence. But the only action on it is the occasional visit of brass thieves looking for remnants of the fixtures of a happier age. Down below, the trucks roar by the rotting, gutted docks that once constituted the busiest port in the world. Today no ships call, but the idea of sailors lingers. One of the gutted piers is called The Pier. To enter, you have to bend down low, crawl through debris, watch out for holes offering direct access to the Hudson and avoid the rats who call the place home. Inside is the promise of perfectly anonymous sex—no witty repartee, no names, no faces, no hangups. The trucks—a row of empty semi's—used to be the meeting place for these strangers. The trucks were dark, but less dangerous. There's something more perfect about the pier.

Then there are the other bars: the Spike, Keller's, Ty's, the Ramrod and the everpopular Eagle's Nest. They define a sensibility, a neighborhood—on a dark night, a religion. Let's face it, New York is the leading exporter of decadent imagery to the world: illusion flows from here to Timbuktu, and West Street is the most advanced decadence in New York. It's not just fluff;

ANDY WARHOL

BY GLENN O'BRIEN

America's greatest artist talks about cutting out paper dolls, fruit, the death of art, turkeys, his favorite color, Campbell's Soup, the Factory, the Velvet Underground, junk food, drugs, why he sleeps with dogs, psychiatry, Marshall McLuhan's daughter, rich people, poor people and happiness.

AW: I had my first coke in ten years.

HT: Really?

AW: I mean Coca-Cola. I used to drink Coke all the time. It was so good. It gives you energy.

HT: Did you ever take acid?

AW: No. Someone thought they slipped it to me once, but I wasn't eating.

HT: Did you ever smoke pot?

AW: No, but I like the smell of it.

HT: Did you ever take any drugs?

AW: No, nothing that ever made me funny or anything. When I was in the hospital after I was shot they gave me drugs, but it was so great to get off those.

HT: Have you ever been drunk?

AW: Yeah.

HT: What happens when you get drunk?

AW: Nothing. I tell everyone they can be on the cover of *Interview*. It's fun getting there, but when you get there, it's such an awful feeling. It's not worth it.

HT: Do you think drugs make people more or less creative?

AW: I don't think they do anything.

HT: Do you think pot should be legal?

AW: Yeah, I do.

Interview, #24, August 1977

MICHAEL KENNEDY

BY RON ROSENBAUM

ANDRE GROSSMANN

Mr. Kennedy is one of the top political lawyers in America and had among his clients members of the Weather Underground, the United Farm Workers, GI-coffeehouse organizers, Los Sieta de la Raza, Wounded Knee, Jack and Micki Scott, who harbored Patty Hearst, and lately the Puerto Rican Socialist Party.

HT: What were those first dope cases like?

MK: Marijuana charges. The first dope case that I took was a kid named Gypsy Peterson, who was the organizer of a GI coffeehouse at Fort Hood, Texas. He had been found with eight seeds in the lining of his pocket and was given eight years—a year a seed—by a Texas court.

HT: Do you feel that dope has helped radicalize people politically?

MK: Definitely. Dope obviously gives you a different perception of the society you live in and causes you to question some of the things that may have been traditionally unquestioned values.

Interview, #17, January 1977

AMANITA MUSCARIA

BY TOM ROBBINS

By far the most significant consumers of the mysterious red mushroom, in terms of historical impact, were the ancient Near Eastern fertility cults and the Sanskrit-speaking Aryans who migrated into India between 2000 and 1500 B.C. Had these peoples not been so fond of the fungus, Vatican City may not have been built, the Ganges would be no more holy than the East River and Billy Graham might be back in North Carolina selling golf carts.

One other indication of the mushroom's last influence: the Greek word *kannabis*—our "cannabis"—has been traced to the much older Sumerian word *gan*, meaning the head of the penis, which the young fly agaric so graphically resembles, as well as the toadstool itself. Thus, marijuana was named for the *Amanita muscaria*, whose more potent properties it was thought to approximate. Isn't history fascinating?

Superfly, #16, December 1976

it's serious play at the end of a spectrum.

Take the Eagle's Nest, perhaps the most famous leather bar in the world. Not much from the outside, it is nevertheless notable for the bedsheet-sized American flag hanging in the window, and the window itself is emblazoned with small eagles of the kind that signify "colonel" in other circles. The awning says "Eagle Open Kitchen." There's often a row of bikes parked out front, but the bikes aren't wild and unkempt like those of outlaw gangs. In fact, these bikers are more than neat. They are obsessively turned out in gear that ranges from traditional (studied Wild One) to futuristically modified SS Death's Head look. At the door there's a sign requesting proper attire, leather or western, and there's a doorman to hold inspection. Regulars might get away with less than leather, but fairy dress and women are not welcome. Not that a few women have not penetrated the portal, but only as an extraordinary courtesy to the escort.

The Eagle's Nest is named after Hitler's mountaintop retreat at Berchtesgaden. So are the little Eagle pins worn on leather jacket collars and the Eagle T-shirts on the guys. And the decor: signs advertising meetings of the Eulenspiegel society, the F.F.A. (Fist Fuckers of America) and Sunday Brunch. The walls are hung with cycling trophies, aquilas of motorcycle clubs who have paid visits, dayglo posters of larger-than-life rough trade, used blue jeans for sale. The help is interesting too. John Dowd, bartender on duty, is a famous artist of the New York Correspondence School, an art movement with strong roots in these environs. Stripped to the waist for action, he rapidly pops the tops off Buds and Cokes (leather men favor cans, since they are less dangerous). A muscular man, Dowd looks ready to quell any disturbance. There never is any. The bar is pure order, but he's ready anyway.

When John Dowd wears a shirt, it's usually a T-shirt that says "FETISH." Over the barstools hang meat hooks, used here as hatracks for helmets. A sign announces the date of the next slave auction. The customers are interesting too. They are dressed like lumberjacks, construction workers, cowboys, motorcycle racers. Funny times we live in. You see a cop off duty, and he's got on a hot pink jumpsuit, platform go-go boots and a ruff; you see an off-duty hairdresser, and he's got on an L.L. Bean flannel shirt and Can't Bust'em overalls with tool pockets. Anyway, most women would be scandalized by just how butch these faggots are. No kidding, if Elliott Gould and James Caan walked in, they'd look swish next to some of these guys. Not all of them, though—the male hustler esthetic isn't foolproof, and the cowboy with his ass actually sticking all the way out of the holes ripped in the back of his jeans would definitely not make it on the range.

It's not hard to understand the psychology behind the scene we have described. It stands to reason that a man who is sexually attracted to men might prefer fucking manly rather than womanly men. Thus we have a convention of masculinity, with femininity (or the passive role) lurking close to yet definitely under the surface. Still, there are definite role choices. S & M is the name of the game, so we have S's and we have M's, and that's where the code comes in. It's a sort of dress code; what you wear conveys what you're looking for. If you're an S, your keys are worn on the left side of your belt. Right is vice versa. A red hankie in the left back pocket means you're into the receiving end of a fist; right pocket means you are the fist. (Fashion note: trade journals report that Puerto Rican youths are busy ripping the sewn-in red kerchiefs out of the back pockets of a popular brand of jeans.) Blue hankies are for scatologists. Those are the basics.

But then again, as we said, sometimes the mind just isn't made up.

Sometimes we lie. You can't wear your keys in the middle. According to Rene Ricard, novelist and retired Warhol leading man, the keys don't mean anything. According to the popularizer of fist fucking, film director Fred Halsted (*L.A. Plays Itself*, *Sex-tool*), 95 percent of gay leather males are M's. "It's usually a competition to see who can be the M fastest." Thus there hangs over the Eagle's Nest and similar establishments an air of hard-edged ambiguity. The keys can lie, or fib at least. But the signals are still all-important. As one regular says, "It's a heavy visual trip. The posing is really much more important than the sex which may or may not follow." Stares penetrate. Love looks threateningly. There's an unspoken tension— a light mist of murder hangs in the air.

But do these guys really want to get hurt? Do they dream of sexy death? Steven Varble, New York's premier costume performance artist, avant-garde playwright, author of a history of the Parke-Bernet galleries and former protege of Liberace, made the following statement to me while standing beneath the totally chromed motorcycle that hangs suspended from the ceiling of the Eagle's Nest.

"If I weren't an artist, I'd be a murderer, I would!" He laughs as if imagining this statement in print in *Art Forum*. "We're all monsters, you know." Steven lists a considerable and impressive catalog of artists who are of the leather persuasion, as if S & M were a kind of initiation required by the state of modern art. He comments that this particular bar gives him the peace he requires to be able to do his work.

"It's kind of like a church in here." he says. "S & M is a religion. It's a way to conquer pain by playing with it. It doesn't work, of course, in the end, but it's a way. I think it's the religion of the white race. The reason we've taken over the world is because we can take pain. The blacks hate pain. They can't stand it. They'll do anything to get away from it. They don't belong to the city. That's why they start taking heroin when they're babies."

Got that? Cut to: Movie theater of film school, where 12 members of the all white, French New Wave seminar are watching a film. On screen is the beautiful actress Anna Karina and Eddie Constantine, who is known in Frogland as "Lemmy Caution" and who functions as their Philip Marlowe. The movie they are watching is *Alphaville*, in which Jean-Luc Godard is making some revolutionary discoveries about the workings of control mechanisms in Western culture in the form of a sci-fi detective story. Karina, a sex surrogate, and secret agent Caution are sitting in a darkened theater watching themselves watch a film we can't see. We hear the voice of Alpha 60, the computer ruler of Alphaville:

> The Central Memory is given its name because of the fundamental role it plays in the logical organization of Alpha 60. But no one has lived in the past, and no one will live in the future. The present is the form of all life, and there are no means by which this can be avoided. Time is a circle which is endlessly revolving. The descending arc is the past, and the rising arc is the future. Everything has been said. At least as long as words don't change their meanings and meanings their words. It is quite obvious that someone who usually lives at the limits of suffering requires a different form of religion from a person who lives securely.

What the college students do not realize is that this last sentence has already been said by William James, famed philosopher brother of Henry, and the man who once saw God while on nitrous oxide. This is because the college students have never heard of William James and are, in fact, asleep.

Cut back to: The only bar in New York named after a home of Adolf Hitler. Steven is still talking while he eyes the eyes in the place, noting costume and demeanor: "The only place that compares to this is jail. I could live in jail. I've been to jail, and everything was the same—how you

GOV'T REPORT DISMISSES POT THREAT

The fifth annual report on marijuana prepared by the National Institute on Drug Abuse is one of the most even-handed "official" reports on the effects of grass yet published. Dr. Robert L. DuPont, director of the institute, reports that research conducted during 1975 failed to confirm several beliefs about marijuana, including those that smoking leads to genetic damage, impotence and lower fertility rates. Although the NIDA report tends to favor legalization, DuPont added that he would like to have more scientific data on what he termed "marijuana intoxication." He asserted that the long-range effects of marijuana use are not yet known, and that heavy users of grass develop a physical dependence on it and a tolerance to its effects.
Health, #10, June 1976

CARTER ENDORSES DECRIM

Surrounded by a phalanx of Secret Service agents, HIGH TIMES news editor A. Craig Copetas recently questioned Democratic presidential hopeful Jimmy Carter on marijuana and the Drug Enforcement Administration (DEA).

"I favor the decriminalization of marijuana," said Carter, "but I'm not sure about the legitimacy of the federal government making this rule. Now in the field of alcohol, for instance, it's been a right reserved for the states and I don't think there are any uniform federal laws on the sale of alcohol except for the taxation of it. I think decriminalization is a matter best left up to the states for the time being."

Carter also said that if elected president, he would "certainly be personally responsible for a thorough investigation and correction of the defects of the DEA." His remarks on the DEA followed an investigation of the agency by Senator Henry Jackson, another Democratic presidential candidate.

"Instead of just investigating it," Carter said, "I intend to run the thing so we can be proud of it."
HighWitness News, #10, June 1976

TIM LEARY DENIED PAROLE

The U.S. Board of Parole has voted three to two to reject Dr. Timothy Leary's request that he be released from prison. Leary is currently serving the second year of a ten-year federal sentence for alleged transportation of marijuana. One joint was found in the vagina of his daughter Susan while they were driving from Texas to California.

The parole board had orginally deadlocked on Leary's request; however, a fifth, unknown official in Washington cast the tie-breaking vote to oppose Leary's immediate release from prison. The board will not entertain another parole request until February of 1978.

HighWitness News, #10, June 1976

HASH BASH '76

Situated on the University of Michigan Diag, once the scene of fraternity house pranks and antiwar demonstrations, the 1976 Ann Arbor Hash Bash brought together over 5,000 tokers. Braving the cold weather and constant drizzle, the congregation of dope smokers, paraphernalia dealers, musicians, mimes, jugglers, food vendors and street performers dubbed this year's bash as "the first dope smokers convention." Police surveillance was minimal. Ann Arbor Deputy Police Chief Harold Wolfson explained that no arrests were made nor had any $5 fines been levied during the Hash Bash.

HighWitness News, #11, July 1976

MARIJUANA SERVES AS INSECT REPELLENT

Police in Winnipeg, Canada, believe they have uncovered a new use for marijuana: as an insect repellent. One elderly couple whose garden boasted seven-foot plants said they didn't know what the weed was but they let it grow because it kept the bugs away. A local farmer reported the same effect. He noticed that whenever his cattle went to pasture during the mosquito season, they would head for one specific clump of bushes. A closer look revealed hemp in the vicinity. The area was remarkably free of flies and 'skeeters, the farmer said.

Health, #13, September 1976

get along. It's all about being a whore, you know. And that's what America is, the biggest whore of them all."

Okay, let's go back for a second. Steven Varble's theory is that S & M is an organized attempt at conquering pain by playing with it. It is, perhaps, the different form of religion required by those who "live at the limit of suffering." The pain is controlled by the M because he wills it himself. The pain is controlled by the S because he learns to exercise it and he learns its limits. Steven says it works up to a point, and then it doesn't work. Why?

John Calendo, a New York film critic, offers another explanation of S & M's appeal: "Usually when you touch someone. when you embrace them, they're warm. But when they're wearing leather and you embrace them, they feel cold. S & M is about playing with death. The leathers come from riding motorcycles, riding on the edge of death and flirting with it. Maybe the reason that it happened has something to do with the bomb. Resentment at the prospect of an untimely death."

One can't help but admire such analysis. Some of these perverts are no dummies; they're consciously obsessed. Take Fred Halsted. Fred is really good copy because what he says assaults the frontiers of the outrageous. Fred Halsted tells interviewers that he is an asshole, but he's not a stupid asshole. I mean, this guy may be sick, but you can't deny that he's an artist who believes in what he says. Fred Halsted is a real S, according to him a rare commodity in his scene. He has an M, Joseph Yale, his slave to whom he was married by an astrologer. Fred ordinarily allows Joseph to participate in his interviews in a controlled way. There is usually a very spirited argument over who will kill whom. Fred insists that at the right time, Joey will kill him. Joey vehemently denies this, stating that he could never hurt Fred, but that Fred will kill him. As you can imagine, this argument could go on forever before anybody settles it, which seems to be the point. Fred feels that this final act will settle his karmic debts and that he will be able to escape the wheel of incarnations, liberated by this magic murder. No shit!

"I'm Russian," Fred explains. "I'm paranoid. I'm nihilistic. I'm a gypsy band that's almost extinct. I have my own peculiar psychic things. I'm a black witch, and I come out with predictions, none of which I want to talk about....

Aw, come on, Fred. You'll talk about it. It's understandable. This really is your religion, and you believe it just like the pope is Catholic. You believe that you must be killed by Joseph, a kind of demon brother or antimatter self, in order to fall off the old karmic cycle. And fist fucking is a magical act, a way of spiritually preparing for the big wipe-out.

Fred is asked how he knows when to stop in the dangerous act of fist fucking. "I know when to stop. I can feel it after the entrance, which is almost bucolic. I mean, there can be massive violence leading up to the entrance. At that point something happens to my psyche in which my arm is not only in the person's body so far that I can feel all of their life functions through my hand...their entire life rests on my judgment of how to use my arm. I could kill that person in one second. However, I find it the most soothing, relaxing thing possible, because I know I am with somebody so much that we're beyond sex. We are dealing with two lives joined together by my arm. And used smoothly, it is the most erotic thing you can feel, because the person I am with knows that they have given themselves to the point of death should I be a maniac."

"Should I be a maniac"? Should I be a fucking maniac? Too much, Fred. You've done it again. What copy! You've given us the equation. "Should I be a maniac" is the X, the unknown part of the equation. Death is invoked, but it can still retreat, granting a new lease on life.

AP-WIDE WORLD

I think there's a tradition here that's not totally obvious. Fred Halsted, talking movie talk, says that he is a filmmaker in the Kenneth Anger school. I don't know if Halsted and Anger are acquainted, but I am sure that Kenneth Anger knows a thing or two about the metaphysics of S & M and why fist fucking is really an act of black magic. Sex and magic are not unacquainted. The Golden Dawn Society, an early twentieth-century magic revival group known for such illustrious members as W. B. Yeats, Arthur Machen, A. E. Waite and Bram Stoker (of Dracula fame), taught a system of Tantric sex exercises intended to channel sexual energy up the spine into the brain. Some branches of the Golden Dawn were involved in heterosexual magic rites, principally an art called karezza, sexual intercourse in which the semen is withheld. However, after the defection of Aleister Crowley, such practices were either discontinued or kept quiet, while Crowley, the self-proclaimed Beast of the Apocalypse, went on to preach sexual magic heterosexual, homosexual and all the shades between—in his secret societies Astreum Argenteum, or Silver Star, and the O.T.O., or Ordo Templi Orientalis. Crowley wrote, "Sex is, directly or indirectly, the most powerful weapon in the armoury of the Magician."

In 1911 Crowley came to the attention of the public in a libel suit stemming from allegations of sodomy. Francis King's book *Sexuality, Magic and Perversion* details certain of Crowley's homosexual rites from 1913 to 1923, and anal sex was prominent in Crowley's grimoire. The uninitiated would have no way of knowing how many rites Crowley devised using the available organs, but it would be surprising to learn that Crowley had not worked rites similar to fist fucking. His interests in anality and cruelty are both well known. No doubt there is a somewhat more esoteric name for fist fucking somewhere in the rites of the Astreum Argenteum. The practice was certainly not invented last year. Fred Halsted may not be a member of the Crowley-inspired Church of Satan, as Kenneth Anger is, but he seems to be as familiar as his film guru with the magical tradition of sexual cruelty.

Through simple analysis, it would seem that fist fucking is a kind of black spiritual exercise that fuses the sensations of the energy centers of procreation and elimination, achieving a kind of metaphoric, if not metaphysical, balance. If the intolerable is the normal, what better exercise to ready us for extinction of the kind Fred Halsted is talking about. In Christianity the body dies, and the soul goes to heaven. At the Last Judgment, however, the body rises glorified for eternal life or is committed to eternal physical punishment.

Of course, the nuns never tell you what glorified means and whether in those Golden Days we'll still have to piss and shit. But this puzzling Christian dogma isn't the only game in town. There's still karma, where you come back again and again, groveling for every bad move until you kick the flesh habit. Fred Halsted is trying to get out of flesh as fervently as George Harrison and his peach-sheeted gaga Krishnas; it's just his methodology that differs.

Let's backtrack a second. We have this S & M craze going on. Mean men in leather and cowboy gear cloning alarmingly. The docks, the streets, the bars are jammed. Almost without exception, these men are white. They are perhaps better educated and more affluent than the partisans of your average peccadillo. They work in "creative" professions, whether they are doing your hair, curating your museums or making the art you hang on your wall. And it would seem that a goodly number of these leather men ascribe their creative impulse to their sexual habits.

Of course, we aren't about to claim that the Eagle's Nest is the fountainhead of American culture. No, we're just looking, thank you. We're

BOWIE BUSTED BY NARC BIMBOS

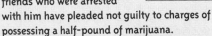

Following his pot bust in Rochester, New York, David Bowie has alleged that he was the victim of illegal search and seizure as well as police entrapment. Bowie and two friends who were arrested with him have pleaded not guilty to charges of possessing a half-pound of marijuana.

Bowie, Duane Vaughns and James Osterberg (a.k.a. Iggy Pop) were arrested after police vice-squad members burst into their hotel rooms, where they allegedly found the weed. Police later admitted that two female undercover narcs had been inside the rooms after being invited by Bowie to a small party. Bowie claims that the two women set up the arrests by being overly friendly to members of the group and encouraging the party.
HighWitness News, #11, July 1976

LAND OF 10,000 LAKES SAYS YES TO DECRIM

Dropping an empty cigarette pack on the sidewalk in Minnesota now carries a stiffer penalty than being busted for carrying an ounce and a half of grass.

Within two hours on March 5, the Minnesota Senate voted to lower the penalty for marijuana possession and to raise the legal drinking age from 18 to 19. Both bills were signed into law by Governor Wendell Anderson one week later, making Minnesota the seventh state in America to liberalize its pot laws and the first in recent memory to tighten booze ordinances.

SOUTH DAKOTA SOFTENS POT PENALTIES

South Dakota's new marijuana decriminalization law was included in the biggest bill of the 1976 legislature—a 122-page revised criminal code containing 19 pages of the Senate Journal, to begin to enumerate. Although the new pot law has a lag period until April 1, 1977, law enforcement officials are stating privately that as far as they are concerned, in most cases, possession of less than one ounce of marijuana will be discreetly overlooked. Beginning April 1, 1977, the penalty for being caught with an ounce of grass will be a $20 civil fine.
HighWitness News, #11, July 1976

LESTER GRINSPOON

CHRISTOPHER S. JOHNSON

BY PHILIP NOBILE
A psychiatrist best known for his upbeat 1971 book *Marijuana Reconsidered*, Grinspoon comes less to praise the substance than to bury misconceptions about it. In their eclectic new work, *Cocaine: A Drug and Its Social Evolution*, Dr. Grinspoon and Boston lawyer John Bakalar have coauthored an impressive treatise on the Andean treasure.

HT: I was fascinated to learn that athletes in the nineteenth century used cocaine as a stimulant.
LG: Which resembles the use of amphetamines by modern athletes.
HT: Why does cocaine improve performance?
LG: We simply don't know the pharmacology on this point. Golden Mortimer, who wrote the big book on cocaine in 1901 [**Peru:History of Coca**], believed it had to do with a saving of energy. That simply isn't so. It's probably a central effect. I mean, I think one can do better at any task if one doesn't feel fatigued. Any time you minimize fatigue and enhance confidence, you improve performance; it isn't that cocaine or amphetamines have a direct effect on performance.
Interview, #18, February 1977

HIGH COURT REJECTS RELIGIOUS POT USE

For the second time in four years, the United States Supreme Court refused to hear an appeal of a marijuana conviction based on a "free exercise of religion" defense. Both appeals were on behalf of the 1,000-member Church of Plenty, a self-sufficient communal farm and spiritual village near Summertown, Tennessee.

Four members of the community were arrested in 1971 for growing marijuana and were convicted and sentenced two years later. At that time, they made their first appeal to the Supreme Court.
Law, #13, September 1976

still trying to figure out this fascination with things violent and Aryan. We're still trying to suss out the sex appeal of SS hobnails and analyze the pleasure in the pain. There seems to be a riddle of the sphincter here. We'll follow any lead.

A few blocks downtown from the Eagle's Nest is The Spike. The Spike is a more laid-back scene than some of the other leather bars, but the menace is still there, glowering cool across the pool table. In the men's room, or rather, in one of the two men's rooms, you might notice this graffito over the urinal: **Piss Slave—Call Jack 691-1385**. In the *Fetish Times* classified ads, they call this kind of behavior Golden Showers. It means that you are interested in piss: pissing, being pissed on, yes, even drinking the stuff. I personally heard a famous pervo New York rock star make an offer of this nature to a girl at a party. Of course, this fellow has a reputation as a great kidder. Still, I don't think Jack, the Spike advertiser, is kidding around. It's apparently quite possible to develop a taste for the stuff. In his *Screw* interview filmmaker Fred Halsted revealed that his slave Joseph has been known to take it warm from the tap, and those guys drink a lot of beer.

In *Scorpio Rising*, by Kenneth Anger, there is a famous scene in which piss is offered up to Satan in a Nazi helmet, parodying the transubstantiation of wine into the blood of Christ in the Mass. By analogy, we might imagine that the point is the transubstantiation (or presto chango) of ordinary piss into the blood of Satan. It's parody, of course, but then again, if these guys really like the stuff, there might be another angle lurking nearby.

Okay, you're gonna love this theory, America! Whatever the Western world is today has quite a bit to do with a people calling themselves Aryans, who swept down from Central Asia into India about 3,000 years before J.C., kicking the shit out of the local small-headed Sumerians living there with a high degree of civilization (flush toilets!) and turning the subcontinent into the headquarters of a sinister plot to conquer the world. The Aryans were bad characters. They were warriors, heavy on the chariots. They bred cattle and grew grain. They ate steak and drank beer. They had a rather frightening tribal religion with a hereditary priesthood—very big on the gods of fire and thunder. The Aryans were no pansies. Not only did they take India, they more or less invented Europe.

Today the meaning of Aryan is much in dispute. Anthropological chic denies the existence of an Aryan race; that theory hasn't been in since Hitler. Instead, we have the opinion that the Aryans were a group of people that does not exist as a specific race today. The dominant thinking of today, in fact, is that brown little wogs of the Gunga Din variety have every bit as much if not more right to call themselves Aryans as your most strapping blond stormtrooper. This is because Aryan is the parent language of both Sanskrit and all European languages.

But whoever these Aryans were, their language, if nothing else, managed to conquer the world. It remains for the reader to determine whether the true Aryan is the blond hulk or the wily Oriental gentleman, which one is more likely to be a warlike, beer-drinking beefeater who swoops down on other peoples' turf. We will just go on the assumption that whoever the Aryan was, his tongue, if not his genes, had considerable effect on what we are in America today. Now our favorite theory on what made the Aryans swoop down out of Central Asia has much to do with a most illuminating book by R. Gordon Wasson entitled *Soma: the Divine Mushrooms of Immortality* (Harcourt Brace Jovanovich, Inc.). Mr. Wasson's starting point is a passage from the Avesta, the sacred word of India, in which old Zoroaster Zarathustra himself is spaking:

When wilt thou do away with this urine of drunkenness with which the priests evilly delude as do the wicked rulers of the provinces in (full) consciousness (of what they do).

These words have long been a problem for scholars of Zoroastrianism reluctant to accept the use of urine as literal. As Mr. Wasson opines, "Surely Zoroaster meant what he said: He was excoriating the consumption of urine in the soma sacrifice. If my interpretation be accepted, there is opened a promising line of inquiry of Zoroastrian scholarship." I hope Mr. Wasson will consider this to be Zoroastrian scholarship in spirit at least, because I think he must be right. It is his theory that the above passage refers to consumption of the divine drug soma, which he goes on to identify as the Amanita muscaria, or fly agaric. The fly agaric contains a powerful hallucinogenic drug, still in use today, though rather discreetly, among Eskimos. One of the properties of this mushroom is that the urine excreted by the user retains the active principle of the drug and is, therefore, reused in this form.

Count Filip von Strahlenburg, a Swedish officer who enjoyed the hospitality of the czar as a prisoner of war in the late eighteenth century, described the use of fly agaric by the Koryak tribe in Siberia. "The poorer sort," he wrote, "who cannot afford...these mushrooms, post themselves on these occasions round the huts of the rich, and watch the opportunity of the guests coming to make water; and then hold a wooden bowl to receive the urine, which they drink off greedily, as having still some virtue of the mushroom in it, and by this way, they also get drunk."

The high produced is far from the laidback passivity of your average acid trip. According to Jesuit missionaries of the North Pacific expedition of 1904-09, the fly agaric was consumed by reindeer hunters to make them nimbler and more ferocious. According to the *Mushroom Handbook* (Louis C. Krieger, Dover, 1967, page 237), "It is said that the 'berserker rage' of the ancient Teutons was induced by partaking too freely of this juice."

The well-documented prevalence of holy-water sports at the dawn of history has given rise to an interesting debate between Wasson and the distinguished scholar of mysticism Mircea Eliade. According to Eliade, fly agaric intoxication was a shamanic shell game introduced after the witch doctors had forgotten (The Lost Secret) the miraculous meditation techniques of their cults' founders. Eventually shamanism evolved into religion as we have it today, rituals in which the hallucinations of the prophets are passed on to the congregation with mushroom substitutes, the purest examples being the wine and wafer, encoding both styles of fly agaric ingestion.

Wasson sees fly agaric itself as The Lost Secret, an evolutionary catalyst because it gave prehistoric man a glimpse of "horizons beyond any that he knew in his harsh struggle for survival" at a time when he had no "heavy" or "far out, " perhaps no word for anything at all. So he was forced to invent language or, if he had language, to invent metaphor, and as an afterthought, religion, philosophy and civilization in general. The names stuck, and we've been blessed ever since with "god" and "immortality" because some lush in a loincloth saw pink mastodons on a cave wall.

Wasson's thinking will probably prevail here, and rumor has it that the two have been in correspondence lately with a view to reaching an accord of learned opinion. Eliade would ultimately have to fall back on Von Daniken anyway, to account for any Lost Secret that wasn't already being nurtured on the cow pies of the bosom of Earth. What's important is that both recognize the mingling of fly agaric with human destiny for better or worse, and the honeymoon lasted long enough to explain everything that

HUNTER THOMPSON

The good doctor tells all...about Carter, cocaine, adrenaline and the birth of Gonzo journalism.

RR: Since we're talking about drug use during the '76 campaign, it's obvious we're talking about people who are now in the White House, right?

HT: Well...some of them, yes. But let's get a grip on ourselves here. We don't want to cause a national panic by saying that a gang of closet coke freaks are running the country—although that would probably be the case, no matter who had won the election.

RR: The inner circle of Carter's people are serious drug users?

HT: Wait a minute, I didn't say that. For one thing, a term like *serious users* has a very weird and menacing connotation; and, for another, we were talking about a *few people* from almost *everybody's* staff. Across the board.... Not junkies or freaks, but people who were just as comfortable with drugs like weed, booze or coke as we are—and we're not weird, are we?

Interview by Ron Rosenbaum, #25, September 1977

CIA & HEROIN

A soon-to-be released report by the House Committee on Government Operations, chaired by Jack Brooks of Texas, charges that the CIA and the Justice Department forced a Chicago prosecutor to drop charges against a CIA agent supplying heroin for distribution in the streets of Chicago. The strongly worded report claims the "forced dismissal of charges...is an example of Justice Department complicity in setting up the intelligence agencies above criminal laws."

HighWitness News, #17, January 1977

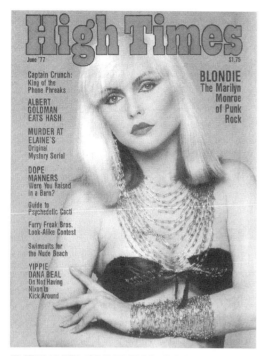

DEBBIE HARRY ON SEX

Sex sells more magazines, books, movies, records, etc., than anything else. Only violence runs a close second, with flying saucers and drugs tied for third. I wish I had invented sex.

The real truth is I learned about sex at the zoo. As a cute but clumsy four year old, I was taken to the Central Park Zoo by my mom. We stood peacefully watching the bears while they sat and scratched themselves, when out of the blue came superjerk in his weather-beaten raincoat (ala Columbo) flashing his worn-out privates. My mom was pissed off. I couldn't have cared less, except he seemed to have three of 'em and I couldn't get much of an explanation from my mom.
Opinion, #38, October 1978

PUNK EDITORIAL

The staff of HIGH TIMES is now bound and gagged. We threw all their dope and drugs down the toilet. We've alerted the FBI. We told them to keep an eye on those middle-aged hipsters and to keep them away from playgrounds and schoolyards. They'll pay for their crimes against the state, don't worry. Now we've taken over this subversive periodical. We are going to tell you the truth. Read it and weep, creep. Your days are numbered. The Age of Aquarius is all over now, baby blue. This ain't the summer of love, and it never was. Everything you believe in is dead and gone. Eldridge Cleaver is an oreo cookie. Jerry Rubin has grown old. Abbie Hoffman is under a rock somewhere. Tim Leary turned his back on you. Jimi Hendrix is rotting away. Gregg Allman finked on his "bruther," man. There's nothing left for you dirty hippies. There never was.
HIGH TIMES Presents Punk, #18, February 1977

happened since.

Wasson offers another scriptural proof of ritual urine consumption of fly agaric in citing the following from the adventures of Krishna (the same of Hare Hare fame) in the ancient Indian epic poem the *Mahabharata*. Wasson suggests that this passage was introduced approximately 1,000 years after mushroom use ceased.

> Krsna had offered Uttanka a boon, and Uttanka said, "I wish to have water whenever I want it." Krsna said, "When you want anything, think on me," and he went away. Then one day Uttanka was thirsty, and he thought on Krsna and thereupon he saw a naked, filthy *matanga* (an outcast) surrounded by a pack of dogs, terrifying, bearing a bow and arrows. And Uttanka saw copious streams of water flowing from his lower parts. The *matanga* smiled and said to Uttanka, "Come, Uttanka, and accept this water from me. I feel great pity for you seeing you so overcome by thirst." The sage did not rejoice in that water, and he reviled Krsna with harsh words. The *matanga* kept repeating, "Drink!" but the sage was angry and did not drink. Then the hunter vanished with his dogs, and Uttanka's mind was troubled; he considered that he had been deceived by Krsna. Then Krsna came bearing his disc and his conch, and Uttanka said to him, "It was not proper for you to give me such a thing, water in the form of the stream from a *matanga*." Then Krsna spoke to Uttanka with honeyed words, to console him, saying, "I gave it to you in such form as was proper, but you did not recognize it. For your sake I said to Indra, 'Give the *amrta* to Uttanka in the form of water.' Indra said to me, 'A mortal should not become immortal; give some other boon to him.' He kept repeating this, but I insisted, 'Give the *amrta*.' Then he said to me, 'If I must give it, I will become a *matanga* and give the *amrta* to the noble descendent of Bhrgu (Uttanka). If he accepts the *amrta* thus, I will go and give it to him today.' As he continued to say, 'I will not give it (otherwise),' I agreed to this, and he approached you and offered the *amrta*. But he took the form of a *candala*. But your worth is great, and I will give you what you wished: on whatever days you have a desire for water, the clouds will be full of water then, and they will give water to you, and they will be called Uttanka clouds." Then the sage was pleased.

Both the *amrta* in the above text and the *soma* in the text previously mentioned are considered to be the "lost drugs" of the Vedic religions, drugs that supposedly conferred immortality or divinity, and consequently are identified with ambrosia. There is a considerable controversy over whether or not *soma* and *amrta* are identical drugs. There is evidence to suggest that there are two different drugs, both divine, but each possessing its own attributes and pantheon: *soma* being lunar, white, a passive psychoactive similar to mescaline or psilocybin; *amrta* being solar, red, possessing qualities associated with cinnabar or mercury. Or *soma* is Woodstock, *amrta* Altamont.

A terrific unsolicited manuscript I read a few years back presented a strong argument for the separate identities of these drugs—identifying them with the solar/lunar, active/passive energy channels of yoga theory. The writer, a Thomas Andrew Angelou, also identified these two divine drugs with the red and white of the Christian Eucharist, the bread and wine, the body and blood of Christ. According to Angelou, by balancing these dual channels/gods/drugs, one achieves immortality, now better known as *samadhi*, or third eye liftoff. An imbalance between these two channels/gods/drugs, would create abnormal, destructive conditions.

The fly agaric is bright red with white specks. If *soma* and *amrta* are different drugs, it is likely that the mushroom is the latter, the divine drug of solar power, rage and destruction. Thus the mushroom would seem to be the body of an angry god, quite suitable to the Aryans' kick-ass, plunder and rape sense of life. World conquest, even if only by language, would seem to require a dei-system built on force rather than on love, and its elixir of immortality would have to be strong enough to send a whole race on a bad trip.

Modern scientific authorities generally consider *soma* and *amrta* to be lost drugs. What is a lost drug? Some consider these substances to be extinct. Others suggest that we have merely lost track of their identity. The latter group has come up with many candidates for the drugs, from wine and hashish to creeper vines and rhubarb. But as Wasson painstakingly points out, fly agaric seems to be the perfect candidate for the divine drug. Did fly agaric become scarce, or was knowledge of the mushroom's properties somehow suppressed or lost?

It's known that the fly agaric is not domesticable. It is found today where it chooses to grow, chiefly in the circumpolar tundra of Siberia, Alaska and points north. Perhaps its range changed because of changes in climate. Or more likely, it was a case of demand far outstripping supply, a condition that might have given rise to some interesting social developments. Before extinction or loss of the drug, there was undoubtedly a period of relative stability of scarcity. How convenient for organizing a kind of metaphysical economy, when the medium of exchange is immortality: that's a better organizing agent than junk.

So when the priests and nobles had dosed themselves full of the body of the god named Red, they called upon their vassals and retainers to drink up their urine. These cocksuckers must have made Hassan I'Sabbah's boys look like dandies, drinking the drug hot, straight from the nethernipple of the boss, with a beer back perhaps. And what's Wasson's theory about the drug's disappearance?

> Why was *soma* so soon abandoned in India, perhaps even before the forms were closed on the canon of the Rig Veda? For one thing, questions of supply, which must always have been awkward, became impossible when the Indo-Aryans spread out over all of India. The mushroom crop in the Hindu-Kush and the Himalayas was each year a fixed quantity. Of course for a time the priests could make do with insufficient fly agarics (as they had to do many times in seasons of short supply, stretching out the Holy Element by utilizing the Second Form).

Okay, the priests are sitting on stools drinking beer and chewing the flesh of the god. The bar is on a caulked platform six feet above the ground. The elite men wear no girdles, but piss on their seats as they drink, and the piss runs down the trough in a stream where the retainers sit with their cups and trenchers of beer. Senior vassals sit nearest the trough at the end under the king and high priest. Sometimes the priests call up a favored young warrior to receive the blessing of a direct infusion of the god from the lords. Thus loyalty was spread through every rank of Aryan society by the physical fealty of worship at the divine faucet. Prices mushroom, if not in money, taking it out in trade. Classes of allegiance form along the lines of supply and demand. The priesthood and kings have more than bread to hold over the heads of the people. The world's first piss slaves got their first taste. Just one taste and they would give their lives and cross a continent to drink of the waters of life. They would swear any allegiance, kick any ass for their fungal fix: "King says there is new land where holy mushroom grow on trees." So they rounded up their animals, made some new leather jackets and sharpened up their spears. And the Aryan race went out to seek its fortune.

A pretty strange fruit, this mushroom. John Allegro, most famous of the Dead Sea Scroll scholars and a distinguished linguist, has written a book, apparently totally independent of Wasson's thought, suggesting that this

JOHN HOLMSTROM

MEET PUNK

Don't believe everything that you read in our special magazine-in-a-magazine starring *Punk* magazine. When these guys came up to our offices the receptionist thought they were a big order from the delicatessen. No, seriously folks, seldom do you meet a more talented bunch of juvenile delinquents than the staff of *Punk*. (Below L to R) Publisher Ged Dunn, resident punk Legs McNeil and editor-cartoonist John Holmstrom all attended the same high school in Cheshire, Connecticut, where punkhood brought them together. Bored with the limitations of suburbia, the three moved to New York, where John pursued art and studied with the famed cartoonist Harvey Kurtzman, Ged pursued money and studied the *Wall Street Journal* and Legs pursued girls and studied with Jack Daniels. Influenced strongly by the rock scene erupting like acne on the face of New York, the Connecticut punks put their talents together and on January 1, 1976, published *Punk*, Vol. 1, No. 1. The rest is history.

Closers, #18, February 1977

ROBERTA BAYLEY

THE FABULOUS GILBERT SHELTON

Back in the early Sixties, Gilbert Shelton, father of the Fabulous Furry Freak Brothers, was a laid-back college student, taking eight years to cop a B.A. from the University of Texas at Austin. His first cartoons were the adventures of Wonder Wart Hog for his college humor magazine. "The Fabulous Furry Freak Brothers" are also from Austin and moved to San Francisco with Shelton. The Brothers appear in their own comic books and in the *Freak Brothers Anthology: The Best of Rip Off Press.* Shelton was among the founders of Rip Off Press in 1969, and he's still around as art director. His work has appeared in magazines from *Esquire* to *Playboy*—not to mention HIGH TIMES, where his work will appear monthly, starting with this action-packed issue.

Closers, #18, February 1977

same mushroom was the origin of Judaism and Christianity. In fact, he goes so far as to suggest that Jesus was in fact a mushroom. A funny thought. Did we have orders not to eat this one, sir? The woman gave it to me.

But let's back up and try to be reasonable about this stuff. We've shown that there are a bunch of influential perverts who like to hurt each other, drink piss and think Aryan. And that the Aryan race may have gotten its start conquering nations because of an interesting drug habit. Still, even if every white housewife in America was secretly into water sports—golden showers and bondage in the sanctuary of their bedrooms—there would be no evidence that the fly agaric is still operative in the Aryan race. It is certainly out of our diet. What we seem to have are a few silly vestiges that like to pop up now and then to embarrass us and remind us that we used to dress up like cows and pour blood on the ground to make the corn grow.

Even if we were to accept the Nazi idea of Aryan—blond, blue-eyed, long-headed, irascible—there is little evidence of continuity of any kind with the early Vedic cults. Even in India there is no evidence of continued existence of *soma/amrta* among the Brahmins. Only the Eskimos seem to have made use of it in modern times, and look where it's gotten them.

Aside from the scarcity hypothesis, there is also the morality argument. Zoroaster reformed Vedic religion, in part by attacking urine consumption as an abomination. Yet broadly speaking, the Aryan race can hardly be said to have distinguished itself on the morals front since this religious reform. Quite the contrary. Since prohibition, the Aryans and their descendants and self-proclaimed scions seem to have become a distinct danger to humanity.

THE DOPE DICTATORS
by Robert Singer

Flying over Jamaica today, you see that about a fifth of the island paradise is brown—burned to the ground. On desert stretches of Mexico, the bones of people and the hulls of fallen aircraft lie bleaching in the sun. On the poppy fields of Turkey, bullet-riddled farmers lie face down in the snow that came too soon this year, blanketing the unharvested opium crop. These are a few snapshots from the Dope War—an undeclared U.S. offensive against liberation movements throughout the Third World, disguised as a war on narcotics.

America's drug laws are actually a secret plot to control the world—just as you always suspected. The plot is the secret weapon of the Nixon Doctrine: the basis of defense against hijackers, kidnappers, terrorists, guerrillas, dissident intellectuals, leftist labor unions, militant peasants and national liberation movements in the Third World in the post-anticommunist era. In the years to come, the rhetoric of Dope War will replace the rhetoric of Cold War as the justification for foreign military intervention. Instead of sending in the Marines, Washington will send in the narcs.

Jamaica, Thailand, Turkey, the Philippines, Bolivia and Chile are all in various stages of Vietnam-style "stabilization" by narcotics actions, and Mexico in particular is taking on the dimensions of another Vietnam—complete with massive military actions, deforestations, herbicides that cause birth defects, and the financing by the U.S. of a corrupt puppet government and its incompetent army against a popular revolution nearly 150 years old.

The plotters include Nixon, Kissinger, Rockefeller, Ford, G. Gordon Liddy, Egil Krogh, CIA Director George Bush, past and present Drug Enforcement Administration chiefs John Bartels and Peter Bensinger and approximately 30 foreign heads of state. Apart from them and their intimates, perhaps a few dozen people in the world understand the meaning of the Dope War, or even suspect that it is being waged. Most Americans learn about drugs from *Kojak* and to follow the tangled skein of drug legislation and law enforcement, let alone the backstage economics of foreign policy, is more than the news media will demand of their audience.

Even dopers are dim in their understanding of the drug laws. To most of us, they are no more than an arbitrary travesty of the laws of God—the prevailing theory among drug users being that the drug laws exist to protect the jobs of narcs, a bureaucratic non sequitur perpetuating itself despite millions of tons of personal testimony and scientific evidence on the benign potential of a few flowers and herbs whose Maker apparently intended us to enjoy. In the 1960s, the drug laws seemed like a simple meaningless relic of Puritanism, an obscene legacy of the 1950s, like fins on cars or Neil Sedaka. But of course the history of drugs and drug laws are the secret history of America, the history they don't teach you in school.

Since the sixteenth century, from the Cold War to the Dope War, industrialized nations got their cheap labor and raw materials and guaranteed markets for their own manufacturers from Latin America, Asia and Africa. But World War II left the colonial powers exhausted, unable to salvage their empires from the prairie fires of nationalism that swept the underdeveloped world in the postwar era.

The Soviet Union, too, was shattered by the war, with 40 million dead and all its major cities destroyed. At the Yalta Conference of 1945, the Big Three (Britain, Russia and America) drew up the battle lines for the Cold War: Stalin demanded Eastern Europe as a buffer zone against the capitalist allies; Britain received carte blanche to repatch its sundered colonies (Churchill little dreaming that the first postwar election would sweep Clement Atlee's socialist Labour Party into power to dismantle that Empire). America's military power was intact, backed up by nuclear weapons and America's overheated economy. Poised to expand, loan, invest, develop and take over, America would build the greatest neocolonial empire the world had ever seen.

The world, of course, was hungry for American aid but hardly ready to see the British, French, Dutch and Portuguese sahibs replaced by simply another set of white faces. Thus in 1947 Winston Churchill "officially" launched the Cold War with his "Iron Curtain" speech in Fulton, Missouri. Harry Truman was on the speaker's platform and in full accord.

The Western investors—the multinational corporations of today— found new partners in the ruling classes of the emerging nations. Latin America was already the first neocolonial empire, thanks to the Monroe Doctrine of 1823. Africa and Asia accepted U.S. financing and technology on whatever terms that were to be had. The terms were participation in the Cold War, suppression of their internal dissidents and acceptance of the U.S. as "world policeman" against communist totalitarianism.

In effect, the local power brokers replaced the colonial powers. The colonies of yesterday became the banana republics of today. Japan was fostered and tolerated as a junior partner in the neocolonial structure as a sop to Third World nationalism; West Germany was welcomed back as an ally against the Soviets. The great disappointments of postwar nationalism smoldered in periodic revolutions, but the U.S. was pretty effective in

ROBERT SINGER

HIGH TIMES resident expert on international politics, Robert Singer, got his start as a foreign correspondent when HIGH TIMES published his epochal interview with the Dalai Lama in November 1975. In "The Rise of the Dope Dictators," Singer unravels the foreign narcotics policy of Nixon, Kissinger and Ford, exposing it as a scheme to transform our anticommunist Cold War allies into antidope police regimes. Not too hard, since most of these countries are military juntas to begin with. Writing with an incisiveness that Singer's heroes— Castlereagh, Bismarck and Metternich—might envy, he says, "In order to analyze Nixon's and Kissinger's master plan, I had to stand back and adopt their total cynicism, their complete indifference to human beings and their callous disregard of ethics and legality for the sake of political expediency."
Closers, #19, March 1977

KNOCKING DECRIM

The concept of marijuana decriminalization came under fire during the fifth annual conference of the National Organization for the Reform of Marijuana Laws (NORML).

Many of the 300 conferees, some of whom came from as far away as the Virgin Islands and Australia, pressed NORML to concern itself less with decrim and more with legalization, particularly in the fields of grass distribution and regulation.
HighWitness News, #19, March 1977

TRANS-HIGH QUOTATIONS MARKET

USA

Regular Mexican	declining supply	oz	20-30
		lb	100-225
Top-grade Mexican	good Oaxacan	oz	50-125
		lb	200-800
Quality Jamaican	good brown	oz	35-55
		lb	150-350
Commercial Colombian	decent availability	oz	25-40
		lb	250-450
Connoisseur Colombian	tight gold buds some red	oz	40-70
		lb	350-650
California sinsemilla	powerful	oz	150-250
		lb	350-1000
Hawaiian Puna buds	sweet and seedless	oz	200
		lb	1000
Moroccan hash	OK green	oz	80-100
		lb	750-1000
Lebanese hash	stale red	oz	100-175
		lb	1200-1500
Afghani hash	good to excellent	oz	100-120
		lb	1400-1800
Nepalese hash	pressed balls good	oz	100-165
		lb	1200-1500
Thai sticks	abundant	one	15-30
		oz	175-225

THMQ, #31, March 1978

AP/WIDE WORLD

ROBERT MITCHUM

The arrest of Robert Mitchum in 1948 was probably the most sensational grass bust in American history. At 31, Mitchum was the rising new idol of the screen, destined, it seemed, to inherit the mantle of Gary Cooper and Humphrey Bogart, the strong, silent, lone-wolf heroes. On the night of August 3, Mitchum and Robin Ford, a Los Angeles real estate agent, visited a house in the Laurel Canyon Hills near Hollywood. The house was rented by Lila Leeds, a 20-year-old platinum blonde starlet who had yet to make her mark on the screen. Staying with her was Vicki Evans, 25, an aspiring dancer.

Unknown to them, the house had been staked out by a team of Los Angeles police and federal narcotics agents. The narcs heard Lila mention "reefers" and they saw her light a cigarette and hand it to Mitchum. Then she lit another.

The Great Grass Trials by Paul Hoffman, #24, August 1977

shoring up its new Cold War allies—"any government friendly to the U.S. and hostile to communism"—against their own populations.

The CIA began to maintain our "necessary presence" if not with the consent of the governed, then at the urgent need of the governors—the Trujillos, Papa Docs, Diems and countless others who without the CIA would be (and often were) swiftly out of power. And if an ally should prove reluctant to embrace the articles of faith, the CIA took care of that, too.

The Cold War worked very well for a long while. The Soviet Union was in terrible shape, thanks to Hitler; the Chinese, especially after the Mao-Khrushchev split, were isolationist to the point of paranoia until well into the 1960s. Everywhere else, the opposition was nothing but a few hundred million backward peasants armed with sticks and mud.

The first turning point was Cuba. The realization that those people needed a revolution, that the U.S. was willing to underwrite the most corrupt dictator in the world in his "whorehouse of the Caribbean," began to break up the Cold War consensus at home in the United States. Ten years later, Vietnam broke America's faith in the Cold War forever.

To everyone's surprise, the American who understood this best was that old Cold Warrior, Richard Nixon. It became Nixon's and Kissinger's conviction, as Leslie Gelb wrote recently in *The New York Times*, that "Soviet military power and influence were on the rise, while America's will to resist was on the decline because of the Vietnam experience. Their strategy was to evolve détente into a new form of containment of the Soviet Union."

By recognizing Russia and China as equal superpowers and giving them access to Western capital and technology, not to mention U.S. grain, America could "draw the Soviet Union into a web of incentives and penalties" and give Mao his first steps on the capitalist road.

With détente, Nixon and Kissinger sought to establish a new balance of power that would inexorably lure the communists into the joys of economic growth, replacing their crude taste for armed aggression with a stake in the neocolonial game and sharing the cheap labor, raw materials and markets with them as our rightful partners in the superpower structure.

But even as they prepared to drop the curtain of détente on the last act of the Cold War, Nixon and Kissinger knew that the Third World would not be a willing turkey in another tripartite carve-up and that the old demons of left-wing nationalism and land reform and the new cacophony of Third World Unity would leave America's old allies without a straw to clutch. The puppet governments would be driven to nationalize foreign corporations, levy protective tariffs, permit labor unions to flourish and take other anti-American steps if they were not to be eaten by their own constituents.

As Robert Scheer wrote recently, "The death of anticommunism as the binding force of American rule here and abroad opened a Pandora's box. When the Arab oil producers became uppity, we could no longer land the Special Advisers Forces to save freedom." Vietnam convinced even Nixon that the Cold War was over—and he realized this as early as the mid-1960s, when he began building the law-and-order/peace-with-honor platform that swept him into the White House in the 1968 election.

The Dope War initially emerged with no apparent relation to the foreign policy that Nixon and Kissinger were then hammering out. The first Nixon Administration brought G. Gordon Liddy, a New York State assistant D.A. notorious for setting up Tim Leary's first acid bust, to the Treasury Department as a special law enforcement adviser. There he began to work with Egil Krogh, the White House narcotics law enforcement coordinator, and Krogh and Liddy soon arranged the first big strike in the Dope War, Operation Intercept.

Operation Intercept—the Mexican border blockade that led to the great grass famine of the summer and fall of '69—was a crude precursor to later twists in Dope War strategy. It was a project typical of the Neanderthal White House plumber types and a point of sure contention in their bitter rivalry with Henry Kissinger. Where Kissinger would later seek to export drug law enforcement as an adjunct of foreign policy, the proto-plumbers merely sought a visible reduction of the volume of *imported drugs*; i.e., a publicity-worthy fulfillment of the law-and-order campaign of 1968.

But judged even by that standard, Operation Intercept was a dismal failure. It too obviously drove tens of thousands of younger pot smokers to heroin while merely increasing the hunger for pot. Intrepid smugglers soon explored the fertile fields of Jamaica and Colombia for the first time. Yet, in the long run, Operation Intercept was a necessary first step in the Dope War, in effect ensuring that millions of Americans would come to feel so threatened by the "heroin epidemic" that they would endorse whatever steps Nixon might take.

The dreaded "heroin epidemic" of 1969 and 1970, along with the rise of recreational drug use throughout the 1960s, drove millions of voters into the law-and-order camp by giving them a bogeyman far more virulent, despicable and immediate than the classical godless communist of yore: the pusher.

An ironic footnote to the Operation Intercept fiasco was the scandal that broke in 1975, when it became known that Nixon's "drug superagency," the DEA, had failed to investigate charges that Nixon's favorite financier Robert Vesco had been involved in heroin trafficking, possibly through both Nixon administrations.

It seems thinkable that Nixon had a vested interest in seeing the U.S. addict population soar. But it would be naive to overemphasize Nixon's peccadilloes of personal corruption—his superfluous paranoia that led to Watergate; the COIN-TELPRO surveillance of radicals; and his enemies list.

The turning point of the Dope War came in 1971, when Henry Kissinger began to replace John Mitchell as the intellectual of the Nixon junta. Until then, Mitchell, Krogh and Liddy had run the Dope War as a domestic vendetta against radicals while permitting the "heroin epidemic" to run amok. By early '71, Kissinger's ascendancy was being demonstrated by the Paris peace talks, the Vietnam troop withdrawals and the press's growing enthusiasm for détente. By June 17, 1971, when Nixon's Message to the Congress declared drug abuse to be "the nation's number one noneconomic problem," the Dope War had hit its stride as the heir to Vietnam. It was the answer to a central dilemma: the exhaustion of the Cold War.

The grand aim of the Dope War was to serve as rationale for sending American troops overseas when the Red Menace could no longer be believed. But the Dope War served several other purposes. It revolutionized the sprawling narcotics-law enforcement bureaucracies that had grown up since the 1930s as a sort of social security program for incompetent cops and federally funded researchers.

The various drug agencies were reorganized into one centralized bureau, the Drug Enforcement Administration (DEA). It transferred responsibility for narcotics from the Justice and Treasury departments to the President, giving Nixon another private police force and placing the political spoils of the Dope War completely in his hands, as was other foreign policy. By staffing the DEA with CIA personnel, Nixon expanded

KEITH RICHARDS

BY VICTOR BOCKRIS

HT: Do you have any advice for the people who read HIGH TIMES?
KR: I don't think I'm in a position to give any advice, as such, but maybe just by talking about it we can make things a bit clearer. It's interesting that they're lightening up on the marijuana laws slowly, and it's accelerating. I mean, since I've come to the states, New York is decriminalized, and once that sort of thing happens it snowballs. Already you hear talk of a commission looking into cocaine to give that a different status. In a way I feel it's all a bit of a game because there's all this flimflam about decriminalization, which isn't legalization, and eventually what it comes down to is money anyway. If they can figure out a way of taking it over and making bread out of it, it'll be legal. The only reason methadone's such a big deal in America is because a lot of people are making millions on it.
Interview, #29, January 1978

DUTCH DOPE CZAR

Michael "Micky" Cesar, who since 1972 has openly bought and sold large quantities of cannabis from six barges in Amsterdam's canals, was recently deported from Holland while attempting to board a plane to the Black Sea, where he was to view a consignment of "People's Hash."

The American dope entrepreneur, who sports an engraved lapel pin of Lenin, left behind a fleet of floating canal boats that paid over $10,000 a year in marijuana sales taxes to Holland.

During his short absence, the cannabis products were sold by his 20 employees, who center operations on board the 100-foot pot barge *Johanna*. Docked on the Wittenburgergracht canal and across the street from a police station, the boat is Cesar's most profitable.

Cesar, who advertises in the Amsterdam Yellow Pages, maintains his cannabis is the finest in Holland.

"There isn't any kind of grass I haven't smoked or sold," related the former electric transformer builder from New Jersey. He was nursing a gunshot wound inflicted last year by a competing marijuana outfit. "Surinamese and African grass are the most popular, especially Congolese and Mozambique varieties."
HighWitness News, #31, March 1978

SUSAN SONTAG

BY VICTOR BOCKRIS
Among American intellectuals, Susan Sontag is probably the only Harvard-educated philosopher who digs punk rock. Sontag became famous in the sixties when her series of brilliant essays on politics, pornography and art, including the notorious "Notes on Camps," were collected in *Against Interpretation*—a book that defended the intuitive acceptance of art against the superficial, cerebral apprehension of it, then fashionable among a small band of extremely powerful, rigid intellectuals who, for example, dismissed such American classics as *Naked Lunch*, *Howl*, *On the Road*, Andy Warhol's film *Chelsea Girls*, etc., as trash.

HT: Do you have any feelings about an increasingly widespread use of drugs?

SS: I think marijuana is much better than liquor. I think a society which is addicted to a very destructive and unhealthy drug, namely alcohol, certainly has no right to complain or be sanctimonious or censor the use of a drug which is much less harmful.

HT: Do you do any of your writing on grass?

SS: I've tried, but I find it too relaxing. I use speed to write, which is the opposite of grass. Sometimes when I'm really stuck I will take a mild form of speed to get going again.
Interview #31, March 1978

ALEISTER CROWLEY

BY DAVID DALTON
Lacking inhibitions, Crowley was the ideal prophet of enlightened drug use. The quality and quantity of Crowley's writings on these substances remain unsurpassed. He is possibly the most documented drug taker of all time, recording his experiences as a series of chemical love affairs.... As their evangelist, Crowley turned on the great minds of his generation: Cole Porter to coke, Katherine Mansfield to opium, H.G. Wells to hashish. It was Crowley who first made peyote (in the form of liquid anaholium) popular in intellectual circles in Europe. His most important convert was Aldous Huxley, whom he introduced to peyote in a Berlin hotel room.
The Dope, Sex and Magick of Aleister Crowley, #35, July 1978

the CIA's capacity for domestic spying and laid the groundwork for the era when the DEA would *supplant* the CIA as the primary instrument of foreign military adventures.

With Kissinger's diplomatic showmanship persuading voters that the war would soon be over, the new emphasis on the Dope War provided the means of pushing Vietnam into the past entirely, a Cold War relic and *fait accompli* making law-and-order the Nixon issue in the 1972 election.

By 1971, there were close to one million heroin addicts in the U.S. The dread "epidemic" had spread to 50 percent of the troops in Vietnam—and the "emerging Republican majority" made no distinction between junkies and the additional millions of pot blowers, acid heads, et al., who threatened all that was still sacred in American life. While George McGovern campaigned against himself, Nixon beat him by running against the smack dealer on the corner.

Now the Dope War began in earnest. Its pusher-bogeymen shouldered aside the senile Cold War commies. The war fused with detente to form the army of the Nixon Doctrine—rushing to the aid of America's "stable and friendly" allies of yesteryear—the new old breed of Dope Dictators.

The head of almost every Third World state is now a potential Dope Dictator. The reason is that some form of "drug abuse" is practiced to a greater or lesser degree in almost every nation in Latin America, Africa and Asia. And wherever the hardy cannabis and poppy flowers thrive, the natives have come to terms with them, incorporating their herbal powers into thousands of years of folk life and legend. For millions of peasants today. the mind-altering plants are the only cash crop that stands between them and starvation. On the political map of the world these peasant plantations are the cradle of both the international drug traffic and the nationalist liberation movements. Thus by cooperating with U.S. narcotics officials in policing the drug traffic, the adroit Dope Dictator can effectively contain revolutionary movements.

In an era when being "friendly" and anticommunist ensured American economic and military support, the dictators of the Third World could afford to modify democracy to their own needs and ignore, suppress or participate in the narcotics trade according to their own inclinations. After Vietnam, it is crucial that the Dope Dictators embrace the American Dope War if they are to rely on American power to shore up their own positions; they must provide the U.S. with an excuse to back up the investments of the multinationals. Here then are the paradoxes of the Dope War in action. The U.S. helps stamp out the drug traffic in order to support friendly dictators. The dictators need the drug traffic in order to receive U.S. support in order to stamp out popular revolution in order to remain dictators. The U.S. needs the drug traffic in order to support the friendly dictators. Hence the Dope War is being waged both to terminate and stimulate the drug traffic—"drug traffic," being understood in the same sense as "communist subversion," is *any* threat to U.S. economic or political or military interests in the country in question. It was in this spirit that Gerald Ford escalated "the illicit export of opium to this country" from "the nation's number one noneconomic problem" to "a threat to our national security."

Ah, national security. As Daniel Ellsberg said of the Pentagon Papers, you can read them till you turn blue looking for an action being taken on behalf of honor, democracy, human decency, common sense or any other ideal, but the only motivation you'll ever see mentioned is the only one the Pentagon takes seriously: National Security, used to justify everything from assassinations to My Lai. Fightin' words.

The commander-in-chief of the Dope War Game is the president. The general staff is the Cabinet Committee on International Narcotics Control. The CCINC was established by Nixon on September 7, 1971, and included many notorious Watergate era names: Attorney General John Mitchell, Treasury Secretary John Connally, Defense Secretary Melvin Laird, CIA Director Richard Helms, United Nations Representative George Bush (who became CIA director after Ford appointed Helms ambassador to Iran), Clifford Hardin and Secretary of State William Rogers. Kissinger sat in as Nixon's special adviser on foreign affairs, taking over the chair from Rogers when Dr. K. became secretary of state in the second Nixon cabinet. The chairman of the White House working group within CCINC, directing the activities of Nixon's various drug agencies and eventually the DEA, was Egil Krogh.

CCINC was the first step in fortifying the politics of détente with the power of the Dope War. As a war council, CCINC dictated policy to domestic local narcs, Customs and the Bureau of Narcotics and Dangerous Drugs (BNDD), which Lyndon Johnson had created as one of his last acts of office. The purpose of BNDD was to streamline the old Federal Bureau of Narcotics to deal with accelerating hippie and housewife drug consumption in the Sixties, but its capacities had been so far outstripped by the realities of the drug scene that it had barely managed Operation Intercept, and had botched that.

Therefore CCINC spawned a series of new agencies to streamline BNDD—the first being SAODAP, which had so little effect that it isn't worth spelling out. It was absorbed along with BNDD into the new Office of Drug Abuse Law Enforcement, organized by Egil Krogh. ODALE suffered from the unsubtle tactics of the Chief Plumber, compounded by the "Dragnet" mentality of its director, former Customs Commissioner Myles Ambrose. ODALE sent several hundred narcs into 33 cities to expedite ongoing grand jury investigations. The ODALE agents turned out to be amateurish Gestapo types who broke down the doors of many innocent citizens, as a result of which many lawsuits arose. ODALE was exploring Gordon Liddy's proposed anti-dealer death squad when the Watergate scandal broke and ODALE was absorbed into the DEA.

These shenanigans were anathema to Henry Kissinger, who desired a discreet dope agency and not a bunch of drunken southern sheriffs to enforce the business end of détente. At Kissinger's behest two more agencies were created by CCINC in 1972 to give a little State Department finesse to the domestic Dope War—the Office of the Senior Adviser to the Undersecretary of State for Narcotics and the Office of National Narcotics Intelligence (ONNI). Finally, in March 1973, all previous agencies were either merged into, or came under the control of the DEA, the drug superagency that would coordinate the Dope War at home and abroad.

Even then, Krogh, who never liked Kissinger, seemed not to understand the delicacy Kissinger desired when he said, "Anyone who opposes us [DEA] we'll destroy. As a matter of fact, anyone who doesn't support us we'll destroy." Under Ford, Kissinger was able to restrain the DEA from what he called the "My Lai syndrome" in drug law enforcement. For the time being, he accepted that compromise gracefully, as one should in a free society.

It would be superfluous here to recount the two Senate probes and the three still secret Justice Department investigations of the DEA. These revealed the DEA's almost consistent brutality and corruption: its tendency to use murder and blackmail as tools of law enforcement, its habit of reselling confiscated drugs, its Bill of Rights violations, its war with the Customs service (the Customs people were particularly provoked by the DEA's trick of smuggling drugs in under their noses to bust buyers by

GANJA IN JAMAICA

BY GLENN O'BRIEN AND GARY STIMELING

When the results of Vera Rubin's ganja study, *Ganja in Jamaica*, became public late in 1974, it immediately drew heavy fire from antipot partisans such as Columbia University's Dr. Gabriel Nahas. Hers was the first scientific research on marijuana that left the laboratory for the homes and countryside of people who smoke pot every day, and she uncovered no reason to stop smoking pot.

HT: Did you investigate whether there was any relationship in Jamaica between violent crime and ganja?

VR: Yes, that's important. Because of what we saw happening in the scientific literature, we went into everything as thoroughly as possible: personal history, family history—including alcoholism, mental illness and so forth. It turned out that, of course, all the smokers had some convictions for possession, but the non-smokers' convictions were for violent crimes. The interesting thing is that marijuana is accused of leading to both apathy and aggression. It's accused of both increasing and decreasing sexual activity. They should make their minds up which way it is. It's as though all the sins and ills of mankind derive from the use of this one substance.

HT: I thought one of the most interesting parts of the study was that marijuana was found to be a benevolent alternative to alcohol.

VR: We didn't expect that. Everybody in the West Indies drinks rum, except Christians. A West Indian Christian is a fundamentalist and a teetotaler. Rum is a national drink, right? Especially in the working class. So we didn't expect to find anybody who did not drink. But our subjects defintely drank less than non-smokers.

Interview, #34, June 1978

KEN WEINER

CIA STUPID BUSH REVEALED!

BY MARTIN LEE

For nearly 30 years the CIA has been devising ever new and more effective ways of inducing psychosis in human beings through the use of drugs, newly declassified documents show. CIA theorists have invented detailed contingency plans for secretly dosing individuals and groups of people with substances that will provoke a broad variety of bizarre mental and physical symptoms.

Among the numerous botanicals listed in this particular report, a few sound especially intriguing. A plant described by the CIA as "stupid bush" (Amaranthus spinogus) was found to flourish in St. Thomas and Puerto Rico. Categorized as both a psychogenic agent and a pernicious weed, the effects of "stupid bush" are shrouded in mystery.
HighWitness News, #36, August 1978

MAIL-ORDER LSD

LSD, 100-percent pure, is available through the mails. The source is Supelco, a government-approved chromatography supply company that manufactures and retails various drugs for use as standards (references) in chromatography analysis (breaking down solutions of closely related compounds).

For $20 Supelco will send you 2 milligrams of LSD-4195, pure LSD bitartrate. The 2 milligrams of bitartrate equal 1,400 micrograms of LSD, approximately four very healthy-sized hits.

Supelco does not require that their customers have a Drug Enforcement Agency (DEA) license to buy from them. The acid comes in methanol (wood alcohol) a toxic solvent. Using a double boiler setup and near boiling water, the methanol can be totally evaporated. Once the methanol is gone, only pure LSD remains.
HighWitness News by Seth Flagsberg, #36, August 1978

entrapment) and the agency's general incompetence and dereliction of duties. Several high-ranking DEA officials were even caught abusing their telephone credit cards in the manner of hippie "phone phreaks."

Such was the legacy of the Plumbers to the DEA. Even its first chief administrator, John Bartels, was powerless to resist the Watergate approach to drug law enforcement, although he later showed a keen grasp of what Kissinger wanted. Bartels was finally forced to resign in June 1975 for his own alleged role in DEA corruption and cover-ups, but his purchase of the "right stuff" was clearly demonstrated by his inclusion on the White House Domestic Council Drug Abuse Task Force.

Now, pay attention. The chairman of the White House Domestic Council was Vice President Rockefeller. Rockefeller, as the world knows, was Henry Kissinger's sponsor for many years before Kissinger's rise to fame, recognizing early that Kissinger's Spenglerian visions of the balance of power were tailor-made for the needs of Rockefeller as leader of the entire neo-colonial system. Thus Rockefeller, Kissinger and Bartels were the true authors of the Domestic Council Drug Abuse Task Force's "White Paper on Drug Abuse," which was presented to President Ford on September 7, 1975.

A stupefyingly boring document, the white paper raised a few eyebrows by recommending low-priority enforcement for pot (a concession to the present decline in anti-marijuana attitudes, made in the hope that anti-heroin fervor, and therefore the Dope War, will remain acceptable to the public). On the whole, however, the media managed to contain its enthusiasm for the white paper, which embodied the first and only full policy statement on the ways and means of exporting the Dope War, as follows:

> No matter how hard we fight the problem of drug abuse at home, we cannot make really significant progress unless we succeed in gaining cooperation from foreign governments, because many of the serious drugs of abuse originate in foreign countries....
>
> In order to encourage the greatest possible commitment from other governments on this joint problem, the task force believes that narcotics control should be discussed at the highest levels.... These discussions should deal not only with illicit opium, but with other drugs as well....
>
> The key objectives of the international program are to gain the support of other nations for narcotics control, and to strengthen narcotics control efforts and capabilities within foreign governments. These objectives can be achieved through internationalization of the drug program, cooperative enforcement and enforcement assistance, and control of raw materials....
>
> In many countries, drug abuse is still seen as principally an American problem. Many countries are unaware of the extent of their own drug abuse....

The report stresses the importance of holding other "victim countries" to their obligations under the U.N. drug treaties and recommends that the U.S. help expedite those obligations through technical and equipment assistance, formal training of enforcement officials and aid in crop destruction or substitution. It is crucial to understanding these recommendations to realize that the equipment to be given includes guns, defoliants and Vietnam-tested "Huey-type" Bell helicopters and that the police forces to receive them are often the de facto standing armies of their nations. The equipment is to be accompanied by special advisers and instructors. Above all, the entire program is directed not against the fabled "kingpins" of heroin traffic but against the opium- *and* marijuana-growing farmers, who profit least from the drug trade. The report hopes that the farmers will eventually discover other cash crops but virtually ensures a standing anti-narcotics army and police force in either case.

Armed with a doctrine of national security and full diplomatic and military support, the DEA has two other powerful weapons. One is the CIA. From its beginning, the DEA has enjoyed the benefit of 64 former CIA agents' membership in the intelligence section alone and has sent an unknown number of narcs for training by the CIA. As late as October 1975, a known 41 DEA narcs were still on the CIA payroll, and George Bush, the former U.N. representative, remains on the CCINC in his present capacity, director of the CIA—which, as he modestly told the House Select Committee on Narcotics Control and Abuse, is "not impotent" in matters of drug law intelligence and enforcement.

Finally the DEA has the controversial "buy-and-bust" system at its disposal. The system allots the DEA a substantial budget ($9,900,000 for fiscal year 1976) to buy drugs from "dealers" whom it then busts—a classic instance of institutionalized entrapment. As used by the DEA in the U.S., "buy-and-bust" has some drawbacks: the high prices offered by narcs anxious for busts virtually force ordinary users to become dealers, while professional dealers smell trouble and stay away; agents have been known to traffic in confiscated drugs; and the infusion of DEA capital actually stimulates the growth of the illicit drug industry itself. Thus as a law-enforcement tool, "buy-and-bust" is far from perfect.

Why, then, does the DEA persist in defending it, despite constant criticism? Would it not be reasonable and prudent to jettison this obsolete precinct-house practice, at least for appearance's sake? On the contrary, "buy-and-bust" is a diplomatic instrument of great subtlety, for lo, it brings forth a "drug problem" where there was none, or no major one, before. Equally important, it gives the DEA access (through resale) to funds that do not have to be voted by Congress, thereby freeing DEA executives from the messy chore of explaining their "covert operations" and dirty tricks to thrifty legislators.

In fact, its relatively small budget makes the DEA look innocuous, on par with, say, Fisheries and Hatcheries. (The whole con was perfected by the CIA years ago: the "front companies," "Delaware corporations" and "proprietaries," whose innocent-looking activities give cover to agents, channel funds to CIA-backed unions, parties, guerrillas, etc., and generate millions of unaccountable dollars that may be put to unspeakable purposes.)

Hoping we have not dwelt overlong on the mechanics of the Dope War, let us now turn to those stable allies, our friendly friends the Dope Dictators, and see how they are faring in their gallant little stands against drug abuse.

Just as Hitler and Mussolini tested the blitzkrieg in Spain in 1937, the DEA fought the first skirmish of the Dope War in Jamaica in 1973. As we have seen, one result of Operation Intercept was the discovery of Jamaica by marijuana smugglers. By 1972, Jamaican marijuana (ganja) exports rivaled and possibly exceeded Mexican exports. Indeed, ganja became the island's third largest industry at a time when the entire economy and political structure had reached a crisis unparalleled in its history. Jamaica's economy is controlled by U.S. corporations: Alcan, Kaiser, Alcoa, Reynolds, Anaconda and Revere, who are the chief miners and buyers of the island's principal export, bauxite, from which aluminum is made. But the bauxite deposits will soon be exhausted. The tourist industry, run by British and American hotel chains, is increasingly hard put to attract tourists aware of Jamaica's growing reputation for racial tension, violence, poverty, martial law and drugs

EMMETT GROGAN

Yeah, I knew Emmett Grogan, knew him well enough to've gone on a half-assed caper with him on behalf of a coke dealer who thought he might've just snuffed the uptown player motherfucker who ripped him off for $20,000 worth of snort, knew him well enough to've long suspected that he boosted a TV set and a hair dryer out of my pad so he could feed his junk habit, knew him well enough to've given him $100 that he never paid back plus a bottle of my dying wife's Percodans as a Christmas present. He later accused me of getting him back on junk with that little gift.
By Al Aronowitz, #37, September 1978

KIDS AND POT

BY DR. PETER BOURNE
In the enthusiasm for the decriminalization of marijuana in recent years, one concerning side effect has emerged which has failed to receive the attention it probably deserves. This problem is the steadily increasing use of marijuana in large quantities by young people before they have reached physical or emotional maturity. Spending too much of this phase in one's life stoned because one does not yet know any better can clearly be detrimental to one's longterm welfare.
Kids Shouldn't Get Stoned, #37, September 1978

DEA TO SPRAY PARAQUAT

BOGOTA—The United States and Colombian governments will soon begin spraying this country's marijuana fields with the deadly herbicide paraquat. Paraquat, used in Mexico to destroy opium poppies, does not kill cannabis, but it leaves a chemical film that is potentially hazardous to the smoker. The spraying follows a $30,000 National Institute on Drug Abuse (NIDA) study into the effects of paraquat on marijuana smokers.

The decision to spray Colombia's fields came after First Lady Rosalynn Carter's trip to Colombia last summer, when the United States promised to supply three Bell helicopters to Colombian narcotics troops. Although the U.S. Drug Enforcement Administration (DEA) has yet to publicize the proposed spraying, sources here indicated that the agency has asked its two top spraying experts to oversee the operation. Over $2-billion worth of Colombian marijuana has been confiscated by the National Police here since 1973. An additional $35-million worth of marijuana was captured and destroyed by DAS narcs.

HighWitness News, #29, January 1978

NORML CALLS ON GOV'T TO STOP SPRAYING

The National Organization for the Reform of Marijuana Laws (NORML) has demanded that the U.S. State Department and the Drug Enforcement Administration (DEA) immediately stop their participation in herbicide-spraying programs in Mexico.

NORML charges that the State Department and DEA have openly encouraged and supported the spraying of the herbicides paraquat and 2-4-D on marijuana and poppy plants for nearly three years without filing Environmental Impact Statements as required by law. These defoliants, according to a letter sent to the DEA, have the potential of doing short- and long-term damage to the environment.

Despite the apparent dangers, NORML director Keith Stroup claims that no U.S. government agency or official has ever thoroughly analyzed any of the potential environmental and health consequences that could result from the spraying, as is required under the National Environmental Policy Act of 1969.

HighWitness News, #34, June 1978

(not to mention the increasing probability of ordinary tourists being arrested and brutally interrogated as suspected smugglers). United Brands—formerly United Fruit—no longer owns plantations in Jamaica but buys most of the country's produce, thus dictating prices. The resulting futility of agricultural life has sent thousands of Jamaicans to Kingston to seek industrial jobs, but industry is abandoning Jamaica to seek bauxite in more stable environments. Jamaica's urban unemployed and rural workers have become the world's leading poverty group outside of India. The marijuana trade therefore offers the island a chance to achieve, for the first time, a decent standard of living.

Unfortunately, ganja is still very illegal in Jamaica, and the influx of money and guns has only made the smoldering racial hatreds and economic desperation more intense. The administration of Michael Manley, elected prime minister in 1972, seemed to offer the Jamaican people some hope, but Manley's sincere attempt to better the lot of the majority of poor blacks was of little avail in the face of the island's economic obsolescence. As the murder rate soared to 2000 a year (on an island of 2 million), including political leaders of all parties and foreign businessmen and diplomats, Manley was forced to ban black power literature and leaders and enact a gun law providing for immediate incarceration for life of anyone caught with a firearm. But Manley's government in Kingston was still troubled by the Rastafarian religious sect, which controlled the countryside and the ganja trade. Though pacifists with a mellow back-to-Africa set, the Rastafarians were now in a position to clear themselves a little breathing space in "Babylon." In short, Jamaica was ripe to become another Cuba in 1974. Then the DEA launched Operation Buccaneer.

The first major DEA action abroad, Operation Buccaneer lasted from June to December 1974 and involved the transfer to Jamaica of numerous U.S. aircraft, air surveillance devices (radar) and narcotics personnel. The DEA used the Jamaican police and military but retained vital control of planning. The DEA also coordinated U.S. Coast Guard and Customs surveillance of Jamaican sea traffic and supplied flamethrowers, helicopters and herbicides for the destruction of ganja fields. On his end, the generally left-leaning Manley introduced massive repression in the form of the Suppression of Crime Act (1974), which allowed secret trials, withholding of bail and indeterminate prison sentences for offenders. Americans and Jamaicans who were apprehended during and after Operation Buccaneer told lurid tales of torture (but nothing to compare with later DEA atrocities in Mexico, Colombia and the Philippines). In addition to massive roundups of suspects and the defoliation of ganja fields, the DEA destroyed the smugglers' mountaintop landing strips (mainly USAF leftovers from World War II) and even planted iron poles on the sides of highways to shear off the wings of aircraft. By December 14, Operation Buccaneer claimed the seizure and destruction of 730,000 pounds of ganja, plus hashish, marijuana seeds and 20 pounds of cocaine en route from Latin America. Numerous firearms, 10 aircraft, 17 vessels and $143,000 in cash were also seized. Five hundred acres of ganja were destroyed and guards set over them. The Jamaican export ganja trade was effectively destroyed (although smoking is still near universal on the island).

In the process, the Jamaican Ministry of Defense, as well as the police, were virtually converted to an auxiliary narcotics force—which, in theory, they remain, keeping a lid on the ganja growers with the help of the DEA. In effect, Manley now has unlimited military force as well as complete control of the judicial system, weapons that may be employed anytime the "drug problem" (it used to be communist subversion) gets out of hand. With Jamaica "stabilized" Manley became the first Dope Dictator.

Unlike Jamaica, Mexico is among the more prosperous nations of the Western hemisphere. However, 95 percent of the nation's wealth is in the hands of 15 percent of the population and its commercial partners in the U.S. and Europe. Of a population of 58 million, 25 million Mexicans are peasants—4 million of whom have no land 66 years after the revolution of 1910, which was fought to win land for every Mexican peasant. The other peasants live on tiny *ejido* farms, generally too poor to buy equipment, grain and fertilizer and under constant pressure to sell out to agroindustrial landholders (who conceal illegally contiguous estates with dummy owners). Mexico's peasants also enjoy chronic underemployment, illiteracy and disease: While they can occasionally pick up two dollars a day as laborers on the large estates, the work is seasonal and many peasants have little alternative to the wetback route.

Mexican political power resides in the Institutional Revolutionary Party (PRI), continuously in office since 1910 and very much the party of the bankers, industrialists, businessmen and foreign interests. The businessmen love their government and are fond of quoting the proverb "In Mexico, government is business and business is government." Apart from enormous investments in Mexico, the U.S. has a vital interest in seeing a politically stable and economically secure neighbor on its southern border. As for the peasants, few are registered voters; the PRI candidates are the only ones on the ballot, and the ministries are corrupt and confusing bureaucracies. As in Jamaica, the short-term solution to the peasants' plight is marijuana; in the long run, only a political and economic reform so drastic that the PRI must regard it as revolutionary can help.

Until recently, the peasants who stuck to the marijuana trade were generally ignored. Gustavo Diaz Ordaz, president from 1964 to 1970, dealt strictly with the radical intelligentsia, jailing most of the leaders of the student movement in 1968 and massacring 300 students at the Plaza del Tlatelolco in Mexico City later that year (for the CIA connection, see Philip Agee's *Inside the Company: CIA Diary*). Diaz's successor, Luis Echeverria (who, as minister of the interior, apparently directed the mass arrests and the Mexico City massacre), freed nearly 900 political prisoners in 1971 but continued to deal harshly with any opposition, suppressing one student march that year by killing 30 marchers. Echeverria then turned to the peasant rebels who had begun to finance their amateurish insurrections with profits of the booming grass trade.

During Echeverria's administration, the violence on both sides has increased to its bloodiest peak since the days of Pancho Villa. Hundreds of peasants and soldiers were killed in pitched battles in 1974 and 1975. Peasant leaders have been bought off as liberally as possible or, in cases like that of the now legendary schoolteacher-turned-guerrilla Luciano Cabanas, relentlessly pursued and assassinated. In one incident, in June 1971, rightwing "shock troops" armed by Mexico City police and businessmen with bamboo staves, automatic pistols and machine guns killed 13 or more antigovernment demonstrators. In retaliation, Mexican radicals kidnapped several U.S. and British diplomats during the next few years. U.S Vice-Consul Terrance G. Leonhardy was abducted on May 4, 1973, by the People's Armed Revolutionary Force. The remains of the most recent abductee, U.S. Vice-Consul John Patterson, were identified in a gulch near Hermosillo in July 1974.

CHEAP "BLOW" ENHANCES SEX

Q◆While I was partying with a lady friend a while back she got kind of sore after a couple of really heavy orgasms, so I dropped a pinch of coke on her clitoris and began licking it. Well of course it numbed my tongue nicely, but I couldn't believe what it did to her. She'd been in a state where she couldn't bear to be touched, but now all of a sudden she was having fantastic orgasms for hours. What accounts of this reaction, and is there any less expensive way to get it?

Tan, Detroit, MI

A◆Coke numbs the exterior nerves of the clit but leaves the inner mechanisms of the female orgasm perfectly functional, making continual stimulation possible for as long as the numbness lasts—two hours or more. You can get precisely the same effect by applying preparations containing procaine, benzocaine or lidocaine. "Solarcaine's better for coming than it is for sunburn," guarantees a woman of our acquaintance. "And lots cheaper than orgy butter."

Though men don't commonly have the same sort of soreness problems as women, it's likely that procaine could act like coke, when dropped on the glans, to retard male orgasm. Pure procaine, dropped onto the back of a person's throat, might enable him or her to give deep-throat head for extended periods of time without gagging.

Adviser, #40, December 1978

YIP VS. NORML

I read with interest about the growing conflict concerning the radical YIP dissent over NORML policies. I see this conflict as a '70s manifestation of the same divisiveness that tapped much of the '60s movements' momentums. What's wrong with NORML being a "middle-class-smokers lobby" as Keith Stroup says? Look how much NORML has accomplished by working within the system.

Jane Becker, Ann Arbor, MI

Letters, #37, September 1978

CARTER'S DOPE CZAR FALLS

Amid national controversy over new revelations that the Jimmy Carter White House is a hotbed of cocaine, marijuana and pharmaceutical use, Dr. Peter Bourne, Carter's top drug aide and the man he called "about the closest friend I have in the world," has resigned following charges that he wrote an illegal prescription for Quaaludes.

Bourne, who tried to cover up the Quaalude scandal after it broke in mid-July, was immediately confronted with charges from columnist Jack Anderson that he had snorted cocaine at a NORML benefit. After NORML chief Keith Stroup confirmed Anderson's story, Bourne resigned his $51,000-a-year job immediately. He is still facing legal charges and possible AMA disciplinary action arising from his bogus Quaalude "scripts."

The Bourne scandal finally brought to light a story the national media, long aware of, has ignored: widespread "drug abuse" in the Carter administration. Following Bourne's resignation, seven junior White House aides told the press they smoked pot regularly, though never in the White House.

Bourne's departure was fraught with tension and drama for the tired and emotional White House staff and press corps. Shortly before handing in his black diplomatic passport, Bourne said there is "a high incidence" of marijuana smoking among members of the White House staff as well as "occasional" cocaine use by a "few" of his former colleagues.

HighWitness News, #39, November 1978

Echeverria, whose term of office (1970 to 1976) coincided with the brief hiatus in Turkish poppy-growing that saw the birth of the "Mexican brown" heroin trade, was an enthusiastic supporter of the Dope War that Diaz had complained of at the time of Operation Intercept (long lines at the border were hurting the tourist trade and truck routes). In 1973 the DEA began a trickle and then a blitzkrieg of paramilitary aid that was to make Echeverria the second Dope Dictator of Latin America.

The cost of our Mexican Vietnam is impossible to estimate. It involves the use of hundreds of aircraft—for example, 28 Huey-type Bell helicopters given to Mexico to spot pot and poppy fields and spray them with defoliants cost the DEA $800 an hour to operate, not counting flight pay. Other DEA-donated helicopters are equipped with heat- and movement-sensitive tracking equipment; troop-carrying landing choppers plus the training machines used by DEA special advisers to recruit local pilots add up to a sizable and costly air force. North of the border at least 89 Customs pursuit planes scramble night and day to intercept homeward-bound smugglers, while the Air Force's NORAD (North American Air Defense) radar system has switched from missile-monitoring to spotting the unscheduled flights of pot pilots.

In Mexico City, DEA special advisers train the *federales* in Vietnam-style search-and-destroy tactics. Others accompany the U.S.-made M-16-toting Mexican narcs to the fields and prisons, which the DEA runs as brutal interrogation centers for Mexican and American prisoners alike. As in Jamaica, the entire Mexican police and military are being retrained to fight the Dope War.

One of the most frightening developments in the Dope War in Mexico is the use of the herbicides 2, 4-D and 2, 4, 5-T, which combine to form a defoliant known as Agent Orange. Agent Orange was banned in Vietnam after it was proved to cause birth defects. Another DEA weapon is paraquat (commercially known as Gramoxone), a nonselective poison that shrivels any leaf it touches—poppy, pot or not. Critics of the Mexican war crimes estimate that as much as 20 percent of the arable land in Mexico could be ruined by the DEA's indiscriminate deforestations. Whether the Dope War can quell the Mexican peasantry in the long run is doubtful; after all, they have little to lose. And the more the pot-consuming public in the U.S. grows aware of the pressures on the growers, the more the importers will seize the opportunity to raise their prices, which DEA agents will routinely double in order to buy and bust. Meanwhile, Echeverria, despite some friction with businessmen over devaluation of the peso and token appropriation of some large estates, has continued the gracious Mexican tradition of accommodating the gringos wherever possible—for instance, by refusing to join OPEC in 1973 and by holding a ceiling on Mexican oil prices. And shortly before leaving office in December 1976, he admitted that the grass trade has been taken over by guerrillas who exchange their crops for weapons.

Former Finance Minister Jose Lopez Portillo, who succeeded Echeverria as president (under Mexican law, a president may not succeed himself but may appoint his successor; with no other parties on the ballot, the PRI remains in power), had to deal with a certain amount of dissatisfaction with Echeverria in the business community. Two days after his inauguration, *federales* expelled 3,500 peasants from large estates that Echeverria had expropriated for their use two weeks before, graphically demonstrating Portillo's allegiance to the business community. However, the tensions between the government and the landless peasants have only been aggravated, so the Dope War seems likely to enjoy a long run in Mexico.

PART 3
THE DIFFICULT
POST-TOM ERA
1979-1983

NO LONGER "THE MAGAZINE OF HIGH SOCIETY,"
WE BECAME "THE MAGAZINE OF FEELING GOOD."

T. COURTNEY BROWN

was a product of the baby boom; spent a quiet but meaningful childhood in New York City, and attended Cooper Union for a BFA.

"Would YOU Trust This Woman With Your Magazine?"

After a stint as associate art director of *Good Housekeeping*, she became the art director of HIGH TIMES magazine in 1975.

Here is Ms. Brown relaxing in the art department during a deadline.

Closers, #26, October 1977

WILLIAM BURROUGHS

BY VICTOR BOCKRIS

After years of exile, the controversial American author of *Naked Lunch* and *Junkie* talks about Jack Kerouac, smack, out-of-body experiences, outer space, brain power, future shock, fascism and the most important novel of the '80s, his own *Cities of the Red Night*.

HT: What's actually causing the growing acceptance of drugs?

WB: Less ill-informed media exposure is making the biggest difference.

HT: What is actually going to happen?

WB: They're going to legalize marijuana, and sooner or later they're going to come around to some form of heroin maintenance. Many people connected with drug enforcement actually think that there's no use going on trying to enforce an unenforceable law and that it's been as much of a failure as Prohibition. That'll make a terrific change. It would destroy the whole black market in heroin and eliminate the whole necessity for the Drug Enforcement Administration.

HT: Is writing on morphine very different than on marijuana?

WB: About as different as you can get. The two drugs are moving in exactly the opposite directions. A pain-killer like morphine naturally cuts down your awareness of your surroundings and whatever's going on in your physical orientation. You can write, you can do anything routine, but I feel that morphine is contraindicated to doing any kind of creative work. It's good for routine work. Doctors and lawyers can function on it, bank tellers, and it's good for writing articles. It's not good for creative writing, because it's dulling your awareness.

Interview, #42, February 1979

YOU ARE WHAT YOU THROW AWAY

by A.J. Weberman

One day in September 1970, Ann Duncan and I were on our way to the Café Gaslight on MacDougal Street and we happened to pass Bob Dylan's town house. For four long years I had been studying Dylan's poetry, trying to crack the code of his symbolism. As I eyed the home of this reclusive poet I wondered what went down behind the door that Dylan had slammed in my face. Just then I noticed Dylan's shiny new steel garbage can and said to myself, "Now, there's something that was inside and now it's *outside*." I lifted the lid, reached in and extracted a half-finished letter written by Bob Dylan himself to Johnny Cash. "Ann, this is no garbage can," I shouted. "This is a gold mine!" Thereby was garbology founded.

Garbology, as we know it today, is the study of human personality and contemporary civilization through the analysis of garbage, and is also known as "garbanalysis."

The basic premise of garbology is "You Are What You Throw Away": Garbage is a reflection of life. Every living thing gives off waste. Living matter excretes; it is a natural, universal process, basic to life itself. The more sophisticated the organism, the more sophisticated the waste it produces. Garbologists, however, do not study urine or feces, even though they are human wastes. We leave this to the medical profession and the CIA, which has been known to analyze the excretions of foreign leaders in order to get an accurate picture of their health. Garbologists stick to other types of human trash for objects of study: refuse, garbage, the ragbag, the dustbin, the junk pile, the trash heap, etc. Archaeologists sift through this kind of stuff, too, but only if it is ancient. The garbologist finds his research material on the street today (or, usually, early in the morning) and from it he derives a mirrored image of human behavior and the modern world we live in.

After my initial discovery in Dylan's garbage (more about this rich find later) I realized that this method of research had great potential. The lives of the rich, famous and powerful could be penetrated, great secrets revealed, plain truths brought to light from beneath the glittery facade. Garbology was a new weapon in the war against lies, injustice and faceless bureaucracy. The study and analysis of garbage could possibly alter the course of history! I resolved at once that aided by this valuable science I would leave no stone unturned, no garbage-can lid untilted, in my quest for truth.

Yet, certain thoughts crossed my mind as my career in garbology blossomed. Was I trampling on other people's rights? Was I becoming the very sort of secret police that I had always opposed? Had I earned the epithets people threw at me—"snoop" and "sneak"? Was Bob Dylan right when he told me, "A.J., you go through garbage like a pig, man"? I wondered long and hard about this.

But history will absolve garbology. For it is nothing less than a journalistic technique, and in this post-Watergate world, the public's right to know is far more important than the privacy of a public figure. The ethics of garbology are parallel to the basic ethics of journalism as put forth in the libel laws; if you are a public figure, you are fair game. I only garbanalyze the rich, famous and powerful. It is beneath the dignity of a distinguished garbologist such as myself to dig through the refuse of any average bozo. When people ask me, "Hey, A.J., when are you going to analyze my garbage?" I often reply, "Just as soon as you stop being a nonentity."

The fact is, however, that America is starting to wake up to garbage. With many of our natural resources rapidly disappearing, garbage, be it ever so humble, is on its way to becoming a highly valuable commodity. It won't be long, I'm sure, before the commodities exchange begins trading garbage futures. Garbology is now taught as a course at several universities. A professor of anthropology at the University of Arizona has his students go through thousands of bags of garbage, sorted according to socioeconomic background, to find out if various social stereotypes pan out. At Queens College in New York City, Professor Warren DeBoer teaches a similar class called "Traces of Human Behavior." DeBoer's students are attempting to find out which socioeconomic groups have the type of trash that is most amenable to recycling. The required literature for the course cites me as the founder of garbology.

Shortly after discovering garbology, the media discovered me. *Esquire* magazine hired me to do a cover story on garbage, and articles about me began appearing in *Glamour, Ingenue* and *Rolling Stone*. The Associated Press did a feature story that appeared in hundreds of newspapers across the country. I began to develop a nationwide network of garbology "stringers" who sent me reports on local trash. I was imitated by Jack Anderson, Robin Moore and other journalists. In order to stay ahead of the competition I was forced to train an associate garbologist—Aron Morton Kay (who would later achieve notoriety as the man who throws pies at celebrities).

With Kay in the field I could devote my time to setting up the National Institute of Garbology, where advanced research and development could be facilitated. The institute is located at 6 Bleecker Street in Manhattan (telephone 212-477-6243) and is not open to the general public although inquiries are welcome. Some of the most significant garbage on file at the institute has been reprinted in this book. Each individual collection of garbage represents months of study and research. But more than that, each is the result of action, sometimes perilous, sometimes hilarious, but always adventurous.

BOB DYLAN'S $1,000,000 TRASH

After recovering from my shock and joy at finding an actual handwritten letter by my favorite poet in the trash can, I pulled myself together and began digging deeper, just barely aware that I was opening up the first chapter of a brand-new science. I confess, though, that the overpowering odor of decaying food, raw onions, dirty diapers and dogshit was a strong argument for turning back. Nevertheless, I pushed onward because I knew that "the answer was blowing in the wind."

My fantasy was that I would find first drafts of Dylan's poetry or a Rosetta stone that would unlock the secrets of his symbolism. But the reality, as I began sorting through the bags, was a harsh one, especially when I hit a layer of disposable diapers. It reminded me that Dylan and his wife Sara had just recently had their fourth child. Dylan is traditional in that respect, producing a kid every year, a big family man, just like my cousin, Rabbi Phineus Weberman. Phineus is super-Orthodox and has fifteen children. To my mind, the dirty diapers were a good example of Dylan's late-'60s conservatism.

I made my way down through a layer of kitchen refuse—vegetable

Interview: The Last Testament of Sante Bario—Did the DEA Poison Its Top Agent?

High Times

May '79 $2.00

NBC CATCHES REEFER MADNESS

THE TRUTH ABOUT CIRCUMCISION

COOKING WITH GRASS
by "R.," Dope Connoisseur

BUY YOUR OWN ISLAND

HARLEM'S HIGH HEYDAYS
Viper Bernie Brightman Enlightens Larry Sloman

L.A.—A TOUR OF THE FAST LANE
by Victor Bockris

Centerfold:
SECRET SMOKE OF THE FAR EAST

Comix:
LAWRENCE OF COLOMBIA

*Satan's Greatest Hits
A Short History of the Devil
by Glenn O'Brien*

JERRY BROWN

We're divided among arbitrary geographical lines, separated into ethnic categories and divided along various linguistic groups, but when we look at the earth and the human species from a few hundred miles up we can't help but sense the oneness of the human race and of this species that has been part of the universe for such a limited period of time.

I also think of the closing frontier, the closing of the west, and what that does to the psychology of people. As long as there is a safety valve of unexplored frontiers, the creative, the aggressive, the exploitive urges of human beings can be channeled into long-term possibilities and benefits. But as those frontiers close down and people begin to turn in upon themselves—that jeopardizes the democratic fabric.

I don't happen to think that frontier is closed. It's just opening up in space. That opening up, that exploration, is first and foremost a discovery of the unknown, a breaking out of the egocentric, man-dominated perceptions that still tie us down here below. As we break out of that narrow perception and see the possibilities, endless and infinite as they are throughout the entire universe, we concentrate the creative energies of the best and most talented of those among us.... Here in this state, where we have witnessed the creation of new industries, where we have witnessed the gold rush, the creation of the airplane industry, the movie industry, the record industry, we are also on the cutting edge of space development and exploration, we are going into space as a species.

Opinion by Governor Jerry Brown of California,
#42, February 1979

PERON'S PRISON MESSAGE

This is Dennis Peron writing from my 5-by-7 foot jail cell in San Bruno. I am in jail ostensibly for running what the media called a pot supermarket. Originally I planned on basing my defense on the "miracle ounce" provision—in California, the ounce you may possess with no more penalty than a fine, so long as you don't buy or grow or sell it. The argument seemed rational to me, but considering I had over 200 pounds of grass and 3,000 hits of acid I figured it was a few more miracles than a jury could accept. So I took a deal for six months in the county jail.

Before my imprisonment I sponsored and placed on the ballot for November in San Francisco an initiative that went to the heart of Pot Prohibition; it would give the supervisors of our high cities the moral authority to cut off the funds to both the district attorney and the police department, who enforce the archaic marijuana laws. Until the laws are changed, the only option of the people is to cut the funds—leave the laws as they are, just don't enforce them, as many laws are not enforced indeed when enforceable. Even the right-wingers agree that their money is being wasted in judges sending their children to jail and protecting us from ourselves.

A battle may have been lost, but the war is not over. Much thanks for your support till the day we may smoke legal weed; I remain a faithful warrior. Watch the light from San Francisco; it will light up the world.

Letters, by Dennis Peron, #42, February 1979

cans, Blimpie wrappers, coffee grounds. His eating habits seemed normal enough. No evidence of "brown rice, seaweed or a dirty hot dog."

Further on, I discovered a form letter to the Dylans from the Little Red School House (around the corner on Bleecker Street) thanking parents for contributing to one of the school's funds. The fact that Dylan sent his kids there was interesting because the Little Red School House is where the children of upper-middle-class and rich liberals of Greenwich Village go.

Next, I stumbled upon a fragment of a fan letter to Dylan from someone in California that read, "Marie will turn to the wind and ask where heroin is available." Very strange, indeed.

My next big revelation was that Dylan and I both shopped at the same Grand Union supermarket! A second layer of kitchen castoffs contained the packagings from Grand Union-brand sweet butter and Grand Union-brand eggs, as well as a Grand Union shopping bag, chicken bones, an empty milk carton, green peas, an empty Balanced apple-juice bottle, and some balled-up aluminum foil. Dylan's dog, Sasha, was evidently fed a diet of Gainesburgers and Ken-L Ration. And that was literally the bottom of that first barrel.

Essentially, the mythic Bob Dylan—romantic, revolutionary, visionary—was dispelled forever by thorough garbanalysis. Instead, he was revealed to be a typically upper-middle-class family man with very ordinary, day-to-day household concerns. From his pail I gathered bills from the vet concerning treatment of Sasha's upset stomach; invitations to Sara to attend private sales at exclusive department stores; dozens of mail-order cosmetic offers and all the high-fashion magazines addressed to Sara; a package from Bloomingdale's addressed to one of Dylan's many pseudonyms and charged to Sara Dylan's account. I also found a bill from the Book-of-the-Month Club, and a memo to Bob Dylan regarding the upcoming monthly meeting of the MacDougal Street Garden Association.

But nowhere did I find any evidence that Dylan was at all interested in politics, causes, activism or world affairs. And at that time, you'll recall, the war in Vietnam was still raging. Nixon was in office, four students had been killed earlier in the year at Kent State and the six o'clock news made it difficult to escape the endless stream of atrocities and injustices. Yet, it seemed to me that Dylan had come a long way from the days when he wrote "Gates of Eden," "Masters of War" and "Blowin' in the Wind." The only remotely political piece of trash I was able to find in his garbage was a poster from upstate New York with a personal note on it from a local folksinger in Woodstock, asking Dylan to please vote in the upcoming election for this particular Democratic county committeeman.

WATERGATE GARBAGE

Watergate was the greatest political scandal in America since Teapot Dome. It afforded endless opportunities for investigative reporting on the people who run America and the kinds of corruption with which the government is often riddled. As a garbologist I became keenly interested in all political garbage that was uncovered during the Watergate scandal, and decided to uncover some of it myself.

I was particularly interested in obtaining the trash of John Mitchell. A New York lawyer, Mitchell had been appointed attorney general by his friend Richard Nixon in 1968. For over four years he was the head of the Justice Department, and as such he was in charge of the FBI, the nation's elite corps of pseudogarbologists. I thought it was about time to turn the tables on Mitchell.

His wife, Martha, was another matter, however. Martha Mitchell had declared, before the whole scandal broke, that something "dirty" was going on in the Nixon administration. In other words, she had the dirt that I was after. But unlike so many others, I never got a phone call from Martha, so I would have to resort to other means.

In August 1973, the Mitchells were living together at 1030 Fifth Avenue. At the time, John Mitchell had resigned from office and was testifying before the House and arrived on target at precisely 7:30. I stood across the street, pretending to be waiting for a bus, while I watched the building superintendent stack about fifty green bags in a neat pile. When he'd finished, I walked over and very casually began making tiny incisions in each bag with a pocketknife in order to facilitate identification.

At last, I hit pay dirt; it was a piece of junk mail addressed to John Mitchell. Working fast now, I whipped a spare liner out of my pocket, poured the Mitchells' muck into it, filled their trash liner with nearby garbage and returned it to the same place in the pile. I was determined that my quarry would not find out he was being garbanalyzed. This time there was going to be a lot of garbage for me to look at. John Mitchell, ex-attorney general, was going to be garbanalyzed to the fullest extent of the garbological law.

The garbage belonged almost exclusively to Martha. It even had a sample of her bleached-blond hair along with many Salem-cigarette butts with lipstick prints on them. I examined these stains with a micrometer and verified the widespread belief that Martha had one of the biggest mouths in America. Many of the butts were smoked only halfway and there were hundreds of them scattered about, along with empty Salem packs and cartons. There was a $7 price tag from a new pair of size 32-medium panties Martha had recently purchased, which read, "Olga—The First Lady of Underfashions." Martha drank Tanqueray imported English gin, with Schweppes tonic, and Canada Dry ginger ale. I came across several pages of handwritten numbers (a score sheet from some parlor game), Dole pineapple cans, Lady Scott toilet paper and toilet-bowl deodorant. Martha's mail included a questionnaire from *Time* magazine and a letter from the Women's National Republican Club. All in all, the kind of boring garbage characteristic of women who spend a lot of time at home.

I went back next morning and found an entire box full of trash that the former attorney general had covered with five copies of the *Washington Post* that he seemed to have obtained from his neighbor, Kennedy-clan member Stephen Smith. John had *The New York Times* delivered each day, and bought the *Daily News* and the *New York Post* at the newsstand. Many of the articles in these newspapers concerned Mitchell, although very few were cut up. It didn't look like he was keeping a scrapbook. I also found four empty bottles—two of Dewar's Scotch, one of Ballantine Scotch and another of Smirnoff vodka. During the Watergate hearings, John Ehrlichman testified that Mitchell was in a bad state of health and was drinking heavily. Here was the evidence. The remains of a Mitchell meal were scattered about—several empty cans of Campbell's soup, some milk cartons, Campbell's franks and beans, chicken bones, Baskin-Robbins ice cream, Coke bottles and Seven-Up cans. His preference was apparently for junk food.

Next came the good stuff—letters—and plenty of them! Mitchell had had to give his address on national television so he received a good deal of mail. One letter read, "If I had my way the lot of you would be stood

TO OUR READERS

Thomas King Forçade was the founder and guiding spirit of HIGH TIMES, *Stone Age* and *Alternative Media*. He was a modest man who, because of certain political and personal beliefs and fears and a disdain of celebrity trips, preserved a strong anonymity. But Tom's ideals, his energy, his enthusiasm and his struggle to insure and expand personal freedom for everyone are evident in every single issue of HIGH TIMES. On November 16, 1978, Thomas King Forçade took his own life.

Tom penned many editorials, features and interviews for HIGH TIMES under various pseudonyms. And every article we've ever published was the result of a collaboration between Tom and a writer, Tom and an editor—ultimately between Tom and an idea. His enthusiasm for change was infectious, his ability to organize and articulate new ideas was unmatched, his clarity of thought was catalytic. Thomas King Forçade was a master communicator.

In 1972 Tom published the first collection of writings that had appeared in various underground publications around the country. This book, *The Underground Press Anthology*, included a poignant biography he himself authored:

Thomas King Forçade was involved in numerous underground scenes. He was associated with *Orpheus* magazine, Underground Press Syndicate, New York Ace, S.D.S., White Panthers, Magic Christian Collective, Youth International Party, Zippies, Amorphia, bus tripping with the Hog Farm and separately, the Caravan of Love, various media conferences, and several rock festivals, including Woodstock, Winter's End, and Randall's Island. He helped promote a series of rock benefits and was the manager of David Peel and the Lower East Side, Teenage Lust, and Evil.

Under pseudonyms, Forçade wrote extensively, including several books, some

unpublished due to U.S. libel laws. He also edited *Steal This Book* and several anthologies.

Forçade is not well known, even to his few friends. His whereabouts and future plans are unknown. **#43, March 1979**

ROBERT BELFIORE

against the wall. If I live long enough, I'm going to see it." Another one asked, "All the lawyers we saw on TV were gay. Are you?" All of these letters and postcards had been ripped to shreds and some of the pieces had been withheld from garbification. Only two of them were intact. One read, "Just for the record I believe Richard Nixon knew about the Watergate cover-up and also that worry has helped to make him ill. I'm one of Martha's greatest admirers. She would never lie. Ha! Ha! Ha!" The other was written over John's picture as published in a small-town Florida newspaper: "You're a damned criminal—may you end up in the penitentiary."

There were three favorable letters in Mitchell's load; one of them came from a small farm in Nebraska. It was nearly illegible and quite illiterate, but after deciphering, it read: "Please stand on testmony i look at that mess evey day. the cross fire you all you all Masson 33 Degree put it to them Make Evey one pay bige fine all so John Deen put a start to it Make you 3 man all pay a fih poor presse dint..." The letter also contained a few pages of literature from the Rev. Gerald L.K. Smith, an anti-Semitic right-wing preacher, which was carefully underlined for the former attorney general's enlightenment. Such were his supporters.

I also found a small scrap of Mitchell's most intimate notes on the Watergate affair. When I was on a television show hosted by Martha Mitchell she told me that she insisted that her husband threw away his important papers a little at a time to thwart souvenir seekers. Martha insisted that I couldn't have got her garbage and brought a sample of it along to compare with her garb-art portrait. If the garbage wouldn't have matched up, I would have been ruined. But the trash was almost identical and Martha had to admit that I had snatched her slops.

Perhaps the most historically significant piece of trash was a manila envelope from the United States Senate Select Committee on Presidential Campaign Activities that bore the signature of Sam Ervin, Jr., in place of a postage stamp. It probably contained his subpoena to testify before the Watergate Committee!

BELLA'S BARREL

Bella Abzug lost her most recent bid for Congress in 1978, but for a long time, "Battling Bella" was one of the most influential women in the country. She's always been on the left side of the political scene, coming out of the labor-movement tradition, leading the Women's Strike for Peace against the Vietnam War and working hard for good social legislation regarding the rights of minorities and women. For this reason, I've always respected Bella, since my sympathies lie in the same direction. But nobody in the public eye is immune to garbology. That's why I started to focus on Bella's barrel. But there were problems right from the start.

Ten years of garbological experience have brought me to the conclusion that America's greatest garbanoids are feminists. Take the case of Kate Millet, author of *Sexual Politics*, who happens to live near the National Institute of Garbology. I spent three years trying to find her heap and the closest I've come to it was some unidentifiable trash with paper plates in it. I have also been unable to obtain *Ms.* magazine founder Gloria Steinem's slops despite repeated predawn raids on her can.

The National Institute of Garbology has devised several methods designed to cure garbanoia. One of them is "daily garbological profiling"—Non-Stop De-Garbification! Sooner or later the garbage will turn up!

Bella was exposed to this sort of scrutiny for about one month. Around the time of the 1972 congressional elections, something turned up—a small paper bag on the bottom of the barrel, which I eagerly scraped up.

Having been strung out for Bella's junk for nearly a month I had to eyeball some of it immediately. I discovered, much to my dismay, that it was a man's garbage—cardboard stiffeners from professionally laundered shirts, containers from foods that required little in the way of preparation, a tube from an expensive cigar. There was also a series of memos from C.B. Richard Securities, Inc., which confirmed my suspicions that much of the trash belonged to Bella's husband, Martin, the stockbroker.

The rest consisted of a bulletin from a drug-plasma plant, a luggage catalog, a gas-and-electric bill for $22.76, a note on a sheet of yellow, legal-sized paper that read, "Katy Industry (pfd) 36 3/4," and some football slips from the office. He also had some duplicate receipts from a local pharmacy for items like Listerine mouthwash (she's got a big mouth) and Miltown tranquilizers (she's very excitable). There were notes reading, "Monday Lamstons [a local five-and-ten-cent store] buy 2 pillow cases"; "Clean my suit"; "Sat-Detroit"; "Sunday-Cincinatti"; "Sat—see Bella in morning/Peter Weiss re: Dellums Viet platform." Aha, left-wing peacenik political garbage!

There was some of the Abzugs' son's stuff in the trash—a bulletin from Hunter College and a request for money from the Center for the Study of Democratic Institutions. Their daughter Eve was represented— an unpaid bill from Boston University.

Finally I got down to the part of the trash that was distinctly Bella's. I noticed something that instantly triggered the muck alarm in my brain: an annual report addressed to her from Litton Industries and an IBM card from American Machine Foundries, Inc. (AMF), with her name and account number printed on it. Both these giant conglomerates specialize in producing complex weapons systems for the United States military.

Bella had made a political career out of opposing the war in Vietnam and had been instrumental in winning the votes of the liberal constituency of her congressional district. Shortly after her election to Congress the Republican-dominated state legislature gerrymandered her district out of existence. This political mugging only made Bella more popular with New York City's voters, and her election was virtually assured in the congressional race. I was in a unique position. Here the election was just a week away and I was in possession of political dynamite. I'd uncovered the fact that Bella Abzug owned war stock.

Since I am always willing to give people like Bella the benefit of the doubt I called her office and asked them to read me a list of the stocks she owned. The gentleman informed me she had shares in a shoe factory, a cement plant, etc.—but he didn't say a word about Litton Industries or AMF. It looked like a cover-up to me. I made a crucial decision. Much as I liked Bella and everything she stood for, I cannot tolerate hypocrisy. I was angry. I felt lied to, cheated, ripped off, bamboozled. And what about her constituents, the people who believed in Bella, who voted for her because they hated the damned war and wanted it stopped? A bunch of chumps!

So I held a press conference the day before the election. The response to it was generally along political lines—the conservative *Daily News* interviewed me and took my picture while the liberal CBS-TV newspeople wouldn't touch the story, accusing me of working for Nixon.

PIE ASSASSIN

BY HARRY WASSERMAN

I first met Aron Kay when I arrived at the Yippies' Bowery headquarters at 9 Bleecker Street, New York City, in the fall of '75. There were some real crazies living there, but Aron was the craziest. I had come from Wisconsin for a live-in job at the *Yipster Times*, America's only national underground newspaper. But 9 Bleecker was more than un underground newspaper office, more than a anarchist commune; it was a nuthouse, a hippie halfway house run by the inmates.

"My first pieing was in May of '73, at Rennie Davis, formerly of the Chicago Seven. Rennie had come to New York's Anderson Theater to proselytize on behalf of our local spiritual hamburger, Guru Maharaj Ji. I tossed a cherry pie at him, which missed, because I was being jostled by security. It ended up on the floor of the stage, and the local gurinoids licked it off the floor."

Soon Aron started on a blitz of successes. William F. Buckley, Daniel Patrick Moynihan, E. Howard Hunt, Phyllis Schlafly, Abe Beame, G. Gordon Liddy, William Colby.... There could be a garbagemen's strike, a blackout or an impending world war, but Aron's pie throw was always funny enough to rate the front page.
Culture Hero, #44, April 1979

POTHEADS SAFER THAN DRUNKS

Scientists have found that grass smokers make conspicuously better drivers than drunks. UCLA's Dr. Sally Caswell gave stoned people visual road-simulation driving tests and compared them with drunks on the same machine. She found that alcohol users typically thought they were doing great on the machine, speeding and taking unnecessary risks, even though their reaction times were dangerously protracted. Grass smokers also had slower reactions, but they were fully conscious of their impairment and conpensated for it by driving more slowly and carefully.

Health, #45, May 1979

WAVY GRAVY

BY RON ROSENBAUM

From psychedelic barnstorming to communal hog farming; from East Coast coffeehouse cool to stoned San Francisco sunshine; from the Beat Generation through the Me Decade and beyond: A conversation with the legendary clown-prince of the counterculture.

HT: How accurate was Tom Wolfe's book about Kesey, *The Electric Kool-Aid Acid Test?*

WG: He got me in big trouble.

HT: Oh, did he? How?

WG: He said I put the acid in the Kool-Aid at Watts. Eight people committed themselves, for heaven's sake. Mothers all over the country were after me at one particular point.

HT: Did you?

WG: No, no, no! I spent the whole night saying to people, "Ladies and gentlemen, this is your friendly invisible man here to inform you that the Kool-Aid on the right is Electric Kool-Aid, get it? Electric Kool-Aid." Because that was the night that LSD became illegal, the night of the Watts acid test.

HT: Who did put the acid in the Kool-Aid?

WG: The same people that always did.

HT: Okay, fine.

WG: But it was the night that I passed the acid test.

HT: What does it mean to pass it?

WG: Well, it's different every time. First of all, Owsley used to get after us. He'd say, alright, how does the group brain work or something. Owsley's so kicked back and together. We were all so intense in those days. We would take all that acid together. We did it hundreds and hundreds of times, and we would just move into one another's genes, into one another's blood. We would surrender ourselves to this thing that wanted to happen. It would move us like marionettes.

Interview, #46, June 1979

Middle-of-the-road WNEW-TV News sent a film crew to my press conference and gave the story a lot of play. The teaser before the news came on that night sounded like this: "Garbage researcher finds evidence of war-stock ownership in Bella Abzug's trash. 'Interview with Muhammad Ali.' Next on the Ten O'Clock Nightly News." The story they ran went something like this: "A.J. Weberman, the man who spends a lot of his time studying the contents of people's garbage, came up with some startling papers in congressional-hopeful Bella Abzug's trash." (Cut to shot of me lifting the lid off Bella's barrel.) The reporter pointed his microphone at me and I told him all I knew, after which the film switched to some shots of Bella doing some last-minute campaigning. The reporter explained, "We confronted Ms. Abzug with these charges while she mingled with voters in Upper Manhattan." The film cut to Bella. "The stock is owned jointly by myself and my husband. It's wrong to profit from this dirty war. I guess you can't hide anything anymore and ya can't win 'em all."

The evidence I presented was overwhelming. Bella held a press conference. Her public-relations man had to admit, "We don't know what stocks she owns anymore." The Associated Press carried the story and the American public's garbage consciousness was raised a couple of notches; people were beginning to get an inkling of just how powerful garbage really is. It nearly altered the course of a congressional election.

DUSTIN'S DUSTBINS

Dustin Hoffman is a great actor; in my opinion, he's the new Bogart. I especially liked him in *Midnight Cowboy*, in his role as "Ratso," a New York City sleazoid who just about starved to death. Too bad Ratso couldn't go through Dustin's trash, because that guy throws away more good food than you could shake a knife and fork at!

I found ham, cheese, hamburger, Oriental sauces, potatoes, lettuce—you name it—in that can, enough to have a picnic in front of it every day! Repeated garbanalyses revealed that cause of disposal was never mold or staleness. Hoffman just wasted good food. On top of that, the actor is sort of a health nut with junk-food tendencies. I found wrappers from natural foods, such as unbleached sugar, organic sunflower seeds, rice and cashew nuts mixed in with empty pop bottles, candy wrappers and stale white bread. I guess he just can't resist that good old junk food.

The most interesting piece was a Xerox copy of an insurance investigator's report on Dustin that had somehow got into his hands. It said the actor suffered from "unsecurity" and saw a $70-an-hour psychiatrist four times a week!

It was downhill from there: cat and dog food, Players Club House passes to tennis games and an empty bottle from a common antibiotic (the insurance report said he had "a minor acne condition of the back"). Mrs. Hoffman attends the French Institute, owns a black cashmere dress that cost $180 at Bloomingdale's, wears Diane Love perfume ($28) and has considered sending her daughter to Fowler Ballet School, which is natural since Mrs. Hoffman is a former ballerina.

MAILER'S MUCK

Norman Mailer has a reputation for being a highly volatile figure, and I approached his Brooklyn Heights town house with extreme caution. To put it bluntly I didn't want to get punched out!

My worst fears were realized when he spotted me one night while I was rifling his cans. Mailer looked at me standing in the rubbish, poking around with a pocket flashlight, and walked on.

From the look on his face he must have thought I was a government agent and if he assaulted me he would have to face federal charges.

Had I been a federal agent, I might have tried to make a case against Mailer for violating the gambling statutes, since his trash was filled with betting slips.

The trash also contained an itinerary for a college lecture tour, remains of instant foods, steel wool, a cheese wrapper, empty toilet-paper rolls and a newspaper clipping with a picture of Mailer. I used this newsprint photo as a model for a garb-art portrait of Mailer.

Mailer had macho garbage and definitely is what he throws away.

RICHIE'S RIGHTEOUS RUBBISH

When some of my friends heard I was after Havens's heap they told me to lay off because "he doesn't deserve garbology." They explained that Havens was a kid from the poor Bedford-Stuyvesant section of Brooklyn who had played for nickels and dimes in the Village's dingy cafés for years before he finally got a record contract. He had paid his dues. His songs often attacked war and racism and he frequently performed at benefit concerts. I told them not to worry. It is a status symbol in the rock world to have A.J. Weberman steal your garbage!

A few days later I was in front of his Greenwich Village town house. I scooped up his trash and schlepped it to nearby Washington Square Park where I performed a public garbanalysis on it while street singer David Peel and the Yippies looked on. The first thing I found was a note thanking Richie for doing a benefit for Americans for Children Relief. Near this was a letter from Richie's management firm, the William Morris Agency, informing him that he'd received a request to do another benefit. Does this guy ever do any paying gigs? I hope so.

On the personal side he has a pet cat (wrapper from cat chow); he drinks a little (Schweppes mixer bottle); and he eats modestly (wrappings from hamburgers and franks and an empty bottle of Seven-Up). He has a daughter named Nancy who likes to play tick-tack-toe, and Havens is a pretty good artist judging from the sketch I found. Richie's righteous rubbish was topped off by ten broken guitar strings, testimony to his passionate, exuberant style of guitar playing.

JACQUELINE'S JUNK

Getting Jackie's junk was no easy task. Two servants had once been fired for selling Jackie's panties for $1,000 each and I was sure she suffered from chronic garbanoia.

In July 1973, Jackie's junk was kept behind iron bars at 1040 Fifth Avenue until the trashman was about to arrive, so I had to get up at the crack of dawn and face 20 bags of trash, only one of which belonged to Jackie. While I was slitting each bag with the razor blade I had brought along, an old lady who lived on the ground floor of Jackie's building spotted me. She called the superintendent who wanted to know what the hell I was doing. "Hey, mister," I insisted, "I don't want to go through this junk. But I have to do it for an ecology class in college. If I don't I might not graduate and could end up becoming a super like you!" Fifteen slits later I discovered Jackie's trash stash when I saw a letter from the Hyannisport Yacht Club addressed to "Mrs. A. Onassis." Near this unopened envelope was another reminder that I was garbanalyzing a former first lady—a bag from a pharmacy with the label reading, "Mrs. Whitehouse, 1040 Fifth Avenue."

12 STATES APPROVE MEDICAL MARIJUANA

Nevada has become the 12th state to pass a bill allowing the use of marijuana for cancer chemotherapy and to alleviate glaucoma. The Carson City legislators emphasized that "only several hundred" people will be permitted to use grass in the preliminary research program.

As this "Reefer Reform" goes to press, the states that permit the use of marijuana or its derivative THC for therapeutic purposes are Nevada, Iowa, Minnesota, Texas, Oregon, New Mexico, Florida, Lousiana, Illinois, Virginia and California. Similar bills are pending in 9 other state legislatures.

Reefer Reform, #52, December 1979

MEDICAL MARIJUANA

States with medical marijuana

States with legislation pending

'QUAT SPRAYING TO CEASE

The federal government is now obliged by law to cut off funds for the spraying of marijuana fields in Mexico with the herbicide paraquat. In 1978, Sen. Charles Percy pressed an amendment through Congress requiring the Department of Health, Education and Welfare (HEW) to assess the health risks to American citizens posed by Mexican paraquat spraying; and the National Organization for the Reform of Marijuana Laws won a federal lawsuit that in effect requires the government to suspend in foreign countries any environment-modifying activities that may pose a threat to Americans. During his last days in office, former HEW secretary Joseph Califano determined through "computer simulation studies" that paraquat-contaminated grass annually endangers the health of at least 2,100 people in the southwestern United States.

HighWitness News, #52, December 1979

NORMAN MAILER

The Champ of American Letters takes all the tough questions on art, life, death, love, hate, war, drugs, etc., from punk contender Legs McNeil.

HT: How do you feel about kids smoking pot now?

NM: I always tell my kids—I don't know if they listen or not—that what I think is, get their education first and then start smoking pot. At least there's something to run downhill with. Because what I find is that pot puts things together. Pot is marvelous for getting new connections in the brain. It's divine for that. You think associatively on pot, so you can really have extraordinary thoughts. But the more education you have, the more you have to put together at that point, the more wonderful connections there are to see in the universe.

HT: Have you done cocaine and other drugs?

NM: Once in a while. I don't like it.

HT: Why?

NM: It doesn't do much for me. It's very much like on a speed trip. It puts me in an ugly mood. It brings out something ugly in me I don't like.

Interview, #49, September 1979

There were two Brut champagne bottles (vintage 1966) and one Cote De Beaune Villages bottle (vintage 1969). Typically, there were empty perfume bottles—Estee Lauder Sport Fragrance Spray, perfumed lavender bath scent, a refillable spray container of Chanel No. 5 and an Avon Fashion Figurine that once held Field Flowers cologne. There was dental floss, toothpaste and five empty packs of Ambassador cigarettes; Wella Care herbal shampoo, Instant Quaker cereal, Melba toast, etc., etc. I also found one of her famous leather gloves, plastic wrappers from panty hose, a perfectly good scarf and two pairs of Jackie's panty hose, one of which I am wearing as I type this.

I also found some ribbons with "Happy 13th, John" and "Sweet Sixteen, Caroline" written on them in glitter along with a piece of stationery with "John Kennedy, Jr." printed on the bottom of it. There was a wrapper from a famous European jeweler, marked "To Mr. Onassis" and another marked "To John." The only traces of Aristotle were boxes from French cigarette filters and half a ticket holder from Olympic Airways.

Jackie's maid's trash was also there. It contained a receipt with Jackie's personal telephone number on it. One of these days I'm going to call Jackie and ask her for a date!

MUHAMMAD'S MESS

Muhammad Ali is perhaps the most famous man in the world. Despite this, Ali gave his garbage to my associate, Ann Duncan, after she rang the doorbell and asked him for it.

The Alis live in a yellow stucco house in Cherry Hill, New Jersey. The house is surrounded by a wall and statues of donkeys, Mexicans and blacks—a bit garish when compared to the colonial homes and landscaping of their neighbors. Their garbage looks different, too, and it's really great that, despite Ali's wealth, he stills grooves on Shabazz bean pie and corn bread. The cans of black-eyed peas and collards made with pork were discarded unopened; I guess because Muslims aren't supposed to eat pig.

No wonder Ali gave the trash to Ann. He had nothing to hide—he is everything he claims to be.

The rest of Ali's trash was uninteresting and unconnected with prizefighting. Ali may be the Greatest, but his trash certainly wasn't!

ABBIE'S BAGS

Although I have been in contact with Abbie Hoffman since he became an underground fugitive in 1973, I have not asked him for his trash. This is one case where privacy is a matter of life and death.

Abbie has always been one of my idols. He fought for civil rights in the South during the early '60s, helped make street theater an art and was a leader of the demonstrations at the Democratic National Convention in Chicago, '68. Abbie has become a legend in his own time.

I first garbanalyzed Abbie in 1971 when he was under intense government surveillance, and I decided that rather than having to compete with such agencies as the FBI and the Red Squad, I'd just ask him for his trash. I went over to his place on 13th Street, a tarpaper shack on the roof of a tall building. "Abbie, I want your garbage, I'm doing an article about it for *Esquire* magazine."

"A.J.," he answered in his combination Lenny Bruce-New Englander accent, "Ya want my gahbage? Tell ya what, I'll make ya up a list of things I throw away and give ya some stuff to put in and make it look really fah-out, okay, A.J.?" I was hoping he'd just walk into his pad and come out with the garbage but if that was the way Abbie wanted it, that was the way it was going to be.

A couple of days later I returned to his penthouse and picked up the stuff he wanted me to plant in his rubbish (pomade from North Vietnam, a hitchhiking ticket, Dear Abbie fan letters, and the like) with some handwritten instructions and suggestions regarding his simulated trash. Here's part of that document, a verbatim account of Abbie's fantasy garbage.

1. American Airlines Envelope. *Say, "That's interesting 'cause in Woodstock Nation he'd said he'd never fly American again 'cause they let the FBI go through his bags."*

2. Cans of asparagus, peas, etc. *Say, "They probably both cook 'cause he was once a chef in a summer camp."*

3. Cans of bacon fat. *Say, "Most freaks pour it down the drain and hope it clogs the pipes, but Abbie has real homing instinct."*

4. Half-finished manuscript. *Say, "Must be Anita working on her next book—her first was called* Trashing*—since Abbie doesn't type."*

5. Torn flag. *Say, "There's a warrant out for Abbie in Kansas for blowing his nose in a flag. When he had his flag-shirt case people sent him hundreds of flags—his kid, America, due July 4th, will have flag diapers."*

6. Moxie bottle. *Say, "Remember in* Revolution for the Hell of It *he wrote Moxie was his favorite drink?"*

7. Record Club Bills. *Say, "See how they're addressed to different names? Abbie must be rippin' them off."*

8. Hitchhiking ticket. *Say, "Judging from the date—April 29—and the location—Connecticut—Abbie was probably hitchin' to Bobby Seales's trial in New Haven. Funny he got busted—*Steal This Book *has a chapter on how to avoid this."*

9. Dear Abbie letters. *Say, "One from an eleven year old who wants to blow up his school and one from Oklahoma for a mail-order copy of* Steal This Book *'cause no bookstore will carry it!"*

Abbie wanted me to collect or forge all these items, then photograph them as his garbage! I had qualms about the ethics involved in fabricating garbological evidence, so I went back to his pad along with a photographer to get some of the real thing, and was about to liberate it when Abbie's wife appeared. I told her that before Abbie left to go on his current speaking tour, he said it was cool for me to take the trash. That fooled her. Steal this trash!

The difference between his imaginary garbage and the real thing wasn't that great and I concluded in my *Esquire* piece that Abbie lived up to his rhetoric because "there were no empty caviar tins in his trash." Actually, the many orange peels, the roses, the box from a ritzy pastry shop and Anita's expensive nightgown all pointed to a contradiction, since Yippies were supposed to lead a more earthy lifestyle. Also, the papers in his real garbage were much straighter than such items as the hitchhiking ticket he wanted me to put in his simulated trash. For example, a model release from an *Esquire* photographer, an estimate on the cost of publishing *Steal This Book* ($13,000) and a prophetic memo to meet Izak Haber at a luncheonette. Izak would later claim he was the real author of *Steal This Book*.

Generally speaking, Abbie was relatively righteous at the time he was subjected to garbanalysis, and I found my phone number—Abbie had given a speech at the Dylan birthday party—along with Dave Peel's,

KINKY FRIEDMAN

BY LARRY SLOMAN

If there weren't a Kinky Friedman, we would have to invent him. A cigar-chomping menorah-glitter cowboy spewing racial epithets while singing some of the most sensitive lyrics ever writ. Kinky's got a terminal case of cultural schizophrenia—a Jew who grew up in the Lone Star State, who came to terms with being a 20th century American while teaching Borneo natives how to use the Frisbee in the Peace Corps.

KF: Betel nuts are the best. Chew betel nut and drink some *tuak*, which is rice wine, and smoke any kind of ganja. And you walk home, you don't know if you're in Hawaii or on Mars or what. You see these giant ants—it's beyond belief. But I wasn't into any Peruvian marching powder over there or anything. I don't know if you know this, but when I lived in Hollywood a few years back, I used to do a lot of your Irving Berlin White Christmas. Other people turned me onto it: the Captain and Toenail, Barry Antelope, The Disappointer Sisters, Olivia Neutron-Bomb, we all took drugs together. Anyway, I finally stopped snorting cocaine about two weeks ago, when Bob Marley fell out of my left nostril. But the Jews have had cocaine around for thousands of years, man; we always just called it horseradish, that's all.

Interview, #52, December 1979

EX-CIA DOC WANTS LIMITS ON HYPNOSIS

Hypnotherapist Dr. Milton V. Kline, former consultant to the CIA's supersecret behavior-modification project Bluebird, is currently campaigning for strict legal constraints on hypnosis, limiting its use to trained members of the health professions. During the early '60s, when the CIA was covertly funneling millions of tax dollars into a variety of brainwashing experiments involving LSD, other hallucinogens and electroshock, Kline provided expertise on hypnosis.

He was outspoken in his belief that one of the central goals of these experiments—to create a hypnotized, remote-control assassin—was entirely possible, though he denies knowledge of any "terminal experiments" that would have tested his theories.

HighWitness News by Jeff Goldberg, #53, January 1980

ROBERT ANTON WILSON

COURTESY ROBERT ANTON WILSON

BY MICHAEL HOLLINGSHEAD
The author of the Illuminatis trilogy expounds on multiple realities, guerrilla ontology, LSD, life extension and things that go bump in the night.

HT: You said just now that you were pissed off with the stupidities of American politics in the late '60s. We are now starting the '80s. Are we less or more free than we were ten years ago?

RW: Oh, I think we are a much freer country today than we were back in 1960, in many dimensions. Of course, there's a bit of a backlash building up against the new freedom, but that was only to be expected. By and large, I think the drug revolution had a good effect on America, despite individual casualties. I wish it could have been handled more intelligently, but I guess you don't have major social changes without a certain amount of upheaval. So it was perhaps only natural that there would be a certain number of bad trips, and a lot of people getting thrown into jail, and scientific research stopped, and so on. You've got to go through these upheavals before a new stage of evolution is stabilized.

Interview, #56, April 1980

JOAN JETT

TODD KAPLAN/STARFILE

At 21, Joan stars with Los Angeles's all-female, heavy-metal punk combo, the Runaways. Joan is definitely part of the new breed who can do what only men used to do.

HT: What kind of rock'n'roll first appealed to you—the Beatles?

JJ: No, heavy metal. I always liked bands like Black Sabbath. I didn't really get into it until I was about 14, the Suzi Quatro era. I really like her.

HT: Has the business changed much for women?

JJ: No, not when you still have to talk with certain pig-headed record people. Women may be liberated in other things but not in the music business.

Women in Rock by Liz Derringer, #51, November 1979

phone numbers belonging to anti-war organizer Dave Dellinger, feminist Kate Millet, radical attorney William Kunstler and Black Panther defendant Lonnie McLucas. There was also a page from a manuscript about the similarities between the Yippies and Black Panthers, which concluded "We both agree that revolution is inevitably armed struggle and that revolutionary violence is the only thing a system in power cannot absorb." Another political piece of rubbish was a reminder Abbie wrote himself to be at a press conference he was holding on the Capitol steps in regard to the charges he was facing for allegedly inciting the May Day, 1971, Garbage Riot!

CABALA:
Tasting the Forbidden Fruit of the Tree of Life
by Robert Anton Wilson

There's a tale they tell at Military Intelligence in London, when the candles gutter low and the fog curls about the windows. It happened in 1914 (they say), when England was losing the first world war and it seemed only a miracle could save her. There was this writer bloke (they say), name of Arthur Machen, never popular or well known, a bloody Welshman in fact and a mystic to boot. Well (they say), this Welshman, this Machen, took it into his head to write a story about the kind of miracle England needed, so he imagined St. George himself leading a group of medieval archers to aid the English troops at Mons. And after the story was published in a magazine, some enterprising newspapers picked it up and reprinted it as fact. And (they say) the whole damned country was gullible enough to believe it. It did as much for national morale as the real miracle would have.

What is even weirder is the sequel—and the chaps at Military Intelligence only discuss this when the candles gutter quite low and the fog is very thick, of course. Soldiers at the front, in Mons, began claiming that they had actually *seen* the phantom archers created out of Machen's imagination. They insisted on it. Some of them were still insisting on it 40 years later. They said they had won the battle because of this supernatural assistance.

Fair gives you a turn, doesn't it?

Stranger still: Machen, the man with the contagious imagination, was a member of a secret society in London. This was known as the Hermetic Order of the Golden Dawn, and it claimed to know the long-hidden secrets of Cabalistic magic.

There were several other members of the Golden Dawn who made a bit of a name. Florence Farr, one of the great actresses of the period, was a member, and it was she who gave Bernard Shaw the ideas about life-energy and longevity dramatized in *Back to Methuselah*; those ideas are currently influencing life-extension research. Algernon Blackwood and Bram Stoker (Dracula's creator) were members; so was the coroner of London; so was an electrical engineer named Alan Bennett who later, as Ananda Maitreya, played a key role in introducing Buddhist ideas to the West.

The egregious Aleister Crowley, who claimed to have come to earth to destroy Christianity, was a member for a while, and I know a good World War I story about him, too. It was Crowley's habit to give his pupils a word to meditate on every year. In 1918, Crowley gave them a number instead of a word: 11. All year his pupils meditated on *11* for at least a half hour every day.... And the war ended on the *11th* minute of the *11th* hour of the *11th* day of the *11th* month.

Did you feel another queer flash then?

The most famous Golden Dawn alumnus, however, was the great Irish poet, William Butler Yeats. In 1894 Yeats predicted that "the right pupils will be drawn to (the Golden Dawn) by dreams and visions and strange accidents...."

Cabala, the working philosophy behind the Golden Dawn, is the science of "strange accidents" which are known as "mere coincidences" to the rationalist or "synchronicities" to Jungian psychologists.

Cabala (also spelled Qabala or Kaballah) was either taught by God to Adam in the Garden of Eden, according to its own tradition, or was invented by a group of rabbis c. A.D. 200 as a means of transmitting the esoteric inner teachings of Judaism after the fall of Jerusalem and the Dispersion. Among the prominent medieval and Renaissance philosophers who were Cabalists one can mention Raymond Lull, Cornelius Agrippa, Giordano Bruno, Dr. John Dee, Pico della Mirandola and Isaac Newton. Cabala became unfashionable in the 18th century and did not begin to make a comeback until the Brain Explosion of the 1960s—the drug culture, the consciousness movement, the importation of Oriental mind-sciences, the popularity of Jung and Leary and Castaneda.

One way to get into the Cabalistic head space is to reflect long and hard on the singular fact that we could not live—could not *breathe*, in fact—without the trees busily pumping oxygen into the air. Yet the trees are not "thinking" about producing life-support for us. To the rationalist, it seems that our need for oxygen has no real connection with the trees' production of that element; sheer chance (or, the more vehement rationalists will anthropomorphically say, *"blind* chance") happens to have produced trees, through natural selection, over many aeons. The fact that we exist is, to this philosophy, a total *accident*, a very strange coincidence.

And, to the same rationalist, Arthur Machen's imagination has no real connection with what was happening on the battlefield at Mons. The magical link between Machen's imagination and the "collective hallucination" of the soldiers is just coincidence—like the magical link between us and the trees.

To the Cabalist, the rationalist sounds like a man found in a closet by a jealous husband, who hopefully explains, "Just by coincidence, while you were away on business I happened to wander into this closet without my clothes on...."

To the Cabalist, the whole universe is a network of *meaningful* connections. *The seemingly coincidental is as full of meaning as anything else.* To begin thinking like a Cabalist you must regard everything as being just as important as everything else. All that *seems* "accidental," "meaningless," "chaotic," "weird," "nonsensical," et cetera is as significant as what seems lawful, orderly and comprehensible.

An elementary Cabalistic training technique is to try every day to "regard every incident and event as a direct communication between God and your soul." Even the license plates on passing cars are such communications—or can be *considered* as such—by the devout Cabalist.

Some will be thinking of Freud at this point; and indeed Nathan Fodor points out in *Freud, Jung and the Occult* that Freud was heavily

HOW TO DO A SMOKE-IN
BY BEN MASEL

The first real step to putting on a smoke-in is publicity: posters, leaflets and so on. But before you commit yourself on paper, you must figure out certain things like where and when the smoke-in should be held. If the event is set for a Saturday, you can have a Sunday rain date publicized with little difficulty. Start at high noon.

Many prefer to key their date to the availability of big-name bands or speakers. This is fine so long as it doesn't force you to schedule the smoke-in prematurely. Lead time is the biggest draw there is. Give yourself at least three weeks from appearance of your posters till the event. Six weeks is much better, giving you time to reach every pothead and pot symp in the state.

Decide on your public-contact address and phone number early. This will enable other people who want to help (and there will be plenty) to reach you. If you are unable to use your own or a friend's, see if a local head shop or food co-op will serve as a message drop. As a last resort get a post-office box or telephone answering service. Having a phone number on the poster lets reporters get hold of you. Bands too.

Find a sympathetic lawyer. This is important not only if there are busts, but also for dealing with the authorities and others who are reassured by the presence of an attorney.

In picking your location, the first priority is your political target. State capitols are an obvious choice. On a local level consider the courthouse, jail, campus or even a certain hill next to the high school. You may want to use the smoke-in to build a community defense of a park in which the local fuzz have been harassing people.

Your political target may not be a good place to lay back and dig on music and smoke, however. In this case start the event at the political target, and then march over to the park where you can get loose.
#56, April 1980

MASSAGE
BY RON ROSENBAUM

First of all, let me assure you that HIGH TIMES correspondent Glenn O'Brien is a man of good taste and judgment. So when he said what he said—however astonishing it sounded at first—I had to take it seriously. We had been talking on the phone one day about the depressing shortage of good herb when Glenn began raving about a massage he'd gotten the day before at a Japanese health spa called Osaka. "Was it really that good?" I asked him. "The best," he said. "I'm still feeling great from it. It's not generally recognized," he added, "but massage is better than sex and drugs."
#51, November 1979

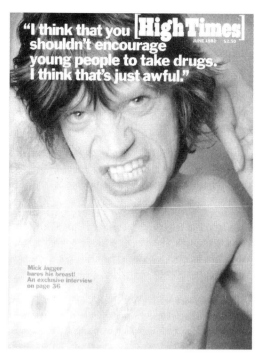

"I think that you shouldn't encourage young people to take drugs. I think that's just awful."

High Times JUNE 1980 $2.50

Mick Jagger bares his breast! An exclusive interview on page 36

MICK JAGGER

BY LIZ DERRINGER

MJ: I don't like drugs. I think cocaine is a very bad habit-forming bore. It's about the most boring drug ever invented. *(Laughs.)* I mean, it's very bad and very debilitating. I can't understand the fashion for it. 'Cause it's so expensive.

HT: That's where you spend your money?

MJ: No, but I see people that do. Grass is a hundred dollars an ounce, a hundred and fifty dollars for an ounce of grass. It's unbelievable. But cocaine, forget it. Anyone that buys cocaine at those prices.... If you want to take it, fine, but if you're spending money on it, Jesus. What a boring drug.

HT: Do you like mushrooms?

MJ: Yeah, mushrooms. Only under medical supervision. No, but mushrooms are more interesting. You really can't take them like cocaine. I think drugs should be used only occasionally.

HT: You sit around and smoke grass.

MJ: Sitting and smoking grass is different.

Interview, #58, June 1980

BEATLE BUST

"I think we could decriminalize marijuana, and I would like to see a really unbiased medical report on it," said pop singer Paul McCartney after being deported from Japan for bringing almost half a pound of marijuana into Tokyo for an 11-concert Wings tour that had to be cancelled. "Cigarettes can kill. They are worse than marijuana."

HighWitness News by Harry Wasserman, #59, July 1980

influenced by a friend who was a Cabalist. The "dreams, visions and strange accidents" that Yeats thought would bring people into the ambience of the Golden Dawn are all Freudian "unconscious material."

A more modern metaphor is to be found in current neurology which points out that the brain is divided into two hemispheres. The left hemisphere is where we do most of our conscious thinking, and it is *linear*; it breaks things down into sequences of A-causes-B, B-causes-C, and so forth. The right hemisphere, on the contrary, thinks in gestalt—meaningful wholes, comprehensive systems.

Cabala, like dope, is a deliberate attempt to overthrow the linear left brain and allow the contents of the holistic right brain to flood the field of consciousness. When you are walking down the street and every license plate seems part of one continuous message—one endless narrative—you are thinking like a very advanced theoretical Cabalist. (Or else you're stoned out of your gourd.)

Practical Cabala (or Cabalistic magic) is the art of utilizing such holistic perception to create effects that will seem like "strange accidents" to the non-Cabalist.

A legendary example concerns an incident when the king of Poland was being urged by his advisers to authorize a pogrom against the Jews. One old Hasidic rabbi—and the Hasidic rabbis spend most of their time studying Cabala—sat down, on hearing of this, and pretended to be writing something; but he did not write. Instead, he deliberately knocked his bottle over three times. His students, who saw this, thought the old man was getting a bit funny in the head. Then, a few days later, came news from the capital: The king had tried to sign the order for the pogrom three times, and each time he had—by "strange accident" knocked over his ink bottle. "I can't sign this," the king finally exclaimed. "God is against it!"

Every Oriental culture has some equivalent to Cabala—some neuroscience of meditations, visualizations and yogic contortions calculated to shift consciousness, or part of consciousness, from the usually overactive left hemisphere to the usually underactive right hemisphere. Cabala differs from all these Oriental disciplines in being as systematic as any natural science—although far weirder.

The system of Cabala is contained in a kind of ontological periodic table of elements. The purpose of this diagram has been nicely defined by the eminent contemporary Cabalist (and Jungian psychologist) Dr. Israel Regardie, who describes it as "a mnemonic system of psychology...to train the Will and Imagination."

The tree is made up of ten circles, called lights, and 22 paths connecting the lights. Each light represents a separate level of consciousness, and hence a separate level of "reality." That is, to the Cabalist, each perceived reality is a function of the level of consciousness which perceives it, and how much reality you can absorb depends on how rich your consciousness is.

The paths, which are more technical than the lights, are techniques for getting from one light (one level of awareness) to another.

The aim of the Cabala is to always know which "light" you are in, which is the level of consciousness that is creating what you are perceiving; and then to know the paths, or tricks, to get from one light (perceived reality) to another.

Dion Fortune, a Cabalist who also practiced psychoanalysis under her birth name, Violet Wirth, sums it all up by saying Cabala is "the art of causing change in consciousness by act of will."

The Tree of Life may be regarded as a map of those parts of consciousness which (a) are active in everybody—the lower parts of the tree; and (b) those which are only active in various orders of adepts—the higher parts of the tree.

The pragmatic theory of Cabala is that each action creates a new "universe," each experiment creates a new experimenter, each dance creates a new dancer. We are growing and evolving all the time, without noticing it usually; but at certain crucial points we can make a mental quantum jump to a level of awareness that puts us in a new reality we have never noticed before. Each of the lights on the Tree of Life represents such a quantum jump.

Concretely, we all start out in Malkuth, at the bottom of the tree, which represents the lowest level of awareness. This is what Freud called the oral stage: We simply drift and wait to be fed. Alcoholics, opiate addicts and most of the people on welfare for "psychological" reasons represent this state in its pure form, but we all contain it and relapse into it under sufficient stress. "I can't cope; somebody come help me." Hear the infant's shrill cry "Maaa-Maaa!" and you know what Malkuth is all about.

Above this is Yesod, the area of strong ego-awareness and what Gurdjieff called conscious suffering. This is where you struggle to be a real mensch, to be honorable, responsible, and self-sufficient. If you never get beyond this, you become what doctors called Type A and are a good bet for an early heart attack.

There are two ways to transcend Yesod's struggles. One takes you to Hod, which can be called the tactic of the rationalist (Dr. Carl Sagan will serve as a model for this), and the other to Netzach, which is the strategy of the ordinary religionist (Jerry Falwell, say).

According to Cabala, both the rationalist and the vulgar religionist are unbalanced; in modern neurological language, the rationalist leans too much on the left brain and the religionist too much on the right brain. The synthesis, or balancing, brings you to the Middle Pillar and is represented by the light called Tiphareth—which charmingly enough means "beauty" in English.

Looking at the tree, you can see that the rationalist has a different path to Tiphareth from that of the religionist. The rationalist must go the path of *nun* ("fish") and the religionist the path of *ayin* ("eye"). Any book on Cabala will tell you what *nun* and *ayin* imply in terms of the psychological transformation involved. Fortunately, the tarot cards were either created or revised by a Cabalist and the meanings of *nun* and *ayin* are vividly conveyed to the unconscious by the two cards called, respectively, Death and the Devil. Anybody with even a rudimentary knowledge of psychology can grasp part of what is meant here—the rationalist must "make friends with" Death and the religionist with the Devil. This is what Jung means when he says each man must face his own shadow.

(Every path on the tree has a tarot card illustrating it, and the quickest way to make the tree clear to your unconscious is to lay out the cards representing the paths between each light. The next step is to redesign the cards in terms of your own understanding. Some Cabalists redesign the tarot every two or three years, as their understanding grows.)

Tiphareth, the balanced center between *and above* both rationalism and religion, means beauty, as we said above. It is the first light that does not appear in normal, statistically average consciousness, and is identified with everything we mean by rebirth or awakening. It is

R.D. LAING
BY ABBIE HOFFMAN
The world's most eccentric shrink talks about sanity, lunacy and the mental-health craze.
HT: You've stated that you're not a political activist, especially after you appeared at the Dialectics of Liberation Conference in 1967 with people like Stokely Carmichael and Herbert Marcuse. But once the psychiatrist goes beyond the individual to examine and treat the family—networks of families—isn't the next logical progression communities and nations?
RL: Yes, indeed. There we go. It's not my ball game, though, if we are talking about activist intervention—more efficient, and more politically backed-up techniques of social engineering; that is, more ways and means of controlling people. The nature of our control system is complex, obscure, full of contradictions, conflicts, paradoxes, confusions, mystifications. My contribution to the commonwealth is an effort to elucidate the nature of this control system.
Interview, #51, November 1979

HYDROPONICS
Science Fiction Comes to the Marijuana Market
Not everyone has access to a secure and suitably camouflaged patch of viable wilderness for growing marijuana. This is how hydroponics came into the grass market. For years hydroponic agriculture was a joke. Dope fiends, though, took hydroponics and secretly turned fantasy into science. Only last fall did word really start to get around. The makers of the Hydropot growing system, who have been quietly advertising in HIGH TIMES since the magazine was a pup, presented one of their patented kits at a West Coast gardening convention. By the time the gardening world heard of it, of course, Hydropot had already saved (and made) millions for pot growers everywhere. Each tub, you see, is good for three to five husky *sativa* plants, trimmed to about six feet tall; each plant is good for about a pound of dope each harvest, so one bin can easily supply an average smoker with a year's worth of exquisite high-test sinsemilla. And a whole cellar full of bins can make one the most prosperous damn dope grower in town, because there are no wholesale fees, transportation costs or expensive legal hassles.
Spring Planting Guide by Ed Rosenthal and Mel Frank, #57, May 1980

71

MARIANNE FAITHFULL

BY ANN BARDACH

HT: During the Rolling Stones' first drug bust, you're the "naked girl in the fur rug..."

MF: We'd gone down to the country to get high on acid. It was the first acid, Owsley acid, we had ever had—any of us. I didn't know the routine yet. I didn't bring a change of clothes. We spent the day having a wonderful time in the woods and everything in the country. When we got back, I had a bath. I had nothing else to wear, but on the bed in the room was a beautiful—not really that beautiful but it looked beautiful at the time because I was very stoned—rug. So while my bath was running—you know, you can't wait to get your clothes off because you've been sweating—I took all my clothes off and put the rug around me like you would a bath towel. Ran the bath, came down and sat down with my rug around me, at which point 25 policemen walked in. That's all.

HT: There wasn't a panic that cops had run in on everybody's first trip?

MF: No, no, no. We were just quietly coming down by then, having a few joints. It only hit us five hours later what had happened. It was really funny.

Interview, #62, October 1980

HAZE BROTHERS

BY FARMER GREEN

Marijuana is now the top cash crop in California, having recently pulled ahead of various fruits, nuts and swamis. This presents a lot of California farm folk with the unenviable chore of hyping their product across the land while doing their damndest to hide every illegal speck of the stuff.

Take the Haze brothers. For four years they've been captivating American potheads with what they brazenly declare to be the "finest pot grown anywhere on earth."

Using seeds from their favorite imported smoke, the Haze brothers came out with "Purple Haze," "Golden Haze" and a range of other colors four years ago, and have been breeding and crossbreeding subsequent generations of those botanical wonders. "The colors are a fluke," says Haze. "We never know what color a crop will come out. One year it's tannish brown, next year it's greenish purple."

Joe Haze says northern-California pot is upstaging his "brand," and without justification. "The stuff they grow up there is mostly *indica*, but it's harvested early to get it in before the frost," he says. "In our county the flowers pump out resin until December, and Haze pot is from *sativa* seeds."

Grow American, #63, November 1980

dhyana in the Hindu system, "Buddha-mind" in Buddhism, the "New Adam" in St. Paul's epistles, Cosmic Christ Consciousness to Christian Cabalists. It represents a total reorganization of the psyche for a higher level of functioning than most humans ever attain. When Dr. Timothy Leary says gnomically that "the nervous system sees no color, feels no pain," he means that the nervous system *on this level* sees no color, feels no pain. You are floating, and this is the first light on the tree that really feels like a light. Acidheads will *know*.

Above Tiphareth are two more unbalanced lights called Geburah and Chesed. Roughly, Geburah is the stage of Nietzsche's superman: he who is much more conscious than ordinary people *and knows it*. In George Lucas's symbolism, Geburah means "being seduced by the dark side of the Force." It needs to be balanced by Chesed, which is humility in the deepest, more ego-destroying sense. In Castaneda's lingo, Geburah is "taking responsibility" and Chesed is doing so while always remembering that "you are no more important than the coyote."

Geburah says "I am God"; Chesed says, "And so is everybody else— and *everything* else!"

There are three more lights on the tree. These are known as the supernals and are much further from ordinary human consciousness than Tiphareth, Geburah or Chesed. Many Cabalists say that you cannot reach the supernals without the direct help of the Almighty. Even *with* such divine aid, reaching the supernals is known as "crossing the abyss" and is regarded as fraught with peril.

The first two supernals are Chokmah and Binah. You will note on the diagram that they are both unbalanced—off the Middle Pillar. Basically, Chokmah is direct contact with the masculine aspect of "God" and corresponds to whatever you associate with Jehovah, Jupiter, Brahma, Zeus, et cetera. Binah is direct contact with the *female* side of divinity and corresponds to Venus, Ishtar, Kali or the White Goddess that Robert Graves is always writing about. Cabala says that each of these Close Encounters has to be "balanced." That is, you have to get beyond both Big Daddy and Big Mommy to arrive at the ultimate light, Kether, the balanced center of all consciousness, which is beyond gender, beyond space, beyond time, beyond words and beyond all categories. In short, Kether is exactly what all the Oriental mystics are seeking: pure consciousness without a blemish of emotion, idea or image, and therefore infinite and formless.

Cabala is very complicated and very, very intricate; the above sketch is no more than a hint of what the Tree of Life contains, on about the level of a discussion of chemistry that tells you there are eight families of elements but does not go on to list the elements in each family. To discuss Cabala fully requires many books; and indeed there is one good-sized book, *Liber 777*, by Aleister Crowley which consists only of *listing* the elements in each light and path of the tree, and *Liber 777* consists of 155 pages with four columns on each page.

The purpose of such lists is to design rituals, and the purpose of rituals is to program your own experience as you navigate from one light to another. As Tim Leary once said, "Ritual is to the inner sciences what experiment is to the outer sciences." Cabalists agree.

For instance, suppose you have had a very powerful experience of the Punishing Father aspect of God, such as John Calvin once had. Within the orthodox Judeo-Christian tradition, you might take this literally and proceed, as Calvin did, to establish a new religion. As a Cabalist, you will recognize it as a Chokmah experience and know that it needs to be balanced by a Binah experience.

You then look on the Tree of Life for a path from Chokmah to Binah. That turns out to be *daleth* ("door"), which corresponds to the Empress card in the tarot. If you look at the Empress you will immediately note that she happens to be a pregnant woman sitting in a field surrounded by vegetation. That should tell your unconscious what the path of *daleth* means. (By a "strange accident" or "mere coincidence" the Empress card, in most tarot decks, contains the women's-liberation symbol and always has, long before there was a feminist movement. That should help jar your consciousness.)

If the Empress card doesn't tell you enough, you look up *daleth* in any Cabalistic textbook, such as Crowley's *777*. You will find that daleth is "in correspondence with" such things as the planet Venus, the color emerald green, the swan, the rose, sandalwood incense, the heptagram (seven-sided polygon), et cetera, and is most powerful on Friday. Thus, to get from Chokmah to Binah, you construct a ritual—a dramatized mind-change operation—to be performed within a heptagram, on Friday evening as Venus is rising, using emerald green decorations, roses, swan feathers and sandalwood incense. If you follow all these correspondences, and know how to write rituals, and have had enough experiences with Cabala to have developed a powerful will and imagination, you should achieve Binah, the vision of the All-Loving Mother.

Similarly there are favorable days, and perfumes, and geometric figures, and other accessories, for every type of brain change operation. Sunday is best for Tiphareth (Christ consciousness), Monday for Yesod (building a stronger ego), Tuesday for Geburah (accumulating power), Wednesday for Hod (wisdom), Thursday for Netzsch (moral strength), Friday for Binah and Saturday for Chokmah.

This is only the skeleton of Cabala, however. Real Cabalistic practice consists of so familiarizing yourself with all the correspondences on the Tree of Life that everything you experience is filed and indexed by your brain as a Cabalistic "message." Thus, if you walk out the door and see a palm tree, you *immediately* (by self-conditioning with Cabala) think of Venus and Hermes—because door is *daleth* is Venus, and palm is *beth* is Hermes. If you see a license plate with 333 on it, you remember that that is the number of egotism and deception, and you must ask what egotism and deception remains in yourself. In short, nothing is trivial; nothing is insignificant; nothing is meaningless. The whole universe, as Crowley says, becomes a continuous ritual of initiation.

A Zen Master was once asked, "What is Zen?" "Attention," he replied. "Is that all?" asked the inquirer. "Attention," the Zen Master repeated. "Won't you say anything else?" persisted the questioner. "Attention," said the Master, one more time.

Cabala creates attention by using the Tree of Life to "key" every possible impression to one of the lights or paths and hence to a stage in the evolution of consciousness. The world becomes—as it was to Plato and Mary Baker Eddy and Sir Humphrey Davy when he tried nitrous oxide—*nothing but ideas*.

Theoretical Cabala is much concerned with *words* and *numbers*, and indeed, insists that every word is a number. This is literally true in Hebrew, because all Hebrew letters are numbers, and the number of a word is the number obtained by adding its separate letters together. Cabala claims that any words having the same number are in some sense identical or "in correspondence with" each other.

August 1980 $2.50

HIGHTIMES

Will success spoil Cheech & Chong? Of course. See page 32.

CHEECH AND CHONG
BY ED DWYER

CG: *Up in Smoke*, we wound up improvising most of it right on the set. We had to.

HT: You guys don't go in with a script when you do a movie?

CH: Do you go in with a script when you get laid? I mean, suppose the script you go in with calls for lots of cocaine and a rubber duck and a Ping-Pong paddle, and then when you get down with the lady you both feel like a six-pack and a shower stall? Same thing with movies exactly.

CG: Yeah, we made that mistake with our first movie; we went in with a whole script. And the studio biggies said change this, fuck that, do some other damn thing. So we rewrote the script and made it better, and they loved it.

CH: Then when we went in to make the movie we just said fuck it, burn the script. And we just shot what we felt like doing, and now we're big Hollywood stars.

Interview, #60, August 1980

TV ADDICTION
BY JUDY BROWN

As habits go, it's clear that TV is a tenacious one—and what's even more frightening, it's got a grip on almost all of us. Here in the States, 99 percent of homes are stocked with at least one set; your average American adult gloms the tube 3.9 hours per day. US kids feed on video from 26 to an almost unbelievable 54 hours a week.

Turned On, Tuned In, Strung Out, #62, October 1980

JIM MORRISON

BY TOM BAKER

Whenever we went to rock clubs like the Whiskey or the Experience, Jim would cause a stir as we walked in and the kids gathered around him. Morrison was usually in a stupor and seemed oblivious to the fans. As soon as we sat down, the resident "groupies" would pounce on him. Sometimes I would share in the spoils; other times I would be ignored as though I were invisible; and still other times Jim would be so comatose I would get them all to myself.

One night we went to the grim little Hollywood flat of two of these "creatures" and sat up till dawn drinking and talking. One girl soon revealed herself to be a practicing junkie and she brought out a plastic vial of pills, blue tablets called New Morthone, a strong synthetic morphine. We crushed them with a tablespoon and sniffed the powder. The high was speedy and euphoric and Jim became loose and talkative, telling us endless tales about himself, including the story of his body being inhabited by the spirit of an old Indian dying by the side of a New Mexico highway. The junkie offered to let us use her "outfit," but we declined. Jim was not inclined to use downers and hated the thought of using a needle on himself, and, aside from this night, I only saw him use cocaine or a hallucinogenic.

#70, June 1981

G. GORDON LIDDY

BY LEGS McNEIL

HT: Didn't your arrest of Timothy Leary make you somewhat of a hero?
GL: He was perceived to be a threat to the children in Dutchess County, New York. And the fact that we got him out of the county was appreciated by the citizens.
HT: Was he really a threat?
GL: Yeah, I think anybody who's preaching—and effectively—that young people should resort to drugs and, in effect, drop out of society is threatening the children. And I think that common sense should tell most people that the ingestion of drugs by children or by anybody for that matter for other than medical purposes is harmful.
HT: Why was LSD always being considered when you thought of doing away with somebody?
GL: It was always being considered by [E. Howard] Hunt. I don't know where he got this affection for lysergic acid diethylamide-25, but he kept proposing we use it for this, we use it for that and the other thing.
Interview, #70, June 1981

For instance, *achad* (I am writing the Hebrew as if it were English, for simplicity's sake) has the value of 13. So does *ahebah*. What does this mean? Well, *achad* translates as "unity" and *ahebah* as "love," so by the mathematical theorem that things equal to the same thing are equal to each other, the Cabalist calculates that love (*ahebeh*) equals 13 and unity (*achad*) equals 13 and therefore love equals unity. And, of course, when you love somebody you are in union with them: You are happy when they are happy; you suffer when they suffer.

Better still, it works backwards, too, according to some Cabalists: 31 is 13 backwards and therefore 31 is mystically the same as 13. And *Al*, the oldest name of God in Hebrew, has the value 31. Therefore, God equals love equals unity.

Which is all very nice and cheerful, and it's pleasant to have our first lesson in theoretical Cabala coming up with such pleasant information.

Unfortunately, *la* (nothing) also equals 31. Is God therefore nothing? Or is it unity that is nothing? or love?

The theoretical Cabalist is not abashed. God *is* nothing, he says firmly—no-*thing*. And in this he is in agreement with the Buddhists and Hindus and, indeed, the most advanced mystics of all traditions. It only sounds queer to those primitives down at the bottom of the Tree of Life in Hod (rationalism) or Netzach (conventional religion); if you persist in Cabala long enough, the divine no-thing will make perfect sense to you.

Unfortunately, before you arrive at Kether—"the Head without a Head," the divine nothing—you will be sure to encounter even worse shocks in theoretical Cabala. Thus, *nesckek*, the serpent in Genesis, the devil himelf, has the value 358. You don't have to look far to find another Hebrew word with the value 358. It jumps up at you, as soon as you start studying Cabala. It is *messiah*.

In what sense is the devil the messiah? Some Cabalists have gone quite batty working on that one.

The charm of Cabala is that the universe adjusts—or in your excited and overstimulated state, *appears* to adjust—in ways that heighten such perplexities. When I first discovered the 358-equals-devil-equals-messiah paradox, I had to go to Los Angeles on business. Arriving at my hotel I found I had been given room 358. That's the sort of "strange accident" that Yeats was talking about, as one of the portals to Cabala....

For several years English biologist Lyall Watson has been collecting the products of Jung's "collective unconsciousness"—dreams, hypnotic states, mediumistic phenomena, automatic writing, et cetera. In his book, *Lifetide*, Watson offers a tentative summary of the data: "...there is a sameness in the tone, the word structure, the feeling, and the delivery of almost all the material. It has a dreamlike quality, and my feeling is that the vast majority of all the evidence I am looking at is a series produced by *one* prodigious dreamer" (italics added).

William Butler Yeats, trying to justify his interest in Cabalistic magic to rationalistic friends, came up with the same metaphor: "The borders of our minds are ever shifting, and many minds can flow into one another, as it were, and create or reveal a single mind...our memories are part of one great memory, the memory of Nature herself."

This "one great dreamer" or "one great memory" can be accessed by Cabalistic practices, or by Zen meditation, or by LSD, or by a dozen other gimmicks. It has the quality of oneness in that it is the same no matter who accesses it or when—whether they are in India 500 B.C or Florence A.D. 1300 or in New York City today. It seems to be "timeless" or unconnected to our conscious notions of sequential time, as even so materialistic an observer as Freud noticed. One of the benefits of the psychological investigations of our times—from Freud and Jung to the LSD research of the '60s and the human-potential movement—has been to make most of us aware again, for the first time since the 17th century, that this level of the psyche exists in all of us and cannot safely be repressed or ignored.

The Cabalist, scorned by the 19th century as a crank or a charlatan, seems to be having the last laugh after all. There may be only one person in 10,000—or in 100,000—who seriously studies Cabala, but the avant-garde third of the population understands Cabalistic logic very well. If you show them the Tree of Life, and explain it, they might say that it is an alternative map of the *chakras*—if they are into Oriental mind-science; or an anatomy of the collective unconscious—if they're into Jung; or the circuits of the nervous system—if Tim Leary is their bag; but one way or another they will *recognize* it. It looked like gibberish to Yeats's contemporaries.

Military Intelligence never could figure out how the "angelic archers" escaped from Arthur Machen's imagination to the perceptions of the soldiers at Mons. But the readers of this magazine understand. Don't you?

WHAT EVERY PARENT SHOULD KNOW ABOUT MARIJUANA

by Dean Latimer

Joe Califano is responsible for all this. One of Califano's final assignments, before he resigned as then-President Carter's secretary of Health, Education and Welfare in 1978, was to the National Institute on Drug Abuse. Assemble everything that's known about marijuana toxicity, he said, review it, and come up with a tract that will persuade kids never to go *near* that awful stuff.

The folks at NIDA, seeing beforehand what a pit-o'-snakes *that* would turn into, shifted the buck to the National Academy of Sciences. The NAS duly set up a panel of 22 respected physicians and educators who'd never voiced a political opinion on the subject, and these people went over the entire cannabis research literature since 1965. This took them until 1981, when Ronald Reagan had become president, and HEW had become Health and Human Services, and nobody in the government *anywhere* wanted anything to do with their report.

By this time, the Big Lie, repeated loud and often, had become fearsome dogma: Marijuana does *so* damage brains, and snap chromosomes, and deform babies, and grow breasts on men and shrink their testicles too, *and* it causes amotivational syndrome, and it leads to the hard stuff and is as impossible to kick as heroin and just as addictive. By 1981, if you didn't come right out and positively say marijuana does all these fabulous things, then you were running dead athwart a highly dangerous New Right coalition of goose-stepping "Parents Power" fanatics with enthusiastic support straight out of 1600 Pennsylvania Avenue. And those *are* the folks who pay the tab for studies like this, now and in the future.

DEAN LATIMER

"Dean Latimer is clearly a Charles Dickens character caught in a time warp," says HIGH TIMES news chief Bob Lemmo of his peculiar office mate. Latimer, who had always thought he was a Samuel Beckett character caught in a space warp, came to us by way of the *East Village Other, National Lampoon, Screw* and a "host of horrible tit magazines." He has never seen *Star Wars* or been inside a disco. He wrote "New Myths from Old Narcs," an exposé of the DEA's latest medical offensive, specifically to pay his $350 Dewars-and-soda tab, two years overdue, at the Bells of Hell. "I wish I knew which Dickens novel Lemmo's talking about," Latimer frets.
Sideshow, #46, June 1979

JUICE

BY DEAN LATIMER

I was not always as you see me now—a middle-aged bachelor of peculiarly repulsive aspect and unmentionable personal habits. At one point in the past I was as pretty and wholesome as anyone else alive at the same point in *their* pasts: ten fingers, ten toes, clear pretty glossy skin all over, bright little eyes goggling around unfocused in their orbits. "It's a boy," everyone exulted. Something intervened 'twixt then and now to shape and misshape the organism through which you are being addressed in the words on this page: a repulsive middle-aged juicehead given over to abominable personal habits. Since my splendid crony and colleague "R." the Connoisseur has heretofore fingered alcohol, in these pages, as the most conspicuous of these reprehensible habits which attach to me, I feel compelled to *absolve* that perfectly innocent, inanimate substance of culpability in the formation and malformation of the organism which now addresses you.

Alcohol is a straight downer, physiologically. It works in a very weird way in the head, by physically softening the membranes between nerve cells, so that all your nerve-conduction juices slop miscellaneously together; makes your brain, texture-wise, a little less spongy and a little more soupy, while you're drunk, and this accounts for the mental clouding and physical uncoordination. At the same time, alcohol directly *stimulates* a certain category of lively nerve juices called acetaldehydes, which accounts for the euphoria. Opium, morphine and smack also tickle up your acetaldehydes. Booze, in this its *premiere* respect, is nothing more nor less than legal heroin.
An Absolution of Alcohol, #73, September 1981

GROUCHO MARX

We ingested those little white tabs one afternoon at the home of an actress in Beverly Hills.

Groucho was interested in the social background of the drug. There were two items that particularly tickled his fancy.

One was about the day acid was outlawed. Hippies were standing around the streets, waiting for the exact appointed minute to strike so they could all publicly swallow their LSD the exact second it became illegal.

The other was how the tour bus would pass through Haight-Ashbury and passengers would try to take snapshots of the local alien creatures, who in turn would hold mirrors up to the bus windows so that the tourists would see themselves focusing their cameras.

There was a point when our conversation somehow got into a negative space. Groucho was equally bitter about institutions such as marriage ("like a quicksand") and individuals such as Lyndon Johnson ("that potato-head"). Eventually, I asked, "What gives you hope?"

Groucho thought for a moment. then he said just one word out loud: "People."
I Dropped Acid With Groucho by Paul Krassner, #66, February 1981

STEPHEN KING

"I think marijuana should not only be legal, I think it should be a cottage industry. There's some pretty good homegrown dope. I'm sure it would be even better if you could grow it with fertilizers and have greenhouses."
Interview by Martha Thomases and John R. Tebbel, #65, January 1981

So this official *Marijuana and Health* report did not come out in 1981, its original due date. It had been *written* by deadline, but the original MS so horrified the politicos at the NAS that they sat on it for six extra months, imposing "balance" onto it. The final report, which is as close to perfect *entropy* as verbally possible, was released late on a warm March Friday afternoon this year, so that it only made the Saturday editions, which nobody reads, and was written up for them by the sort of third-string copy hacks who have to work late on warm Friday afternoons in spring. None of these hacks, of course, read anything but the "Conclusions" section here, which—in its isolated context—manages to make grass sound vaguely but emphatically scary: MARIJUANA "CAUSE FOR NATIONAL CONCERN," SAY SCIENCE BIGS.

All this time, *another* NAS report, on marijuana-control policy, was being held up even longer by the petrified politicos there. This one had been put together by some real heavies: Louis Lasagna, hard-line drug-policy adviser to every administration since Eisenhower, was the chairman, and Jerome Jaffee, who writes the basic reference text on addiction for "Goodmall & Gilman," was typical of the rank of the authors. And this one didn't merely recommend decriminalization as a nationwide model for grass control, but suggested that a policy of *licensed sales to adults* might help to minimize the special health hazards that marijuana undeniably poses for growing young people.

The panicked reviewers at the NAS sat on this, then, until the accompanying list of the established, *proven* health hazards of marijuana could be appended to it, taken out of *Marijuana and Health*. And this Lasagna Report, *An Analysis of Marijuana Policy* came out with a special preface from NAS president Frank Press, an oil-development geologist, who said in it that *he* disagreed with all these pharmacologists and psychiatrists and law-department chairmen. And it was not presented to the media at all, but just sat unnoticed at the NAS for over a month until "grumblings from the scientists" brought it to the attention of *The New York Times*.

At HIGH TIMES, since some of our readers are said to smoke marijuana, we feel obliged to publish this summary of what the U.S. government has established to be the worst toxic effects of the said substance. This is the whole thing, word for word, nothing altered or censored, even unto the routine pitch for more money to study further the effects of this *incredibly* well-studied drug.

We *have* made bold, here and there, in the particularly murky sections, to hang a few elucidatory footnotes. Though supposedly written for layfolks by academic experts, this tract does get confoundedly dense and spacy in places. We've tried to clarify it without fear or favor, and—by golly—we *did*, too.

Appendix: Summary of Marijuana and Health

The Institute of Medicine (IOM) of the National Academy of Sciences has conducted a 15-month study of the health-related effects of marijuana, at the request of the Secretary of Health and Human Services and the Director of the National Institutes of Health. The IOM appointed a 22-member committee to:

• analyze existing scientific evidence bearing on the possible hazards to the health and safety of users of marijuana;
• analyze data concerning the possible therapeutic value and health benefits of marijuana;

• assess federal research programs in marijuana;

• identify promising new research directions, and make suggestions to improve the quality and usefulness of future research; and

• draw conclusions from this review that would accurately assess the limits of present knowledge and thereby provide a factual, scientific basis for the development of future government policy.

This assessment of knowledge of the health-related effects of marijuana is important and timely because marijuana is now the most widely used of all the illicit drugs available in the United States. In 1979, more than 50 million persons had tried it at least once. There has been a steep rise in its use during the past decade, particularly among adolescents and young adults, although there has been a leveling-off in its overall use among high-school seniors in the past two or three years, and a small decline in the percentage of seniors who use it frequently. Although substantially more high-school students have used alcohol than have ever used marijuana, more high-school seniors use marijuana on a daily or near-daily basis (9 percent) than alcohol (6 percent). Much of the heavy use of marijuana, unlike alcohol, takes place in school, where effects on behavior, cognition and psychomotor performance can be particularly disturbing. Unlike alcohol, which is rapidly metabolized and eliminated from the body, the psychoactive components of marijuana persist in the body for a long time.[1] Similar to alcohol, continued use of marijuana may cause tolerance and dependence.[2] For all these reasons, it is imperative that we have reliable and detailed information about the effects of marijuana use on health, both in the long and short term.

What, then, did we learn from our review of the published scientific literature? Numerous acute effects have been described in animals, in isolated cells and tissues and in studies of human volunteers; clinical and epidemiological observations also have been reported. This information is briefly summarized in the following paragraphs.

Effects on the Nervous System and on Behavior

We can say with confidence that marijuana produces acute effects[3] on the brain, including chemical and electrophysiological changes. Its most clearly established acute effects are on mental functions and behavior. With a severity directly related to dose, marijuana impairs motor coordination and affects tracking ability and sensory and perceptual functions important for safe driving and the operation of other machines; it also impairs short-term memory and slows learning. Other acute effects include feelings of euphoria and other mood changes, but there also are disturbing mental phenomena, such as brief periods of anxiety, confusion or psychosis.

There is not yet any conclusive evidence as to whether prolonged use of marijuana causes permanent changes in the nervous system or sustained impairment of brain function and behavior in human beings. In a few unconfirmed studies in experimental animals, impairment of learning and changes in electrical brain-wave recordings have been observed several months after the cessation of chronic administration of marijuana. In the judgment of the committee, widely cited studies purporting to demonstrate that marijuana affects the gross and microscopic structure of the human or monkey brain are not convincing; much more work is needed to settle this important point.

Chronic relatively heavy use of marijuana is associated with behavioral dysfunction and mental disorders in human beings, but available evidence

R. BUCKMINSTER FULLER
BY ROBERT ANTON WILSON

HT: In *Critical Path* you say that there are now four billion billionaires living on earth. Would you explain that?

BF: I simply mean that in terms of real wealth, defined as the capacity to nurture and accommodate human life, everybody on this planet could have a standard of living as high as that of any billionaire.

HT: You say that nationalism is obsolete.

BF: Yes. We simply cannot continue navigating Spaceship Earth with a hundred and fifty separate and supreme admirals all steering in different directions.

HT: Suppose we get through the "critical path" of the 1980s. What do you forsee in the '90s?

BF: There will be no more jobs. Employment as we understand it will vanish along with the nation as we understand it.

Interview, #69, May 1981

THE CONSPIRACY

When I returned to HIGH TIMES recently it was almost six years to the day that I first helped launch it. We were fresh from the underground press and quite comfortable in our Greenwich Village basement. We took a weird pride in the fact no national magazine distributor would handle HIGH TIMES and more than 40 major printers wouldn't print it.

In those days we called ourselves "The Magazine of High Society." We said we were the only magazine dedicated to getting high...really high." But there was always something more—a certain character. As founding editor Tom Forçade put it, "We're not just a magazine about things you put in your mouth."

It was never simple to figure out what would work in the pages of the magazine. Everyone involved with HIGH TIMES felt part of a conspiracy. Not only staff members and contributors but readers as well.

I spent more than two years away from the operations of the magazine. In the interim it became "The Magazine of Feeling Good." However, judging from the response, some loyal readers began to have doubts.

I returned with the luxury of a fresh perspective. There was one thing I noticed immediately—HIGH TIMES was slipping away from the conspiracy. Joggers were beginning to read the magazine.

Opinion by Editor & Publisher Andy Kowl, #61, January 1981

THOMAS SZASZ

BY RON ROSENBAUM

The gadfly of the psychiatric establishment takes on sexologists, moral entrepreneurs and drug-happy shrinks.

HT: You believe in the abolition of all drugs laws?

TS: The drug laws are the drug problem. The people who promote the drug laws are in some way moral criminals.

HT: People have a craving from meaning in life and some will get it from religion, some from drugs. Is that to be condemned?

TS: Absolutely not. It should be no more condemned than the craving for food or water or air...Consider the following: a hundred years ago in the United States a human being had an unqualified right and opportunity to buy and ingest any drug he wanted. Nobody stood in his way. Not the state, not the politicians and not the doctors. But supposing he wanted to publish a picture like is now in *Playboy*. He would have been in jail for years and years and years, right? Now you can do all these things in a sexual realm, but the drug realm is completely closed off.

Interview, #73, September 1981

H. ROSS PEROT

The Texas wiretapping law is commonly called BEW, short for Breaking, Entering and Wiretapping. In precise technical language, it effectively empowers any state or local cop to break into any home, business, organization, church or school and plant hidden eavesdropping devices. The federal "antidrug" law, proposed by Sen. John Tower last spring, allows for the confiscation of any private property the police may characterize as belonging to anyone involved in buying or selling "controlled substances."

Both laws were drafted in close consultation with a political organization called the Texans' War on Drugs Committee, chaired by ultraright international industrialist H. Ross Perot, who independently invaded Iran with corporate mercenaries in 1979 to extract some of his company personnel there, and is broadly reputed to have ties to high-tech paramilitary groups both in the US and abroad.

HighWitness News, #75, November 1981

---

does not establish if marijuana use under these circumstances is a cause or a result of the mental condition. There are similar problems in interpreting the evidence linking the use of marijuana to subsequent use of other illicit drugs, such as heroin or cocaine. Association does not prove a causal relation, and the use of marijuana may merely be symptomatic of an underlying disposition to use psychoactive drugs rather than a "stepping stone" to involvement with more dangerous substances. It is also difficult to sort out the relationship between use of marijuana and the complex symptoms known as the amotivational syndrome. Self-selection and effects of the drug are probably both contributing to the motivational problems seen in some chronic users of marijuana.

Thus, the long-term effects of marijuana on the human brain and on human behavior remain to be defined. Although we have no convincing evidence thus far of any effects persisting in human beings after cessation of drug use, there may well be subtle but important physical and psychological consequences that have not been recognized.

Effects on the Cardiovascular and Respiratory Systems

There is good evidence that the smoking of marijuana usually causes acute changes in the heart and circulation that are characteristic of stress, but there is no evidence to indicate that a permanently deleterious effect on the normal cardiovascular system occurs. There is good evidence to show that marijuana increases the work of the heart, usually by raising heart rate and, in some persons, by raising blood pressure.[4] This rise in work load poses a threat to patients with hypertension, cerebrovascular disease and coronary atherosclerosis.

Acute exposure to marijuana smoke generally elicits bronchodilation; chronic heavy smoking of marijuana causes inflammation and pre-neoplastic changes in the airways, similar to those produced by smoking of tobacco. Marijuana smoke is a complex mixture that not only has many chemical components (including carbon monoxide and "tar") and biological effects similar to those of tobacco smoke, but also some unique ingredients. This suggests the strong possibility that prolonged heavy smoking of marijuana, like tobacco, will lead to cancer of the respiratory tract and to serious impairment of lung function. Although there is evidence of impaired lung function in chronic smokers, no direct confirmation of the likelihood of cancer has yet been provided, possibly because marijuana has been widely smoked in this country for only about 20 years, and data have not been collected systematically in other countries with a much longer history of heavy marijuana use.

Effects on the Reproductive System and on Chromosomes

Although studies in animals have shown that delta-9 THC (the major psychoactive constituent of marijuana) lowers the concentration in blood serum of pituitary hormones (gonadotropins) that control reproductive functions, it is not known if there is a direct effect on reproductive tissues. Delta-9 THC appears to have a modest reversible suppressive effect on sperm production in men, but there is no proof that it has a deleterious effect on male fertility. Effects on human female hormonal function have been reported, but the evidence is not convincing. However, there is convincing evidence that marijuana interferes with ovulation in female monkeys. No satisfactory studies of the relation between use of marijuana and female fertility and childbearing have been carried out. Although delta-9 THC is known to cross the placenta readily and to cause birth defects when administered in large doses to experimental animals, no adequate clinical studies have been carried out to determine if marijuana use can harm the human fetus. There is no conclusive evidence of teratogenicity in human offspring, but a slowly developing or low-level effect might be undetected by the studies done so far. The effects of marijuana on reproductive function and on the fetus are unclear; they may prove to be negligible, but further research to establish or rule out such effects would be of great importance.

Extracts from marijuana smoke particulates ("tar") have been found to produce dose-related mutations in bacteria; however, delta-9 THC, by itself, is not mutagenic. Marijuana and delta-9 THC do not appear to break chromosomes, but marijuana may affect chromosome segregation during cell division, resulting in an abnormal number of chromosomes in daughter cells. Although these results are of concern, their clinical significance is unknown.

The Immune System

Similar limitations exist in our understanding of the effects of marijuana on other body systems. For example, some studies of the immune system demonstrate a mild, immunosuppressant effect on human beings, but other studies show no effect.

Therapeutic Potential

The committee also has examined the evidence on the therapeutic effects of marijuana in a variety of medical disorders. Preliminary studies suggest that marijuana and its derivatives or analogues might be useful in the treatment of the raised intraocular pressure of glaucoma, in the control of the severe nausea and vomiting caused by cancer chemotherapy and in the treatment of asthma. There also is some preliminary evidence that a marijuana constituent (cannabidiol) might be helpful in the treatment of certain types of epileptic seizures, as well as for spastic disorders and other nervous system diseases.[5] But, in these and all other conditions, much more work is needed. Because marijuana and delta-9 THC often produce troublesome psychotropic or cardiovascular side effects that limit their therapeutic usefulness, particularly in older patients, the greatest therapeutic potential probably lies in the use of synthetic analogues of marijuana derivatives with higher ratios of therapeutic to undesirable effects.[6]

The Need for More Research on Marijuana

The explanation for all of these unanswered questions is insufficient research. We need to know much more about the metabolism of the various marijuana chemical compounds and their biologic effects. This will require many more studies in animals, with particular emphasis on subhuman primates. Basic pharmacologic information obtained in animal experiments will ultimately have to be tested in clinical studies on human beings.

Until 10 or 15 years ago, there was virtually no systematic, rigorously controlled research on the human health-related effects of marijuana and its major constituents. Even now, when standardized marijuana and pure synthetic cannabinoids are available for experimental studies, and good qualitative methods exist for the measurement of delta-9 THC and its metabolites in body fluids, well-designed studies on human beings are relatively few. There are difficulties in studying the clinical effects of marijuana in human beings, particularly the effects of long-term use. And

PAULINE MORRIS

PETER TOSH

Captured Dread and Alive
BY JOHN SWENSON

HT: It seems really weird, I guess, the way that you were harassed politically when you went on your own. And then Bob Marley, they tried to assassinate him. Do you see that as part of one mind trying to stop both of you or what you stood for?

PT: I see it was politically motivated. There are always elements there to try to stop anything that is awakening to black people. If there is one who try to give a message to black people, there is always obstacles.

HT: What do you think of the fact that now Bob Marley is dead, people are saying that you are the king of reggae?

PT: I am not no king of reggae. It was me who put Bob Marley's first finger on a guitar and said "This is a C, this is a G, this is a A." It is I who taught Bob Marley to play music. I was born with music to me. Bob Marley has exposed himself and has become international superstar or whatever you call it. I am not a superstar. I am an architect. Don't want to be a superstar, there are no kings. "In my father's house are many mansions." And all of them is beautiful. So I am just doing what I am here to do. I am a messenger, see? I am a missionary, see? Bob Marley's a musician or a superstar, so they say. I am a missionary preaching the words of righteousness decorated by music.
Interview, #75, November 1981

PETER BAGGE

ZOMBIE GENERATION

Since sex is out of fashion, people will have to use artificial insemination, or have "test tube babies." But raising kids will be a breeze, because their brains will be totally hypnotized by all their computerized toys. Maybe when these kids grow up they'll be called the..."Zombie Generation."
"It" Generation by Peter Bagge, #78, February 1982

WOMEN, SEX AND COCAINE

HIGH TIMES

August 1981 $2.50

Exposé:
**The Cocaine
Fascists
Who Rule
Bolivia**

**Growing Dope
in the Desert**

Interview:
**Tommy Rettig's
Life After Lassie**
The Sordid Details start on p. 32

**LSD '81
Designer Acid**

Moroccan OO Kif
by Cherniak & Latimer

BOYCOTT BOLIVIAN

WHY I HATE COCAINE

BY SHEERA STERN

Coke doesn't produce the perceptual changes that give other drugs their serendipitous effect. There's nothing that's more fun on coke—except more of the same. As a party drug, it's a laugh. Coke becomes a dumb substitute for the party itself; you really feel good without expending anything but money. Acid gave us the yellow submarine; coke gave us Steve Rubell.

What makes coke such a lousy drug is that no one ever forgets how much it costs. I had to ban it from the house. When I lived alone, I used to get calls from men bearing coke. "Hey, baby, I have some coke. Wanna party?" I thought it was a pretty tacky way to get invited over, waving a C note in my face. For while I made up excuses. "No, I'm busy wrapping Christmas presents. And it's such a bad night—why don't you wait until the snow melts?"
Cocaine Confidential, #76, December 1981

PRICE INCREASE

As I'm sure you've noticed, this month HIGH TIMES has raised its price to $2.95 an issue. Now while to some of you that'll mean cutting one or two of your buds a little closer to the stem, others may find the increase a bit more inconvenient; at any rate, I feel an explanation is necessary. First off, in the past two years our production costs have gone up well over 20 percent. Secondly, the last few years have brought an avalanche of repressive legislation down on our heads.
Flashes by Andy Kowl, #76, December 1981

yet, without such studies the debate about the safety or hazard of marijuana will remain unresolved. Prospective cohort studies, as well as retrospective case-control studies, would be useful in identifying long-term behavioral and biological consequences of marijuana use.[7]

The federal investment in research on the health-related effects of marijuana has been small, both in relation to the expenditure on other illicit drugs and in absolute terms. The committee considers the research particularly inadequate when viewed in light of the extent of marijuana use in this country, especially by young people. We believe there should be a greater investment in research on marijuana, and that investigator-initiated research grants should be the primary vehicle of support.[8]

The committee considers all of the areas of research on marijuana that are supported by the National Institute on Drug Abuse to be important, but we did not judge the appropriateness of the allocation of resources among those areas, other than to conclude that there should be increased emphasis on studies in human beings and other primates. Recommendations for future research are presented at the end of Chapters 1-7 of this report.

Conclusions

The scientific evidence published to date indicates that marijuana has a broad range of psychological and biological effects, some of which, at least under certain conditions, are harmful to human health. Unfortunately, the available information does not tell us how serious this risk may be.

The major conclusion is that what little we know for certain about the effects of marijuana on human health—and all that we have reason to suspect—justifies serious national concern. Of no less concern is the extent of our ignorance about many of the most basic and important questions about the drug. Our major recommendation is that there be a greatly intensified and more comprehensive program of research into the effects of marijuana on the health of the American people.

Footnotes

1. The metabolic end products of marijuana *may* have a half-life in the body of about 14 days after a single dose. During this time they exert no "psychoactive" effects, or any known biological effects, either. Refer Dr. Monroe Wall and Dr. Mario Perez-Reyes, Research Triangle Park, North Carolina.

2. Tolerance development and dependence seen with marijuana are not really "similar to" that seen with alcohol. Compared to alcohol these phenomena with marijuana are virtually nonexistent and cannot even be measured by the same scale of symptoms. Refer Dr. Reese Jones and Dr. Neal Benowitz, Langley Porter Psychiatric Institute, San Francisco.

3. "Acute" in this context does not mean "heavy" or "dramatic." In fact, it means "transient." Refer to any dictionary.

4. The most commonly observed effect of marijuana on blood pressure in humans is a transient *lowering* of blood pressure. Though this is no health hazard for healthy people, in persons with low blood pressure to begin with, a charge of high-THC grass *can* conduce to marked vertigo if the smoker rises rapidly from a supine position. In some people, particularly small persons, faintness amounting to a momentary blackout can occur. Though this is all well-established in the cannabis research literature, for some unaccountable reason it goes unmentioned as a

plausible health hazard of marijuana in either of these NAS reviews. But since a person *can* fall down and sustain a nasty bump on the head in such a situation, we're volunteering it here. Seen it happen scores of times.

5. This does not mean persons with epilepsy should try self-medicating with street grass. There is almost *no* cannabidiol in street marijuana; in some commercial tropical strains of grass, cannabidiol only occurs in molecular trace quantities. This is because cannabidiol directly antagonizes and abolishes all the effects of delta-9 THC and vice versa. Drug strains of grass are therefore bred specifically to minimize CBD content, and maximize THC content. Since THC in some people actually appears to *promote* seizures, the use of street grass is not to be recommended to epileptics.

6. This is shameless special pleading for the pharmaceuticals industry. If the word "probably" in this sentence were changed to "possibly," it would've been a great deal more accurate and infinitely more honest.

7. Several "cohort" studies, in which both marijuana smokers and carefully selected nonsmoking peers are observed over long periods of time, have been published in recent years. None has shown any even slightly adverse effects from grass smoking, which is quite surprising, because that's what they were *structured* for specifically. Some responsible party, such as a Ph.D. candidate looking for a *historic* dissertation, really ought to review them someday. Refer Vera Rubin and Lambros Comitas, *Ganja in Jamaica*, 1974; William Martin, ed., *Cannabis in Costa Rica*, 1982; Sheppard Kellam *et al.*, *Paths Leading to Teenage Psychiatric Symptoms and Substance Use*, University of Chicago, 1982.

8. This is shameless pleading for the academic research community, which has been mortally savaged by Reagan budget cuts in "social" areas. One thing the NAS reviewers definitely discovered is that a lot of terrific social research that might never otherwise get funded can be done under the guise of "marijuana" research.

REEFER MADNESS: THE RISE OF HARRY ANSLINGER

by Larry Sloman

There was fun in the House Health Committee during the week when the Marihuana bill came up for consideration. Marihuana is Mexican opium, a plant used by Mexicans and cultivated for sale by Indians. "When some beet field peon takes a few rares of this stuff," explained Dr. Fred Fulsher of Mineral County, "he thinks he has just been elected president of Mexico so he starts out to execute all his political enemies. I understand that over in Butte where the Mexicans often go for the winter they stage imaginary bullfights in the 'Bower of Roses' or put on tournaments for the favor of 'Spanish Rose' after a couple of whiffs of

ABOMINABLE SLOMAN

Larry Sloman interviewed Dr. James Munch, the government scientist whose testimony in 1937 before Congress was responsible for the banning of marijuana, while working on his book *Reefer Madness: A History of Marijuana in America*—which is going to cause quite a stir when Bobbs-Merrill publishes it later this year. Among other things, Sloman will document the government plan to round up Louis Armstrong, Billie Holiday and every other black jazz musician in America on dope charges in the 1940s. Sloman also has the evidence to prove that the authors of the original federal antipot laws never intended to punish personal possession. It's another journalistic coup for Sloman, whose past scoops include: "The Case for Valium" and the bestselling Bantam paperback *On The Road with Bob Dylan: Rolling with the Thunder.*
Sideshow, #39, November 1978

WILD ABOUT HARRY

The reason you're reading HIGH TIMES this month and not something like, let's say, New-Wave QuicheEater, is on account of a man named Harry Lipsig. In fact, if our subscribers only knew how close they came to being stuck with a year's worth of centerfolds showcasing the talented young cheeses of France (just imagine, wheels of brie dressed up in little black leather jackets) and articles like "I Ate Foie Gras with the Egon von Furstenburgs," letters would be pouring in from all over the country demanding to know more about the guy who saved their grass. For the past two years we've been locked in a court battle with Gabrielle Schang, widow of HIGH TIMES founder Tom Forçade and once publisher of HIGH TIMES, over control of this magazine. The best and brightest lawyers in New York couldn't bring about a settlement, and, to be honest, for a while there most HT staffers wouldn't have given you a legal stimulant for our chances of making it through last summer. Enter Lipsig, and within a matter of months the widow Schang is settling for cash and we get to keep the magazine. Mr. Lipsig was asked by the court to try and settle the HIGH TIMES case because, in the words of presiding judge Marie Lampert, "if anybody could save the magazine and the money for the estate it was Mr. Lipsig."
Flashes, #80, April 1982

ANOTHER SIDE OF TOM FORÇADE

BY BOB LEMMO

The first time I met Forçade, it was so he could sell me some pot, and the way he went about it shows that the guy had a certain amount of Kool. In 1973, Andy Kowl and Bob Sacks, two personages currently mastheaded on this magazine, and I were publishing an alternative (née underground) paper called the *Express* out of the town of Hicksville, Long Island. Now Hicksville was nestled deep in the eastern bowels of Nassau County, a land then fabled as absolutely glutted with idle, snoopy cops and as one of the easiest places in New York State to get busted for pot.

The three of us had talked to Forçade a number of times, since the *Express* belonged to the Alternative Press Syndicate, and when he one day mentioned that he had some great Colombian pot for sale, we indicated our interest. He said fine, he'd run some out to us. The next day he arrived at our office decked out in a cowboy hat and toting a paper shopping bag that was cross-my-heart-and-hope-to-die *brimming* with sun yellow Colombian. We mentioned to him that it was kind of risky toting the pot up from his car all exposed like that, in this neck of the woods. Nah, he said, he hadn't taken a car. He had just spent the last hour or so on the Long Island Rail Road, sitting with his pungent bag of buds, stopping at every village and burg and hamlet between lower Manhattan and the potato farms of Long Island. Then he walked the half dozen or so blocks from the train station to our office. Foolhardy, yes, but I was not left with the impression that Forcade felt ill at ease around marijuana.

#82, June 1982

Marihuana. The Silver Bow and Yellowstone delegations both deplore these international complications." Everybody laughed and the bill was recommended for passage.
—Montana Standard, *January 27, 1929*

While the Montana legislature was "debating" their marijuana bill, a career bureaucrat, whose name would later go down in history linked hand-in-stem with the Marijuana Menace, was having a difficult time enforcing the prohibition of America's favorite recreational drug: alcohol. Harry Jacob Anslinger had just been appointed assistant commissioner of Prohibition, after working three years on the problem in Washington as chief of the Division of Foreign Control with the Treasury Department.

If there was ever a better prohibitionist, Uncle Sam had never received his service application. Anslinger was born on May 20, 1892, in Altoona, Pennsylvania, a Taurus on the cusp of Gemini. Of sturdy Pennsylvania Dutch parentage, the young lad suffered a traumatic experience at the age of 12 that was to change the course of his life. In *The Murderers—The Shocking Story of the Narcotic Gangs*, Anslinger painfully recalled that incident:

As a youngster of twelve, visiting in the house of a neighboring farmer, I heard the screaming of a woman on the second floor. I had never heard such cries of pain before. The woman, I learned later, was addicted, like many other women of that period, to morphine, a drug whose dangers most medical authorities did not yet recognize. All I remember was that I heard a woman in pain, whose cries seemed to fill my whole twelve-year-old being. Then her husband came running down the stairs, telling me I had to get into the cart and drive to town. I was to pick up a package at the drug store and bring it back for the woman.

I recall driving those horses, lashing at them, convinced that the woman would die if I did not get back in time. When I returned with the package—it was morphine—the man hurried upstairs to give the woman the dosage. In a little while her screams stopped and a hush came over the house.

I never forgot those screams. Nor did I forget that the morphine she had required was sold to a 12-year-old boy, no questions asked.

But not only did young Harry harbor a crusader's zeal against the narcotic menace; he was possessed of a hankering for sleuthing and a remarkable aptitude for that work that produced results. At 20 he was an investigator for the Pennsylvania Railroad, while working his way through State College. A woman had been killed by the Broadway Limited at a grade crossing, and her aggrieved husband was suing for $50,000 damages, claiming that her shoe had become caught in the track while crossing and that the oncoming train was not visible due to a sharp curve in the track. Just as the railroad company lawyers were about to settle the claim, Anslinger came forth with evidence that the accident was, in fact, suicide. Suspicious that anyone would cross at such an isolated spot, the young sleuth searched the area and found the victim's market basket in some bushes. On questioning the couple's neighbors, he learned that the pair had quarreled violently the morning of the accident. Finally the husband admitted that his wife had threatened to kill herself, and the spurious suit was dropped.

Anslinger's work impressed his superior, who, on promotion to head the state police, enlisted Anslinger to take charge of arson investigations. Harry left college and investigated fires until World War I. At 25 he became an inspector for the War Department; after a year he applied for foreign service and in 1918 was assigned to the American Legation at The Hague. Situated behind enemy lines, young Anslinger carried out many espionage missions. As a result, he somehow obtained the field utility kit and other minor personal possessions of His Imperial Highness Kaiser Wilhelm II, which were donated to the Smithsonian Institution in 1957. "How I obtained them must remain a state secret," the modest official wrote later.

From The Hague, he became vice-consul at Hamburg, Germany, which was at that time a worldwide center for illicit drugs. After two years Anslinger was promoted to a consulship at La Guajira, Venezuela, where he encountered pearl-smuggling. These were good times for the Altoona native, and he and his wife, the former Martha Denniston, enjoyed the life of the foreign corps.

But duty reared its ugly head and interrupted Anslinger's idyllic stay in Venezuela, when he was transferred to the Bahamas as consul in 1926. In Nassau Anslinger came face to face with rumrunning, and his prohibitionist instincts were honed. And on the creative front, being in the Bahamas gave him insight into another social problem: the shark scares. In his spare time, Harry wrote an article exposing the myth that sharks attack humans, and revealed that it was, in fact, barracudas who are the culprits of the deep. Published in the June 12, 1926, issue of the *Saturday Evening Post*, Anslinger debunked the shark's bad image with: "It may be safely stated that unless a shark is ravenously hungry he will not attack a human being, unless he is positive that the man has been drowned or is absolutely helpless. He has never been known to attack anything that is perfectly healthy."

It didn't take long for a torrent of letters to swamp the magazine's desks. People from all over the world sent in protesting letters, documenting horrible experiences where sharks had attacked humans. The editors at the *Post* forwarded the letters to Anslinger and asked for a follow-up article.

The result was "Shark Fins," and it bears scrutiny:

Australians regard with astonishment persons who claim that the vicious barracuda is responsible for attacks by sharks. They have many arguments to back up their claim that the shark is a man-eater.

Early in 1927, a fifteen-year-old boy died as a result of being attacked by a shark at Port Hacking, Australia.... It was found that the flesh of the right leg had been torn completely off from thigh to ankle, leaving the bones exposed and causing death shortly thereafter....

A sailor shipwrecked on Surprise Island reef in New Caledonia in 1916 saw a native Kanaka disappear in a flurry of blood and foam. The Kanakas remarked, "Too much blurry shark"....

In the summer of 1926, a shark captured at Koolau, Hawaii, was found to contain human bones and a pair of swimming trunks. The bones consisted of more than half of the upper part of a skull, a hand, a knee, two whole arms, one leg bone and the first and second cervical vertebrae. (Photograph) A quantity of short black hair was attached to the skull....

At last this document reveals the full maturation of the inimitable Anslinger style, the style that would titillate thousands of readers of *The Murderers*, *The Protectors* and *The Traffic in Narcotics*. It was two-

DREW FRIEDMAN

THE TAXMAN
BY BRUCE JAY FRIEDMAN
"Listen," said Gowran, "how's the grass situation up here?" The question put Ullman right on the spot. He had some, but what if he produced a few joints and Gowran slipped the cuffs on him, booking him not only on tax evasion but also on a drug rap. Maybe that's what Ingrid's presence was all about. On a simpler level—if he brought out grass it would be clear-cut evidence that the apartment was more than just an office. Still, a certain inevitability began to surround the evening. He went and got some.
#69, May 1981

CONFESSIONS OF A PORN QUEEN
BY CANDIDA ROYALLE
I'd like to briefly discuss drugs on porn-film sets. Very simply, there are none. And when there are, it's kept very quiet for fear of the producer finding out. Coke is regarded very unfavorably on the set. There've been a couple of times when guys spent the previous evening partying with sex and cocaine, resulting in a torturous day for all on the set. Most people become erotic performers for one or both of the following reasons: good money and/or a tremendously active libido. Each of these reasons provides enough motivation to perform sexually without the aid of drugs on the set.
#83, July 1982

TATTOO YOU

BY SPIDER WEBB

It has been argued that tattooing is our oldest art. It belongs in the spectrum of body arts that ranges from such extreme practices as the head deformation of infants through scarification, circumcision, piercing, teeth filing and insertion of labrets to clothing, cosmetics and—traveling full circle—plastic surgery.

The dark ages of tattooing began in Europe in the seventeenth century when the Catholic Church began taking a dim view of what it considered a pagan practice. Up until then, tattooing had been practiced by Christians, who wore various symbols on their bodies, including the cross, the fish and the eye inside a triangle. But this sensibility was crushed, even though several passages in the New Testament imply special tattooed marks on the forehead to identify followers of Jesus. In 787, Pope Hadrian I banned all tattooing, and by the Middle Ages it had been forced underground, turned into an esoteric and criminal activity.

#89, January 1983

CHARLES BUKOWSKI

MICHAEL MONTFORT

I stopped at the liquor store, got two bottles of wine, went to the Hotel Helen, which was right across the street from the bar I had been in. I had a girlfriend there, an alky, she was 10 years older than I, she worked as a maid there. I walked up two flights, knocked on her door, hoping she'd be alone.

"Jane," I knocked, "I'm in trouble. I've been fucked over."

The door opened. Jane was alone and drunker than I was.

I closed the door and walked in.

"Where's your drinking glasses?"

She pointed and I peeled a bottle and poured two. She sat on the edge of the bed and I sat in a chair. She drained her drink and I passed her the bottle. She lit a cigarette.

"I hate this place, Hank. How come we don't live together anymore?"

"You started running the streets too much, baby, you drove me crazy."

"Well, you know how I am—"

"Yeah."

Notes of a Dirty Old Man, #91, March 1983

fisted journalism, pulling no punches, leaving no bone unturned. Here we have our first inkling of his tremendous feel for anatomical detail. Here we see the first usage of the litany of case histories. Finally, we note the obvious concern for the individual as opposed to the statistic. Nine years later Anslinger would be published again in a mass-media magazine. This time it would be the *American Magazine* of July 1937, but the style echoes the Bahamas, 1928. It began:

The sprawled body of a young girl lay crushed on the sidewalk the other day after a plunge from the fifth story of a Chicago apartment house. Everyone called it suicide, but actually it was murder. The killer was a narcotic known to America as marijuana, and to history as hashish. It is a narcotic used in the form of cigarettes, comparatively new to the United States and as dangerous as a coiled rattlesnake....

It was the flowering of a long, distinguished career. In one paragraph one can hear the echoes of the bloody railroad tracks that the Broadway Central hugged, the moans of the innocent swimmers cut down during a moment of relaxation by a dark vicious denizen of the deep. And, of course, the shriek of that desperate woman in that lonely farmhouse. Harry Anslinger was 45 when his article appeared, and he was the head of the Bureau of Narcotics. And he had finally found his sharks in America, masquerading as a harmless little weed the Mexicans called marijuana, or "good feeling."

As Anslinger assumed control of the newly formed Bureau of Narcotics, which was subsumed into the Treasury Department of the federal government, the concern over marijuana was just beginning to have a national impact. In the states where marijuana usage was visible, namely, the Southwest and Louisiana, pressure began to mount to enact legislation against its use. Although most Americans couldn't care less about this strange exotic drug, a handful of newspaper editors, legislators and concerned citizens began to put pressure on Washington to move on the issue.

Anslinger took over as acting commissioner of an autonomous Federal Bureau of Narcotics in June 1930, fully cognizant of the increasing demand for federal regulation of marijuana and at least in some sense familiar with the drug itself. For in April of that year, Anslinger, in his position as secretary of the Federal Narcotics Control Board (under the Prohibition Unit), had instituted a survey of sorts into the cannabis problem. The survey was prompted by proposed legislation that sought to bring cannabis under the purview of the Narcotic Drugs Import and Export Act.

One of the people to whom Anslinger addressed a series of fundamental questions about cannabis was William Woodward, the director of the Bureau of Legal Medicine and Legislation of the American Medical Association. The AMA, which by 1930 was a potent political force in medical matters, had uneasy relations with the Treasury Department, especially since the Harrison Act had set the stage for a large number of cases where doctors were arrested and prosecuted for treating drug addicts by maintaining their habit.

So Woodward's reply to Anslinger on April 28, 1930, reeked with sarcasm and ill-disguised contempt.

To his chilly letter Woodward appended a 13-page document consisting of extracts from letters he had received from pharmaceutical manufacturers relative to the pharmaceutical use and habit-forming properties of cannabis. Twenty-nine out of the 30 respondents objected strongly to including cannabis under the Narcotic Drugs Act. One pharmacist railed "Absolute rot. It is not necessary. I have never known of its misuse." A few maintained that the government should let sleeping dogs lie:

With refererence to Cannabis Indica, also Cannabis Americana, as far as our exprience goes, the drug is practically abandoned in regular medicine. In veterinary medicine it is used to some extent. We make and offer the tincture and fluid extract and sell almost none. As far as we know there are only three products we offer in which it is one of the unimportant ingredients. Our opinion is that an action of this kind would only call attention to something which is already dormant and of no consequence, at least in the Eastern section of the United States.

The one respondent who cautioned Woodward about cannabis was saved for last. This correspondent reported meeting a physician from India who contracted the cannabis habit during World War I. "He said that for three years he was as much a slave to the addiction of the drug as was ever a user of opium in any of its forms.... He had to take treatment, which he described as being similar to the treatment for morphine addiction. He said it was at least four months after he left the sanatorium before he fully regained his strength and nerve equilibrium: This may be an exceptional case."

That it was. Of 30 responses, only one reported negatively about cannabis. And, predictably enough, that was the one answer that Anslinger marked off in the margin of the letter with a broad bracket, destined to be filed for future use in the rapidly expanding file marked "Marihuana" of the infant Bureau of Narcotics.

Anslinger had also asked some of his field agents in the Prohibition Unit to investigate the cannabis situation. In June 1930, one narcotics agent made purchases of marijuana cigarettes and interrogated the vendors. He found that most of the marijuana sold in New York was sold by Spaniards and East Indians to trade consisting mostly of members of those races. The drug was obtained by these street peddlers from crews of boats belonging to the United Fruit Lines. Up in Harlem the marijuana was selling for twenty-five cents a cigarette, $1 to $1.50 for 15 to 20 grams and $75 to $100 a pound. However, the agent noted that the price was considerably cheaper along the border and in cities of the Southwest and West, where single cigarettes went for five cents and pounds could be purchased for $5 or $6.

The agent concluded:

Marihuana is used for smoking by Indians, Mexicans, Philipinos [sic], Spaniards, and East Indians. In the larger cities of the United States it is used, distributed and sold in the Spanish, Philipino, Greek, East Indian and Mexican quarters, and it is used by some white habitués of the Tenderloin districts. In Texas, Oklahoma, and Southern California it is used to a great extent in cities surrounding the oil fields where there is a large population of Mexicans and Indians, and by habitués of the Tenderloin. The smokers use it for its enlivening effect which is described as making things appear brighter, and relieving the user of care and worry. Overindulgence in smoking it causes temporary insanity, makes the user irresponsible and vicious, and deeds of violence have been committed under its influence.

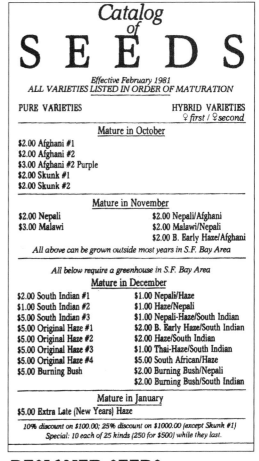

DICK GREGORY

Everybody'd been in a Crackerjack box. People were breaking out for the first time, and for the first time guidelines had to be set. I told people a long time ago that the whole drug scene was government—that whole thing of just putting people to sleep, and that's why I had a strong thing then about drugs. Nobody in the movement in the '60s ever saw me with any drugs, never saw a time when I wasn't talking against it. I said then "You want to destroy the movement? This is how you're going to do it." But I could understand it. People were jumping out of the box...I always said white children were becoming niggers. And when you become a nigger, you play your music loud, you wear loud clothes so you can be seen. You learn to dance. Once somebody makes me invisible, I'm like a little child...I don't think anybody has really analyzed the significance of what the '60s meant to a white status-symbol ethics and integrity, which was not what you *did*, but what you *looked* like. Young whites came through and broke out of that. Your father couldn't take you to the country club because he had talked about them hippy faggots.... The '60s was the turning point. The '60s were just *beautiful*; and I saw *no* mistakes in the '60s....
Interview by Bob LaBrasca, #94, June 1983

SINSEMILLA

BY ED ROSENTHAL

Government reports which discuss the perils of marijuana often refer to new sinsemilla marijuana strains that have a potency of 8 to 10 times the marijuana available 10 years ago. As usual, the government has messed up again. First of all, after working in the marijuana business for all these years, they should know that sinsemilla is a technique, not a variety.

Sinsemilla is derived from the two Spanish words, "sin" and "semilla," meaning "without seed." Connoisseurs prize sinsemilla, partly because the marijuana has a greater potency and a richer aroma than the seeded, and partly because of its enhanced appearance. In order for the flowers to ripen unseeded, they must remain unfertilized.
Grow American, #95, July 1983

By December 18, 1930, Anslinger had finally attained Senate confirmation as the commissioner of the new Narcotics Bureau, a confirmation that came on the heels of a record $5-million dope bust in New York the day before. It was a perfectly timed publicity play, something Anslinger would become very adept at, and it so moved one senator that he entered a newspaper report of the arrest into the *Congressional Record* with a preface: "This commendable act gives evidence that Mr. Anslinger is going to make an effective and useful commissioner."

Anslinger's rise to commissioner of the Bureau of Narcotics seemed meteoric, since he had spent only three years in the Prohibition Unit. However, some commentators have pointed out the fact that his wife Martha came from the well-connected Denniston family who made a fortune in steel, and was also a niece of Andrew Mellon, who, as treasury secretary, was Anslinger's immediate superior. At any rate, Anslinger was a good solid Republican, taking office during the Hoover administration, and it would be two years before the New Deal would threaten his control over the Bureau.

When Anslinger took over, the Narcotics Bureau had an annual budget of $1,411,260 up from the previous year's total of $1,350,440—not bad for a depressed economy. But, operating with a staff of only some 300-odd agents, it was clear that priorities would have to be set with respect to law enforcement. While morphine and opium addiction were known evils, Anslinger, during 1931, received many queries from all over the country regarding this new "menace," marijuana. Typical of these was a letter sent to the Narcotics Division on March 14, 1931, from Carl Murphy, the president of the *Afro-American* which billed itself as the "World's Biggest All-Negro Weekly." Murphy wrote:

I find theatrical folk smoking a cigarette which they term Reefer of Magijuana (the spelling is phonetic and probably incorrect), a Mexican importation.
I understand that it is a drug and injurious to the health.
Please advise what the real name of this plant is and what its effects are on the human body.
Its use has spread so that it seems necessary to call attention to it if it is injurious.

Anslinger replied with a standard letter describing *Cannabis indica*, detailing its deleterious effects, and noting the "grave question" as to its constitutionality if it were to be placed under the Harrison Act. Instead, he borrowed Surgeon General Dr. Hugh Cummings's ideas and raised the possibility of placing interstate commerce controls on its distribution and/or preventing its growth within the country.

But if Anslinger essentially passed the political hempball, newspapers all over the country began agitating for federal regulations with respect to the new drug. In New Orleans, where marijuana consciousness had been high since the 1920s, a number of magazine articles helped to increase the pressure on the newly formed Bureau to act on this grave social issue.

One of these agitators was Dr. A.E. Fossier, an M.D. from New Orleans, who, on April 14, 1931, read a paper before the Louisiana State Medical Society called "The Mariahuana [*sic*] Menace." Fossier's paper began with a recounting of the legendary Assassin myth, a myth that links hashish to the commission of brutal murders in Persia around 1090. Although the myth was later discredited, it served as demonstrable proof that marijuana use was intimately tied up with brutal crime. Fossier argued that one in every four people arrested in New Orleans was "addicted to mariahuana." Seventeen of the 37 murderers smoked "muggles," the marijuana cigarette.

But Fossier revealed the implicit racism that the early antimarijuana crusaders shared when he speculated on the causes for the alarming rise of "mariahuana addiction":

As far as it can be ascertained this addiction has assumed formidable proportions since the advent of that "noble experiment," that fiasco, prohibition. In fact, it is the offspring which bids fair to surpass its dissembling parent in destroying moral inhibition. The lesser of the two evils is alcohol.... The debasing and baneful influence of hashish and opium is not restricted to individuals, but has manifested itself in nations and races as well. The dominant race and most enlightened countries are alcoholic, whilst the races and nations addicted to hemp and opium, some of which once attained to heights of culture and civilization, have deteriorated both mentally and physically.

The paper was very well received, and much praise was heaped on the hemp theories of Dr. Fossier during the discussion period. Dr. Frank Gomila, the commissioner of Public Safety of New Orleans, assured the good doctors present that the police department had been ordered to crack down on the muggles trade, since it was a drug "in the same class as heroin." In closing, Fossier had one last warning:

If overnight, after the advent of prohibition, this nation became so adept in the brewing of beer, the making of wine and the distilling of alcohol, so much so that even children are adept in their manufacture, what will happen in the near future, with such a dangerous plant that may grow in our very backyards?

Another influential article which appeared that year was "Marihuana As a Developer of Criminals," by Eugene Stanley, the district attorney of New Orleans. Originally published in the American Journal of Police Science, it recommended that marijuana be placed among the narcotic drugs covered under the Harrison Act. Again the old Assassin myth was trotted out, along with the notion that the drug is favored by the underworld for its value in "subjugating the will of human derelicts to that of a master mind." As if that weren't enough, Stanley further cautioned that it is commonly used as an aphrodisiac, although its continued use leads to impotence.

Stanley's article was widely circulated among law-enforcement officials, and one copy was sent to Anslinger by the New Orleans Narcotic Agent in Charge. In an accompanying letter, the perceptive agent wrote:

This is forwarded for information of the Bureau, and of any interest the Bureau may have in the proposition now and in the future, as Mr. Stanley had given newspaper interviews along the same line urging public opinion to compel the Federal Government to have a law passed with regard to "Marihuana" similar to the anti-narcotic statutes.

Of course, it is a self-evident fact that the Federal Government would be seriously handicapped in the enactment and enforcement of law upon "Marihuana." Here in New Orleans, and in the Southland, this plant grows promiscuously. The Police Department here in New

AIDS

There has been growing concern over the relationship of AIDS (Acquired Immune Deficiency Syndrome) and certain patterns of drug abuse. To date, correlations between AIDS and some kinds of drug abuse have been established. We know that certain disease syndromes are related to drug abuse, either in their formation or in their transmission among individuals. Among these are the malnutrition and cirrhosis of the liver typically seen in alcoholics, though these are not infectious diseases. With intravenous drug users— those who shoot heroin, speed, etc.—infectious "serum" hepatitis Type B is a special hazard, however. And AIDS, a recently recognized disease entity, appears also spread among I.V. drug users in much the same way as hepatitis B. Some researchers have also speculated that AIDS may be associated with the inhalation of butyl and amyl nitrate, but the Centers for Disease Control (CDC) have since virtually ruled out this connection.

To date, the CDC has reported 1,500 cases of AIDS, and 58 associated deaths. The cause of AIDS is at present unknown, but recent research has isolated a T-cell leukemia virus (T-cells comprise a major part of the body's immune systems) in humans; this virus may infect exposed individuals, suppress their immune systems and render them susceptible to opportunistic infections.

The patterns of contagion of AIDS are becoming clear: the disease seems, like hepatitis B, to follow traceable patterns of human contact: by blood contact with I.V. drug users who share their syringes, by blood contact with hemophiliacs receiving transfusions, and by blood, and perhaps semen, among homosexuals.

Abuse Folio, by David Smith and Rick Seymour, #97, September 1983

CLONING YOUR CROP

BY COLE STEVEN

During a recent trip to Amsterdam, where the police have a funny out-of-sight, out-of-mind attitude about marijuana in general and growing in particular, I saw a large cloning operation and want to pass on some of the info to you.

Actually, cloning is a misnomer that has become a popular name for propagation through cuttings. What is so great about cuttings? For one thing, you can grow a genetic duplicate of the parent plant, so that if you have a terrific female, you can have a repeat performance via a cutting.

Ordinarily, presexing is done through the manipulation of the photoperiod: you cut the light cycle back to 10 hours, tricking the plant into believing that winter is on its way and the plant goes into bloom. Once the plant "declares" itself, the males are eliminated, the photoperiod put back to 18 hours and the remaining females have to scramble to get back into a vegetative cycle. This process takes two to three weeks and can traumatize the plants. By using a cutting, you eliminate all those problems. You can presex by proxy.

Grow American, #97, September 1983

GOING SMOKELESS

..."R." has turned down joints at parties. He has turned down free samples from dealers and growers. In fact, for two full months he hasn't smoked any grass at all.... He's just decided it was time to get some perspective on potsmoking.

Connoisseur by "R.," #99, November 1983

MIKE BLOOMFIELD

There was a piano player that played with Muddy Waters. He was said to have been his half brother. He's passed on, so I can mention his name, Otis Spann—he was a real good friend of mine. On occasion he would be known to deal pot, and Otis always dealt nigger nickels—tiny little bits of amorphous vegetable matter, wrapped up in many pounds of tinfoil. You didn't know what the hell it was—he didn't know, I didn't know, no one would know. Otis would say, in his gravelly voice, "Mike, dis some good shit." I wouldn't know what it was. It was shit, I'll tell you it was shit.

Copping, #94, June 1983

Orleans advises this office that this vegetable is grown generally on vacant city lots and out in the open country. The difficulty of enforcing a restrictive law with regard to production of Marihuana is obvious. It would appear that the suppression of the growth, use and dealing in Cannabis Indica is very clearly a police matter, hardly to be reached effectively by an Internal Revenue Statute of the Federal Government.

In his reply, Anslinger agreed with the agent's views and further stated that before federal legislation could be proposed, "it would be necessary to give the subject very careful consideration, particularly with reference to the extent to which *cannabis sativa* is grown in the United States, the extent of its use for bona fide medical purposes, and whether such use could be supplied by the substitution of a less harmful drug." He then requested that these views be communicated by the agent to Mr. Stanley.

So, early in his first year in office it was clear that Anslinger did not desire to burden his small staff with the additional responsibility of regulating traffic in a weed that was so widely available. The pressure on the Bureau to do so was coming from the southwestern, western and Gulf states and, by and large, the users of this new drug were minorities.

In an interview with Yale professor David Musto in 1970, Anslinger recalled that early enforcement was directed at Mexicans whom the "sheriffs and local police departments claimed got loaded on the stuff and caused a lot of trouble, stabbing, assaults, and so on." But the New Orleans authorities were the first to warn the nation of the real danger marijuana offered. It was one thing that Mexicans were cutting each other up in the barrios during these lean Depression years. It was quite a different cause for concern when the muggles were actually being sold to impressionable white schoolchildren. Gomila, in one of his mid-1930 articles on the dangers of marijuana, reported: "One gentleman of the byways explained: 'The worst thing about that loco weed is the way these kids go for them. Most of them, boys and girls, are just punks and when they get high on the stuff you can write your own ticket.'"

But by 1931 the hysteria was largely confined to New Orleans, and Anslinger sought to temper it in the Bureau's annual report: "The Traffic in Opium and Other Dangerous Drugs." He wrote:

This abuse of the drug (Marihuana) is noted particularly among the Latin-American or Spanish-speaking population....

A great deal of public interest has been aroused by newspaper articles appearing from time to time on the evils of the abuse of marihuana, or Indian hemp, and more attention has been focused upon specific cases reported of the abuse of the drug than would otherwise have been the case. This publicity tends to magnify the extent of the evil and lends color to an inference that there is an alarming spread of the improper use of the drug, whereas the actual increase in such use may not have been inordinately large....

Anslinger urged state laws to regulate marijuana use, and this remained the position of the Bureau over the next few years; all inquiries to the Bureau with respect to marijuana got the standard reply that it was a matter for the states and their localities to deal with. It was clear that marijuana was not a priority of the Bureau.

During 1933 and 1934 the pressure on the Bureau mounted. Newspapers carried lurid accounts of the spread of the marijuana habit. For example, the *Los Angeles Examiner*, on November 5, 1933, screamed: MURDER WEED FOUND UP AND DOWN COAST—DEADLY MARIHUANA DOPE PLANT READY FOR HARVEST THAT MEANS ENSLAVEMENT OF CALIFORNIA CHILDREN. Two days later the *San Francisco Examiner* headlined: DOPE OFFICIALS HELPLESS TO CURB MARIHUANA USE.

However, in 1934 the marijuana phenomenon received attention from professional quarters as well as the sensationalistic press. At Bellevue Hospital in New York, Walter Bromberg, an assistant psychiatrist at the time, reported a clinical study of Cannabis *sativa* in the September issue of the *American Journal of Psychiatry*. Bromberg, who was presenting the first scientific data on marijuana since the scare began in the early 1930s, found that marijuana itself was not primarily responsible for crime. Rather, he argued that the drug simply uncovers the underlying anti-social aggressive and sadistic elements of persons who may use it. Using as an informant "an intelligent Negro who has had an extensive criminal career and a wide acquaintance in the underworld," Bromberg delved into the sociological aspects of marijuana use. "Most folks in show business smoke it," Bromberg quoted his source as saying. "For the last five years it has increased to my knowing.... You can leave it at the start but not after a while. You want the exhilaration it gives you.... After a while, you just go on the bum. You can't do anything. You are dull.... Dancers especially like it because it makes you feel light. Only a few of those who smoke marihuana go in for morphine or heroin. Most of those who have the habit are satisfied with it and stay in it, increasing the dose."

Returning to the crime thesis, Bromberg reported that not a single case of confirmed marijuana addiction was found in a group of 2,216 criminals convicted of felonies in the Court of General Sessions in New York City in 1933. "None of the assault crimes could be said to have been committed under the drug's influence. No crimes were committed in this group at a time during or after the intoxication," he concluded.

One year later, in 1935, in an article for *Medical Record* called "The Menace of Marihuana," Bromberg continued to debunk the "breeder of crime" theory regarding marijuana:

In considering marihuana as a "breeder of crime" one must bear in mind the psychopathic types that use the drug. It is more than probable that alcohol is at least as responsible for crime as is marihuana. It is inaccurate to assign such a role to the drug when the basic antisocial nature of the persons who use it is understood. From the material quoted and the experience with users, it is clear that marihuana cannot be considered a primary cause of crime. We cannot fasten on it responsibility for each new crime wave that appears....

From all indications, Bromberg's empirical work had little effect on Anslinger. The commissioner did appropriate the quotes from Bromberg's Negro source for the Bureau files; as for the doctor's thesis, Anslinger seemed to have little interest. That is, until February 1937, when he wrote to the assistant surgeon general inquiring whether Bromberg was in good standing in the medical profession.

However, we must note that Anslinger had other preoccupations at the time. After narrowly surviving when FDR and his Democratic New Deal swept into office, Anslinger came under serious attack near the end of 1934. A slew of letters descended on the White House, criticizing the running of the Bureau of Narcotics. One such letter, addressed to Roosevelt intimate James Farley, went:

THE FIRST ASK ED

Dear Ed:

If marijuana plants are growing close to each other and their roots entangle, will this hurt the plants' growth or kill them?

Dwayne A.
Susquehanna, Pa.

No. In areas where marijuana is grown using broadcast seeding, up to 35 plants are grown per square foot. Plants that are grown close together vie for air space. They grow few side branches and tend to grow tall. When removing plants with entangled roots, it is best to cut rather than pull them out, because otherwise the other plants' roots may be disturbed.

Ask Ed, #99, November 1983

COOCHY COOCH

ROBERT WILLIAMS

TOM ALEXANDER

BY BOB LABRASCA AND DEAN LATIMER

The publisher of *Sinsemilla Tips* is a walking encyclopedia of marijuana information: from evading NASA's spy-in-the-sky satellites to combating red spider mites.

TA: The indoor scene is rapidly exploding. Out here more is grown indoors now than outdoors. I mean, you look at the combined sales of lights and it's been a thousand and twelve hundred lights a month.

HT: How about large-scale indoor growing operations in warehouses?

TA: I've reported and seen some large-scale operations in warehouses. People are also buying second houses. But this is the type of approach that gets people busted. If you grow in a warehouse and you don't have a front—say, a machine shop or something—you are giving the authorities the excuse to suspect you of growing.

Interview, #100, December 1983

Anslinger, shaking and trembling, knowing you are going to can him, is making a big noise recently (seeking publicity) pinching a lot of poor sick addicts. And here's the sad part—a genuine tragedy—he conveys to society the impression that drug addicts are desperate criminals.

Mr. Farley, drug addicts are the most harmless class of people in the country. A smart dick will tell you the same. Not a narcotic agent.

But the protests came from higher places, too. In a letter to Stephen B. Gibbons, the assistant secretary of the treasury and one of Anslinger's superiors, newly elected senator Joseph Guffey of Pennsylvania called for Anslinger's dismissal:

Enclosed herewith please find copy of a circular letter issued by Mr. J. Anslinger, Commissioner, Bureau of Narcotics, Treasury Department to District Supervisors and others concerned regarding Mr.————.

This circular letter has become public and the colored population of the State of Pennsylvania have been advised thereof. I am being deluged with complaints from our colored population because Mr. Anslinger has been so indiscreet as to refer to one of their race as a "ginger-colored nigger."

It would seem to me that a man in such a responsible position as that held by Mr. Anslinger should have more discretion than to refer to one of such a large part of the population of this Country in the manner quoted above, and I doubt very much that one so indiscreet should be allowed to remain in such a responsible position. Personally, I think he should be replaced, and I submit the matter to you for your consideration.

But Anslinger had developed a strong following which included many highly placed pharmaceutical executives, many right-wing newspaper editors and some influential congressmen; and, in the pre-Earl Butz atmosphere of the 1930s, he weathered the storm of his indiscreet remarks.

BAN THE BUD

BY "R."

As the Ralph Nader of the recreational reefer consumer, I cannot stand by passively any more and see marijuana grown in America, once a pleasure and a delight, turned into what it is—a stupid, bad drug. I'm talking about *indica*.

I am calling on all growers all over the United States to stop planting any *indica* or *indica*-blend seeds for an entire season, so that we, the mass of American ganja smokers, can get some perspective on the plague of uselessly stupefying sinsemilla that's being force-fed into our heads. That's right—I'm calling for a freeze on *indica* growing in order to save *sativa* from self-destruction.

When I tell people about my plans to call for a freeze on *indica*, most think it's a foolish, quixotic crusade. "You can't take on a billion-dollar industry, 'R.' " they tell me. "Even with all the respect you've built up over the years, even with your reputation as a devoted consumer cannabis advocate, the big growers are too strong, they're too deeply committed economically to their *indica* seed strains. They'll never go along."

But then I remind these sceptics of the humble origins of the anti-nuclear power movement. It began with one defiant symbolic act. A young idealist named Sam Lovejoy toppled a power transmitting tower in the rural New Hampshire hills that was designed to carry power to the notorious Seabrook Nuclear Reactor. From that act, from the attention it generated, the entire mammoth, evil nuclear-power industry was slowly brought to a halt. Stopped dead in its tracks.

Indica *Madness, #98, October 1983*

PART 4
CULTIVATION
CARRIES THE MAGAZINE
1984-1988

AT THE HEIGHT OF THE DRUG WAR, INDOOR CULTIVATION OF
MARIJUANA BECAME A BOOMING COTTAGE INDUSTRY.

ED ROSENTHAL

As far as cannabis history goes, it qualified as a momentous event: after years of anonymity, Ed Rosenthal, the guru of ganja, agreed to appear on the Morton Downey, Jr. Show to debate the feasibility of the government's decision to spray paraquat.

If the quality of the opposition is any indication, surely we must be closing in on legalization. Never have so many myths and mistakes concerning cannabis been so fervently held up as fact, including such statements as "Paraquat is biodegradable...paraquat is the safest herbicide in the world...marijuana smoking is a progressive disease that leads to AIDS...."

Sad to think that after all these years, the same lies continue to perpetuate. The Parents for Drug-Free Youth won't end their crusade until they've turned every child in America into a corporate-loving yuppie zombie.

However, they'd better watch out 'cause now they have Ed Rosenthal to contend with. Why not join Ed, readers? Step out of that cannabis closet you're hiding in. Support NORML, attend cannabis rallies, and help remove the stigma surrounding marijuana.

Page Six by Steven Hager, #158, October 1988

SMALL IS BOUNTIFUL

As outdoor cultivation becomes increasingly risky, more and more people are bringing their plants inside. Through trial and error they've developed "closet growing" techniques that allow maximum yield with minimum space. Even if all you have is a bit of unused shelf space, you can harvest a 1984 crop.

The main problem with closets is that there is usually little air circulation, so that once the CO_2 that plants need for photosynthesis is used up, growth stops. A fan blowing air out of or into the area will help.

Thin, rectangular closets are served better by a fluorescent unit hung from the ceiling. Additional tubes can be used to supplement the top lights. Patio and outdoor furniture shops, and discount stores, sell small-wattage mercury vapor and low-pressure sodium vapor lamps. These lamps are as efficient as fluorescents and are often more convenient to use since banks of tubes are not required. And remember, areas with odd shapes are illuminated better by several sources of light rather than one central source.

Grow American by Ed Rosenthal, #101, January 1984

INTERVIEW WITH ED ROSENTHAL
by Larry Sloman and George Barkin

HIGH TIMES: When did you first start smoking pot?

Ed Rosenthal: I first started in 1966. I had tried it a couple of times in 1965 but I never got high. Then in 1966 I bought a lid and I smoked it with my roommate in college.

I knew as soon as I got high that this was an ally of mine in the same way Carlos Castaneda spoke about little smoke or big smoke being an ally. And that this was really a good friend of mine, and by the second purchase that I made I was a dealer. I started dealing.

HIGH TIMES: What do you mean when you say that the pot was a "friend" of yours?

Rosenthal: I have such an affinity for being high, for that state. That almost is my normal state of consciousness, or felt that it should be. So the pot becomes an ally.

I learned to work on it, play on it, and somebody once said that pot wakes me up in the morning and puts me to sleep at night. Basically, I live my life to be high. It happened twenty years ago.

HIGH TIMES: You were never able to obtain that state previously, without smoking pot? That highness?

Rosenthal: Well, psychedelics...I think marijuana is a mild psychedelic and I had had a very unhappy childhood and adolescence. I had gone through therapy and things, but through my teens and early twenties I still suffered periodic states of depression. First, marijuana helped me to get out of myself and see what was going on, helped me to put everything in perspective in a way many, many, many hours and many, many, many thousands of dollars of therapy hadn't done. In 1967 I came back to New York where I went to a be-in in Central Park and Abbie Hoffman was onstage—he jumped down from the stage and started handing out acid and said to me, really impersonally, as he had been for thousands of others, "Wanna trip?" and I said, "Yes" and he put a tab on my tongue and I swallowed it and went through a most powerful experience. I went through a really horrible experience. All the shit and all the negativity that had accumulated all my life started coming out. I didn't say, "This is a bad trip, this is terrible, this is terrible." I realized what was going on. It wasn't the acid or anything—it was what was in my own head that was coming out. Shortly after that I never suffered from depression again. I really learned to control my state of consciousness.

HIGH TIMES: A lot of people smoke pot, but what led you to make it become your life's work, your business?

Rosenthal: I think everyone should live their fantasies. Most people don't like what they do for a living and I've always tried to vocationalize my avocations.

HIGH TIMES: You've traveled all across the world searching out the various ways of cultivation. Where have you seen marijuana growing?

Rosenthal: Throughout the United States. That's actually where I've seen the most. Maybe not in quantity but at least in operation. Then, I was to India, to Morocco, Amsterdam, Spain, Colombia.... I was in Colombia for a day. I did a consulting job down there.

HIGH TIMES: What do you mean, "consulting job"?

Rosenthal: These people had a field that was suffering from some problems and they consulted me to try to find out what the problems were and to try and correct them.

HIGH TIMES: Were you successful?

Rosenthal: I don't know—I never got to see the field a second time.

HIGH TIMES: In which area did you find the best pot?

Rosenthal: The best pot is in the United States. There is no doubt about it. American growers really understand marijuana, the plant, more than any other cultivators. Of course, it's the difference between the first-world and third-world countries because most of the other growing places are third-world countries, and in Europe they're really ten years behind us in cultivation in general.

HIGH TIMES: Also, the cultivators here tend to be in more cases users, than, for example, in South America. There they're just growing it for an export group.

Rosenthal: Mostly. And in India, I've got a feeling that perhaps the farmers used it but the processors didn't. The retailers do.

HIGH TIMES: When you're in Morocco or Colombia, how are you perceived by growers of other nationalities? Are you perceived as an American *El Exigente* or are you perceived as a cannabis researcher?

Rosenthal: I'm taken very seriously and I'm very well respected.

HIGH TIMES: Do you get hassled a lot by authorities?

Rosenthal: When I went to India I wanted to see the Legal Fields. We were on the train and we looked out the window and there are these pot fields, and I went to the people who were there and asked what town this was. They said Khandwa. So we went to the Department of Agriculture. I walked in and said, "You have marijuana fields growing in Khandwa and I would like to go see them. What procedure do I follow?" They said there is no ganja growing in Khandwa, there's no ganja growing in Madhy Pradesh. I said, "Oh, no, I saw it and I know that it's growing there." So they called the Department of Agriculture in Khandwa and they said, "Oh, yes, yes." They said that it wasn't under their jurisdiction, that it was under the jurisdiction of the Excise Tax Department. But anyway, they wrote a letter to the Department of Agriculture.

Then I arrived in Khandwa.... Meanwhile, I had copies of my book and I'm showing them, and as soon as I pulled out the book, you know, this is serious, an American scientist is here. That's the kind of reaction I got. So the next day a convoy of four vehicles drove up. And they pulled us into the jeeps, and we went first to the processing plant and then to visit the fields and then we came back from the fields. I asked if we could pick. They said, "Sure, go ahead, pick anything you want." So here was this field with all kinds of plants, mixed seeds, and they said to just take anything. So we got down enough for our needs the next couple of weeks. Well, we didn't cut down the plants, we just took the nicest buds. They were beautiful buds.

And the next day when we were in our hotel room, we hear this knock on the door. The door just opens—it was like a raid, only it was the excise guy and he had come to bring us dope. He had a handful of dope that he gave to us—which was the first and last time a government agent ever brought me dope.

HIGH TIMES: Do the cultivation methods in Morocco differ from those in West Virginia, stuff like that?

Rosenthal: Yeah, they do. Most people in America, because of the political and the unprotected situation therein, tend to grow very big

LSD'S 40TH BIRTHDAY

After disappearing from the headlines for almost a decade, psychedelics are again being talked about and consumed copiously by the US public. Two recent West Coast conferences, featuring a host of researchers famed for their work with psychoactive substances, reflected this resurgence of interest. Even Dr. Albert Hofmann, who discovered LSD 40 years ago at Sandoz laboratories in Switzerland, was on hand to receive the adulation of the conferees.

After a standing ovation from the crowd, Hofmann, now 76, described in detail what he had "learned from LSD" in his own self-experiments. LSD, he said, had shattered the belief he had held before he discovered the drug (in Berne, Switzerland, during World War II), that there is "only one true picture of the external world." Entheogenic and meditative experience, he said, were capable of uniting the duality created by the intellect's "subject-object" or "I-you" barrier and could lead to a true religiosity—"an embracing of reality which could provide us with confidence, with love, with thanks and with tranquility."

One of the principle topics discussed at the first of two afternoon panels was the role played by Timothy Leary in the psychedelic trauma of the '60s. Many of the pioneers in LSD studies, whose work had been shut down by antipsychedelic backlash during that period, harbored manifest animosity toward the former Harvard professor, whose campaign to popularize the drug, they felt, had provoked the repressive attitude. He had strong defenders, though, some of whom had originally been "turned on" by Leary at his Millbrook, New York, estate.

HighWitness News by Peter Stafford and Bruce Eisner, #101, January 1984

JOE COLEMAN

BY COPPER JOHN V

JOE COLEMAN

He entered the stage dressed in ancient priest's robes, and a necklace of human bones, a wrathful messiah about to wreak out an apocalyptic justice. At this point there was an oozing in the audience of primordial fear.

Without any warning the professor smashed a bottle of wine on his head, then began growling and spitting insults at the confused crowd. He called upon the demons that have haunted him from the house on 99 Ward Street. His body twisted, writhed and catapulted around the stage and into the audience, his face contorted in a godless obscenity.

Suddenly, Professor Momboozoo rose again to his feet. Blood was now dripping from his forehead, into his eyes and mouth, the result of the bottle he had crashed into his skull. The professor then pulled out a lighter and ignited the explosives he was wearing beneath his shirt. The explosives went off in a thunderous blaze, scaring away much of the audience.

Joe Coleman: Geek Cartoonist, #102, February 1984

JOHN KEEL: MR. UFO

JK: I was one of the few people who attended the first flying-saucer convention in 1948. They had a convention on 14th Street here in New York, and there were about thirty people there, and I remember it rather well. I can't remember who staged the damn thing, but I do remember that everybody was shouting at everybody else. It was a screaming match, but even in 1948 they'd all decided that the government was withholding information about flying saucers and that something should be done about the air force.

HT: I think from the people I've read, you came the closest to solving it by suggesting the UFOs are not extraterrestrials, but linked to psychic and occult phenomena. By linking the whole sort of tapestry of human history, fairies, elfs, tricksters, you've done a job of looking at it in a different perspective than anyone else has, so to that extent you did succeed.

JK: Well, there are a lot of European books that have been written in which they glorify me and say that I've solved the mystery. Well, I don't feel that I solved it.

Interview by Jim Cusimano and Larry Sloman, #102 and #103, February 1984; March 1984

plants. Several big plants or, in other words, they put a lot of work into the individual plant. In other parts of the world for the most part sinsemilla is not grown. People grow the way they would grow corn or any other field crop. In India maybe they grow them three feet apart, the rows are three feet apart, and spaced out about a foot apart in each row. In Morocco they grow maybe fifteen to twenty to thirty plants per square foot. There it just comes up as a stalk. There have been pictures of it in HIGH TIMES.

HIGH TIMES: What are your feelings about hash?

Rosenthal: Well, hash usually comes from the thirtieth parallel. As HIGH TIMES readers know, the thirtieth parallel has a heterogeneous grouping of plants so that it will survive under a variety of environments, so hash can be very varied. Some people swear by hash, and to them that's it, but me, I much prefer a *sativa*, cannabis.

HIGH TIMES: Why is that? Because of the variable quality of it?

Rosenthal: I think that different varieties of grass give you different highs. "R." talked about that a lot. Those different varieties, those different heads, different people prefer different heads. Although "R" exaggerates it, he is correct that a *sativa* head is like this soaring high, a very psychedelic type of head, and that the Afghanis tend to be more down.

HIGH TIMES: Do you think that's a cultural predisposition? Do you think that most Americans like the get-up-and-go of *sativa*?

Rosenthal: No. I think that most Americans like to be drunk. I think that there are a few individuals who really do like that sort of head, but I think that most Americans like Afghani.

HIGH TIMES: Why isn't hash more popular?

Rosenthal: It's too hard to light and you can't put it in a cigarette. If you put it in a joint you burn your clothes.

HIGH TIMES: Let's backtrack. Let's go back to when you were in college. You said that the second time you smoked pot you immediately started dealing.

Rosenthal: Yeah, the first time I bought a lid, the second time I bought a half-pound.

HIGH TIMES: Was that because you were an entrepreneur? Did you say, "Wow, this is a great way to make money and have fun"?

Rosenthal: I think I felt more like a missionary.

HIGH TIMES: This is around 1966?

Rosenthal: BY 1967 I dropped out of school.

HIGH TIMES: So everything they say about marijuana is true.

Rosenthal: The reason I dropped out of school was because I had gotten my 1-A for the draft, which meant I was prime meat. Then I went to work at a series of straight jobs, like on Wall Street. I had always wanted to work on Wall Street.

HIGH TIMES: Really, why?

Rosenthal: It was fascinating. Here were for sale these things which had no tangible value, except what people wanted to pay for them. They weren't really worth anything. They were only worth what people thought they were worth. So that became a really good, interesting time. I became an assistant compliance officer who takes care of in-house enforcement of the FCC Rules and Regulations. So I was doing that for a while. Then I got fired.

HIGH TIMES: You were an internal cop for Wall Street.

Rosenthal: Yes.

HIGH TIMES: And you were smoking pot at the same time?

Rosenthal: Yes. You've heard of the Stock Exchange, and then there's the over-the-counter market, well, I was running the under-the-counter market. Once my supervisor came in...I mean, I had this brown bag with me and he said, "What's that?" I said, "My lunch." Then he opens it up and sees a plastic bag with pot in it and says, "Don't bring lunch to work."

HIGH TIMES: So you left Wall Street by when?

Rosenthal: 1969. I started making candles. Then somewhere around that time I moved back to the Bronx to a six-room apartment and I started growing dope in one of the rooms. That led via a natural evolution to my sitting here today.

HIGH TIMES: What compelled you to do that?

Rosenthal: When I was a kid I had always wanted to be a plant scientist and a writer. I was really into plants. I used to take classes at the Botanical Gardens and so it was just natural for me to grow these plants if I had the room. So I started growing them and I knew very little about it and there were no books on it. Actually, there were a couple, but one of the books, I don't know if I still have it. It was written by this guy who had given his whole life story. He had been in the army, then he smoked pot, he saw the errors of his ways and got a discharge and was growing pot in his apartment on the Lower East Side and he had filled this whole room with soil and was growing.... All you had to do was put a foot of soil in your room, but I decided to grow it in pots instead.

I had these fluorescent lights and I didn't know about buds, so I was smoking leaf primarily. And this stuff is getting me so high and everybody else who lived in the apartment house was getting high. Everybody was living off my harvesting a few of these leaves every day. I mean, we were really getting wiped out.

HIGH TIMES: But you were supporting yourself with your candles?

Rosenthal: Yes. Then I thought growing was so great, so I cleaned up my room, got rid of the pot and decided to sell greenhouses to grow pot. So that's what I did. I started selling indoor greenhouses for growing marijuana. I would come and install it in your home, everything but the seed.

That was how I met Mel Frank, we were both interviewed by *Rolling Stone* magazine, and we decided to write a book in six weeks about it, and a year later we came up with the book, and that was the *Indoor-Outdoor Marijuana Growers Catalog*, and from then on after the book was published we started taking it more seriously.

HIGH TIMES: What year is this now?

Rosenthal: 1972-'73 we started getting into it. We went down to the University of Mississippi and met Carlton Turner who is now the drug-policy adviser for the federal government. But at that time he was running the Mississippi Project—the dope-farm contract to the government. Turner turned us on to the Mississippi bibliographies of all of the different scientific papers on pot which had been published in the years 1968 to 1972, '74. We bought that. We were able to decide what scientific papers we wanted to read and put together a synthesis of their information and our information and develop some theories about it. From that came the *Growers Guide*.

HIGH TIMES: What kind of guy is Turner?

Rosenthal: New South. He is an example of the soft machine and I think he's way over his head.

HIGH TIMES: What do you mean by "soft machine"?

Rosenthal: Well, it's a fascist mentality clothed in gentle words and seeming reasonableness. I think perhaps the Bill of Rights doesn't mean as much to people in the South.

BOB IS THE DRUG

The Conspiracy *encourages*, BLATANTLY, a useless, empty pattern of social drug abuse in its slaves. The anti-reality sleepdrugs like alcohol and "downs" are *legal*, pretty much, while the "wake-up" drugs are only *available*. You can tell which ones They'd *rather* you take.

There are certain crucial things they don't tell you about their drugs. For instance, did you know that different drugs put your body on different vibrational levels?

The depressants (alcohol, tranquilizers, cough medicine, TV, etc.) make your molecular structure more *dense*, according to their severity. The stimulants (coffee, soda pop, sugar, speed, nicotine, etc.) cause less molecular density. The alcoholic is more "solid"—he feels more invulnerable, and in fact is. The acidhead, however, *is* more "gaseous"—there are vast spaces between his molecules; wotrons and neutrinos pass through him more easily...he may even *feel* them.

The Book of the SubGenius, #101, January 1984

SANDEE BURBANK

Founder of Mothers Against Misuse and Abuse (MAMA), Burbank heads one of the most unique parents organizations in the country.

"Drugs are not for kids. Kids are too young and too immature—no, that's not the word I want. Let's put it like this. When I was growing up we were not allowed to drink coffee because it stunted your growth. You did not smoke cigarettes because children did not smoke cigarettes. You did not use alcohol because children did not use alcohol. And I feel that children should use no drugs at all if at all possible, and that includes aspirin, or any of the other drugs that are out there. If a child gets a temperature, parents will give him drugs, because children are supposed to have this perfect temperature all the time. I have a lot of problems with the drug use that I see occurring with our kids, not just illicit drug use but legal drug use as well. You know, we program our kids to take drugs for every little bitty thing that bothers them, from the time they're babies on. Then, when it comes to recreational drugs—alcohol, I guess tobacco would have to fall into that category, marijuana and illicit drugs— they're already programmed into the system of relieving every anxiety or pain with a drug."

Interview by Bob LaBrasca, #104, April 1984

WHAT TO FEED YOUR PLANTS

HIGH TIMES

JUNE 1984 — USA $3.25

TENTH ANNIVERSARY ISSUE

THE GOSPEL ACCORDING TO TOM

This interview was conducted by Tom's wife, Gabrielle, the very week before his tragic death.

HT: If you had to state your occupation in a couple of words, what would you call yourself?

TF: A social architect. I have to take mega concepts and make them work in mass and in macro scale.

HT: Do you sometimes worry about going to jail for some of the things you've stood up for?

TF: Effectively, I've already spent the last ten years in jail—I've been under such close surveillance. My only real crime is not agreeing with the straight media. I think that *Tass* and *Pravda* in Russia are probably as independent as *Time* and *Newsweek*, *The New York Times*, the *Washington Post* and CBS. In the past twenty years the media has been bought up and has become a subsidiary of big business. There is no media self-criticism in this country. The result is inevitable. What we read here is tightly controlled. Therefore, Americans are very provincial and have little idea what's really going on in the world.

HT: What was HIGH TIMES like in the old days?

TF: First, there was just me and Ed Dwyer, who is an able writer and editor. We were usually so wiped out we could barely crawl up to put our hands on the keyboard of our typewriters. That went on about four months and then I hired six or seven other people. Then I got this weird fellow named Michael Gibbons, who was a systems analyst, to become publisher, and he managed to bring order out of chaos. We always manage to stay high and come out on time. It's an efficient worklike office, but there is room for creativity in it. There's not too much pressure and that's healthy.

Flashes by Gabrielle Schang-Forçade, #106, June 1984

HIGH TIMES: Do you think they're like Anslingerarian-type wolves in sheep's clothing? Do you think there is a continuity?

Rosenthal: Yes, I think that even though individual members in this group may not be bigoted, I think there are certain key words and code words which are really words that bigots recognize. Just the same way that every Republican presidential candidate always makes some nasty antiblack slip—it's just to let the bigots know they're with 'em—it's no slip at all. They have these code words and people understand them, and I think that their real feeling is that there are certain people that are undesirable. Like pieces of shit that won't flush down the toilet. These people that we need laws to control, and whatever laws we need to control these people and this mentality we'll use. That's how the drug laws came to be and that's how they still exist. Most HIGH TIMES readers are classed in that category. Even if they stopped smoking pot the government wouldn't like them because of the way they think. They are independents, they are unwilling to be wards of the state.

HIGH TIMES: What happened to the psychedelic revolution?

Rosenthal: It's still going on, it's just not going on in the big cities because the rents are too high. More acid, more mushrooms are sold every year than ever before.

HIGH TIMES: Do you see marijuana as effecting change in people's attitudes or has it just become a totally hedonistic thing?

Rosenthal: I think that people are still changing through pot and we don't even realize that, as we look back at changes over the last thirty years, our society has changed tremendously. Twenty years ago an unmarried woman and an unmarried man, even if they were just roommates, people would talk.

HIGH TIMES: What is the most overrated pot you ever smoked?

Rosenthal: I think a lot of the early Mexicans were overrated.

HIGH TIMES: You mean stuff like Acapulco Gold.

Rosenthal: A lot of them are overrated. Then there's the "mystery pot"—I never actually had Panama Red. After all these years we've heard about it, how many people have actually smoked Panama Red? It's a fable to me. I'd like to see it.

HIGH TIMES: What pot gave you the best for your potsmoking dollar?

Rosenthal: Wacky Weed. The fabled New York Wacky Weed. Boy, that stuff sure was psychedelic. I wish I had some seed.

HIGH TIMES: Do you ever smoke any commercial?

Rosenthal: I don't like the Colombians coming in now so I don't smoke them. But I smoke some of the new Mexican and Mexican sinses and they are very reasonably priced. Colombian has a real problem. The quality of the pot is going down. They don't really seem to care.

HIGH TIMES: Do you talk to your marijuana plants?

Rosenthal: It's illegal to cultivate plants in California but I will say this, they're more fun to grow than tomatoes.

HIGH TIMES: Is there any degree of spiritual communion between you and your plants?

Rosenthal: Sometimes I think that maybe I'm an agent of the marijuana plant come here to help run the world. I have thought that.

HIGH TIMES: There he goes. When you talk to your plants do you feel any communion? Do you think plants have a consciousness?

Rosenthal: No. I don't think that plants have the kind of learning ability or the genetic ability to express themselves the way we do. I don't think talking to a plant or playing it music is gonna help.

HIGH TIMES: You don't.

Rosenthal: I do think proper nutritional health is important.

HIGH TIMES: And you don't think along the lines of some of the Rastafarians or some of the more mystical thinkers—that God puts plants here for the spiritual enlightenment of man?

Rosenthal: Well, let me tell you a few things about cannabis. To many groups of people cannabis was the plant that helped them make the transition from a herding, nomadic society to an agricultural society, and that's still going on today. The pygmies grow only one plant, cannabis, and with that plant they made the transition from a nomadic society to an agricultural society, so this tends to be re-played many, many times.

HIGH TIMES: In what way? I don't understand.

Rosenthal: Well, in a nomadic society you just travel all over. Well, if you start planting something, then you have to start caring for it, right?

HIGH TIMES: So why do they plant? What's the motivation?

Rosenthal: They sell it. They smoke it and they sell it to the other tribes.

HIGH TIMES: You're out of your mind. Have you ever bought pot from a pygmy?

Rosenthal: No, I've never been there.

HIGH TIMES: Let's talk about marijuana activism. The political side of Ed.

Rosenthal: Well, I'll tell you how it started. I was vacationing in Florida in 1971 and I met these college kids who were making bongs, and they made a bong for me as a going-away gift. We had all tripped the night before on this acid and it was really incredible—very beautiful, so they gave me this bong and we smoked one toke each out of it and started hitchhiking back to New York City and got busted in Bowling Green, Virginia, for hitchhiking. And then they open my suitcase and find this bong and they busted me for residue and a pipe. It cost me $500 and two trips back to Virginia. I'm sure that if it weren't for that I wouldn't have had any interaction with the law.

HIGH TIMES: That was a real radicalizing experience.

Rosenthal: Yes.

HIGH TIMES: Were you brutalized by the police?

Rosenthal: No, but at the end the cop wanted to shake my hand, after the trial. You know, "No hard feelings, son," and I said, "You're a pig."

Right in that time frame NORML had its first conference, which was the first people's pot conference, and this was the only real...legitimate activist conference. It was great. It was held in the basement of a church and people were camping out. I had been asked to come down and give a speech on cultivation.

HIGH TIMES: By who?

Rosenthal: Keith Stroup.

HIGH TIMES: This was before your book came out.

Rosenthal: It was before the book, but while I was making indoor greenhouses.

HIGH TIMES: That's how Stroup had heard of you?

Rosenthal: Yes, I had been in *Rolling Stone*, so I went down there and then I met Mike Aldrich at the conference and he said, "Come out to California, we're having a '72 initiative." So I decided to go to California. At this conference I made a speech on marijuana cultivation and it was very, very well accepted and I knew from that that people were into it. By this time we were still working on the book. I went out to California to work on the initiative.

HIGH TIMES: Through the years you have been known as a gadfly in the marijuana movement. You've had great disagreements with NORML and the marijuana establishment. Can you briefly highlight some of

THE FORÇADE BE WITH YOU

Tom also actively engaged himself in the Yippie movement. With his love of guerrilla theater and media shock tactics it was a natural preserve for him. But he quickly fell out with the reigning hierarchy—Jerry Rubin, Abbie Hoffman and their followers—and formed his own splinter party, the Zippies.

The Zippies, mainly Forçade and a handful of dedicated, hardcore followers, denounced the Rubin/Hoffman nexus as "dinosaurs" and "sellouts," and Tom ferreted out and published the information that Hoffman, Rubin and Ed Sanders had received $30,000 for their book, *Vote*. At the same time the Zippies endorsed Democrat George McGovern for president. The Yippies, traditionally opposed to all candidates, preferred to vote with their feet. They saw the endorsement as a betrayal of principle. At the 1972 Republican National Convention in Miami the confrontation between the two factions came to a head.

The Zippies clearly outclassed the Yippies in creative, imaginative protests. At one point Forçade managed to steal a 20-foot portrait of Lyndon Johnson from the convention hall and the Zippies paraded up and down Collins Avenue displaying it. As a result of such bravado, Tom and his girlfriend Cindy Ornstein were busted on a phony firebombing rap at the end of the convention, though the case was soon dropped. Following the convention Rubin and Hoffman publicly resigned from the Yippies.

It was at the convention that the idea of HIGH TIMES was born. There have been many explanations as to how the bizarre scheme was hatched, many of them fostered by Forçade's flair for inventing history. He was fond of telling people the magazine was simply the product of a nitrous-oxide vision. In fact, the concept for HIGH TIMES was based on a much more specific inspiration: the short-lived but ferociously successful Pot People's Party.

The Pot People's Party was an ad hoc group that organized for the Miami convention and set up headquarters under a huge eucalyptus tree in Flamingo Park. At the demonstrators' campsite, where a number of Left groups were ensconced—Vietnam Vets Against the War, National Welfare Rights Organization, etc.—the PPP consistently drew the largest crowd. This wasn't lost on Forçade.

"When I saw that huge crowd under the eucalyptus tree," Forçade would later recall, "I saw the politics of the '70s."

Trans-High Market Analysis by Bud Bogart, #106, June 1984

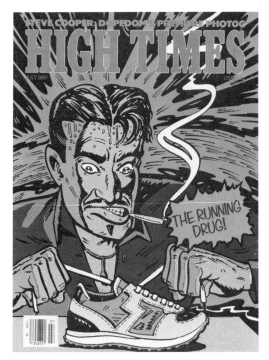

I GOT A NEW DRUG

BY "R."

I want to tell you about a new drug. A fabulous drug, better than grass. It costs practically nothing; gets you higher than Colombian Gold in a profound, lasting way; doesn't give you a hangover the next day. And best of all—it's legal.

The drug is called "beta-endorphin." You get it, free, from your own body, simply by running half an hour a day at least five times a week. Think of it: That's a mere 150 minutes—you spend at least that much time on the phone trying to reach your dealer....

In fact, I think historians of our era will come to recognize that the suburban-fitness, jogging craze was, in fact, a drug-addictive phenomenon. All the Yuppies out there becoming as addicted to their own internal morphine as the urban junkies (the Juppies) are to street heroin. And how all of it is part of a deeper phenomenon—the desire to be in touch with the undistorted precivilized high of natural man.

#107, July 1984

CAPT. WHIZZO

your disagreements?

Rosenthal: First of all, I wouldn't call NORML the marijuana establishment; I think they're not really in the center at all.

HIGH TIMES: What do you think of Stroup?

Rosenthal: I think that he started an organization, and in order to keep control of it, because it was getting successful, he decided to sacrifice the organization for himself, and in other words, they needed professional people in there but they had never gotten professional organizers to do anything. They have amateurs and then they train them and then they go on. Same as the Yippies do, and they never really tried to make it into a mass-movement organization.

HIGH TIMES: I don't think they ever wanted it to be a mass-movement organization.

Rosenthal: The problem is that they never had a clear definition and they still don't know what they want. That's NORML's main problem. They want to be all things to all people. They can't be.

HIGH TIMES: Doesn't NORML serve now as a way to educate drug lawyers?

Rosenthal: Well, it does do that, that's one very important role, and also it does a lot of trial work against these laws, especially paraquat. But in terms of actually doing activist legislative work, it's not doing anything.

HIGH TIMES: But was that their intent?

Rosenthal: I think the original intent was to be in Washington to lobby at Congress. What they got was that nobody is going to listen to lobbiers unless they have one of two things—money or votes. And you don't have votes unless you have membership. And that's one instance where the NRA, the National Rifle Association, is so effective. They have millions of members.

HIGH TIMES: Yes, but hasn't there in fact been just a kind of a co-optation of millions of smokers in all of this de facto legalization where the government then is able to use the marijuana laws more selectively? Most people don't get busted. Most people can smoke marijuana and not feel that threatened now. People are busted for other reasons.

Rosenthal: Well, that's true. It is true that most people who smoke marijuana really aren't threatened. Except that the government is trying to change that—make no mistake about it. Under the Reagan administration we've had a real change in attitude. The percentage of drug arrests for marijuana has skyrocketed. And also they are trying, you know...like they are saying that they are trying to get urine testing in the workplace, so that if you smoked marijuana last night, you are going to show a positive the next day. So I think that pot smokers today are under greater and greater pressure.

HIGH TIMES: How about the future of marijuana referendums?

Rosenthal: Well, in California we couldn't even pass a return-bottle bill, so I think it would be very difficult.

HIGH TIMES: What do you see in terms of the issue of legalization?

Rosenthal: One possibility—I think that NORML, and the marijuana movement in general, has to align itself and make itself known as a human-rights movement, part of that broad coalition of environmentalists, gays, minority groups and so on. And when that... when the issue gets recognized that way, then it's going to rise and fall with the other issues. That's one scenario that I see.

Another scenario I see is a basic break in world politics, which will affect the United States. Spain has legalized possession, and I think that Italy is pretty far along. I think that some of the African countries are gonna break it, and I think that India is going to unilaterally break it. Or there is a good possibility of those countries breaking it. And I think that the world...there is going to be a new polarization based on that.

HIGH TIMES: Breaking with the Single Convention Treaty?

Rosenthal: And the United States and Britain, for instance, might go far out on a limb and get real right wing about it, especially under Reagan, and I think that what ultimately the government has in mind is rehabilitation, and for chronic users, maybe something worse.

HIGH TIMES: You are an advocate of marijuana and it's an ally of yours. Do you see any dangers to marijuana use?

Rosenthal: Yeah. You know, I don't think that marijuana is totally harmless. It changes the liver and metabolism slightly. And pot smoke does do damage to your lungs.

HIGH TIMES: How about the whole notion of a-motivational syndrome?

Rosenthal: Well, I don't have it. I smoke a lot and I don't have it.

HIGH TIMES: How much do you smoke?

Rosenthal: Depends. You know, the better the dope is, the more you smoke.

HIGH TIMES: On the average?

Rosenthal: Between a quarter- and a half-ounce.

HIGH TIMES: A day?

Rosenthal: No, a week.

HIGH TIMES: Every day. But every day? Do you smoke every day?

Rosenthal: Yes. Only when I'm living.

HIGH TIMES: Ed, you have a new son. When your son grows up, when he's maybe about twelve or thirteen years old and he starts asking about pot—what will you tell him about it?

Rosenthal: Well, he'll probably ask a lot before twelve or thirteen.

HIGH TIMES: All right, let's assume he can start speaking. And his first words are "pot, pot."

Rosenthal: I think the problem with pot and kids these days is that it's such an illicit thing that it makes it more attractive to them, and they tend to overdo it a little because of that. But I think I would rather see kids using pot than alcohol.

HIGH TIMES: Do you have any friends that you think are better off without pot? Do you ever say to yourself, "Hey, I've been smoking too much lately"?

Rosenthal: Yes. And I cut down sometimes. I have also gone without pot for extended periods.

HIGH TIMES: How long?

Rosenthal: I went to Mexico for three weeks, a year ago, and I didn't smoke anything.

HIGH TIMES: You are doing a regular "Ask Ed" column for us. What's the single most common question that people ask you?

Rosenthal: "How can I tell a male from a female?"

HIGH TIMES: And how do you answer it—by pulling down their plants, ha-ha.

Rosenthal: Buy a *Growers Guide*. The pictures are right in the *Growers Guide*.

HIGH TIMES: You've just completed a Special Cultivation issue for us. What're the estimates on the number of people cultivating?

Rosenthal: Well, I have an interesting way of looking at it. You notice how many ads for cultivation equipment there are in HIGH TIMES every month over the past five years. And you realize how much those ads cost and how many lights have to be sold just to pay for the ad. And then you realize that there are a lot of people out there cultivating. And there are

RICHARD BELZER

I used to go onstage every night. I'd be fucked out of my mind on drugs that you guys can't pronounce. Okay? I've done everything. And things have done me. I've gone onstage using every type of drug and I've embarrassed myself; I've been great; I've been okay; I've given every level of performance on drugs.

And then I stopped using drugs. Not totally, but to go onstage with. I was on the road with Warren Zevon, touring, opening up for him in these clubs all over. And every night before we went on, you know, it was like "Get out the shovel."

He introduced me to Stolichnaya, by the way. So, we'd be drinking Stoli from the bottle and doing coke like, you know, Jimi Hendrix's nephews, and before I went on I had to have that, you know [snorting], and I just felt I had to do it. And one night we were late. the bus was late and for whatever reason, I had to go on straight. God forbid I should go on straight.

And I had this moment: I said, "Wait a minute. I'm funny. I'm not high. Okay."

So I went on and I fucking killed. And it just taught me a little lesson. Because since I first started, I always had to have a couple of drinks, I always had to do something before I went on. First it was drinking. Then it got to be pot. Then it got to be coke. There were nights onstage I was on heroin. There were nights onstage on every fucking drug known to man.

Interview by George Barkin and Larry Sloman, #107, July 1984

REPORT FROM THE FRONT

BY GENE WHEELWRIGHT

On a recent whirlwind tour through the nearer reaches of northern California, we found that hard times had fallen on our grower friends of the region, and that drastic new strategies for coping with the law were being devised.

The forces of oppression have redoubled their efforts this year and are coming on heavy—thanks to the billion-dollar subsidization by the Reagan administration's DEA in Washington and its subordinate bootlickers in Sacramento. Recruiting primarily Southern California police officers for the federal-state-local task force known as CAMP (Campaign Against Marijuana Planting), the big boys are turning up the heat on the marijuana economy by hiring the more fervent antidrug zealots. Well-armed and uniformed, and often with long hair to match their camouflage fatigues, these right-wing commandoes (politically akin to Ronnie's "freedom fighters" in Nicaragua) have been landing in helicopters, leaping from four-wheel-drive trucks and jeeps, and outraging the citizenry up and down the state.

Trans-High Market Analysis, #113, January 1985

thousands of people buying lights every month.

HIGH TIMES: How do you see the marijuana-growing industry changing in the next ten, fifteen or twenty years? Do you think it's all going to become indoor growth? Assuming that the status of its illegality remains unchanged.

Rosenthal: More and more people will grow indoors.

HIGH TIMES: Can you get as good a product indoors?

Rosenthal: I am glad you brought that up. In most parts of the United States I think the indoors is better. Your own homegrown is better than any commercial because commercial growers have a different interest in mind than homegrowers. The commercial growers' interest is to put out as much product as possible over the shortest period of time. Homegrowers are growing for a different reason. They are growing to get the best. They grow to get their own stash. So they have a different motivation, they don't necessarily want to have the most quantity or the best yields or the earliest plants. In other words, a commercial grower might be able to have 120-day turnaround, while the homegrower might be going on 150 to 180 days.

In order to get the really true connoisseur grades, you know, the sinsemilla Colombian hybrid or a sinsemilla Thai or most of the Africans—those plants take longer than the Afghanis and the Kushes. So I see more people growing indoors and I think more and more people are going to say, "I don't want this Afghani."

HIGH TIMES: What's the story on *ruderalis*? Is there really any in the United States?

Rosenthal: I haven't seen it, and Shultes described a short plant with low branches...eighteen to twenty-four inches high with no THC in it. That wouldn't be a pleasant smoke.

HIGH TIMES: But wouldn't it be possible for commercial growers to hybridize it because its life cycle is over in ten weeks?

Rosenthal: If you were able to hybridize some hotshot *indica* with *ruderalis* it would theoretically bring in a crop in a few months or so. Well, I have dealt with Moroccan weed. And that comes in in late August.

HIGH TIMES: Remember the *Rolling Stone* article about a year ago that talked about a whole generation who smoked in the late '60s and now we're in the '80s and they have stopped smoking. You are somebody who started smoking in the '60s and then continued smoking to this day. Was that hype or do you think that there was a significant drop, and why?

Rosenthal: Well, I think there are a lot of exploitive articles about the '60s generation. For instance, I found out why the guy killed himself in *The Big Chill*. It was because he couldn't stand his friends anymore.

And the reason why that woman in *Rolling Stone* doesn't smoke is because she's not getting good stuff, and the reason she's not getting good stuff is...well, I don't want to get into that. But I presume that that's part of it. But I think that drug use naturally slows down as people hit middle age.

HIGH TIMES: Do you see the day, or do you ever foresee the day that you might just stop smoking? Outgrow it?

Rosenthal: I don't know, anything could happen. I haven't got religion yet.

HIGH TIMES: Have you been thinking about religion?

Rosenthal: I have been. I've been thinking lately about life and death. Do you go to heaven or hell or is it more complex than that. But I'll tell you, when I die, I just want to be compost. Then I'll be happy for eternity.

CLONING FOR SEX

by Jorge Cervantes

In August marijuana shows several signs of sexual differentiation. Male plants usually grow tall and lanky while females grow denser with shorter spaces between the sets of leaves. Sometimes there are a few premature flowers at the joint of the leaf and stem, between the eighth and twelfth internode. The male flower is about 1/16" to 1/8" long and looks like a ball on the stem. The females have two antennae protruding from an elliptical base, and no stem. If you are growing Afghani, kush or *indicas*, the sex should be evident by now.

Flowering is triggered by the photo-period. Plants that receive 18 hours or more of light a day will remain in the vegetative growth stage. If the ratio is changed to 12 hours each of light and darkness, the plants will think it is fall and start to bloom.

Marijuana is dioecious: It has either male or female flowers. Occasionally a hermaphrodite develops. "Herms" have both male and female flowers. Most gardeners remove them from the garden because they may pollinate the other plants.

If the young adult plants have not shown their sex by this time, there is an easy way to tell who's who: "Cloning for Sex." There are many ways to tell the sex of a plant, but few are as certain, basic and simple as Cloning for Sex. The beauty of this method is that anybody can do it, without altering the life cycle of the "parent" or "donor" plant. One commonly used sexing method makes the parent start flowering by giving it 12 hours of darkness per night. With Cloning for Sex, the parent plant is allowed to grow continually under "normal" conditions. It does not have to flower and then revert back to vegetative growth, which takes about six weeks, mutates growth and diminishes harvest.

Why do people grow clones or cuttings indoors? Reasons: safety, yield, quality and growing time are just some. (For more about clones see: HIGH TIMES, "Cuttings," by Ed Rosenthal, Feb. '82 and "Better Smoking Through Cloning," by Robert Connell Clarke, Jan. '81.) With an indoor crop, using clones and a 1000-watt "super" halide, the horticulturist is able to grow a room full of females, beginning to end, in less than four months. This translates from an investment of $300-$500, depending on the cost of electricity and your indoor needs, to a harvest of 8 to 38 ounces of dried, primo, sinsemilla tops, depending on your level of expertise and care. This harvest may be taken three to four times a year, regardless of what the weatherman says! In fact, clones may be taken from clones for "generations" with no genetic breakdown. You may never want to go back to seeds again!

To Clone for Sex, take two cuttings from each parent in question. Two clones are taken in the event that one dies. (See Step-by-Step instructions on how to take clones.) Make sure to label each clone and corresponding parent plant when sexing more than one, and always use waterproof labels.

When rooting, give clones only 12 hours of light by placing a cardboard box over them each night or by simply placing them in a dark cabinet, drawer or closet. The 12 hours of "uninterrupted total

KENNY SCHARF

KENNY SCHARF

"Every day I'd collect junk in the street, paint it flourescent and put it in the closet. I never painted on mushrooms and I don't do them anymore, but I really got a lot of inspiration from them. On the ceiling I painted a fluorescent blue and orange spiral. I used to take mushrooms, lie on my back and stare at the spiral until it slowly dropped from the ceiling. I'd leave my body, go inside the spiral and float around in endless space. After that, I always stared at the spiral when I took mushrooms."
Mutants From Outer Space by Steven Hager, #114, February 1985

ACID DREAMS

The bad rap on acid was sensationalized in the establishment press, which had been focusing on the detrimental effects of LSD since the Harvard scandal. Typical scare headlines from the mid-1960s read: "Girl, 5, Eats LSD and Goes Wild"…"A Monster in Our Midst—A Drug Called LSD"…"Thrill Drug Warps Mind, Kills." In March 1966 *Life* magazine ran a front-page spread entitled "LSD: The Exploding Threat of the Mind Drug That Got Out of Control," which described the psychedelic experience as chemical Russian roulette in which the player gambled with his sanity. Pictures of people on acid cowering in corners, beyond communication, were used to underscore the message that LSD "could be a one-way trip to an asylum, prison or grave." *Life*, whose publisher, Henry Luce, had once spoken favorably of psychedelics, didn't pull any punches: "A person…can become permanently deranged through a single terrifying LSD experience. Hospitals report case after case where people arrive in a state of mental disorganization, unable to distinguish their bodies from their surroundings…it brings out the very worst in some people."
by Martin A. Lee and Bruce Shlain, #128, April 1986

BILL BURROUGHS

All writing is autobiographical in a sense. All novels are autobiography and also, all novels are fiction at the same time. So many people thought that Jack Kerouac was writing straight autobiography. He wasn't at all, he was writing fiction. *On the Road* could not possibly be written now any more than *The Great Gatsby* could be written now. A book is as much context as anything else. Besides which, the present is very much influenced by *On the Road*. Time is everything.
Interview by John Howell, #115, March 1985

TV EVANGELISTS

BY ANN MAGNUSON

In fact, much of Christian TV is dazzling to watch. For these ministries are tailor-made for your Sony Trinitron, the altar for the New Church of Immaculate Reception. Day of Discovery with Paul van Gorder comes to us from the Hallmark greeting-card idyll of Cypress Gardens, America's very own Garden of Eden. From this acrylic Xanadu, bland hymns are sung by a consciously racially-mixed chorus dressed in three-piece sky-blue polyester suits and conservatively cut bridal gowns of flowing pastel chiffon. Carefully arranged on meticulously manicured lawns or around mini-Monticello gazebos, the choristers roam amidst the many fountains and purple hyacinths, highlighted by dissolves to spectacular cloud formations, waterfalls, lush oases, sunrises and sunsets superimposed on glowing crucifixes, giant Bibles, happy homes, superhighways, marching bands, frolicking fawns and whooping cranes. One wonders, if Leni Riefenstahl were directing today...
TV's Electronic Evangelists, #124, December 1985

darkness" is the actual signal for marijuana to flower. If they do not get 12 hours of uninterrupted darkness they may not flower. The clones *must* be light-tight at night! If this creates heat buildup, move the box to a cooler location for the evening to prevent wilt. *Note:* Clones will flower whether or not they have roots! However, the stronger the root system, the more pronounced and stronger the flowers.

During the day, the tender little clones may be placed in a sunny southern window, on a patio, under a halide or HP (high pressure) sodium lamp. For best results, place the clones under an HID (High Intensity Discharge) lamp or in natural sunlight; this will promote rapid flower formation. Heat build-up may become a problem if clones are placed too close (less than three feet) to the HID. Most growers place the clones in the subdued light behind older plants, a foot or more away from the HID. Heat will dry the soil out rapidly if there is no humidity tent over the clones, and the little cuttings will therefore quickly dry up, get stunted or die from the lack of moisture. However, with a humidity tent, moisture condensation may become a problem. This is remedied by setting the clones up off the floor on blocks so that the soil underneath is able to "breathe." Very High Output (VHO) fluorescent lamps work fairly well when Cloning for Sex, and the less luminous "standards" also can be used.

The clones will show their sex in 5 to 15 days. The earliest way to detect this is by using a small magnifying glass. Simply match the labels of the clones with the corresponding parents to decipher males from females. The little clones that were sexed as females make excellent early smoke, and if they *are* smoked, gardeners will be less likely to steal leaves or undeveloped foliage from plants still in the vegetative stage. Remember, leaves are the food factories of a plant—they are necessary for a healthy crop!

Now that you know the boys from the girls, take your cuttings from the best female plants. Which females will give the best clones? The females selected should have fast, squat, bushy growth with early, sustained, high THC potency. Clones will be exact replicas of the female they are taken from. Cannabis *indica* usually has all of these characteristics and is the favorite of most indoor growers. The bushier and healthier the outdoor female, the more clones she can produce.

Before a branch can grow roots from the stem, some very important changes must take place. First, the stem must stop green vegetative growth; then, undifferentiated growth or cells must form on the subterranean stem. Undifferentiated cells must form before roots are able to grow. The "mother's" lower, slow-growing branches have less nitrogen and a higher carbohydrate (starch) content than the upper branches. Nitrogen promotes green leafy growth while a high carbohydrate content promotes undifferentiated growth. These are the branches to consider first when taking clones. However, stay away from weak or sickly branches; they tend to root slower.

CLONING, STEP BY STEP

(1) With a sharp blade (do not use scissors), take cuttings from firm healthy branches about 1/8" to 1/4" in diameter and 2" to 8" in length. Trim off one to three sets of leaves and buds (nodes) so the stem can fit in the soil. *Immediately* place the little clones in fresh water after cutting and stripping lower leaves off.

(2) Fill containers with coarse, washed sand, fine vermiculite or

soilless mix, and water until saturated. Use a pencil to make holes in the rooting medium a little larger than the stem. If this is your first time cloning, it will probably be easiest to use peat pots or rooting cubes.

(3) Many growers prefer to use a rooting hormone and they get a better "stick" rate than those who do not. Almost all rooting hormones contain a fungicide. A fungicide is very important for clones because they grow best in a humid environment that promotes fungi. Some of the most common brands are: Hormex, Rootone-F, Hormodin and Superthrive. Swirl the cutting(s) in the diluted liquid hormone for ten seconds, or dip the stem in powder hormones. Place the cuttings in the hole in the rooting medium. Pack it gently but firmly around the stem.

(4) If Cloning for Sex, give plants 12 hours of natural sunlight or halide light. Make sure they get 12 hours of uninterrupted total darkness. If cloning known females, give them 18 hours of fluorescent light to ensure vegetative growth.

(5) Place a humidity tent over rooting clones to keep the humidity high at 80+ degrees. The tent may be constructed of anything transparent. The tent helps retain moisture since there are no roots to supply the leaves with water. Soil surface should be kept evenly moist. Watering may only be necessary once or twice when using the tent.

(6) The humidity tent should maintain a temperature of between 70 and 80 degrees. If the temperature should fall below this level, rooting will be slower, and if much warmer, it might kill the plants.

(7) Some of the cuttings might wilt for up to three days, which is normal. If they wilt for over a week, clones will be stunted or die and should be yanked.

(8) In two to four weeks, the cuttings should be rooted. The tips of the leaves will turn yellow, roots may be seen growing out drain holes, and clones will start vertical growth.

(9) Transplant rooted clones into 5-gallon pots or set in a hydroponic unit.

If the little clones get a competitive edge at an early stage in life, they will maintain it throughout life. Likewise, if they get off to a slow start, they may never catch up! It is superimportant to keep them healthy and growing fast at all times.

It is easy to maintain clones by making sure all the basic needs, especially heat and humidity, are met. But if you are not into just maintaining the little clones, and want to give them a head start on the world, use the proper fluorescent. One of the ways to maintain this competitive edge is to root clones under the brightest fluorescent, with the best spectrum possible. Fluorescents that are VHO produce about two and a half times as many lumens and use three times the amount of electricity as the standards. Combine "warm white" and "cool white" VHO tubes to get a very bright, cool lamp for rooting clones. *Note:* The warm white and cool white must be used together to get the proper spectrum. Using two 4-foot VHO tubes, a total of 215 watts is available. Another lamp that is very popular and works extremely well is marketed under the name "Vita-Lite."

VICESTYLES OF THE RICH AND FAMOUS

BY DAVID HARRISON

One of the longest-running dope tales has been the one involving Stacy Keach, best known as TV's Mike Hammer (although we remember him most fondly as the drug-crazed narc Sgt. Stedenko in two Cheech & Chong flicks). Keach was busted at a London airport attempting to smuggle 1.3 ounces of coke into England and was sentenced to nine months' hard time in a British prison. While in the slam, Keach promised to give *mea culpa* antidope speeches in England and the US once he was released. But when he got out after serving six months, Keach took off on vacation, snubbing the House of Lords and copping out on his stateside lectures as well.

Yet another TV personality whose drug involvement made headlines was Dan Haggerty, one-time second banana to a bear on *Grizzly Adams*. Rumored to be heavily into freebasing, Haggerty allegedly sold less than three-quarters of an ounce of blow to undercover narcs. The narcs were part of a six-man "entertainment squad" formed by the Los Angeles Police Department to entrap celebrity dopers. (Now *there's* a total waste of taxpayers' money.) Haggerty was convicted on one count of sales, but the jury acquitted him on the other count by reason of entrapment. As for the "entertainment squad," it has busted no other big-name stars but continues to squander valuable police man-hours in the attempt. According to Richard Szabo, head of the squad, "We decided, hey, we have to do something about these people living in the fast lane and making it look glamorous."

#120, August 1985

MILTON KNIGHT

SOLO SILO

My neighbors on both sides of me are narcs. My wife and dog have left me to join a Right Wing nudity cult. I live in a missile silo as far away from the 2-D conservative world as possible and my only salvation is the slot I have cut in the ceiling of my bunker through which current copies of HIGH TIMES are shoved by passersby who know it is best for everyone concerned if I am kept underground and occupied.

B. Lowe Sealevel
Minister of Sanity
Elkbladder, Montana

Letters, #134 , October 1986

GROW LIGHTS

BY FARMER IN THE SKY

There is much statistical evidence to suggest a causal relationship between high UV levels found at higher altitudes and high THC content in the pot grown there.

If you have a multi-light grow room, you should place UV fluorescents in the space between grow-light reflectors, as well as around the edge. The UV fluorescent reflectors around the edge should be relatively deep with a sharper angle, and direct the light horizontally toward the plants; while the ones in the middle should be shallower, and direct the light downward at various angles and horizontally.

The UV-B light should only be used the last two to four weeks of budding, because of its harmful effect on plant growth.

Other stressful conditions can also increase THC or other flavinoid-compound production. Too much stress, however, will too-greatly reduce plant growth or yield.

#126, February 1986

CRACKDOWN: A GROWER SPEAKS OUT
by William Meyers

Look at a relief map of California, and you can clearly see the long, almost preternaturally straight line of the San Andreas earthquake fault, rising somewhere east of Los Angeles in the Mojave Desert and slicing northwestward for hundreds of miles through the mountains of the Coast Range. The faultline transects the San Francisco and Marin peninsulas, whose point of closest approach forms the Golden Gate; then continues its unvarying course through the Olema Valley, up the Sonoma County coast, and at Point Arena, passes out to sea. Only after another 110 submarine miles does it visibly emerge again, at Cape Mendocino—the westernmost point of California—before disappearing into the northern Pacific.

It's estimated that the earth has been in upheaval along this major fracture zone—where the two geological plates of the Pacific basin and the North American continent are in frictional collision—for at least 20 million years. The tremors from the constant "creep" of an inch and a half a year can be felt, to some degree, every day. The strain is always cumulative, and, at varying but theoretically predictable intervals, it's released suddenly and violently. In 1857, fissures as long as 40 miles opened up, and the earth was displaced in places (the Pacific side moved northward) by as much as 30 feet. In 1906, half the city of San Francisco was destroyed by such an earthquake.

In 1982, just before dawn, a large tremor emanating from that dark canyon in the ocean between Point Arena and Cape Mendocino and west of the coastal King Range, could be felt throughout Humboldt County. South of Eureka, a freeway overpass collapsed, blocking whatever traffic there was on U.S. 101.

High atop the King Range, and asleep in bed, the Sinsemilla Farmer and his wife were awakened by the sound of rocks rolling down the hillside, and the entire frame of the house around them creaking and popping in a most unsettling way. Thinking only of the massive foundation they had laid under their house and whether or not the whole thing might be sliding, the Farmer and his wife clung to each other until the force over which they knew they had absolutely no control subsided at last, and the deep subterranean rumble lapsed into quiet.

That was his peak year, the Sinsemilla Farmer now realizes—the year he sold 35 pounds of manicured buds out the front door, at $1,600 to $2,000 a pound, and made enough to have achieved an independent income from growing high-grade marijuana—if that had been his aim. It was the year he and his wife were able to afford to open the organic garden-supply store down in the town of Manzanita as an investment in their not-so-certain future. Things were going so well for a while that they put some of their money into another piece of land, for leasing out to a sharecropper friend, and even rented a house in Mexico for chilling out over the rainy winter months.

Here, in the large living room of their mountaintop house and during the height of the growing season, they'd hired a bunch of migrant manicurists to clip and trim the pungent product at an hourly wage that was better than anything they could find in town. Even the people most vehemently against pot had to admit that, with the Farmers' garden-supply store, their two pieces of property on either side of the county with the taxes they paid on them, and the number of people they had helped to support with their wages and their business, they'd made a pretty fair contribution to the local economy.

And now? In April of 1985—everything is changed. The bright living room seems more spacious without the drying plants hanging from the ceiling and the mounds of buds among the manicurists on the floor. Everything is comfortably and immaculately furnished now in late-hippie, down-home décor. The radio quietly cooks with a program of pop music of past decades that, at this altitude, you can tune in from Fort Bragg, 100 miles down the coast. And we sit, drinking the Farmers' favorite wine, from a winery a few ridges over, watching the sun go down in splendor behind a distant, roseate bank of Pacific Ocean fog.

We have just climbed up an incredibly steep slope, which, having been logged before the Farmer bought his land, gives his house its year-round, panoramic view, of both sunrise and sunset. We've seen his self-sufficient energy set-up, with the methane generator down the hill by the outhouse, the windmill on the hilltop and the photovoltaic solar panels on the roof supplying all the good-karma electrical energy they could ever need. And we've noticed that, even now in early spring, the vegetable garden behind the house is looking juicy and luxuriant from the Sinsemilla Farmer's customary magic touch with growing things.

But the plants of utmost interest—this year's *cannabis indica* starts—are in the greenhouse: a bunch of one- to two-feet high, translucent-green seedlings in individual pots. Looking vibrant and healthy in the sunlight coming through the opaque, fiberglass roof, they're just on the verge of flowering, and ready to transplant. But there are only about thirty in all—and the males haven't even been identified and pulled out yet.

Is that all then? Are there others, stashed elsewhere? The Sinsemilla Farmer, it seems, is only prepared to grow maybe 15 or 20 plants this year, not a whole lot more than the maximum of 10 for "personal use" that's the current, informally but not officially declared limit for avoiding harassment by the heat. Even accounting for the refinement of his horticultural techniques over the years to the point where he can now get more pounds of manicured buds from one plant than one would think possible, it's a drastic cutback from the level of two seasons past.

So the truth comes out. This is his last year of sinsemilla cultivation in Humboldt County. He'll either quit growing entirely, in order to go on living here, or he's going to pick up and move out.

With that, the Sinsemilla Farmer fires up the colossal joint he's been rolling—almost a spliff—from a stash of his choicest buds. The smoke curls languorously in the air around his head, and after a mere couple of tokes the oils from the crushed and resinous bud are staining the joint paper. It's the finest of *indica* sinsemilla—the best buds he knows of in the county.

We pass the joint. Under the circumstances, we get cosmically ripped.

Rivers of fog, tinted violet by the sunset, are moving in from the ocean and spilling over the smaller hills. The whole undulant landscape of grassy mountain meadows and dark, forest-filled ravines is glowing a dull red now, and the shadows in the room are darkening.

With the kind of appreciation of good pot that the Sinsemilla Farmer has, we wonder how he can even consider quitting what is obviously his calling. He could take on any kind of job, of course, involving agricultural know-how—or construction skills, for that matter. But we've seen him

ROCK CRITICS

FLICK FORD

BY JAMES MARSHALL
What is a rock critic indeed if not the most droll subject for an article imaginable? Picture Waldo (the nerd with glasses and knickers on the Little Rascals) in an R.E.M. teeshirt, or Thurston Howell III in high-top sneakers, and you get the picture.

First, however, let me clarify the difference between rock critics and journalists. There have been (and still are) many fine music journalists. I certainly wouldn't demean Nick Tosches or Peter Guralnick by calling them "rock critics." No, the breed of which we speak can best be understood as an essential cog in the great wheel of the music industry. The true rock critic reports on and reviews the latest happenings in the wonderful world of pop music. It is his thankless task to make sure the Corporate River of Hype is kept flowing at all times, clogging and stupefying the minds of the record-buying public.
#134, October 1986

IT HAPPENED IN THE HAIGHT

BY COOKIE MUELLER
I moved on to Golden Gate Park. As usual, the sky over Hippie Hill was dark with frisbees, kites, and sea gulls. Hundreds of hippies' dogs were barking and walking on the people laying on the grass. The air was thick with the smell of marijuana, patchouli oil, jasmine incense and Eucalyptus trees. The music was deafening. Black guys were playing congas; white guys were playing flutes, harmonicas, and guitars. It was as crowded as Coney Island on the Fourth of July. Hippie Hill was like this every day of the week.

I ran into some friends and sat around drinking wine. Around noon I stopped back at 1826 Page Street. An acid capping party was in progress. It was the sort of party that only happened where an acid dealer lived. The object of the party was to put acid powder into gelatin capsules, but since the acid assimilated through the skin, everyone got pretty high. Consequently, the party usually went on in shifts and when someone got too stoned to continue, another person would take their place. So when Kirk, one of my roommates, dropped out, I slipped into his place in front of a large mound of white powder. After filling around 300 capsules, I decided I was quite high enough. Someone took my place and I went back out on the street.
#129, May 1986

AYAHUASCA

BY PETER GORMAN

With the one remaining candle Alphonse lit a black tobacco cigarette and, still chanting, blew the smoke into the little pot of ayahuasca. He filled the gourd with the thick yellow-brown liquid, chanted, and passed the serving gourd to Chuck.

By the time the gourd reached me I decided to forego my fears and trust my instincts. I raised it to my friends, wished them luck and drank. It tasted like burnt grapefruit juice that had been infused with dark, dank smoke. I almost choked.

Alphonse drank last and then passed the bottle of aqua diente around. We were invited to drink a little and smoke cigarettes. Suddenly Alphonse leaned over the unwalled platform and vomited. We'd been warned we would all vomit, but there was something unusual in the way Alphonse did it...his vomiting sounded like a rushing river crashing against rocks and stones, boiling up like rapids, louder and louder until the clarity of a mad spring seemed to pervade everything. I couldn't believe the sound was issuing from his stomach.
#130, June 1986

CAPTAIN WHIZZO

It's held in a small bar called Tramps, costs only $6 to get in, and no one has to run the gauntlet past snotty doormen. The club features some of the best bands on the East Coast, draws a fun-loving crowd, and boasts one of the finest light shows in America. "I asked the girl in the sound booth if she knew of anyone who did lights," says Ivy Vale. "She gave me the name of someone called Captain Whizzo.... He's not just a lighting man. He's an artist."
Journey to the Mind's Eye, #144, August 1987

doing this growing thing for seven years now, always getting better at it, always doing better with it—a plant geneticist of the people—basically because he loves smoking it: loves getting stoned on the best, and turning people on to the best. He believes in it. It's his astral ally—his healing herb.

There were times, in years past, when we had seen him in the midst of the harvest, with his long hair and beard full of leaf trimmings and his hands and fingers stained bright green from days of cutting and picking and manicuring, when he seemed to embody the very essence of cannabis—the happiest kind of wedding of psychedelic substance with human form.

He also likes to make money when he can, and, if possible, have a lot of it around in reserve. All very typically American—a quality common to both growers and corporate executives—and especially for someone with a wife, an ex-wife and four kids in all to help support. But, brought up as a Presbyterian Kansas farmer's son and trained to derive the utmost return from the utmost effort, he'd probably be industrious at whatever he did.

Still—however big and juicy you grow your organic vegetables, for whatever rip-off price you can get for them in San Francisco, there is *nothing* you can grow that even approaches the profit margin of lovingly grown marijuana *sinsemilla*. Given that fact, what could have possibly brought our increasingly productive and successful Sinsemilla Farmer to make his sudden decision to stop growing?

Any regular reader of HIGH TIMES *will be familiar by now with the depredations of California's Campaign Against Marijuana Planting (CAMP), funded by Ronald Reagan's Justice Department and implemented with enthusiasm by California's Republican Governor Deukmejian and his Attorney General, John Van de Kamp. Up and down the north coast of California, but concentrating on Humboldt County, armed troopers and 'copter jocks were allowed to run amok and terrorize the general populace in the course of their crop confiscations. [June and July '85* HIGH TIMES.*]*

Last October, the CAMP forces were formally enjoined from engaging in activities that are in clear violation of constitutionally protected civil liberties (such as having your property invaded and searched without a warrant, should your property happen to be near a marijuana plant). As of May of this year, that injunction is still in effect. CAMP's recent appeal, at the beginning of the new growing season, to have the injunction overturned, was summarily rejected.

Bear in mind that, although it has such practical advantages for growers and nongrowers alike as preventing helicopters from hovering closer than 500 feet over one's house, the injunction is only a disciplinary corrective for a campaign that has already begun again this year in full force.

"I don't see any future in growing marijuana this way anymore," says the Sinsemilla Farmer, in tones reminiscent of laments for the passing of the Haight-Ashbury. "Not around here anyway. The government is against it, and it's been made too big a risk to grow it—especially here."

But isn't that just a temporary condition? Isn't it just a matter of waiting for the conservative tide to ebb?

"Humboldt County will never go back to being what it used to," he says. "The general feeling is that everybody's cutting back or not growing at all— or moving out. All the bigger, more mercenary type of growers are looking for other places to move to. They won't come back—they know their roll is over. And then there's a lot of people like us who would just as soon get out of all commercial growing in order to go on living here—but can't afford it otherwise."

Could that mean the Farmer himself is planning to move away from Humboldt County, after spending the last eight years putting together this beautiful spread—this independent, life-supporting, new-age microbiosphere? What about his house, every one of whose heavy timbers and joists he's had to haul out from town and up miles of winding dirt road to the top of this mountain? What about the 2,000-gallon irrigation tank he's built around the spring and into the hillside out of concrete blocks? Can he just turn his back on the hard-won fruits of these labors? Can he just walk away from all this?

Not if the Farmer's wife can help it. She was brought up Irish Catholic, in the row-house slums of Baltimore, and has escaped a bleak east-coast scene that, from her current point of view, might as well be Lebanon. Having two kids of her own—and four when the Farmer's two older ones are visiting—she's not all that averse to giving up the built-in paranoia of growing pot. They're both vegetarians and subsist on organically grown vegetables, so why not grow *them* for a living and stop sweating spotter planes?

She turns us on to medjool dates—oversized sweet globs of explosive energy for our cannabinolized brain chemistry. And the Farmer rolls up another number.

They obviously haven't resolved the issue. They love the land and their home and the community of growers that's evolved here in this part of the country. Having followed an unbroken thread from the psychedelic revolution of past decades to the agrarian independence and voluntary simplicity of today's northwest-coast communities, they feel most at home in a community of people who have not only put their energy into growing marijuana but have allied themselves with the politics of the preservation of the earth and respect for all life. They know no one, except maybe transient "river people" in town or shadowy absentee landowners, for whom smoking marijuana or making money growing it is the single or even most important reason for being here.

$2.1 million was spent this year to employ 600 people to eradicate over 150,000 marijuana plants in the State of California. Of that number, slightly over 100,000 were growing in Humboldt County. Out of the 114 people actually arrested in connection with the confiscations of pot, 53 of those arrests took place in that county alone. CAMP's claim to have cleansed the county of 25 to 40 percent of its annual crop is confirmed by growers to be true only of specific, "scoured" local areas—such as the town of Manzanita, site of the Farmers' store. In such locations, many families have already moved out, school enrollments have declined, and businesses such as the Farmers' have been folding. It has become obvious to everyone that, due to its media-hyped reputation as the very hotbed of flagrant growing, Humboldt County has been singled out for a concentrated antidope blitzkrieg—as a media display, some say, for the Latin American countries whom the DEA is pressuring into taking similar measures—but most certainly as a taxpayer ripoff for the right-wing advocates of militant law-enforcement who helped to re-elect Ronald Reagan. As we watch the pattern of persecution repeat itself as it has so many times in the past, we can come to no other conclusion than that the marijuana-smoking and growing-based subculture of the North Coast has attracted this kind of heat because it presents the threat of not only an alternative economy but one for whom old social barriers and ideological allegiances have crumbled. This is what really scares them about marijuana-growing and has convinced the feds that the subculture itself must be nipped in the bud: because the ethics and politics of the most highly evolved grower

ACID FLICK FIEND
BY ROGER BERRIAN

In late 1967, Roger Corman took the psychedelic cinema to the masses with the first acid epic, *The Trip*. Written by Jack Nicholson, *The Trip* starred Peter Fonda as an executive who scores a hefty dose of micrograms from his groovy pal Dennis Hopper.
#133, September 1986

MY LAST ACID TRIP
BY ERIC BOGOSIAN

I guess everything began when I dropped that acid Mike gave me for my birthday. When I got off, I decided to take a bath and I was watching the water...just thinking about how beautiful it looked, how I've never really noticed how beautiful bathwater looked before...when out of nowhere I heard this incredible music—like chimes. Eventually, I realized it was the front doorbell and I thought, I better go answer it, you never know. I stood up and realized I was wet and naked. And then I thought, so what? What difference does it make in the grand scheme of things. So I went to the door and it was this girl from down the street, who I never met before. I invited her in, and this is the really strange part. She came in.
#133, September 1986

LAST TIME THE ANGELS CAME UP

BY KEN KESEY

Now Bert is kicking his old chopper over. Same one he took to London, years ago. The girl puts the record player in the black car then shuffles around, uncertain. Awful Harry rolls his big luxury model out of the garage, declares he's got brakes again. The girl looks from Old Bert's old bike with its skimpy seat, to Harry's new Electro-glide with elaborate leather cushions and sissybar. Harry shakes his head at her.

"Oh no you don't bitch! He balls you, he hauls you."

She climbs on behind Old Bert and wraps her sunburned arms around his waist. He grins at me.

More popping, roaring, backfiring, churning brown dust and blue smoke…stalling and stalling…then, all at once, they are leaving, whooping and roaring, rolling in a long detonating wave out of our dirt road to the pavement, west, rap-bab-babbing up the grade toward Mt. Nebo, then out of sight, south, echoing their way through the smoky afternoon.

"Right off!" Rumiocho squawks when the last one is gone.

A civilization begins to drift back over the farm, like the settling dust. The silence is a thunderclap of relief.

Me, I'm gonna change out of these boots and back into my moccasins.

#136, December 1986

ELDRIDGE CLEAVER

I started following the drug laws in 1962, so I've seen a lot of changes. And I particularly watched in the last couple of years, the DEA in its attempt to stamp out drugs and coming up with nonsensical programs, like spraying paraquat and the CAMP activity in the northern counties. I've documented how the DEA and all these task forces admit that they cannot stop the drugs at their source. So, they're starting this mandatory drug testing thing and, at the same time, doing these terroristic attacks on the farmers. Nowhere are they dealing with the issue, which is the right of the American people to use these substances…. I think the farmers should be left alone to produce a superior product. I believe the government should regulate it in the marketplace. I believe we won the struggle between the psychedelic and the alcoholic culture, but now it seems we're being called upon to refight those old battles….

Interview by John Holmstrom, #131, July 1986

community in the country are basically opposed to those of Reagan's resurrected American Empire.

Once CAMP got underway during the harvest season of 1983, the Sinsemilla Farmer and his wife knew it was time to convert whatever investments they had into cash and keep as low a profile as possible. They cut loose of their rental in Mexico, and were hot to sell their extra piece of land but decided to hold on to it mainly because the couple who were renting it from them—the Stalwart Sharecropper and his lady—were good friends, and were trying to get it together to buy the land. So the Farmers let them live and grow on it for another year, and grew a crop on their own land about half the size and more spread out than the previous year's, trusting to their collective luck and smarts to get them through the season.

The Farmer's land was remote from everything—up at the end of a 10-mile dirt road that traversed some of the more breathtaking sheer escarpments of the King Range. Anyone intent on busting him would have to plan on at least a two-hour trip in a four-wheel drive just to reach him. Doubly cautious after the last year's raids, he adopted the most discreet planting pattern possible, placing his plants in individual grow-holes he'd dug in the sunnier patches of the woods. Everything stayed cool there that year—not even an attempted rip-off by a teenager or town boozer.

But late in September, he got word from the Sharecropper that CAMP was in the area, and it could be a matter of days, or even hours, before they hit the small field where he had his patch of about 75 plants (a not so discreet planting pattern). So the Farmer headed down to the Alder Creek area for a little premature harvesting.

He and the Sharecropper went alone together in the Sharecropper's flatbed. Everything was still there as they'd left it, hemmed in all around by reddening madrone and poison oak, and humming with insects in the hot afternoon, but otherwise quiet. They had cut down about 45 of the 75 plants, according to the Farmer, and had loaded them onto the flatbed when they suddenly stopped still and agreed that they could hear truck engines not far away in the woods. Then—very faintly—the sound of men's voices.

The road they had used to come on to the property was the less accessible "back way" where they were less likely to run into paramilitary types. So when they found themselves back in the truck on top of a huge adrenalin rush, they drove back up the wooded hillside, the same way they came in. Through the window of the truck and through the trees, the Farmer could see the khaki uniforms of some men coming onto the field even as the truck was climbing the hill.

Just before it got to the top, though, the straining and still cold engine coughed out. The Stalwart Sharecropper put the floor-stick in neutral to restart the truck, but it wouldn't start. *"Fuck!"* said the Sharecropper. It was all telepathic, and happened in what seemed like either a split-second or a timeless space. They both knew there was a leak in the hydraulic brake line and the truck hadn't had an emergency brake in years. The Sharecropper was stretched out straight and stiff as a board with his foot crammed against the brake pedal, but the pedal just sank to the floor. *The truck started rolling back down the hill toward the field.*

As the Sharecropper tried desperately to shove the floor-stick into gear the Farmer could see their only chance was to do what he did: He grabbed up the 50-pound concrete block that they kept with them for parking on hills, threw open the door and jumped out with it. When he hit the ground, he knew he'd torn the ligaments in his right knee, and tried to keep from crying out with the pain as he lunged back toward the truck and rammed the block behind the rolling front wheel. The truck was moving so fast that it almost completely bounced over the concrete block. But it didn't. It crashed back on the uphill side and stopped.

The sound of a helicopter engine came wafting through the woods at that point. As the Farmer was lying in the ditch by the side of the road, clutching his knee, he could see, through the blur of his tears, the chopper passing over the treetops in its descent to the field for the pickup of the contraband load. He says he can remember thinking to himself *"What the fuck am I doing here?"*

After much cursing and choking of engine, the Sharecropper got his truck started at last, pulled the Farmer inside and took off over the hill. He forgot the concrete block, but he didn't go back for it.

In addition to its achievements on the paramilitary front, the U.S. government has begun to revive some of its favorite old methods from the Vietnam years for generating paranoia from within. As evidence for this, we cite these recent developments:

• On October 12, 1984, a new federal law—the Comprehensive Crime Bill—was enacted in California, allowing the government to confiscate any property where marijuana is cultivated, if the grower is convicted of a felony. Cultivation of marijuana for commercial sales is, of course, a felony.

Five days after the law was enacted, helicopter-borne federal agents descended on a 208-acre ranch in Mendocino County (the next one south of Humboldt). There they busted Rique Kuru and his wife Natasha, owners of the ranch, for growing 52 marijuana plants and holding one pound of packaged pot.

In the opinion of their attorney, Ron Sinoway, the scope or (amount) of land forfeiture could have been minimized—or the felony charges reduced to the misdemeanor level and the forfeiture averted entirely. His case was made irrelevant, however, as the government, just before the impending trial, offered a plea-bargain too tempting for the Kurus to refuse: all marijuana-cultivation charges, both misdemeanor and felony, subjecting them to the prospect of 2 to 30 years in prison, would be dropped if they agreed to surrender all legal claims to their property to the federal government. Having lived on the property for only a year, their total equity representing only $20,000, the couple was moved by this powerfully persuasive offer and readily accepted.

Assistant U.S. Attorney Peter Robinson, orchestrator of the deal and chief expediter of California's stepped-up rate of pot-bust convictions, announced in San Francisco that the Kurus' property would be auctioned off, the $95,000 mortgage paid, and the remainder of the proceeds turned over to the Mendocino County sheriff's office to finance further marijuana-eradication efforts. (To the government's chagrin, however, the public auction which was held on May 20th elicited only two offers from the unruly crowd gathered on Ukiah's courthouse steps—one for ten cents, and the other for thirty pieces of silver.)

• In March of this year, about 50 residents of southern Humboldt County received photocopied letters in the mail, postmarked Virginia and signed "Om Shanti." They were warned that extensive personal profiles of at least 500 people suspected to be major marijuana growers were being compiled, and that in the coming months the data would be made available to the new Grand Jury being seated in Eureka for investigation of the grass-growing scene. They were also warned that the government would be simultaneously attempting a variety of methods to spread fear, distrust and paranoia within the community.

JOHN WATERS

BY JOHN HOWELL

Some call Waters' movies camp fun. Others dismiss them as disgusting filth.

JW: Crack is the first drug that I haven't tried—and I don't want to. I'm really down on all drugs. I don't think people who smoke pot should be arrested, but I think pot makes you satisfied with less in life. I smoked pot every day for years, then got tired of it.

HT: Ken Kesey talked about not having to keep taking acid any more after certain changes had taken place in the mind.

JW: I can't imagine taking LSD now. I may sound like some old hippie, but I think the big difference is that when we took drugs in the sixties, the spirit was to learn and think more. Now, it's to think less, to just blot yourself out. Then, it was political, something was changing because of it. Now, nothing changes.

Interview, #137, January 1987

HOWARD STERN

The FCC announced it would no longer limit its definition of indecent language to the infamous "seven dirty words" made famous by George Carlin. Its redefinition was apparently inspired by charges from Morality in Media, a right-wing religious group of nuts and fruitcakes, and the accusations of "filth" have been principally directed against New York radio personality Howard Stern.

HighWitness News by John Holmstrom, #143, July 1987

J.D. KING

YOU GOTTA FIGHT, KILL AND MAIM FOR YOUR RIGHT TO PARTY!

BY KEN WEINER AND THE GENERAL

Take drunk driving. They're always telling us not to drink and drive. Why not? There's nothing more fun than getting a little loaded, smashing into someone's house, and running over a boring yuppie.

Booze and dope don't cause car accidents: cars cause car accidents! So let's cut the crap and outlaw cars!

We should start building trolleys, streetcars, bullet trains, moving sidewalks. When this country had a good mass transit system, nobody worried about drunk driving. They just staggered into a trolley!

The enemies of fun don't want you to get laid, either! All they talk about is AIDS, herpes, and stuff like that. What we really need is a disease to wipe out all the yuppies, like a deadly, unseen virus found only in Perrier.

#144, August 1987

HEP CAT

JOHN HOLMSTROM

As of May, some residents had been notified by the IRS itself that they were under investigation.

• Financial records of many car (and especially van and truck) dealerships, real estate companies, and travel agencies in southern Humboldt County have indeed already been subpoenaed by the federal government, in preparation for what is anticipated to be a campaign in conjunction with the IRS to indict growers on tax-evasion charges. Helplessly compromised, many of the local businesses in the area now suffer from the reluctance of their customers to expose themselves to further violations of their privacy.

In the meantime, there's a lot of money made from sinsemilla-farming frozen in proxy mortgages. Or buried out there in the hills. Or being laundered in some entirely other part of the world. Or being spent on cocaine...

All of us are seated now in the Sinsemilla Farmer's rooftop, solar-heated hot tub—the Farmers, the Sharecroppers, and the two of us from far-away New York. Unusually early this year after a dry winter, California's already hot inland valleys have begun their annual cycle of drawing the ocean's cool fog into all the valleys and hollows and low-lying recesses of the coastal mountains. The fog is just below us and all around us—above us, the stars. In the distance, other mountaintops protrude from the moving, billowing fogbank, like islands in a grey sea. Out in the remotest audible reaches is the roar of surf.

The water is still hot, even late at night, and the Farmer sighs with relief as he massages his knee—which he strained again only recently while he was trying to pull one of his goats out of the garden. We pass around the latest spliff, using a chopstick roachclip to keep it from getting any wetter than the night air has already left it.

"I guess the crackdown was inevitable," he says. "Given all the circumstances involved, I'm not really surprised by it. The feds have probably concentrated in this area because of all the publicity in the media, which they have to respond to. What they most want to do is come here and rip up thousands of pot plants, and make sure it's shown on TV, so they can say, 'Here is this terrible problem—and here we are.' But then, of course, there's also what's going on here."

So what's going on here? For one thing, the evolution of a whole community whose economy is based on growing—a community which has attracted a diversity of people from all over the country, but whose politics are predetermined by the illegality of its livelihood. Independence from the system has become the guiding principle for every homestead family, resulting in self-sufficient energy setups for every home; organic grocery and garden-supply cooperatives; grower-built and maintained schools and clinics; and a soft-spoken but widespread network of midwives for home birthing, itself an illegal activity subject to state prosecution. And yet the ties to the parent culture are deep-rooted and powerful—it's unavoidably where the money comes from, not to mention all the things so often attendant upon acquiring lots of money all at once.

We ask innocently enough, yet knowing full well it's the kind of question a HIGH TIMES interviewer would feel obliged to ask, "Is there more tooting up going on around here than there used to be?" Putting out this charged subject into our hot-tubbed group mind is like throwing a turd in the punchbowl. It brings out strong convictions.

"Cocaine?" says the Sinsemilla Farmer. "Some people are quitting smoking because they're doing coke and just growing so they can afford it. And then other square-type people are hearing about it through the media and lumping the whole drug scene together like it was one thing, and using the coke scene to condemn the grass scene. They've seen what happens to addicts, of course. The whole thing is a turn-off.

"The problem we have around here is not like the one you'd have in Oakland or New York. Most of these growers can afford their habits. But that's the problem—they usually end up taking themselves out of the action. Maybe they 'base out, and you never hear from them again. Coke tends to make you self-absorbed and into your own trip. Remember how speed and smack destroyed the Haight? If there is anything that has contributed more than CAMP to the breakdown of this community over the last few years, it's coke. The heat couldn't have planted a better weapon for their purposes. It's a vital weakness they're already exploiting."

The Farmer says that he tried coke for a while but didn't like the way it made his body uptight, so he avoided it thereafter.

The Sharecropper's Lady says she likes it, really, but has the strength of will to do without it. "It's not hard to stay away from it once you see what it's doing to your friends," she says.

"Personally," says the Farmer's wife, betraying her east-coast upbringing, "I think I could even quit smoking grass if I was convinced it would make me more productive."

"You could get more uptight, too, being that productive," admonishes the smiling Farmer, always the defender of the sacrament. "And that could lead on to harder stuff."

We can think of another thing going on here besides pot-farming and coke-snorting that, while admirable and appropriate, could attract just as much heat in the long run: the radicalization of political consciousness that is occurring all over the region, as invariably happens wherever in the world the oppressor-behemoth tries to crush a popular movement by lunging around in an excess of destructive fury. (Can you think of other examples?)

The people who settled in this region over the last 20 years in order to leave behind them the insanities of urban blight and malled-over America have, in the last two years, experienced a rude awakening. The police state has caught up to them at last, and is informing them that they will no longer be allowed to grow the one viable crop that affords them their economic subsistence here. There can be no mistaking the intentions of the county to use this means of running them out entirely. The local district attorney has been quoted as saying he expected small-scale growing to continue as ever, but would concentrate on getting the bigger, commercial-scale growers to move away. In the face of a threatened prison term, moving away would appear to be an appealing option.

Otherwise unemployed in a region where there are few other jobs, the growers' choice in responding to these tactics is to leave or fight back. Some have already left; some have begun to fight back—with lawsuits, with community meetings, with political-environmental newspapers; and by organizing in groups to monitor and publicize violations of what we all still assume to be our civil liberties.

We ask if anyone has suffered any direct consequences from all those Garberville and Redway business records being subpoenaed.

So far as anybody knows, just the businesses themselves. "The owner of the auto dealership in town," says the Farmer, "he worked out a compromise with them, where he had to turn over all his financial records that involved more than $2,500 per person, and didn't have to turn in anything else, which actually eliminated just about everybody. It really hurt

DOCK ELLIS

BY ERIC BROTHERS

Dock woke up late. Why shouldn't he? As far as he knew, the team had an off day and he planned to take full advantage of it. Three hits of LSD were ready and waiting in the refrigerator.

"Say baby, how about breakfast?"

A few minutes later, his girlfriend returned with the coffee, donuts, and the morning paper. At noon, they dropped acid. Dock put on a record, while his girlfriend read the paper.

"Dock, it says here you're pitching today!"

"Whaaa...?" said Dock groggily.

Dock Ellis and the Electric Baseball Game, #144, August 1987

PERPETUAL HARVEST

BY KYLE ROQ

Angel runs a Perpetual Harvest. Clones are put into flowering and buds are harvested at staggered times. It's a bud harvest, as opposed to a Continual Harvest, which is letting a plant vegetate 'till it drops, while clipping leaves...Equally important to starting cuttings at the same height, is keeping them from shooting up. Super Sativa Seed Club research has found high humidity, especially when combined with high grow room temperatures, a culprit in taller plants. The reason is simple: Plants absorb water through their roots and transpire through their leaves. When a plant can't transpire freely, because the hot, muggy air can't hold more humidity, the water stays in the plant's cells, pushing against the walls, elongating the cells still further, making the plant taller.

#150, February 1988

SUPER SATIVA SEED CLUB

BY STEVEN HAGER

Holland is not a particularly good place to grow. It is cold, rainy, and cloudy most of the year, the soil is rocky, and much of the land is reclaimed ocean bottom. But the Dutch are an ingenious and persistant race, and over the years they have achieved a victory against this harsh environment. The secret of their success was to move indoors and grow hydroponically. Flowers, plants, and produce are cheap and abundant in Holland. Although they have been farming this way for many years, marijuana cultivation is still a relatively new concept. The Super Sativa Seed Club (SSSC), a consortium of growers located throughout the country, comprises some of Holland's first commercial marijuana growers.

"We are ten years ahead of most of the growers in Holland," says Kees, one of the company's founders. "Our approach is the most technical and the most sophisticated."

The cornerstone of the SSSC method is the ebb and flow table. Several times a day, the table is flooded with nutrient solution. Three-week-old clones are placed on the table and flowered immediately, a system that produces small, portable plants of incredible potency. The system is designed for maximum harvest out of minimum space.

"I don't really approve of weed grown out of Rockwool," counters Robert Connell Clarke, a typical organic researcher. "I have a hard time eating food produced by chemical agriculture. But I have to admit the results from SSSC have been amazing."

#145, September 1987

his business for a while, though—took him some time to gain back the confidence of the people. He's had to go out of his way to preserve his business integrity—to protect his customers. He sent them all an apology in the mail. And he's doing okay now. But I think it's outrageous that the government could come in and almost put him out of business that way, by making him comply—to give them what they wanted."

We mention our feeling that the surveillance techniques of the Nixonian era are on the ascendant again, and reminiscent of methods employed in Berkeley and the Haight-Ashbury.

"The problem is," says the Farmer, "every single subculture we've seen come on in the last 20 years is represented somewhere around here. There are so many trips involved in this whole scene that it just can't be kept cool."

"Tell 'em about the Who-Dos," says the Sharecropper's lady.

"Ever hear of the Who-Dos?" says the Sharecropper. "They're some kind of church that believes the world's made up of those who do and those who don't. So they're the Who-Dos. They came up here from the city and settled on a piece of land right near us. I've picked up members of their church hitchhikin' up the road that have just been really unable to communicate. Really spaced out. Kind of displaced people in general—a lot of former addicts, I think.

"Anyway, there was this spotter plane flyin' around our ridge last summer, and I watched it flyin' around for weeks—the same plane. For three or four days a week, every week, it'd come up and fly in these lazy circles up and down our ridge and the Who-Dos' ridge too. The feds must have seen every single pot plant that was growin' around there, because they were at it for weeks. It was the sort of thing that can kind of get to you after a while—whether you got grass growin' in the woods or not.

"So it got to the Who-Dos finally, and one of them—supposedly it was the head of their thing—he fired off a couple of shots at the plane with a rifle. The plane didn't come back after that. But about a week later, around eight o'clock in the mornin', a couple of helicopters came in and dropped teams on their ridge that's back behind ours, lookin' for the person who had shot at them. And they arrested him and took him away. I don't know about the rest of them, but I don't think there's hardly anybody left there now."

The Farmer pulls himself out of the tub and sits now on its side, his body steaming in the finer moisture of the gathering fog. The island mountaintops have disappeared, and our serene scene here on the rooftop is all that's left visible.

"Eventually," he says, "they identified the plane the Who-Do shot at as a DEA training plane. And it'd been training agents from all over California and several other states. It'd been doing training missions. It turns out the Feds are using this area as a training ground for paramilitary types from all over California and Oregon—training them in tactics for spotting and busting marijuana. It's pretty obvious that what they're hoping to do is start a grassfire here that will eventually spread all over the country. After all, they're growing marijuana commercially *everywhere* now, not just here."

"Legalize it," says the Sharecropper.

"Right on," says the Sharecropper's lady, still the old Berkeley firebrand. "It's the only answer."

Are they kidding? Do they know what legalization would mean for the price structure that's enabled them to do what they've done so far and end up here at this physical and karmic pinnacle of their lives?

"I think the majority of growers have always preferred that grass be legalized," says the Sinsemilla Farmer. "The minority, which I think is who they're mainly after, have been making a great deal of money because it's illegal. But that's maybe five or ten percent of the growers in the county. Even though there's just a few of them who are self-supporting, there's a lot of farmers like us who would have a hard time making it here any other way.

"But *everyone* right now would be willing to make a lot less than they've been making if it means getting to go on living here without having to be paranoid. I mean, we're people—we're homesteading, and the reason we moved here was to raise our families in a quiet, clean environment. That's not so out of the ordinary, is it?

"*It would be such a godsend* if grass were legalized. You could take the unemployed people out of the cities and put them in the country and give them something to do that they could make a living at. Regulations could be written that would limit an individual to, say, no more than $20,000 a year—or that would limit any one person to a certain number of plants. All you've got to do is figure out how much is consumed across the board and come up with the most number of people who can produce that, instead of the fewest number of people."

He sighs and slips back into the water. "But I suppose that would be anti-American."

The irony is that the Sinsemilla Farmer is in many ways the kind of self-made man that good American boys have always been encouraged to be. He's worked hard for his money and the security of his family, he's built his own version of a new-age, energy-efficient dwelling, he's established a successful organic farming operation, and he's plowed a great deal of his money and energy back into the community he lives in. What mainly marks him and keeps him apart from all the other successful burghers with master bedrooms throughout the state of California is that his cash crop—*California's number-one cash crop*—is, even now in 1985, still outlawed.

We pack it up the next morning and say goodbye to our friends and their two kids. The Farmer needs to do some things in town, so he takes his truck, and we follow him down the mountain—far enough behind him on the winding dirt road to avoid the heavier clouds of dust that his truck kicks up. By the time we've reached the valley floor, the morning fog is already burning off.

Two hours and forty miles of winding road later, we've parted ways with the Farmer and have arrived in Garberville. The town's nondescript main street is busy with all the everyday goings-on that you would expect to see in any town across America. Except that there is something heavy in the air.

We drop in on a real estate office to ask how business is doing. The receptionist informs us that her boss prefers not to talk to us—and, when asked why, says that he refuses to talk to any media representative whatsoever. Apparently he was misquoted by somebody at some point, misunderstood and publicly embarrassed. We can only imagine some out-of-context snippet of this law-abiding citizen on prime-time boob-tube news, saying, "Some of my best customers are growers," or something to that effect. We respectfully take our leave.

The situation is much the same at the downtown feed store. "Don't want to talk to anybody." *Everywhere we go we find guarded glances, glazed stares. We have the feeling that we've arrived at ground zero after the media bomb has hit, and the radioactivity of national attention is still intense. The last thing anybody wants is another good jolt. We have an appointment, though, with the editor of the local newspaper, the* Redwood Record, *and we pick up the latest edition, along with the* San Francisco Chronicle, *to get a feel for what's going on at that level.*

RHAPSODY IN PINK
BY LENNY KAYE

As they cemented each brick in the wall, oohing and aahing the audience with their crashing airplane, animated cartoons, and inflatable pig, it looked as if the Floyd had made their ultimate statement on the repercussive price of societal square pegs in a polygonal hole. Despite the band's triumphal Joshuan reentry at the climax of the show, the personality riffs between Floyd members had compartmentalized them from one another. Passions that had reached boiling point in the studio during the recording of *The Wall* now exploded during the making of *The Final Cut*, which consisted of [Roger] Waters' extending musing on the death of his father in World War II. The rest of Pink Floyd felt they were in danger of becoming a disposable adjunct to Roger's seizing the creative reins, and they parted unamicably in 1984.
#150, February 1988

ENGLISH ART ROCK
BY JAMES MARSHALL

Syd Barrett was the most overrated guy in music. Pink Floyd is the Henry Mancini of an entire generation of junior high potheads. And don't kid yourself—Henry Mancini sold a lot more records than Little Richard ever did. Pink Floyd is actually pretty ignorable, but what came in its wake was worse—Yes, Jethro Tull, Eno, and worst of all Genesis and its offspew, the ultimate in overblown pomposity.
Ten Worst Things That Happened to Music,
#144, August 1987

BIG BUD: SUPER INDOOR CLONE!

HIGHTIMES

MARCH 1987 · $3.95

INSIDE CANNABIS CASTLE!

THE INCREDIBLE STORY
OF THE MAN WHO WOULD BE
KING OF CANNABIS
BY STEVEN HAGER

MADISON '87

No one knew what to expect when Ben Masel announced the 7th annual Great Midwest Harvest Festival. In 1985 the event (one of the oldest of its kind), had drawn a paltry 300 protesters. But perfect autumn weather and a new spirit of activism combined to inspire 10,000 protesters to defy their governor's orders and storm the Capitol grounds, with NORML National Director Jon Gettman and HIGH TIMES Senior Editor Ed Rosenthal leading the charge.

The event drew widespread media coverage, much of which was sympathetic: the Wisconsin *State Journal* took a potshot at their governor with the headline: "Thompson's Vows Go to Pot." (The day before the governor had emphatically announced "there would be no more pot rallies on Capitol grounds.") The police came to arrest the protesters, but changed their minds quickly after seeing the size of the crowd. Jon Gettman, who only recently became NORML's national director, seized the day and rallied the crowd. Once at the Capitol, the crowd taunted the governor with calls of "Tommy can you hear me?" Rosenthal was described in local papers the next day as a "rabble rouser." The angry crowd alternated between chants of "Free the Heads, jail the Feds" and "Pot's an Herb, Reagan's a Dope!"
HighWitness News, #149, January 1988

The headlines tell the story—the epicenter of the next big earthquake has been pinpointed at Parkfield, California, halfway between San Francisco and Los Angeles. Elaborate exercises in L.A. in preparation for its next big 'quake come off like Keystone Kops confusion. The Diablo Canyon nuclear power plant, less than 100 miles away from Parkfield, and lying astride a major fault itself, has finally been licensed to go on-line, full-power. Off the pristine coastline of Mendocino and Humboldt Counties, oil "developers" have begun exploratory offshore drilling, using "air cannons," which have a deadly effect on marine life, and uncased wells with no blowout protection. In burned-out Marin County, cocaine rehabilitation clinics have become the fastest growing industry—blowout protection for those who can afford it. And in San Francisco, at the Golden Gate, the Coast Guard has just nabbed a fishing boat packed with 31 tons of primo Thai weed.

Times are tough in California.

The story you've just read is true; some names of people and places have been changed.

INSIDE CANNABIS CASTLE
by Steven Hager

It is Thursday, November 6, 1986, and Nevil has just returned from his daily pilgrimage to a nearby post office. It is raining lightly and a cold breeze blows off the Rhine River. Although the sun made a brief appearance early in the day, it has since been obliterated by massive, billowing clouds.

As Nevil enters his house, he is assaulted by his watchdog, Elka. He climbs the stairs to his living room, flops on an old couch, and starts opening his mail. "Breeding is a matter of bending nature to your will," he says while drawing a toke on a joint of Skunk #1. "There's not a coffee shop in Holland that can produce better weed than this. But I don't sell it. I give it away—or I throw it away."

In a few short years, Nevil has made an incredible transformation from penniless junkie to wealthy entrepreneur. Although he's an effective and efficient businessman, marijuana is his business, so things are run a bit differently around here than at most companies. For example, resinous buds of exotic types of cannabis are strewn haphazardly about the room, as are large chunks of hash and bags filled with seeds.

Nevil is a displaced Australian of Dutch heritage, and has a quiet, understated sense of humor. He lives in relative seclusion on his estate, breeding marijuana, playing pool, watching video, waiting patiently for his many cannabis experiments to bear fruit. He has his doubts about the future of the marijuana business in the Netherlands, but these doubts are likely to disappear in a whiff of smoke whenever he samples a new, successful hybrid.

"In the beginning I was quite keen for people to come here and visit me, but I found it takes large amounts of my time," he says. "I have to sit around and smoke with them. Now it has to be someone worthwhile, someone who has a large project in mind. Most American growers are looking for the same thing: strong, overpowering, two-toke *indica* with huge yields. My number one seller is Northern Lights."

After the mail has been sorted and delivered to the in-house accountant, Nevil visits the basement to inspect his prize plants. The doors to four grow rooms are wide open, disclosing the blinding glare of dozens of sodium and halide lights. Powerful exhaust fans circulate the air, and the smell of cannabis is overpowering. Three of the rooms are devoted to young seedlings, while the largest contains 40 flowering females in their spectacular resinous glory.

It's no secret that an explosion of indoor marijuana propagation has taken place in America: Grow stores are sprouting across the nation and sodium and halide lights are selling faster than Christmas trees in December. The reason for this sudden interest in indoor growing is no secret either: For the past two years high-quality marijuana has been nearly impossible to find—unless, of course, one personally knows a grower. But any pot farmer will tell you good equipment does not guarantee a good harvest. The most important element, in fact, is good seeds. And until recently, good seeds have been as rare as a $15 lid of Colombian gold.

Thanks to Nevil, however, this sad situation has changed. Every day letters pour into his post office box, letters containing American dollars wrapped in carbon paper to avoid detection. The money is for seeds. Not ordinary pot seeds, but the best, most potent seeds on the market, seeds that will grow gargantuan buds dripping with resin, seeds that cost between $2 and $5 each.

Nevil's seed factory has been in business for three years and is perfectly legal. The Dutch government views Nevil as a legitimate, tax-paying businessman. Seed merchants are held in esteem in Holland, and even though Nevil is something of a small fry by seed merchant standards, he is a protected national asset nonetheless. Last year his company supplied $500,000 worth of seeds to 15,000 American growers. If you smoked high-quality marijuana sometime in the last three years, chances are good the buds were grown with Nevil's stock.

There is a big difference between growing marijuana and breeding for quality. The best-known example of the long-term effects of breeding are the *cannabis indica* plants that arrived in the United States in the '70s. For hundreds of years *indica* plants were bred by Afghani farmers for disease resistance, early flowering, large buds, and wide leaves. The strain was developed for hash production, but it was also useful for American growers who had difficulty with *sativa* strains, most of which require longer growing cycles.

Ever since *indica* arrived in this country, breeders have been creating hybrids that take advantage of *indica*'s hardiness and *sativa*'s clear, bell-like high. The results of these experiments first appeared at secret harvest festivals in California, Oregon, and Washington. Then, in the early '80s, a legendary underground organization called the Sacred Seed Company began distributing these remarkable hybrids. Nevil's company, The Seed Bank, sells many strains originally developed by the Sacred Seed Company, including the famed Skunk #1, Early Girl, and California Orange. In the past three years, however, some of the most mindblowing strains have come out of the Pacific Northwest area: Northern Lights, University, Big Bud, and Hash Plant are adequate proof that Seattle and Portland now hold the breeding crown. Needless to say, Nevil's Seed Bank has obtained cuttings and seeds of all these varieties and will soon be offering them for sale.

Who is Nevil and how did he come to found this amazing company? As usual, the truth is wilder than anything HIGH TIMES could invent.

MY AMERIKA

BY ED HASSLE

Why isn't our holy weed legal yet? Why can't we toke up in peace? It makes me madder than a pothead who just soaked his stash in rancid bong water whenever I think about this pathetic situation. I was reading a report the other day written in the late '60s that predicted marijuana would be legal by 1986. Well, it's 1986 and there's not a single Congressperson willing to support legalization. In fact, the entire country seems to be undergoing a wave of anti-drug hysteria.

I was talking to my Bangladesh guru Ramjam the other day and he told me we live on one of the few planets in the universe that has outlawed pot. According to Ramjam, aliens have made frequent forays to this planet just to sample the local sinsemilla.

Flashes, #130, June 1986

HASH BASH '88

The word at HIGH TIMES spread like wildfire—PARTY IN ANN ARBOR!!! So a bunch of us rented a bus, packed up our stuff, and drove out to the Diag at the University of Michigan. Not only that, but we invited along everyone we could think of. Besides sending out invites to all of our subscribers in the area, we dragged along The Black Orchids and The Rat Bastards, two cookin' rock bands. (After all, it wouldn't be a party if we didn't bring some music!)

We made our entrance to the Diag in grand style. Chef RA led a procession of freedom fighters down the street, while pounding on drums and cowbells.

by Buford Bosko, #155, July 1988

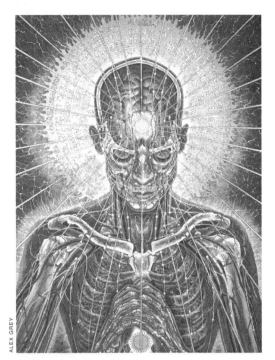

ALEX GREY

HIGH ART

BY CARLO McCORMICK

When people take mind-expanding drugs, they can be propelled into states of awareness that may forever change the way they perceive reality, and many artists so enlightened express these new feelings and thoughts in art, music and writing. Two contemporary artists who have used psychedelics to explore the universe of cosmic energy within the self are Alex and Allyson Grey, a couple who translate their experiences onto canvas.

#139, March 1987

QUEEN'S DAY

BY ROBERT CONNELL CLARKE

Queen's Day in Amsterdam is one of the premier street festivals of our time. Each year, the Dutch set aside April 30th to commemorate the birth of their Queen. (Queen Beatrix has been on the throne for seven years, but Queen's Day is still celebrated on the birthday of her mother, Queen Juliana.)

Although Queen's Day has been celebrated since shortly after World War II, its significance increased in the early '80s as Beatrix took the throne amidst street riots between squatters and police.

Queen's Day is a "free market day," which means anyone can sell anything anywhere in the city without a license, taxes, or any other hassles. For a day, Amsterdam becomes the world's largest flea market, and the bargains are amazing.

#145, September 1987

THE MAKING OF A SEED MERCHANT

The man who would be King of Cannabis is the son of Dutch migrants who settled in Perth, Australia, in 1954. His father worked as an instructor for telephone technicians, while his mother became a counselor for unwed mothers. They were adventurous, hardworking Catholics, and they raised their six children strictly, sending them to Catholic schools.

"I wasn't the most malleable child," admits Nevil. "From an early age I had an aversion to authority. I was the first-born, and I saw myself as a sort of pathbreaker for the rest of the children."

Despite his rebellious nature, Nevil was intelligent enough to jump two years ahead of his peers, a leap that resulted in his being the smallest in class. "I got beat up a lot," he admits. "A typical day would start with the teacher calling me up in front of the class to smell my breath. 'Yep,' she'd say, 'You've been smoking.' And I'd get six of the best straight away. And that was just to start the day! Usually a thing like that would put me into a bad mood, so the rest of the day wasn't much good either. It worked out I got the strap 900 times in one year, the school record."

Nevil was not your typical juvenile delinquent. At age seven, he began raising parakeets; two years later he joined the Parakeet Society of Western Australia. "My best friend across the road got some parakeets," he explains, "and I got extremely jealous. After he started breeding I became quite adamant I'd do the same."

He eventually became friends with one of Australia's leading parakeet breeders, Bob Graham. "I learned an awful lot from him," he says. "He was a quadriplegic and he was incredibly intelligent." Nevil learned Mendel's laws of breeding and began charting dominant, recessive, and intermediate traits for his birds (something he would later do with cannabis plants). "I bought some of Graham's stock and got immediate results," he says. "When you breed parakeets, you breed to an ideal. It's like sculpting with genes."

When he was 15, Nevil was sent to a state school and forced to repeat his third year of high school. Consequently, he caught up with his classmates in size. "I got into a few fights," he says with a smile, "just to get back for all the times I'd been beaten up."

Although discipline at the school was considered harsh, it proved a cakewalk after Catholic school. "The first time I was brought before the headmaster to be punished, he made me hold out my hand and he tapped it twice with a cane," recalls Nevil. "I thought he was just aiming. I closed my eyes and waited for the real pain, but it never came. I was quite shocked. I thought, 'Well, now I can do anything I want.' I ignored the dress code and dressed how I pleased. That didn't go over well and I managed to get kicked out within three months."

He also discovered marijuana.

NEVIL'S FIRST HIGH

"I had an American friend who suggested we buy some," he says. "I remember thinking, 'Okay, I'm not scared.' We both pretended we'd done it before, when in fact, neither of us had. After scoring from someone at school, we went back to a shed outside his house. I volunteered to roll joints, even though I'd never done it before. There were three of us and I rolled three joints, one for each of us, hahaha. It seemed logical at the time, still does, actually, even though it was more normal to pass joints. But we didn't know any better. It was Indonesian weed and we got extremely ripped. I really liked the sense of time distortion—everything happened so slowly."

There was plenty of high-quality reefer going around Australia, and to insure a steady supply for himself, Nevil made the jump from smoker to dealer in a matter of weeks. Meanwhile, to satisfy his parents, he found a legitimate job.

"As long as I couldn't be the pope, my mother wanted me to be a doctor or a veterinarian," he says. "My father didn't see this as a possibility and just wanted me to get a job. Fortunately, I was offered work as a lab assistant at a local university, which was semi-professional, eh? And I was working, so they were both satisfied."

Nevil did well at the position. So well, in fact, that he was made acting head of the anatomy lab with responsibility for the operating room, animal room, and office. He was given the only set of keys to the drug cabinet and placed in charge of ordering drugs when supplies ran low. For someone interested in sampling illicit chemicals, it seemed like the perfect job.

"Having heard horror stories about cannabis and how horrible it was for you, I decided everyone in authority lied about drugs," says Nevil. "I knew cannabis wasn't harmful. I concluded the harmful effects of other drugs must be exaggerated as well. I started with barbiturates. I knew many people used them for sleeping tablets. Eventually, I tried morphine. I was quite good at giving injections. There's something very professional and doctorlike about giving yourself an injection. I had to inject rabbits and mice all the time, and if you can hit a vein in a rabbit's ear, you can get any human vein. I veined the first time I tried. Morphine made me feel good. I had friends who were already addicted to heroin and they encouraged me. Soon, I had a bag filled with tablets, pills, and chemicals of all sorts from the lab." Unfortunately for Nevil, this situation was not destined to last. Within a few months, he was arrested for drug possession. And it didn't take long for the police to figure out where the drugs had come from.

The head of the anatomy department suggested Nevil be sent to a treatment center. His parents agreed and had their son committed to a university psychiatric ward for six weeks. "I wasn't addicted at the time," says Nevil. "I used far too large a variety of ingestibles to become addicted to any one thing. After I was released I had the option of working part-time at the University—to build up my position again. But, uh, I felt the stigma of being a known user. It was a bit unbearable. So I left and started hanging around with people who supplied smack. Even though I started shooting smack, I never sold it. I just sold weed."

One day Nevil woke up with a terrific backache. His hips and the base of his spine hurt terribly. He went to a doctor and was given some pain pills, which proved useless. The doctor couldn't find anything wrong. Nevil went home and the pain still wouldn't go away. "Then I realized, 'Shit, I'm addicted," he says. "It was quite a substantial shock even though I knew it had to come eventually." He enrolled in a methadone program, which proved to be an extremely dehumanizing experience. "They made me beg for drugs," he says. "I didn't like that. I was scoring weed in Melbourne and shipping it back in huge speakers, telling people I was in a band. I was making what seemed like a huge sum of money—$5,000 a week."

Unfortunately, Nevil gave a free sample to a girl who was later arrested by the police. The girl identified Nevil as her supplier and a long court case ensued, one that eventually reached the Australian version of the Supreme Court. Throughout the trial, Nevil was enrolled

JAMES ROMBERGER

MAINTENANCE RUN

BY OWL

I cleaned the traps, then baited them with peanut butter. Rats love it; can't resist it.

They also love hemp fiber shredding. Rats need to chew or else their front teeth out-grow their bite, resulting in starvation. One big pack rat can strip a six-foot plant on a single fun-filled afternoon—and not eat any of it, just drag off stems to shred, then weave the fiber into his nest.

Rabbits are another story. The little hopping humpers love juicy growing tips. The nervous rodent bastards can't sit still long enough to eat a lethal dose of poison. They just hop from plant to plant eating whatever grows through the hoop from the ground level to a foot and a half high.

Jackrabbits are the worst. They're too paranoid to sleep; eat day and night, venting perfectly round pellets in a constant trail wherever they go.
#150, February 1988

PSYCHEDELIC MECCA

BY GREG SHAW

Since about 1982, neo-psychedelic music has been one of the strongest underground trends in American music, and its creative home has been Los Angeles.

Until recently, the Cavern Club on Hollywood Boulevard was a prime showcase for '60s music, a supportive home for the growing cult scene and a showcase for more than 100 new bands....

The Mods are a sizeable contingent in Southern California; for the most part a very conservative—if not reactionary—society, a few of them had developed an interest in borderline Mod psych bands of the '60s, like Creation and The Smoke, and from there went on to discover...The Chocolate Watchband, Seeds, The Standells....
#141, May 1987

AMERICA'S SECRET TEAM

BY JONATHAN MARSHALL, PETER DALE SCOTT AND JANE HUNTER

A relevant example is the so-called "Defection Program" authorized in 1947 (by National Security Council Intelligence Directive 4, a document still withheld in full). Despite explicit Congressional prohibitions, this program was designed to bring Nazi agents, some of them wanted war criminals, to this country, to develop the covert operations capability of the United States.

According to a US special warfare veteran, William Corson, some of these ex-Nazis became pilots in the 1950-52 supply operations of Civil Air Transport (later Air America) to opium-growing Chinese Nationalist guerrilla forces in Thailand. In his book *The Armies of Ignorance: The Rise of the American Intelligence Empire* (1977) Corson notes that those knowledgeable about an in-house murder and resulting "Thailand flap" have theorized "that the trafficking in drugs in Southeast Asia was used as a self-financing device to pay for services and persons whose hire would not have been approved by Washington."

Another book, Alfred McCoy's *The Politics of Heroin in Southeast Asia* (1972), documents that KMT forces were...supported with arms by an American company, Sea Supply....

#145, September 1987

---

in a methadone program and under psychiatric supervision. "I got the feeling things were coming to a head," he says. "My drug problem seemed quite insurmountable and the case didn't look promising. So I flew to Thailand."

ESCAPE TO BANGKOK

For several weeks Nevil lived in a cheap hotel in Bangkok, shooting heroin until his money ran out. He skipped out on the bill, moved to another hotel, and began hawking his valuables to raise money. "I found a taxi driver who would take me to exclusive shops in the city," he says. "The driver would get a kickback from the store for delivering Europeans to the shop, whether they bought anything or not. After we left, the driver and I would split the kickback."

However, after they'd visited every shop in Bangkok (and were no longer welcome at any of them), Nevil telephoned his parents and asked for a plane ticket home. Unfortunately, the police had already appeared at his house with a warrant for his arrest. "It didn't seem prudent to return to Australia," says Nevil with typical understatement. His parents sent him a ticket to the Netherlands and the address of an uncle living in the countryside.

After Thailand, Nevil's habit was really out of control. Upon arriving in Holland, he immediately enrolled in a methadone program and discovered he required 24 tablets a day to stay straight. "I handled that for about six months," he says. "I was trying to cut down, trying to fit in. I had unemployment benefits, which is enough to survive in Holland. But I was feeling quite lonely." Six months later, he moved to Tillberg, the center of Holland's smack scene.

Obviously, Tillberg was not the sort of environment conducive to kicking heroin. Junkies had taken over the city, converting pubs and hotels into shooting galleries. "My first day in town, I went to a bar called the Lawyer's Purse," says Nevil. "Smack was being sold up and down the counter. It was a madhouse. Apparently, the police didn't—or couldn't—do anything about it. It went on like that for quite some time. When the police would close one place down, everyone would move to another bar. It was a fairly rough town and I went through a time of hardship. I had no money except welfare. I had a raging habit. I was living in a town known for being tough and criminal. I cost the state large chunks of money as I went through all the available drug rehabilitation programs. After having made numerous failed attempts at stopping, I decided no one could help me. Which is true. No one can help a junkie. He can only help himself. So, I decided to kick heroin on my own. I convinced a doctor to give me 'ludes to sleep and a synthetic opiate, which probably didn't do anything. I stayed home and suffered for six weeks until I reached the point where I could handle alcohol. Then I started drinking every day, a half bottle of Scotch in the morning, a half bottle at night. I used the 'ludes to sleep, so that there was always a certain part of the day blocked out. Eventually, I got sick of hangovers and turned to grass. I decided it was probably the only acceptable drug."

In 1980, while still trying to kick his habit, Nevil stumbled across a copy of the *Marijuana Grower's Guide* by Mel Frank and Ed Rosenthal. "I'd grown some weed in the bush in Australia," he says. The book helped reawaken Nevil's interest in genetics. Why not combine his two favorite pursuits, breeding and drugs? Nevil applied for a loan to build an indoor growing chamber for marijuana. Only in Holland could such a request be taken seriously. "The drug program I was enrolled in gave grants to drug addicts to get them started doing something useful," he explains. "I told them I wanted to grow weed indoors. They weren't thrilled with the idea, but they gave me the money anyway." The unit consisted of eight 5-foot fluorescent lights. "There was a vacant lot behind my apartment and I filled it with weed. I had Nigerian, Colombian, and Mexican seeds. The Mexican was the best. I still have the strain. My dwarfs come from it." Although there wasn't much demand for homegrown weed in Holland, hash oil was a valuable commodity and could be sold easily. So Nevil became a professional hash oil maker.

THE FIRE

Nevil used petroleum ether, an extremely flammable liquid, for the distillation process. "I was heating it with thermostatically controlled electric plates," he says. Unfortunately, however, Nevil didn't realize that the thermostat on the heater had to be placed in another room because the thermostat sparks when turned on. He had a sink filled with 40 liters of petroleum ether, as well as a can with another 10 liters on the floor. One day he turned on the thermostat and it sparked. The spark turned into a flame, which instantly turned into a raging fire.

With eyes closed, Nevil ran to the adjoining room and dove out the window, bouncing off a roof and rolling onto a sidewalk. "My first thought after hitting the ground was to save my dope," he says with a laugh. He ran back inside, grabbed whatever hash oil he could find, and buried it in the backyard. He went back again and collected whatever valuables he could find. "Then I went next door to tell the neighbors," he says. "They were shocked by my appearance. I didn't realize my hair was singed, my face was black, my clothes were torn. I thought I had first-degree burns, and I was covered with blisters."

Twenty minutes later the police arrived, followed by the fire brigade and an ambulance. At the hospital, the burn specialist told him he was lucky to be in such pain because it meant the burns weren't first degree. He was given a shot of morphine to kill the pain. The next morning, however, Nevil refused further shots. "I knew I'd turn into a junkie again," he says.

Despite horror stories from his doctors about being scarred for life, Nevil was released two weeks later with no visible damage. There was one permanent change, however: Nevil decided not to make hash oil anymore.

Since Nevil had been reading HIGH TIMES, he knew revolutionary new *indica* strains were appearing in the United States, even though none were available in Holland. If only he could grow weed the Dutch would consider palatable, then he'd be in business and could sell marijuana instead of hash oil. He searched through copies of HIGH TIMES, hoping to find an *indica* seed supplier. "I looked for hidden meanings in all the ads," he says. "Of course, it was just fantasy on my part. I knew how diffcult it was to get good Nigerian and Indonesian seeds in America and I wanted to trade with someone."

Eventually, Nevil realized there was only one way to obtain good seeds, and that was to become a seed merchant himself. He hired a lawyer to investigate the legal implications and discovered it was possible to sell cannabis seeds in the Netherlands. Within a matter of months, he sent his first ad to HIGH TIMES.

"I expected there were thousands of people just like me, and as soon as they saw the ad, I'd be in business," recalls Nevil. Business, however, was

THE COCAINE-CONTRA CONNECTION

BY JOEL MILLMAN

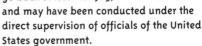

Three ex-smugglers, all currently in jail, have given testimony to federal officials that links the Nicaraguan Contras to illegal arms and drug shipments that go back at least to 1983, and may have been conducted under the direct supervision of officials of the United States government.

According to George Morales, Gary Betzner and Micheal Tolliver, the trafficking consisted of ferrying arms shipments to Contra supply depots in Honduras, El Salvador and Costa Rica, then returning cargoes of illegal drugs to the United States. The arms-for-drugs operation also offered the pilots the option of "freelancing," that is, running their own shipments of drugs up from Central and South America as an additional payment for making the arms runs. The three say they believe both ends of their missions were sanctioned by federal authorities.

George Morales, a three-time offshore powerboat champion, may be the most important witness.

#147, November 1987

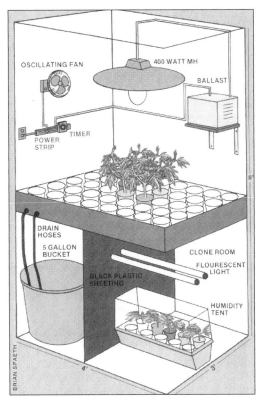

THE DR. INDOORS GUIDE TO CLONING

BY BRAM

The secret to a successful garden is cloning. Cloning insures females for harvest and allows the grower to take full advantage of his or her gene stock. Just like Dr. Mengele, who cloned Hitler with the future in mind, you can clone cannabis with your future gardens in mind. The immediate harvest is a bonus. What you're looking for is to establish a baseline on continual, identical gardens.

Let's assume you have a closet that can be turned into a mini-garden. The closet is 3'x4' (see diagram). The top two thirds of this space will be the main grow area and the bottom third will contain your clone room.

The Buds From Brazil, #158, October 1988

POLYMERS

BY DR. ZEE

Polymers looks like crystals when dry; when wet, they swell and retain moisture and nutrients. Without polymers, most of the water runs off too quickly to be absorbed by the root system. With polymers, water loss through evaporation is virtually eliminated. Polymers retain and release 90 percent of the moisture added to the soil.

#160, December 1988

disappointingly slow for the first few months. Why? Probably because most readers found it hard to believe high-quality seeds could be obtained so easily. Nevil doesn't discuss his distribution system, but there is no doubt the seeds were getting through. Most of the money Nevil received went back into improving his seed strains. Nevil went to great expense to obtain seeds, a commitment that is best illustrated by a secret trip to Mazar I Sharif in Afghanistan. According to the Moslem legend, one of Mohammed's sons died in the city. Consequently, it is a very holy city. It is also known for high-quality hashish. Although hash from the area had been readily available in Holland in the '70s, the Soviet invasion of the country greatly reduced exports. In 1985, an Afghan refugee told Nevil the fields around Mazar I Sharif were being destroyed. "That was all I needed to hear," says Nevil. "I caught the next plane to Pakistan to save the strain."

The story of this adventure was first reported in *Regardies* magazine and written by former HIGH TIMES reporter A. Craig Copetas. "After being smuggled into a refugee camp near Peshawar while lying on the floor of a car, Nevil made contact with a 30-year-old Muslim fanatic who had a throbbing vein that ran from between his eyes straight up his forehead," wrote Copetas. "The man took a lump of black hash out of his pocket and told Nevil that it had been processed by his uncle, a man known as Mr. Hashish. Surrounded by four men who were pointing machine-guns at him, Nevil set about negotiating with Mr. Hashish, a Mujahedin commander, and finally persuaded him to send a squad of his men 280 miles into Soviet-occupied territory and come back with two kilos of healthy Mazari seeds."

"He thought I was ridiculous because I didn't want to buy hash or opium," recalls Nevil. "Nobody had ever come there before to buy seeds, and at first he had no idea what I was talking about. I stood there trying to explain genetics to this tribal hash leader in sign language. When he finally figured out what I wanted, he asked for too much money. I took a zero off his price and gave him ten percent up front. He called me a bandit, but I had the seeds four days later."

Nevil also went to great lengths to obtain *ruderalis* seeds, a little-known cannabis strain that grows primarily in Russia. Although some American growers have sold so-called *ruderalis* strains in the past, Nevil undertook the necessary trip to the Russian-Hungarian border to authenticate the plant. *Ruderalis* is not known for spectacular resin content, but it flowers automatically—regardless of photoperiod, which makes it an extremely useful hybrid, especially for outdoor growers. Nevil plans to cross *ruderalis-indica* hybrids with his Mexican dwarfs. The result? The ultimate cannabis strain: a potent indoor/outdoor bonsai marijuana tree that matures within two months and never reaches a height over two feet. The plant would be nearly impossible to detect from the air and it could take years before the DEA even figured out what it was. Nevil is so close to perfecting this strain that seeds could be available by the time this article is published. This and other miracles can be expected soon from Cannabis Castle.

"Since becoming a seed merchant, I've directed all my energies and money into finding people with superior strains of cannabis and getting seeds out of them," says Nevil. "And I can honestly say, I've never heard of a strain I wanted that I wasn't able to get—one way or another. Theoretically, there is someone out there growing better stuff than I am using my seeds. Why? Because tens of thousands of plants are being grown with my stock. Selection from tens of thousands gets phenomenal results, while I can only select from a few hundred. I'm not holding back anything. Any grower in America can experiment with the same stock I do."

HOW TO BEAT A DRUG TEST

by Robert Freeman

We, the American people, are now facing the biggest threat to personal liberty of this century. It is not coming from communists or from another government, but from the American government itself—the drug urinalysis-test. First used on the Armed Forces, this test is slowly invading every aspect of our lives. For the occasional (or more) drug user it means the constant fear of losing one's job, or even one's freedom. Drug testing sets a bad precedent in the American judicial system, the ability to search someone not suspected of committing a crime—an act specifically prohibited by the Constitution of the United States.

But this is not news. Everyone's been hearing about urine testing in the media, as more and more companies and organizations start using it. What can the individual concerned with protecting him or herself do? As with all things, the test for marijuana is not infallible; it can be fooled. Especially if one is armed with the proper knowledge beforehand. This article will give you the knowledge to beat the urine test.

I was a Drug and Alcohol Officer for the United States military and now teach emergency medicine for an American university. I was a D&A officer because that was the safest job I could have in the military, considering my enjoyment of recreational drugs. In the course of a three-year hitch I helped many soldiers enjoy their personal freedoms without the encumbrances of the urinalysis test.

First one must look at the test itself. The urinalysis test for marijuana measures major metabolites of the chemical delta-9-tetrahydrocannabinol (THC), the active ingredient in marijuana. The standard for the test is a ratio measurement of solute (drug) to solution (water) measured in nanograms of solute per milliliter of water. There are only two sure ways to defeat this nemesis of personal freedom: lower the amount of solute or increase the amount of solution.

The first method is to lower the amount of solute in the body. THC is stored for up to 30 days in the fatty tissues of the body and slowly released into the urine over this period of time. We do not yet know a substance which will block the absorption of the drug into the fatty tissues, therefore the only way to effect a reduction of THC in the body is to stop the intake of the drug. Obviously this is not the purpose of this article, and we will not consider this option.

The second option is to increase the amount of solution. Think of it this way: There is a test that will detect the presence of oil in water if there is more than one part of oil in 1,000 parts of water. Theres a bucket that holds 5,000 drops of water but only has 1,000 drops of water in it. If two drops of oil are added to the bucket our oil test will detect the presence of oil. However, if 2,000 more drops of water are added to the bucket, then the ratio of oil to water drops from two parts per thousand to .6 parts per thousand and is no longer detectable by our test. This effect can be achieved in urine.

The easiest way to achieve this is with a drug known as Lasix[1]

ERIC DROOKER

WHAT TO DO IF YOU'RE FIRED BY A URINE TEST

So far, drug-urinalysis testing has twice gotten the Greyhound Company in bad legal trouble. Greyhound has twice fired drivers and mechanics after drug-testing them, and both times the employees went into labor arbitration, and were awarded reinstatement with back pay.

If you want the exact legal chapter and verse—care names, file numbers, etc.—on these and scores of other important legal decisions that have ruled against drug-testing you can write...NORML [1001 Connecticut, Suite 1119, Washington DC 20036, (202) 483-5500]. **HighWitness News by Dean Latimer, #135, November 1986**

FIRST ANNUAL CANNABIS CUP

Although the Cannabis Cup Awards were a lot of fun, they did have a serious motive: to establish an international standard for marijuana seeds. Since it is legal to sell marijuana seeds in Holland, and anyone visiting the country can sample the same brands the judges were smoking, that standard should only be a few months away.

Growers from around the world are encouraged to enter the Cannabis Cup Awards next year. However, since the contest is limited to Dutch seed merchants, growers outside Holland must locate a Dutch intermediary. This is actually quite easy: most seed companies are constantly looking for new strains. However, before rushing off to Holland with a handful of seeds, please keep in mind that most marijuana sold in the US is far below the standards of what is already available in Holland. *Judging the Cannabis Cup by Ed Hassle, #153, May 1988*

(generic name: furosemide). This is a diuretic and causes the kidneys to step up the excretion of water. Take 80 milligrams prior to the urinalysis test and urinate at least two or three times prior. Believe me this will not be hard. However, be sure and increase your water intake both before and after taking this drug so as to avoid dehydration.

Furosemide is a prescription drug, but is not controlled like narcotics and is usually easy to get your hands on.

If furosemide cannot be acquired the next best solution is fluid preload. However, this requires knowing when your urinalysis test is going to be and this is not always the case. If you do know then the night before the test drink **massive** amounts of water. The more the better. Then, the morning of the test (or right before, if it is the afternoon) drink copious amounts of coffee. Caffeine is a mild diuretic and will cause an effect similar to furosemide although not nearly as effectively. But, if you smoke less than two or three times a day, this should get you through your urinalysis with no drug detected.

So much for the chemical means, now for the mechanical. The best, easiest, and least detectable means is taping a 250cc intravenous solution bag under your arm. These can be purchased at most drugstores or from medical supply houses without a prescription. Use only normal saline as this is undetectable as a contaminant. Tape the tubing to the front of your body and run it to the urinary meatus (opening). When it is time to urinate, fill the sample bottle with very little urine, then use your arm to squeeze the fluid out of the bag and into the sample bottle. The bag placed under the arm early enough insures that the sample will be warm enough when it is handed back to the tester.

One of the myths about urine tests is that putting salt, aspirin, and other contaminants into the sample will alter the results of the test. This is not likely. The test measures only the drug and not the contents of the solution. Other substances, short of causing damage to the machine, will not alter the results. In addition, if whomever is testing detects the presence of a contaminant in your urine, then they will probably test you again or not hire you, if your test is a pre-employment test.

Another common myth is that urinalysis can be defeated by the drinking of vinegar prior to a test. The principle behind this is that the kidneys tend to excrete more of a solute when the blood is slightly alkaline. Drinking vinegar (an acid) in sufficient amounts would cause the blood to become acidic and suppress the excretion of metabolites (drugs). You would have to drink a *lot* of vinegar to accomplish this. This would alter the pH balance of the blood, a dangerous thing to do even in a hospital and rather stupid to do outside of one.

So you see, the drug urinalysis test is not a hard test to take, if you study. When enough people can defeat this menace to society its usefulness will become nil. But merely defeating the test is not enough—let your congressman know how you feel. The freedom you preserve may be your own.

1. Lasix is a registered trademark of the Hoechest-Roussel Company.

PART 5
LAUNCHING THE
HEMP MOVEMENT
1989-1994

SALES BEGAN TO SKYROCKET AFTER WE BEGAN PROMOTING THE
ENVIRONMENTAL BENEFITS OF HEMP

JACK HERER

BY STEVEN HAGER

HT: When did you first become aware of hemp?

JH: In 1973, when I began working on the California Marijuana Initiative (CMI). The guy who got me involved was called Captain Ed. He convinced me to donate some of my time to the legalization movement. We made a pact that we wouldn't stop working for legalization until marijuana was legal, or we were 84 years old, or we were dead. Captain Ed and his CMI friends introduced me to all this esoteric information about hemp paper and fiber.

HT: When did you reach the conclusion that legalizing hemp would reverse the Greenhouse Effect?

JH: About 1979 or 1980, I began to figure out that it was the only thing that would work. You see, the Greenhouse Effect is the direct result of burning fossil or old carbon fuels. There is only one plant that can completely substitute for fossil fuel. The plant is an annual that grows in all 50 states. It is the fastest growing sustainable biomass on the planet. It can produce paper, fiber, food and fuel. One of the most amazing things I found was the first issue of HIGH TIMES, which had an article titled "Hemp Paper Reconsidered" by Jack Frazier.

HT: Why do you think marijuana was made illegal? Did the oil industry play a role?

JH: I believe that DuPont is either the most criminal corporation in the history of the world or the most ignorant.... About 80% of DuPont's business would not exist if hemp was legal. I base this figure on paint, varnish, plastics, fiber, and from the sulfide process used to produce wood pulp paper.

Interview, #176, April 1990

CAN POT SAVE THE WORLD?

by Jack Herer

DID YOU KNOW...
That hemp (marijuana) production played a major role in the War of 1812, a fact that has been written out of every history book in America?

1700's and Early 1800's
Cannabis hemp is, as it has been for the thousands of years before, the biggest business and most important industry on the planet.

1710 on...
Russia, because of its cheap slave/serf labor, produces 80 percent of the western world's cannabis hemp, finished hemp products, and is, by far, the world's best-quality manufacturer of cannabis hemp for sails, rope, rigging and nets. Cannabis is Russia's number one trading commodity—ahead of its furs, timber and iron.

1710 to 1807
Great Britain buys *90%* or more of its marine hemp from Russia; Britain's navy and world sea trade runs on Russian hemp. Each British ship *must* replace 50 to 100 tons of hemp every year or two.

1793 to 1799 on...
The British nobility is hostile toward the new French government primarily because the British are afraid that the 1789-93 French Revolution of commoners could spread, and/or result in a French invasion of England and the loss of its Empire and, of course, its nobility's heads.

1803 to 1814
Britain's navy blockades Napoleon's France, including Napoleon's allies on the Continent. Britain accomplishes the blockade of France by closing their (France's) English Channel and Atlantic (Bay of Biscay) ports with its navy; also, Britain controls absolute access to and from the Mediterranean and Atlantic, by virtue of its control of Gibraltar.

1803 on...
The **Louisiana Purchase** gives rise to some Americans', mostly Westerners', dreams of "Manifest Destiny"—that is—the United States should extend to all of North America, from the top of Canada (furs) to the bottom of Mexico, and from the Atlantic to the Pacific.

1803 to 1807
Britain continues to trade and buy 90% of its hemp directly from Russia.

1798 to 1812
The fledgling United States is officially "neutral" in the war between France and Britain. The United States even begins to solve its own foreign problems by sending its navy and marines (1801-1805) to the Mediterranean to stop Tripoli pirates and ransomers from collecting tribute from or for American **Yankee traders** operating in the area. "Millions for Defense—not a penny for Tribute" was America's rallying cry, and the incident came to be reflected in the second line of the Marine hymn: "...to the shores of Tripoli."

1803
Napoleon, needing money to press war with Great Britain and pursue control of the European continent, bargain-sells the *Louisiana Territory* to the United States for $15 million, or roughly two-and-a-half cents per acre.

Photos from the
HIGH TIMES
archives

ALLEGRA, OF THE NEW YORK CITY BAND FEEL FUZZY, HAS APPEARED ON THE COVER OF HIGH TIMES MORE THAN ANY OTHER MODEL.

REPUTED TO BE SOME OF THE FINEST POT IN HARLEM, THIS STRAIN BECAME KNOWN AS "THE CHRONIC."

THIS AMAZING BUD WAS GROWN ON A FIRE ESCAPE IN NEW YORK CITY.

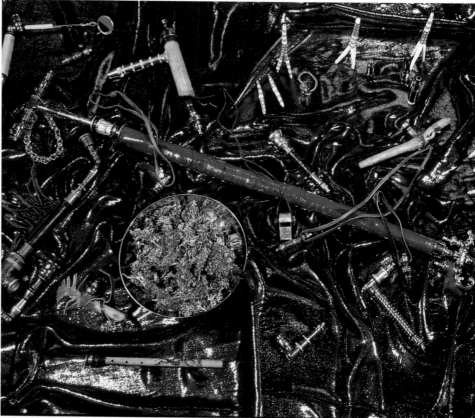

ALL THE SMOKING DEVICES SHOWN HERE WERE MADE BY THE INFAMOUS JOE PIPE.

The Cannabis Cup

EVERY YEAR, HIGH TIMES SPONSORS A MARIJUANA CONTEST IN HOLLAND. IN 1993, ROBIN LUDWIG DESIGNED THIS SILVER TROPHY FOR THE WINNING STRAINS.

HOLLAND IS THE ONLY COUNTRY IN THE WORLD WHERE COFFEESHOPS LIKE THE ONE SHOWN HERE OPENLY SELL MARIJUANA.

THE MAJOR SEED PRODUCERS OF HOLLAND PROVIDED THE POT SHOWN HERE FOR THE 6TH ANNUAL CANNABIS CUP, HELD OVER THANKSGIVING WEEKEND IN 1993.

IN THE LATE '80S, A NEW BREED OF CANNABIS ACTIVISTS BEGAN APPEARING ON COLLEGE CAMPUSES ACROSS THE COUNTRY.

HIGH TIMES RESPONDED BY CREATING THE FREEDOM FIGHTERS, WHO TRAVELED ACROSS THE COUNTRY IN A PSYCHEDELIC BUS, SPREADING THE MESSAGE THAT OUR FOUNDING FATHERS GREW HEMP.

The Freedom Fighters

WHEREVER THE BUS STOPPED, CHEF RA PROVIDED FREE FOOD FOR THE ACTIVISTS.

THE ASSASSINETTES, LUCY, KIMONA 117 AND ABBEY, WERE FEATURED PERFORMERS WITH THE OFFICIAL FREEDOM FIGHTER BAND, THE SOUL ASSASSINS.

HI! I'M NEW IN THE NEIGHBORHOOD! I JUST THOUGHT I'D DROP OVER AND GET ACQUAINTED!

BARK! BARK!

WE COULD HAVE A "GET-ACQUAINTED" PARTY" RIGHT HERE THIS AFTERNOON!

I'M "INTO" ALL KINDS OF THINGS... MASSAGE, BODY PAINTING, PHOTOGRAPHY, NUDE SWIMMING, AND ALL KINDS OF "INDOOR GAMES!"

I'VE GOT A FRIEND! WE COULD DO A THREESOME!

MAYBE YOU'D LIKE FRENCH LESSONS? HOW ABOUT GREEK CULTURE? ARE YOU INTERESTED IN UNDERWEAR?

S. & M.? B. & D.? GOLDEN SHOWER? ANIMAL LOVER?

ER, UH... NECROPHILIA? COP... UH... COPROPHAGIA???

(WHAT THE HELL IS "COPROPHAGIA?")

SLAM SLAM

WHY DID YOU SLAM THE DOOR IN THAT LADY'S FACE PHINEAS?

THAT SOUNDED LIKE A LOT OF FUN!

THAT WAS NO LADY! THAT WAS NOTORIOUS NORBERT IN DRAG! HE MUST'VE BEEN DEMOTED TO THE VICE SQUAD!

GET BACK IN THE SQUAD CAR, PATROLMAN NORBERT!

CAN'T YOU DO ANYTHING RIGHT!

AW, COME ON, LIEUTENANT O'FLYE! TAKE IT EASY! I'M NEW ON THE "DOOR-TO-DOOR ENTRAPMENT" DETAIL!

THE END

1807

Napoleon and Czar Alexander of Russia sign the Treaty of Tilset, which cuts off all legal Russian trade with Great Britain, its allies or any other *neutral nation* ship acting as agents for Great Britain in Russia.

Napoleon's strategy and his most important goal of the treaty is to stop Russian hemp from reaching England, thereby destroying Britain's navy by forcing it to cannibalize sails, ropes, and rigging from other ships; and eventually, Napoleon believes, with no Russian hemp for its huge Navy, the British will be forced to end its blockade of France and the Continent.

1807 to 1809

The United States is considered a neutral country by Napoleon as long as its ships do not trade with or for Great Britain, and the United States considers itself to be neutral in the war between France and Great Britain. However, Congress passes the 1806 Non-Importation Pact. British articles which were produced in the U.S., which could be produced elsewhere were prohibited. Congress also passes the 1807 Embargo Act to wit: American ships could not bring or carry products to or from Europe. These laws hurt America more than Europe; however, many Yankee traders ignored the law anyway.

1807 to 1809

After the Treaty of Tilset cut off their Russian trade, Britain claims that there are no neutral countries or shipping lanes. Hence, any ship that trades with Napoleon's "Continental System" of allies are the enemy and are subject to blockade. On this pretext, Britain confiscates American ships and cargo and sends sailors back to the United States at American ship owners' expense. Britain "impresses" some American sailors into service in the British Navy. However, England claims that they only "impress" those sailors who are British subjects and whose American shipping companies refused to pay for the sailors' return fares.

1807 to 1810

Secretly, however, Britain offers the captured American traders a "deal" (actually a blackmail proposition) when they "overhaul"—board and confiscate—an American ship and bring it into an English port. *The deal*: Lose your ship and cargoes forever, or, go to Russia and secretly buy hemp for Britain, who will pay the American traders, in gold, in advance, and more gold when the hemp is delivered back. At the same time, the Americans will be allowed to keep and trade their own goods (rum, sugar, spices, cotton, coffee, tobacco) to the Czar for hemp—a double profit for the Americans.

1808 to 1810

Our shrewd Yankee traders, faced with the choice of either running British blockades and risk having their ships, cargo, and crews confiscated, or acting as secret (illegal) licensees for Britain, with safety and profits guaranteed, mostly chose the latter. John Quincy Adams, later to become president, who was in 1809 the American Consul at St. Petersburg, noted:

"As many as **600 clipper ships**, flying the American flag, in a two week period, were in Kronstadt [the Port of St. Petersburg, now called Leningrad, Russia], loading principally cannabis hemp for England [illegally], and for America, where quality hemp is in great demand also."

The United States passes the *1809 Non-Intercourse Act* which resumes legal trade with Europe, except Britain and France. It is soon replaced with the *Macon Bill* resuming all legal trade.

1989: YEAR OF PROTEST

BY ED HASSLE

If you're a cannabis consumer, you probably don't realize the extent of your repressed anger over this country's insane drug policies. Most of this anger is the result of the persecution you have suffered from family, police and the court system.

For hundreds of years black Americans were persecuted and they made very little headway until the Civil Rights Movement. The anger of black America was never felt until the freedom marches and sit-ins of the '60s. That is why it is so important for every pot smoker in this country to become actively involved in the pro-cannabis movement.

For the first time, I marched in Madison this fall. I was totally unprepared for the emotions that overtook me as I marched down State Street to the Wisconsin State Capitol with 15,000 others. A tremendous cathartic release was unleashed from the depths of my soul.

#161, January 1989

ABBIE HOFFMAN

"There are now over 200 colleges that have kicked South Africa out of the stock portfolios of their university—some six billion dollars. That's not exactly a career/marriage/yuppie interest. There's over 180 schools that have kicked the CIA off campus in terms of recruiting. As I speak at college campuses, I see schools that are fighting curfews, fighting campus controls of newspapers, holding pot protests, protesting the absence of minority programs, fighting a growing racism that's happening on campus—fighting all kinds of battles. At the same time, this generation went three to one for Bush. That's pretty far out.

"I would say we're in a state of great transition. We're passing out of a period of passivity on the part of the citizenry, a kind of nihilistic pessimism on the part of the youth, and headed towards a period of increased participatory democracy and increased activism. I would also say that since we lost the Vietnam War, America has been on the decline as an empire, which means things happening in other countries are going to have a tremendous effect on us."

Interview by John Holmstrom, #165, May 1989

OLIVER NORTH

ERIC DROOKER

BY ERIC DROOKER During the public investigation of the Iran/contra scandal, the testimony of Oliver North was broadcast throughout America. Regularly scheduled TV shows were preempted. North was portrayed as a national hero because, though he broke the law, he did it in the name of fighting communism. US senators were very gentle in their questioning of North, and the issue of drugs was barely touched upon. Television cameras ignored the banner that was unfurled by a spectator at the hearings which read: "ASK ABOUT COCAINE!" (This spectator was instantly jumped and arrested, and is now serving a three-year prison sentence.)

Another key personality questioned during the Senate investigation was Ramon Milian Rodriguez.... In an interview with journalist Leslie Cockburn in June, 1987, Rodriguez stated: "There seems to be a big to-do about the CIA having connections with drugs. It might be news now, but it's something that has been quite prevalent for quite some time. Outside of the United States, drug dealers are very powerful people. They have the ability to put governments in power or topple them, if they do it subtly. They have cash. The CIA deals primarily with items outside of the US. If they want to deal in foreign countries' policies and politics, they are going to run up against, or run with, the drug dealers. It can't be done any other way...if the end result is for the benefit of everyone, it usually works."

Guns, Drugs, and Money, #165, May 1989

BEN MASEL

If 1989 is truly the year of protest, then Ben Masel certainly qualifies as our counterculture hero. Almost single-handedly Ben has kept the cannabis reform protest movement alive. His annual Midwest Harvest Festival in Madison, Wisconsin, is an event no self-respecting pothead should miss. At this year's Madison Rally, HIGH TIMES will be accepting votes for the 1990 Counterculture Hero of the Year. Hope to see you there!

Page Six by Steven Hager, #161, January 1989

1808 to 1810

Napoleon insists that Czar Alexander stop all trade with the independent United States traders as they are being coerced into being illegal traders for Great Britain's hemp. Napoleon wants the Czar to allow him to place/station *French* agents and troops in Kronstadt to make sure the Czar and his port authorities live up to the treaty.

1808 to 1810

The Czar says "Nyet!" despite his treaty with France, and turns a "blind eye" to the illegal American traders probably because he needs the popular, profitable trade goods the Americans are bringing him and his Nobles, as well as the hard gold he is getting from the Americans' (illegal) purchases of hemp for Great Britain.

1809

Napoleon's allies invade the Duchy of Warsaw.

1810

Napoleon *orders* the Czar to stop all trade with the American traders! The Czar responds by withdrawing Russia from that part of the *Treaty of Tilset* that would require him to stop selling goods to neutral American ships.

1810 to 1812

Napoleon, infuriated with the Czar for allowing the life blood of Britain's navy—hemp—to reach England, builds his army and invades Russia to punish the Czar and ultimately stop hemp from reaching the British Navy.

1811 to 1812

England, again an ally and full trading partner of Russia, is still stopping American ships from trading with the rest of the Continent. Britain also blockades all U.S. traders from Russia at the Baltic Sea and insists that American traders have to now buy other strategic goods from them, secretly, mostly from Mediterranean ports, i.e., from Napoleon and his allies on the Continent who by this time are happy to sell anything to raise capital.

1812

The United States, cut off from 80% of its Russian hemp supply, debates war in Congress. Ironically, the representatives of the Western states argue for war under the excuse of "impressed" American sailors. However, the representatives of the Maritime States, fearful of loss of trade, argue against war, even though it's their shipping, crews, and states that are allegedly affected.

Not one senator from a Maritime State votes for war with Great Britain. Virtually all Western senators vote for war, hoping to take Canada from Britain and fulfill their dream of "manifest destiny," in the belief that Great Britain is too busy in European wars with Napoleon to protect Canada.

The Western states win in Congress, and on June 18, 1812, the United States is at war with Britain. America enters the war on the side of Napoleon, who marches on Moscow in June of 1812. Napoleon is soon defeated in Russia, by its harsh winter, the Russian scorched-earth policy, 2,000 miles of snowy and muddy supply lines, and by Napoleon not stopping for the winter and regrouping before marching on Moscow as was the original battle plan. Of the 450,000 to 600,000 men Napoleon starts with, only 180,000 ever make it back.

1812 to 1814

Britain, after initial success in war with the United States (including the burning of Washington in retaliation for the earlier American burning of Toronto, then the colonial Canadian capital), finds its finances and military stretched thin—with blockades, war in Spain with France, and a tough new America on the seas. Britain agrees to peace, and signs a treaty with the United States in December, 1814. The actual terms of the treaty give little to either side. But, in effect, Britain agrees to never again interfere with American shipping and the United States will give up all claims to Canada forever (which we did with the exception of "54-40 or Fight").

POT SEED AS THE BASIC WORLD FOOD

Hemp seed was used in porridge, soups, and gruels by virtually all the people of the world regularly, until this century.

Monks were required to eat it three times a day, make their clothes, and print their Bibles from paper made from its fiber.

(See "Research Institute For The Study Of Man," Dr. Vera Rubin; Eastern Orthodox Church; *Therapuetic Potential of Marijuana*; E. Abel, Marijuana, The First 12,000 Years; Ency. Brit.)

WHY AS FOOD?

The marijuana hemp seed (which is technically a fruit) is the second-most "complete" (has the eight essential amino acids) vegetable protein source on our planet!, only soybeans have a bit more protein. However, hemp seed is *many* times cheaper and its protein potential can be utilized better than soybean by the human body.

In fact, the marijuana seed is the highest in enzymes and overall amino acids of *any* food on our planet, including soybeans. Hemp seed extracts*, like soybeans, can be made to taste like chicken, steak, or pork. Hemp seeds, like soybeans, also can be used to make tofu-type curd and margarine, and at only **ten to twenty percent** of the cost of soybeans. (*U.S. Agricultural index; The Marijuana Farmers*, 1972, Frazier.)

Please Note: **When marijuana is grown for seed** the **half weight** of the full grown plant is **seed!!!**

*No!, like the shirts, hemp seeds won't get you high either.

MARIJUANA METHANE AS THE BASIC WORLD FUEL

In the 1920s and '30s, most American cars and farm vehicles were sold with the option to run either on methanol *or* gasoline or both. During the gas shortages of World War II, methanol was widely used by farmers and even the military. It is still used by most racing cars today.

Methanol does not pollute! When burned it emits only carbon dioxide and water vapors; and while growing it takes three times as much carbon dioxide out of the air before eventually putting (when burned) one-third of it back...whereas oil or coal only can pollute—never clean—because its source—vegetation or dinosaur—died millions of years ago.

The early Oil Barons (Rockefeller, Standard; Rothschilds, Shell; et al.) paranoically aware in the '30s of the possibilities of Ford's methanol scheme* and its cheapness, dropped and kept oil prices incredibly low—between $1.00 to $2.00 per barrel (there are 42 gallons in an oil barrel)—for almost 50 years until 1970. So low, in fact, that no other energy source could compete with them...and when they were sure of the lack of competition, the price jumped to almost $40.00 per barrel in the next ten years.

Suddenly, for whatever reason, we are now in an era when oil is not only prohibitively expensive, but embargos or wars by foreign nations,

TOMMY CHONG

BY EILEEN POLK

HT: When were you turned on to pot?

TC: It was neat—when I first got turned on to pot, it was almost legal in the sense that no one really knew what it was, so no one really cared about it, especially in Canada. I remember smoking it behind this jazz club with the guys that turned me on, and the police came and searched the car for booze. And we were all laughing hysterically. They wanted to know what kind of tobacco that was, and we told them it was Italian tobacco.

HT: Do you feel like you're doing something that could get you into trouble, or do you welcome that?

TC: No, I don't want to get in trouble.... I've seen too many martyrs go down. Their lives are ruined, because that's what those old fucks want, a target. They love a target, then they'll eat you up. Because you see, it's all money....

It's the same thing with the government. The very people doing the biggest anti-drug thing are usually involved with keeping it happening. They scare the shit out of you and then say, "I'll save you, but pay me. I need all this money." The great minds of this country have already figured out how to make this country a paradise, but nobody listens to them.

HT: The drug war is a billion dollar industry now.

TC: They burn up the billion dollars worth of drugs, and then they create all this corruption, all this crime—can you imagine being a narc who's making $20,000, $30,000 tops $50,000 a year, busting kids who have that much in their pockets? And all he has to do is lose half of it on the way to the police station. And the minute you start doing that you're a thief. The temptation is ridiculous.

Tommy Chong Smokin' Solo, #166, June 1989

127

HASH BASH '89

BY BUFORD BOSKO

The Hash Bash itself was the biggest blast since the Madison Harvest Festival—we figured it was about 5,000 people. The diag was crammed with people who had heard about last year's Bash. In 1988, we guessed there were 2,500 people, and this year it looked like twice as many, even though the local newspapers said it was only 1,000 people. But that's the way it is nowadays—the media is out to destroy the movement.

At noon, the festivities started. For the second year in a row, the HIGH TIMES marching band made its appearance, made up of assorted Freedom Fighters and psychedelic bus crew members, and even a couple of ROTC guys (it turns out that they were charter members of Ed Hassle's Freedom Fighters, but I heard they got busted for wearing their military uniforms at a pot rally!).

#167, July 1989

BATTLE OF THE HEMP BALES

BY GUY KINNISON

In the summer of 1861, the state of Missouri had not seceded from the Union, but rebels from Missouri set up their own government in exile and fighting broke out in the state....

A local resident came up with a plan to defeat the Federals. By soaking the giant hemp bales and pushing them up the hill, the hemp could be used as moving breastworks.... Behind each bale, three or four men pushed toward the Federal trenches.

The Yanks tried in vain to set the bales on fire by using hot shot in their cannons. A few bales broke apart only to be replaced by other bales.

The Missourians kept pushing closer until the Federals ran out of food, water and supplies and the Union men surrendered to the rebels.

#168, August 1989

i.e. OPEC, Khomeni's Iran, etc., can virtually hold the U.S. hostage. Methanol and other methods deserve serious investigation—and certainly no governmental or bureaucratic impediment to the most efficient growing celluloses of all—hemp, cornstalks, sugarcane. In fact, Brazil in 1984 ran 1,200,000 cars on methanol made from sugarcane stalks.

Depending on the method used to produce it, methanol can be *retailed* for about $6.00 per barrel or 15 cents per gallon. The cellulose used in methanol production may be obtained from cornstalks, wood, or even lawn trimmings. *Science Digest* (a Hearst publication) reported in 1983 that *"over"* 50% of America's automotive gasoline needs could be fulfilled through an aggressive program of recycling the cellulose contained in just our waste paper alone!—That bears repeating: 50% of all America's gas for cars can come from recycling waste paper, right now!

Then—depending on which U.S. agricultural report is correct—a full-grown hemp plant can provide about 4 to 50—to even 100 times the cellulose found in cornstalk, the planet's next highest annual cellulose plant. Hemp can, in most places, be harvested twice a year, and in warmer areas, such as Southern California, Texas, Florida, and the like, it could be a "year round" crop.

The United States government pays (in cash or in "kind") for farmers to refrain from growing on 89 *million* acres of farmland each year, called the *soil bank*. Ten million of these acres in hemp would be the *equivalent of 40 million to 500 million acres of cornstalks*—(given the difference for C-3 plants and C-4 plants **METHANE POTENTIAL**) enough to run America, with the recycling of paper, etc.—virtually without oil except as petroleum fertilizer. And 10 to 89 million acres of hemp or cornstalks plus its corn would make it (energy) a whole new ballgame.

*Henry Ford even grew marijuana on his estate after 1937 to prove the cheapness of methanol.

NEW BILLION DOLLAR CROP

Popular Mechanics, February 1938
In 1916, Lyster H. Dewey, Botanist in Charge of Fiber Plant Investigations, predicted that once the necessary machines were invented, it would be cheaper to make paper out of cannabis than wood pulp. Below is the front page of his report. An employee of the U.S. Dept. of Agriculture, Dewey felt that hemp would again become America's number one farm crop.

Twenty-two years later, the machinery was finally available, as outlined in Popular Mechanics, *February 1938. However, just as this invention and the cannabis plant were about to revolutionize the fiber industry, cannabis was made illegal.*

"American farmers are promised a new cash crop with an annual value of several hundred million dollars, all because a machine has been invented which solves a problem more than 6,000 years old. It is hemp, a crop that will not compete with other American products. Instead, it will displace imports of raw material and manufactured products produced by underpaid coolie and peasant labor and it will provide thousands of jobs for American workers throughout the land.

"The machine which makes this possible is designed for removing the fiber-bearing cortex from the rest of the stalk, making hemp fiber available for use without a prohibitive amount of human labor.

"Hemp is the standard fiber of the world. It has great tensile strength and durability. It is used to produce more than 5,000 textile products, ranging from rope to fine laces, and the woody "hurds" remaining after the fiber has been removed contain more than 77 percent cellulose, and can be used to produce more than 25,000 products, ranging from dynamite to Cellophane.

"Machines now in service in Texas, Illinois, Minnesota and other states are producing fiber at a manufacturing cost of half a cent a pound, and are finding a profitable market for the rest of the stalk. Machine operators are making a good profit in competition with coolie-produced foreign fiber while paying farmers fifteen dollars a ton for hemp as it comes from the field.

"From the farmers' point of view, hemp is an easy crop to grow and will yield from three to six tons per acre on any land that will grow corn, wheat, or oats. It has a short growing season, so that it can be planted after other crops are in. It can be grown in any state of the union. The long roots penetrate and break the soil to leave it in perfect condition for the next year's crop. The dense shock of leaves, eight to twelve feet above the ground, chokes out weeds. Two successive crops are enough to reclaim land that has been abandoned because of Canadian thistles or quack grass.

"Under old methods, hemp was cut and allowed to lie in the fields for weeks until it 'retted' enough so the fibers could be pulled off by hand. Retting is simply rotting as a result of dew, rain and bacterial action. Machines were developed to separate the fibers mechanically after retting was complete, but the cost was high, the loss of fiber great, and the quality of fiber comparatively low. With the new machine, known as a decorticator, hemp is cut with a slightly modified grain binder. It is delivered to the machine where an automatic chain conveyor feeds it to the breaking arms at the rate of two or three tons per hour. The hurds are broken into fine pieces which drop into the hopper from where they are delivered by blower to a baler or to truck or freight car for loose shipment. The fiber comes from the other end of the machine, ready for baling.

"From this point on almost anything can happen. The raw fiber can be used to produce strong twine or rope, woven into burlap, used for carpet warp or linoleum backing or it may be bleached and refined with resinous by-products of high commercial value. It can, in fact, be used to replace the foreign fibers which now flood our markets.

"Thousands of tons of hemp hurds are used every year by one large powder company for the manufacture of dynamite and TNT. A large paper company, which has been paying more than a million dollars a year in duties on foreign-made cigarette papers, now is manufacturing these papers from American hemp grown in Minnesota. A new factory in Illinois is producing fine bond papers from hemp. The natural materials in hemp make it an economical source of pulp for any grade of paper manufactured, and the high percentage of alpha cellulose promises an unlimited supply of raw material for the thousands of cellulose products our chemists have developed.

"It is generally believed that all linen is produced from flax. Actually, the majority comes from hemp—authorities estimate that more than half of our imported linen fabrics are manufactured from hemp fiber. Another misconception is that burlap is made from hemp. Actually, its source is usually jute, and practically all of the burlap we use is woven by laborers in India who receive only four cents a day. Binder twine is usually made from sisal which comes from Yucatan and East Africa.

"All of the products, now imported, can be produced from home-

THE DAY TOM KILLED HIGH TIMES

BY JOHN HOLMSTROM

When Tom Forçade received his FBI files on January 16, 1975, he now had tangible proof that his most paranoid fears were true—the government had been keeping track of his activities since he was working in Phoenix on *Orpheus*, way back in 1968. The discovery at about the same time that an undercover police officer was working in the office also unsettled him. So did the visit to the HIGH TIMES offices by the DEA. When they threatened to arrest him unless he revealed his sources, Tom merely put out his wrists, and dared them to take him away. They left, but the message they delivered remained.

There was a dark side to Tom Forçade. He suffered from a manic-depressive disorder, and from severe seasonal mood swings usually in the fall and winter. In the autumn of 1976, after an absence of four months, Tom returned to the HIGH TIMES office. He ordered all of the art boards for the latest issue immediately delivered to his office before they went to the printer. Upon inspection, he threatened to rip the whole magazine into shreds and force the staff to create a new one from scratch. As Andy Kowl recalls, Tom commanded, "I want you to close the magazine. Your job is terminated. Everybody's job is terminated. Fire everybody on the staff."

Tom stormed into the office, ripping the telephone intercom system out of the reception room. Then he headed for the newsroom. "Everyone was running around scared to death," Craig Copetas relates. "I jacked him up against the wall and said, 'Tom, go home. We're putting out a magazine.'"
The Ultimate Hippie: The Life and High Times of Thomas King Forçade, #170, October 1989

NORML'S NEW DON

ANDRE GROSSMANN

BY STEVE BLOOM

NORML has a new leader. His name is Don Fiedler. He was appointed by the organization's Board of Directors in June and began full-time work as the national director in November....

Fiedler, a Nebraska lawyer, helped lead the fight for decriminalization of marijuana in Nebraska. He started the state's chapter of the National Association of Criminal Defense Lawyers. Fiedler was elected to the NORML Board in June, 1988. A year later, on June 25, he became the eighth director in NORML's 20 year history....

Most important for Fiedler is pulling NORML out of debt. "Obviously, something has been wrong with our marketing approach," he says. "All we need is one dollar each from every pot smoker. I'm going to try to stir things up, to energize the casual smoker."

HighWitness News, #172, December 1989

TEUN VOETEN

One day in 1988, I got a phone call from a Dutch photographer who said he was in New York for a few days and wanted to meet me. Since we do a lot of photography in Holland, I thought it was a good idea. A few hours later, in walked Teun Voeten, a young anthropology student from Leiden University in Holland. Teun was armed with an outstanding portfolio of architectural photographs. The work was good enough that I immediately offered him the job of photographing the Cannabis Cup Awards.

While Teun was in the office, I happened to mention how much I admired the Dutch Provos, a group of radicals based in Amsterdam in the '60s. Although little-known in this country, the Provos were the most innovative social revolutionaries of their era.

Suddenly we both got very excited about the possibility of publishing the first definitive history of the Provo movement. Since so little has been written about the group, the job required a lot of research. Teun flew back to Holland and spent nearly a year tracking down all the original members for interviews. The result is a great article and presenting it provides my proudest moment as a magazine editor.

Page Six by Steven Hager, #173, January 1990

grown hemp. Fish nets, bow strings, canvas, strong rope, overalls, damask tablecloths, fine linen garments, towels, bed linen and thousands of other everyday items can be grown on American farms. Our import of foreign fabrics and fibers average about $200,000,000 per year; raw fibers alone we imported over $50,000,000 in the first six months of 1937. All of this income can be made available for Americans.

"The paper industry offers even greater possibilities. As an industry it amounts to over $1,000,000,000 a year, and of that, 80 percent is imported. But hemp will produce every grade of paper, and government figures estimate that 10,000 acres devoted to hemp will produce as much paper as 40,000 acres of average pulp land.

"One obstacle in the onward march of hemp is the reluctance of farmers to try new crops. The problem is complicated by the need for proper equipment a reasonable distance from the farm. The machine cannot be operated profitably unless there is enough acreage within driving range and farmers cannot find a profitable market unless there is machinery to handle the crop. Another obstacle is that the blossom of the female hemp plant contains marijuana, a narcotic, and it is impossible to grow hemp without producing the blossom. Federal regulations now being drawn up require registration of hemp growers, and tentative proposals for preventing narcotic production are rather stringent.

"However, the connection of hemp as a crop and marijuana seems to be exaggerated. The drug is usually produced from wild hemp or locoweed which can be found on vacant lots and along railroad tracks in every state. If federal regulations can be drawn to protect the public without preventing the legitimate culture of hemp, this new crop can add immeasurably to American agriculture and industry."

DUTCH PROVOS
by Teun Voeten

It all started with the Nozems. Born out of the postwar economic boom, the Nozems were disaffected Dutch teens armed with consumer spending power. Part mods, part '50s juvenile delinquents, they spent most of their time cruising the streets on mopeds, bored stiff and not knowing what to do. Their favorite past-time? Raising trouble and provoking the police.

"Provo" was actually first coined by Dutch sociologist Buikhuizen in a condescending description of the Nozems. Roel Van Duyn, a philosophy student at the University of Amsterdam, was the first to recognize the Nozems' slumbering potential. "It is our task to turn their aggression into revolutionary consciousness," he wrote in 1965.

Inspired by anarchism, Dadaism, German philosopher (and counter-culture guru-to-be) Herbert Marcuse, and the Marquis de Sade, Van Duyn, a timid, introverted intellectual, soon became the major force behind *Provo* magazine. But while Van Duyn presided over the Provo's theoretical wing, another, more important, element was provided even earlier by its other co-founder, Robert Jasper Grootveld, a former window cleaner and the original clown prince of popular culture.

More interested in magic than Marx, Grootveld was an extroverted performance artist with a gift for theatrical gesture. During the early '60s, he attracted massive crowds in Amsterdam with exhibitionistic "Happenings." At the core of Grootveld's philosophy was the belief that the masses had been brainwashed into becoming a herd of addicted consumers, the "despicable plastic people." According to Grootveld, new rituals were needed to awaken these complacent consumers. While the writings of Van Duyn greatly appealed to the educated crowd, Grootveld found his followers among street punks.

The Provo phenomenon was an outgrowth of the alienation and absurdity of life in the early '60s. It was irresistably attractive to Dutch youth and seemed like it would travel around the world. However, in only a few short years it disappeared, choked on its own successes.

"Every weekend in 1962, I paid a visit to a police officer named Houweling," explains Grootveld. "During these visits, I often dressed like an American Indian. We always had very friendly chats about marijuana. Houweling didn't know anything about it, so I could tell him anything I wanted."

Thus began the "Marihuettegame," a disinformation game played by Grootveld and his friends. The idea was to demonstrate the establishment's complete ignorance on the subject of cannabis. The players were supposed to have fun, fool the police and, of course, smoke pot. Other than that, there were no rules. Anything that looked remotely like pot was called "marihu": tea, hay, catfood, spices and herbs included. Bonus points were collected when a smoker got busted for consuming a legal substance. The players often called the police on themselves. A raid by blue-uniformed nicotine addicts, looking for something that didn't exist, was considered the ultimate jackpot.

"One day a whole group of us went by bus to Belgium," says Grootveld. "Of course I had informed my friend Houweling that some elements might take some pot along. At the border, the cops and customs were waiting for us. Followed by the press, we were taken away for a thorough search. The poor cops...all they could find was dogfood and some legal herbs. 'Marijuana is dogfood,' joked the papers the next day. After that, the cops decided to refrain from hassling us in the future, afraid of more blunders."

The following year, Grootveld and artist Fred Wessels opened the "Afrikaanse Druk Stoor," where they sold both real and fake pot.

The marihuette game became the model for future Provo tactics. Surprisingly, games proved to be an effective way of shattering the smug self-righteousness of the authorities. The police would usually overreact, making themselves seem ridiculous in the process. There was, however, a seriousness underlying the method. The ultimate aim was to change society for the better.

In the late '50s, Grootveld was already well-known as a kind of performance artist. His inspiration, he claimed, derived from a pilgrimage to Africa, where he'd purchased a mysterious medicine kit formerly owned by a shaman. Somehow, the kit helped Grootveld formulate a critique of Western society, which, he came to believe, was dominated by unhealthy addictions. A short hospital stay soon convinced Grootveld that the worst of these was cigarette smoking. "All those grown-up patients, begging and praying for a cigarette was a disgusting sight," he recalls. (Even after this realization however, Grootveld remained a chain-smoker.)

Smoking, according to Grootveld, was an irrational cult, a pointless ritual forced upon society by the tobacco industry for the sole purpose of making profits. The bosses of the "Nico-Mafia" were the high priests of a "cigarette-cult"; advertisements and commercials were their totems. Ad agencies were powerful wizards, casting magic spells over a

OPERATION GREEN MERCHANT

BY PETER GORMAN

On Thursday, October 26, 1989, the Drug Enforcement Agency conducted raids on retail stores and warehouses specializing in indoor garden supplies in 46 states, in an attempt to shut down the indoor production of marijuana in this country. The raids were the culmination of a DEA plan, dubbed "Operation Green Merchant," which began in 1987 as the brainchild of DEA agent Jim Stewart....

According to *U.S. News & World Report*, Stewart, who was unavailable for comment to HIGH TIMES, conceived Operation Green Merchant while thumbing through a copy of this magazine. Struck by the number of ads for both indoor gardening supplies and marijuana seed banks, he began mapping out a plan for undercover agents to visit garden centers and request information regarding the growing of pot. The responses of the store owners to their employees were, in some cases, revealing enough to give the DEA the legal authority to "subpoena United Parcel Service records from 29 of the equipment firms," *U.S. News & World Report* said. The records produced more than 20,000 names of customers who had done business with those supply stores.

While the DEA officially denies the allegation that one of the main motives of the operation was to close down HIGH TIMES and *Sinsemilla Tips*, when reached at the Justice Department in Washington, the DEA operator responded to this reporter's announcement that he was with HIGH TIMES by saying, "What? Are you still in business over there?"

HighWitness News, #173, January 1990

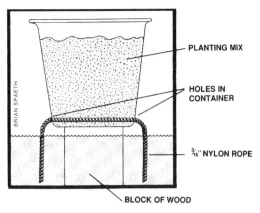

BRIAN SPAETH

— PLANTING MIX

— HOLES IN CONTAINER

— ³⁄₁₆" NYLON ROPE

— BLOCK OF WOOD

THE WICK SYSTEM

Nylon rope is an ideal wick because it draws water well and lasts for years.

To construct a wick pot, a nylon rope is drawn through two holes of a container, leaving a four- to five-inch end coming out of each hole. A six-inch container needs one to two cords; larger containers may need four. The container is filled with a moist planting mix or with most planting mixes sold in nurseries and garden stores.

A Tale of Two Gardens by Ed Rosenthal, #170, October 1989

DRUG ARRESTS '88

BY JON GETTMAN

For the first time in US history, more than one million people were arrested in 1988 for "drug abuse offenses," according to the Uniform Crime Reporting division of the FBI. This demonstrates the impact of political rhetoric on state and local authorities and the worsening of the drug crisis.

While arrests for the sale of marijuana declined by a few hundred from the previous year, total arrests for marijuana rose from 378,000 in 1987 to 391,600 in 1988. The lucrative cocaine market led to tremendous increases in the number of drug arrests; as a result, marijuana arrests declined from more than 50 percent of the drug arrest total in 1986 to 34 percent in 1988.

HighWitness News, #176, April 1990

CANNABIS CUP '89

The Winner: Early Pearl/Skunk #1 x NL#5/Haze.
In the United States a few brave souls have tried to develop and sell superior varieties. But success and fame have usually been followed by legal problems. That's why your five judges had to go to Holland to test samples provided by four Dutch seed companies: Cultivator's Choice, S.S.S.C., The Seed Bank and Sensi-Seed.

by Ed Rosenthal, #169, September 1989

hypnotized public. At the bottom of the heap lay the addicted consumers, giving their lives through cancer to the great "NicoLord."

Grootveld began a one-man attack on the tobacco industry. First, he scrawled the word "cancer" in black tar over every cigarette billboard in town. For this, he was arrested and put in jail.

After his release, Grootveld began going into tobacco shops armed with a rag soaked in chloroform. "I spread that terrible hospital odor all around," he says. "I asked if I could make a call and spent hours on the phone, gasping, coughing and panting, talking about hospitals and cancer and scaring all the customers."

A rich, eccentric restaurant owner named Klaas Kroese decided to support Grootveld's anti-smoking crusade. He provided him with a studio, which Grootveld dubbed the "Anti-Smoking Temple." Declaring himself "The First Anti-Smoke Sorcerer," Grootveld started holding weekly black masses with guest performances by poet Johnny the Selfkicker, writer Simon Vinkenoog [see HIGH TIMES, June '86] and other local underground artists.

But Grootveld was soon disappointed by the small media coverage these performances received, blaming it all on the Nico-Mafia who controlled the press. He decided to do something really sensational. After a passionate speech and the singing of the "Ugge Ugge" song, the official anti-smoking jingle, Grootveld set the Anti-Smoking Temple on fire, in front of a bewildered group of bohemians, artists, and journalists. At first everyone thought it was a joke, but when Grootveld started spraying gasoline around the room, the audience fled to safety. Grootveld himself came perilously close to frying, saved only by the efforts of the police who came to rescue him. Although the crusade had only begun, the fire cost him the support of Kroese, his first patron.

In 1964, Grootveld moved his black masses, now known as "Happenings," to nearby Spui Square. At the center of the square was a small statue of a child, "Het Lievertje." By coincidence, the statue had been commissioned by a major tobacco firm. For Grootveld this bit of evidence proved the insidious infiltration of the nico-dope syndicates. Every Saturday, at exactly midnight, Grootveld began appearing in the square, wearing a strange outfit and performing for a steadily growing crowd of Nozems, intellectuals, curious bypassers and police.

Writer Harry Mulisch described it this way: "While their parents, sitting on their refrigerators and dishwashers, were watching with their left eye the TV, with their right eye the auto in front of the house, in one hand the kitchen mixer, in the other *De Telegraaf*, their kids went at Saturday night to the Spui Square.... And when the clock struck twelve, the High Priest appeared, all dressed up, from some alley and started to walk Magic Circles around the nicotinistic demon, while his disciples cheered, applauded and sang the Ugge Ugge song."

One night in May 1965, Van Duyn appeared at one of the Happenings and began distributing leaflets announcing the birth of the Provo movement. "Provo's choice is between desperate resistance or apathetic perishing," wrote Van Duyn. "Provo realizes eventually it will be the loser, but won't let that last chance slip away to annoy and provoke this society to its depths...."

Grootveld read the first Provo manifesto and decided to cooperate with the publishers. "When I read the word 'anarchism' in that first pamphlet, I realized that this outdated, 19th century ideology would become the hottest thing in the '60s," he recalls.

The leaflets were followed by more elaborate pamphlets announcing the creation of the White Plans. Constant Nieuwenhuis, another artist, was instrumental in shaping the White Philosophy, which considered work (especially mundane factory labor) obsolete. Provo's renunciation of work appealed to the Nozems—and marked an important ideological split with capitalism, communism and socialism, all of which cherished work as a value in itself. Provo, however, sympathized more with Marx's anarchist son-in-law Paul Lafargue, author of "The Right to Laziness."

The most famous of all white plans was the White Bike Plan, envisioned as the ultimate solution to the "traffic terrorism of a motorized minority." The brainchild of Industrial designer Luud Schimmelpenninck, the White Bike Plan proposed the banning of environmentally noxious cars from the inner city, to be replaced by bicycles. Of course, the bikes were to be provided free by the city. They would be painted white and permanently unlocked, to secure their public availability. Schimmelpenninck calculated that, even from a strictly economic point of view, the plan would provide great benefits to Amsterdam.

The Provos decided to put the plan into action by providing the first 50 bicycles. But the police immediately confiscated them, claiming they created an invitation to theft. Provo retaliated by stealing a few police bikes.

The White Victim Plan stated that anyone causing a fatal car accident should be forced to paint the outline of their victim's body on the pavement at the site of the accident. That way, no one could ignore the fatalities caused by automobiles.

Other White Plans included the White Chimney Plan (put a heavy tax on polluters and paint their chimneys white), the White Kids Plan (free daycare centers), the White Housing Plan (stop real estate speculation), and the White Wife Plan (free medical care for women).

Some White Plans were elaborate, others were just flashes of inspiration. "It seemed that proposing a White Plan was almost a necessary exam to becoming a Provo," says Grootveld. The most hilarious of all was the White Chicken Plan, proposed by a Provo subcommittee called Friends of the Police. After the police began responding to Provo demonstrations with increased violence, the Provos attempted to alter the image of the police, who were known as "blue chickens." The new white chickens would be disarmed, ride around on white bicycles, and distribute first aid, fried chicken and free contraceptives.

The police failed to appreciate this proposal. At one demonstration they seized a dozen white chickens which had been brought along for symbolic effect.

Van Duyn's theories of modern life were quite similar to Grootveld's: labor and the ruling class had merged into one big, gray middle-class. This boring bourgeoisie was living in a catatonic state, its creativity burnt out by TV. "It is impossible to have the slightest confidence in that dependent, servile bunch of roaches and lice," concluded Van Duyn.

The only solution to this problem lay with the Nozems, artists, dropouts, streetkids and beatniks, all of whom shared a non-involvement with capitalist society. It was Provo's task to awaken their latent instincts for subversion, to turn them on to anarchist action.

As later became clear, Provo didn't really enlighten the street crowd, although they did offer an opportunity to intellectuals and punks alike to express their feelings of frustration and rage.

Van Duyn's writings combined an equal mixture of pessimism and idealism. Too much a realist to expect total revolution, he tended to follow a more pragmatic and reformist strategy. Eventually he

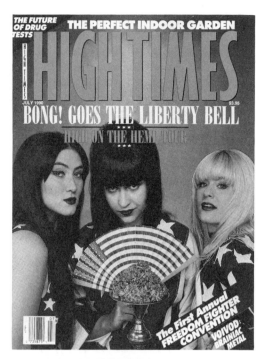

FIRST FREEDOM FIGHTERS' CONVENTION

BY MARK BARNET

When it looked like most of the members attending the convention had made it to the hotel, Steve Hager issued marching orders. Everyone moved out and boarded Rodger Belknap's inspiring Purple Psychedelic Bus. He generously donated his fantastic purple cruiser and services as pilot to the cause. Everyone was smiling and laughing as we experienced what the Freedom Fighters are about: the freedom of knowing you're doing The Right Thing. Even though we all knew we were being closely watched by Big Brother, our unity made us invincible! We didn't care! And let me tell you friends, when you throw down the chains of oppression, even if only for a weekend, it feels like paradise!

There were almost 100 of the faithful present as the State Leader nominations and speeches took place.... All were obviously committed to the movement and there was much optimism.... After the meeting, it was time to relax and everyone mingled around the bonfire as Chef RA arrived. Rasta RA made up a huge dose of real Jamaican Jerk Chicken that was truly a breeze of up-vibe flavor from the islands! From then on, the party and good feelings of freedom kept going well into the night.

Back at HIGH TIMES, we were talking about the Freedom Fighters and what we need to accomplish. There is a lot more to be done than just make pot-smoking legal. We have got to get cannabis legalized for our environment, for our economy and for justice.... Freedom Fighters! We are the few who are brave enough to stand up at the very beginning of this struggle. We must stand together and win this war! We will.

Freedom Fighters Come Together, #179, July 1990

KEEPING THE ELECTRIC BILL COOL

BY D. GOLD

Many indoor growers are justifiably concerned these days with keeping their electric bills as low as possible. This can be difficult with a growing operation utilizing multiple metal halide or high-pressure sodium lights. A 1,000 watt light puts out almost as much heat as an electric space heater drawing the same amount of wattage.

In many cases, the costs are not just reflected in the electricity to run the lights, but in the electricity necessary to keep the air temperature down within acceptable limits. This has usually meant that growers need to install expensive-to-operate air conditioners.

There are many solutions to the heat problem. Like the air conditioner, some are simple—and expensive to set up and operate—and others are complicated, but inexpensive.

#175, March 1990

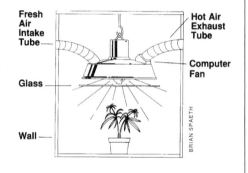

Fresh Air Intake Tube

Hot Air Exhaust Tube

Computer Fan

Glass

Wall

BRIAN SPAETH

HEMP CLOTHING IS HERE!

Suddenly, out of nowhere came Stoned Wear, a new line of hemp clothing and products from Sativa Creations, located in Vancouver, Canada and Joint Venture Hempery, Inc., in Tempe, Arizona. Most HIGH TIMES readers barely noticed their advertisement in the October 1989 issue. Even HIGH TIMES editors were skeptical, as the clothing samples sent were only 55% hemp and 45% cotton. Is this the real thing or not, we asked?

Then we met Matthew Cheng and Alex Shum, the two men who are importing the hemp fabric. Matthew and Alex feel that the way to legalize marijuana is to sell marijuana legally. When you can buy marijuana in your neighborhood shopping mall, IT'S LEGAL! So, they are going to produce every conceivable thing out of hemp: hemp shirts, hemp pants, hemp jackets, hemp hats, hemp oven mittens, hemp towels, hemp pot holders, hemp books, hemp comics, hemp scratch pads, and hemp stationery. Anything and everything you can think of will be made from hemp.

#175, March 1990

advocated participating in Amsterdam council elections. Other Provos denounced this as an outrageous betrayal of anarchist ideals.

One Provo leaflet hit the newsstands folded between the pages of *De Telegraaf*, Amsterdam's biggest newspaper. The perpetrator of this action, Olaf Stoop, was immediately fired from the airport newsstand where he worked. No big deal for a Provo. It was important to demonstrate a disdain for careerism in general.

When the next leaflet, Provokaatsie #3, was published it aroused indignation all over the Netherlands by alluding to the Nazi past of some members of the Royal House, a sacred institution in Dutch society. Provos threw the leaflet into the royal barge as it toured the canals of Amsterdam. Provokaatsie #3 was the first in a series of publications that were immediately confiscated by police. The offical excuse was that Provo had used some illustrations without permission. A lawsuit followed and Van Duyn was held responsible. But instead of showing up in court, Van Duyn sent a note stating it was "...simply impossible to hold one single individual responsible. Provo is the product of an everchanging, anonymous gang of subversive elements.... Provo doesn't recognize copyright, as it is just another form of private property which is renounced by Provo.... We suspect that this is an indirect form of censorship while the State is too cowardly to sue us straight for lese majeste [an offense violating the dignity of the ruler].... By the way, our hearts are filled with a general contempt for authorities and for anyone who submits himself to them...."

In July 1965, the first issue of *Provo* magazine appeared. "It was very shocking to the establishment," recalls Grootveld. "They realized we were not mere dopey scum but were quite capable of some sort of organization."

The first issue contained out-of-date, l9th century recipes for bombs, explosives and boobytraps. Firecrackers included with the magazine provided an excuse for the police to confiscate the issue. Arrested on charges of inciting violence, editors Van Duyn, Stoop, Hans Metz and Jaap Berk were released a few days later.

Actually Provo had an ambivalent attitude toward the police, viewing them as essential non-creative elements for a successful Happening. Grootveld called them "co-happeners." "Of course, it is obvious that the cops are our best pals," wrote Van Duyn. "The greater their number, the more rude and fascist their performance, the better for us. The police, just like we do, are provoking the masses.... They are causing resentment. We are trying to turn that resentment into revolt."

By July 1965, Provo had become the national media's top story, mostly due to overreaction bv the city administration, who treated the movement as a serious crisis. Even though only a handful of Provos actually existed, due to Provo media manipulation it seemed as though thousands of them were roaming the streets. "We were like Atlas carrying an image that was blown up to huge proportions." recalls Van Duyn.

At the early Spui Square Happenings, the police usually responded by arresting Grootveld, which was no big deal. Grootveld was considered a harmless eccentric and always treated with respect. Privately, he got along quite well with the police. "They gave me coffee and showed me pictures of their kids," he says. And Grootveld remained grateful to the police for rescuing him from his burning temple.

However, trouble started at the end of July. A few days before, the White Bike Plan had been announced to the press. The police were present, but hadn't interfered. At an anti-auto happening the next

Saturday, however, the police showed up in great numbers. As soon as some skirmishing began, the police tried to break up the crowd.

The following week, after sensational press coverage, a huge crowd gathered at Spui Square. Again the police tried to disperse the crowd, but this time serious fighting broke out, resulting in seven arrests. The next day *De Telegraaf*'s headlines screamed, "The Provos are attacking!" Suddenly, the Provos were a national calamity.

In August 1965, some Provos met with the police to discuss the violent interventions in the Happenings. "Since Amsterdam is the Magic Center, it is of great cultural importance that the Happenings will not be disturbed!" declared the Provos in a letter to the commander of police. Unfortunately, the talks produced no results. "We stared at each other in disbelief like we were exotic animals," says Van Duyn.

The same night, the police surrounded the little statue in Spui Square, Rob Stolk recalls, "like it was made out of diamonds and Dr. No or James Bond wanted to steal it."

About 2,000 spectators were present, all waiting for something to happen. At exactly twelve o'clock not Grootveld, but two other Provos showed up. As they tried to lay flowers at the Het Lievertje statue, the crowd cheered. The police arrested them on the spot, after which a riot broke out. Thirteen were arrested, four of whom had nothing to do with Provo, but just happened to be hanging around the square. They all ended up serving between one and two months in jail.

In September 1965, Provo focused their actions on another statue, the Van Heutz monument. Although Van Heutz is considered by most Dutch to be a great hero of their colonial past, Provo branded him an imperialistic scavenger and war criminal. The following month the first anti-Vietnam war rallies were organized by leftist students who were slowly joining Provo. "Our protests against the Vietnam war were from a humanistic point of view," recalls Stolk. "We criticized the cruel massacres but didn't identify with the Vietcong like Jane Fonda. That's why later on we didn't wind up on aerobics videos."

Although the Happenings at the Spui Square were still going on, the Vietnam demonstrations became the big story of 1965. Hundreds were arrested every week. Meanwhile, the Provo virus was spreading throughout Holland. Every respectable provincial town boasted its local brand of Provos, all with their own magazines and statues around which Happenings were staged.

At the end of the year the administration changed tactics. Instead of violent police interventions, they tried to manage the Provos. Obsolete laws were uncovered and turned against Provo. But when a demonstration permit was refused on this basis, the Provos showed up with blank banners and handed out blank leaflets. They still got arrested. Provo Koosje Koster was arrested for handing out raisins at a Spui Happening. The official reason? Bringing the public order and safety into serious jeopardy.

Public opinion on the Provos began to get more polarized. Although many were in favor of even harsher measures against the rabble-rousers, a growing segment of the public sympathized with the Provos and began having serious doubts about police overreaction.

The monarchy became the ultimate establishment symbol for the Provos to attack. Royal ceremonies offered ample opportunities for satire. During "Princess Day," when an annual ceremonial speech was delivered by the queen, Provo made up a fake speech, in which Queen Juliana declared she'd become an anarchist and was negotiating a transition of power with Provo. Provo Hans Tuynman invited the Queen

CANNABIS CUP '90
BY JOHN HOLMSTROM

Cannabis Cup 1990, the third annual marijuana connoisseur awards, was clouded by controversy. The Seed Bank swept the field, winning all four categories and the grand prize. Weeks later, it was forced to close down operations, and now faces an uncertain future—it might even be impossible for anyone to get their hands on the 1990 Cannabis Cup winner. The competition was further complicated when two judges, Robert Jasper Grootveld and Kees Hoekert, staged a Provo demonstration at the awards ceremony. Worst of all, the overall feeling one got from being in Amsterdam was that the party might be over, and recriminalization is on its way back to Holland.

In spite of all the drug-war rumblings and rampant paranoia, three of the four major Dutch marijuana seed companies entered the contest: The Seed Bank, S.S.S.C., and Sensi-Seed.

The competition itself was thisclose. Only a half-point separated the winner, Northern Lights #5, from the runner-up, Super Skunk. As always, the competition was based on a ballot system that gave a maximum of 10 points for color and condition, 10 for taste and aroma, and 15 for strength and quality of high. Northern Lights #5, (which was marked PI-2, for pure *indica*-2 in the judges' sample kits) received 90 points (out of a possible 105), while Super Skunk received 89 1/2 points. Gilbert Shelton and Paul Mavrides, the Freak Brothers cartoonists, gave their highest scores to NL#5. According to one of their ballots, it had "a nice resinous sheen, bud is well-formed, good balance of leaf to flower."
#183, November 1990

GARRICK BECK

GABE KIRCHHEIMER

GB: So we moved into communal houses in Portland. We created food co-ops. We sought a larger vision and there it was: Go back to the land! What a vision! The vast green earth. People all over the world left the cities and attempted to live an ecological lifestyle. A group of us got together, located a piece of land, and bought it. We were new to gardening, water pumps and chainsaws. There was the question, are we self-sufficient? But it seemed to me there was always an interchange of supplies and materials. We grew organic wheat, organic apples, organic carrots. We learned that by living close to the earth, we could survive.

HT: You must have had some problems.

GB: Some people were on heavy guru trips or political power trips. We were on a circuit filled with hipsters, tripsters, dipsters, and every kind of lipster. Romances happened, babies happened. Lots of babies happened. People screamed at each other. We had the vegetarians versus the meat eaters, new age Christians versus born again Christians. In the many attempts to find the beautiful alternative society, we tried a lot of things that didn't work. We tried group marriage. We tried living without property. We learned the first basic truth: People are basically very good to each other, thus dispelling the myth for the need of standing armies.

Interview by Steven Hager, #182, November 1990

JURY POWER

BY LYNN AND JUDY OSBURN

Every jury in America has the right to reverse any law they feel is unjust or unfair. Strangely enough, they are never informed of this right. Don't you think it's time they were told?

The Fully Informed Jury Amendment/Initi-ative (FIJA/FIJI) is a grass roots movement intended to compel state governments to require that judges tell juries of their power, right and responsibility to judge whether a law is unjust or misapplied. FIJA requires jurors to be allowed to hear evidence about the defendant's motives, and would reaffirm their authority to acquit or convict according to the dictates of conscience.

"Jury nullification," as it is sometimes called, is a traditional American right defended by the Founding Fathers. Those patriots intended the jury to serve as one of the tests a law must pass before it assumes enough popular authority to be enforced.

#181, September 1990

to hold an intimate conversation in front of the palace, where he and some other Provos had assembled some comfortable chairs. Although the Queen did not show, the police did, quickly breaking up the Happening.

The climax of this anti-royal activity came in March 1966, when Princess Beatrix married a German, Claus von Amsberg, a former member of Hitlerjugend, the Nazi youth organization. Coincidentally, Grootveld had been doing performances based on "the coming of Klaas," a mythical messiah. Sinterklaas, the Dutch version of Santa Claus, and Klaas Kroese, Grootveld's former sponsor, served as the inspirations for these performances, but by March, Provos identified the coming of Klaas with the arrival of Von Amsberg.

"Grootveld objected to this corruption of his symbolic Klaas mythology," recalls Jef Lambrecht. "He wanted to keep Klaas pure and undefinable, but the link was soon established."

The Provos spent months preparing for the March wedding. A bank account was opened to collect donations for an anti-wedding present. The White Rumor Plan was put into action. Wild and ridiculous rumors were spread through Amsterdam. It became widely believed that the Provos were preparing to dump LSD in the city water supply, that they were building a giant paint-gun to attack the wedding procession, that they were collecting manure to spread along the parade route, and that the royal horses were going to be drugged. Although Provo was actually planning nothing more than a few smoke bombs, the police expected the worst acts of terrorism imaginable. Foreign magazines offered big money to Provos if they would disclose their secret plans before the wedding, plans that didn't exist.

A few days before the wedding, all the Provos mysteriously disappeared. They did this simply to avoid being arrested before the big day. Meanwhile, the authorities requested 25,000 troops to help guard the parade route.

On the day of the wedding, Amsterdam—the most anti-German and anti-monarchist city in the country—was not in the mood for grand festivities. Half the City Council snubbed the official wedding reception. A foreign journalist put it this way: "The absence of any decorated window, of any festive ornament, is just another expression of the indifference of the public."

Miraculously, by dressing up like respectable citizens, the Provos managed to sneak their smoke bombs past the police and army guards. "The night before, the cops made a terrible blooper by violently searching an innocent old man who was carrying a suspicious leather bag. So the fools gave orders not to search leather bags any more, fearing dirty Provo tricks!" says Appie Pruis, a photographer. The first bombs went off just behind the palace as the procession started. Although the bombs were not really dangerous (they were made from sugar and nitrate), they put out tremendous clouds of smoke, which were viewed on television worldwide. "It was a crazy accumulation of insane mistakes. Most of the police had been brought in from the countryside, and so were totally unable to identify the Provos." A violent police overreaction ensued, witnessed by foreign journalists, many of whom were clubbed and beaten in the confusion. The wedding turned into a public relations disaster. "Demonstrations of Provo are Amsterdam's bitter answer to monarchist folklorism," commented a Spanish newspaper.

The week after the wedding, a photo exhibition was held documenting the police violence. The guests at the exhibition were attacked by the police and severely beaten. Public indignation against the police reached new peaks. Many well-known writers and intellectuals began requesting an independent investigation of police behavior.

In June, after a man was killed in a labor dispute, it seemed as if a civil war was ready to erupt. According to *De Telegraaf*, the victim was killed not by the police, but by a co-worker, an outrageous lie. A furious crowd stormed the offices of the paper. For the first time, the proletariat and Provo were fighting on the same side.

By the middle of 1966, repression was out of control. Hundreds of people were arrested every week at Happenings and anti-Vietnam rallies. A ban on demonstrations caused them to grow even bigger. Hans Tuynman was turned into a martyr after being sentenced to three months in jail for murmuring the word "image" at a Happening. Yet around the time, a Dutch Nazi collaborator, a war criminal responsible for deporting Jews, had been released from prison and a student fraternity member received only a small fine for manslaughter.

Finally, in August 1966, a congressional committee was established to investigate the crisis. The committee's findings resulted in the Police Commissioner's firing. In May 1967, the mayor of Amsterdam, Van Hall, was "honorably" given the boot, after the committee condemned his policies. Strangely enough, Provo, which had demanded the mayor's resignation for over a year, liquidated within a week of his dismissal.

The reason for Provo's demise, which was totally unexpected by outsiders, was its increasing acceptance by moderate elements, and growing turmoil within its ranks. As soon as Provo began participating in the City Council elections, a transformation occurred. A Provo Politburo emerged, consisting of VIP Provos who began devoting most of themselves to political careers: Provos toured the country, giving lectures and interviews. When the VIP Provos were out of town attending a Provo congress, Stolk staged a fake palace coup by announcing that a new Revolutionary Terrorist Council had taken power. Van Duyn reacted furiously, not realizing it was a provocation against Provo itself. When the Van Heutz monument was damaged by bombs, Provo declared that "although they felt sympathy for the cause, they deeply deplored the use of violence." The division between the street Provos and the reformist VIPs began growing wider. Some Provos returned to their studies, others went hippie and withdrew from the movement.

Provo was a big hit as long as it was considered outside of society. But as soon as the establishment began embracing it, the end was near. Moderate liberals began publicly defending it and social scientists began studying the movement. The former Secretary of Transportation joined forces with Provo. "As a real supporter, he should have proposed a crackdown on Provo," Van Duyn said later.

Provo's proposal to establish a playground for children was now greeted by the City Council with great enthusiasm. The real sign of Provo's institutionalization, however, was the installation of a "speakers-corner" in the park.

Van Duyn encouraged this development, but Stolk saw it as a form of repressive tolerance—the Provos were now free, free to be ignored. "Understanding politicians, well-intentioned Provologists and pampering reverends, they were forming a counter-magic circle around us to take away our magic power," says Stolk. So Stolk and Grootveld decided to liquidate Provo. "The power and spirit had vanished," says Grootveld. "Provo had turned into a dogmatic crew. Provo had

SEED BANK BUSTED

BY PETER GORMAN

Nevil Martin Schoenmakers, operator of Holland's Seed Bank, was arrested in Australia at the request of the US government on July 24. At presstime, extradition proceedings were underway to transport Shoenmakers to Federal court in New Orleans, where he will face charges of violating the Controlled Substances Act.

The 44-count indictment alleges that Schoenmakers, "in concert with at least five other persons," knowingly distributed, through the US Postal Service, a total of 1,921 seeds to marijuana growers and DEA agents (251 total seeds) in the New Orleans area from 1985 to 1990. The indictment also alleges that Schoenmakers, an Australian native who makes his home in Holland, "did knowingly...manufacture [grow] more than 1,000 marijuana plants, a Schedule I drug controlled substance." If convicted on all counts, Schoenmakers (as well as a second unnamed "co-conspirator") faces a possible life sentence. Schoenmakers's indictment is closely tied to the ongoing grand-jury investigation of HIGH TIMES being conducted by US District Attorney John Volz. The government has been seeking to determine whether or not conspiracy charges can be brought against the magazine for allowing advertisers to offer products through the mail which may later have been used in indoor-growing operations in the New Orleans area.
HighWitness News, #182, October 1990

BUILDING THE HEMP BOOTH

BY GEORGE HEMPMAN WASHINGTON

Want to get more involved in the pro-cannabis movement? Build a hemp booth—the fun easy way to educate friends and neighbors to the real facts about hemp and the environment. The first step is to buy a copy of *The Emperor Wears No Clothes* by Jack Herer. Hemp can be an international issue in a short time if we all work at it. Go to a different flea market every weekend. Start a NORML chapter and sell hemp shirts and hemp bird seed at the booth. Show cloth and rope samples or sell them. Sell copies of *The Emperor Wears No Clothes* and give away free literature. You can do this in the name of a non-profit group like NORML, BACH, HEMP or the Freedom Fighters, or make money doing it. Just get the truth out.
#180, August 1990

STEVEN HAGER

ANDRE GROSSMANN

HT: When do you think cannabis will be legal?
SH: The forces keeping pot illegal are among the strongest in the world. They include the oil and petrochemical industries, liquor and tobacco companies, and the pharmaceutical industry. People tend to make fun of the pot movement. Like it's a bunch of hippies who just want to smoke dope. That's what the government would like you to think. The truth is legalizing hemp would restructure our national economy and put more money in the hands of American farmers, while devastating the petrochemical industry—the major source of world pollution. They have billions of dollars and all the thugs and narco cops in the world on their side, but the truth is on our side. One day the truth will prevail.

HT: Why is it so hard to get the real facts to the people?
SH: HIGH TIMES has been bombarding the national media with hemp information for two years and no one wants to publish the truth. It's scary. All knowledge of hemp has been deliberately erased from our national memory. But why should that surprise us? Look at the Kennedy and King assassinations. Congress figured out years ago that the Mafia and the CIA conspired to kill both men, but they're too intimidated to do anything about it. Our country is in a really bad state. I think the worst drug is television. It has turned the nation into a bunch of mindless consumers.
Interview, #179, July 1990

degenerated into a legal stamp of approval."

At the liquidation meeting, Stolk said: "Provo has to disappear because all the Great Men that made us big have gone," a reference to Provo's two arch-enemies, the mayor and commissioner of police.

Provo held one last stunt. A white rumor was spread that American universities wanted to buy the Provo archives, documents that actually didn't even exist. Amsterdam University, fearing that the sociological treasure might disappear overseas, quickly made an offer the Provos couldn't refuse.

HERITAGE OF STONE

by Steven Hager

Although John F. Kennedy was neither a saint nor a great intellectual, he was the youngest president ever elected, which may explain why he was so well attuned to the changing mood of America in the '60s. Americans had grown weary of Cold War hysteria. They wanted to relax and have fun. Like the majority of people across the planet, they wanted peace.

The President's primary obstacle in this quest was a massive, power-hungry bureaucracy that had emerged after WWII—a Frankenstein monster created by anti-Communist paranoia and inflated defense budgets. By 1960, the Pentagon was easily the world's largest corporation, with assets of over $60 billion. No one understood this monster better than President Dwight D. Eisenhower. On January 17, 1961, in his farewell address to the nation, Eisenhower spoke to the country and to his successor, John Kennedy.

"The conjunction of an immense military establishment and a large arms industry is new in the American experience," said Eisenhower. "We must guard against the acquisition of unwarranted influence, whether sought or unsought, by the military-industrial complex."

At the beginning of his administration, Kennedy seems to have followed the advice of his military and intelligence officers. What else could such an inexperienced President have done? Signs of a serious rift, however, first appeared after the Bay of Pigs, a CIA-planned and executed invasion of Cuba that took place three months after Kennedy took office. The invasion was so transparent and misconceived that Kennedy refused massive air support and immediately afterward fired CIA Director Allen Dulles, Deputy Director General Charles Cabell and Deputy Director of Planning Richard Bissell.

Kennedy's next major crisis occurred on October 16, 1962, when he was shown aerial photos of missile bases in Cuba. The Joint Chiefs of Staff pressed for an immediate attack. Instead, Attorney General Robert Kennedy was sent to meet with Soviet Ambassador Anatoly Dobrynin. In his memoirs, Premier Nikita Khrushchev quotes the younger Kennedy as saying: "The President is in a grave situation.... We are under pressure from our military to use force against Cuba.... If the situation continues much longer, the President is not sure that the military will not overthrow him and seize power." Military hopes for an invasion of Cuba evaporated as Khrushchev and Kennedy worked out a nonviolent solution to the crisis. In return, Kennedy promised not to invade Cuba. Angered over the Bay of Pigs fiasco, the CIA refused to bend to Kennedy's will and continued their destabilization campaign against Castro, which included sabotage raids conducted by a secret army, as well as plots against Castro's life, which were undertaken with the help of such well-known Mafia figures as Johnny Roselli, Sam Giancana and Santos Trafficante. A bitter internal struggle developed around Kennedy's attempts to disband the CIA's paramilitary bases in Florida and Louisiana.

On August 5, 1963, the US, Great Britain and the Soviet Union signed a limited nuclear-test-ban treaty. Engineered by President Kennedy and long in negotiations, the treaty was a severe blow to the Cold War warriors in the Pentagon and CIA. On September 20, 1963, Kennedy spoke hopefully of peace to the UN General Assembly. "Today we may have reached a pause in the Cold War," he said. "...If both sides can now gain new confidence and experience in concrete collaborations of peace, then surely, this first small step can be the start of a long, fruitful journey."

"Years later, paging through its formerly classified records, talking to National Security Council staff, it is difficult to avoid the impression that the President was learning the responsibility of power," writes John Prados, in his recent book *Keepers of the Keys*, an analysis of the National Security Council. "Here was a smoother, calmer Kennedy, secretly working for rapprochement with Fidel Castro and a withdrawal from Vietnam."

Although Kennedy's Vietnam policy has not received widespread publicity, he turned resolutely against the war in June of 1963, when he ordered Defense Secretary Robert McNamara and Chairman of the Joint Chiefs of Staff General Maxwell Taylor to announce from the White House steps that all American forces would be withdrawn by 1965. At the time, 15,500 US "advisors" were stationed in South Vietnam, and total casualties suffered remained a relatively low 100.

On November 14, Kennedy signed an order to begin the withdrawal by removing 1,000 troops. In private, Kennedy let it be known the military was not going to railroad him into continuing the war. Many of the hard-line anti-Communists—including FBI Director J. Edgar Hoover—would have to be purged. Bobby Kennedy would be put in charge of dismantling the CIA. President Kennedy told Senator Mike Mansfield of his plans to tear the CIA "into a thousand pieces and scatter it to the winds." But these plans had to wait for Kennedy's reelection in 1964. And in order to win that election, he had to secure the South. Which is why Kennedy went to Texas later that month. Could John Kennedy have stopped the war in Vietnam, as was his obvious intention? America will never know. His command to begin the Vietnam withdrawal was his last formal executive order. Just after noon on November 22, President Kennedy was murdered while driving through downtown Dallas, in full view of dozens of ardent supporters, and while surrounded by police and personal bodyguards. Twenty eight years later, grave doubts still linger as to who pulled the trigger(s), who ordered the assassination, and why our government has done so little to bring justice forth. In 1963, no American wanted to believe that President Kennedy's death was a coup d'état planned by the military establishment and executed by the CIA. Today, such a claim can no longer be dismissed. Why has the national media done such an abysmal job of presenting the facts to the American people? Hopefully, some light will be shed by Oliver Stone's upcoming film, *JFK*, a $30-million epic starring Kevin Costner, scheduled for release later this year. As his

SIRHAN SIRHAN

[Robert Kennedy's] killing was a set-up too. After just winning the all-important California primary and giving his victory speech, he was led from the podium thru the kitchen pantry to where Sirhan Sirhan served as a diversionary gunman. In the confusion Kennedy was shot four times directly from the rear, the fatal wound being fired from just three inches from the back of the head above the ear. The true assassin was named Thane Eugene Ceasar, a last-minute security guard stand-in with mob connections who disappeared directly after the killing.

The assassination of Robert Kennedy was the result of years of research and hard work by the CIA in the area of mind control and behavior modification through drugs and hypnosis, specifically hypnotically controlled assassins. Sirhan Sirhan was hypnotically programmed by a Hollywood psychiatrist named William Joseph Bryan, Jr. Bryan worked extensively with the CIA and in this case went as far as having Sirhan stay at his ranch for weeks while being programmed.
A Hippy's History of the Sixties and Beyond by Lewis Sanders, #172, December 1989

WAS WILLOUGHBY THE MASTERMIND BEHIND JFK'S ASSASSINATION?

Willoughby was clearly a man with open fascist sympathies. In the 1920s he had journeyed to Spain to meet with the right-wing extremist General Francisco Franco. In 1952, the Pentagon exploited Willoughby's connection with the fascist dictator, sending him on a high-level US military delegation to Spain to discuss establishing US air bases there.

In 1946, when Willoughby was a top administrator in the US occupation of Japan, he granted immunity to imperial Japanese military men who had conducted germ warfare experiments on Chinese civilians in exchange for the data from their grisly "research."

Willoughby was also an admirer of Italian fascist dictator Benito Mussolini: "Historical judgment, freed from the emotional haze of the moment," wrote Willoughby, "will credit Mussolini with wiping out a memory of defeat by re-establishing the traditional military supremacy of the white race."

In the 1960s, Willoughby worked with the Hunt family's private probe into the JFK killing, and pushed the theory that JFK's accused assassin, Lee Harvey Oswald, had been working for the KGB.
JFK & The Fascist Connection by Bill Weinberg, #219, November 1993

WILLIE NELSON

"Hemp is petroleum. Hemp is food. Hemp is clothing. Hemp is paper. Hemp is over 10,000 different things from dynamite to cellophane to rope to canvas. It's a shame that our farmers aren't allowed to grow this again. They used to do alright with it, and when you take the hemp away from the Kentucky farmers, it's like taking the cotton away from the Texas farmers or the wheat away from the Kansas farmers. Why did they take it away? Because hemp is petroleum. It's big business again.

"I believe in the War on Drugs, I just don't think hemp is a drug. I think hemp is a flower and an herb and I don't believe in a war on flowers. I am in favor of a War on Drugs, but I am not in favor of a war on flowers and herbs. We should take the money that it's costing us to keep hemp illegal and use that for the education and rehabilitation of people who are addicted to hard drugs.

"At one time the cannabis part of the plant was being used widely by the medical association and the doctors. They were refused the right to do that. Some of them are still doing it around the country. I still talk to doctors who say, 'Yeah, we still use cannabis for cancer patients and for glaucoma patients,' and wherever they use the pills that the government makes them use—which are not as good as the real thing, but they're better than nothing. At least they know the value of the medicine there, and I think if the doctors were allowed to use it that it would be a great relief for all the human suffering that's going on in the world, for all the people who would really benefit by it and who are not having that opportunity."
Interview by Steve Bloom, Steven Hager, and John Holmstrom, #185, January 1991

focal point for the story, Stone has chosen former New Orleans District Attorney Jim Garrison, the only prosecutor to attempt to bring this case to court, and a man subjected to one of the most effective smear campaigns ever orchestrated by the US government. It is a frightening story of murder, corruption and cover-up. Even today, 24 years after he brought the case to court, a powerful media disinformation campaign against Garrison continues.

Born November 20, 1921, in Knoxville, Iowa, Earling Carothers Garrison—known as "Jim" to friends and family—was raised in New Orleans. At age 19, one year before Pearl Harbor, he joined the army. In 1942, he was sent to Europe where he volunteered to fly spotter planes over the front lines. Following the war, he attended law school at Tulane, joined the FBI, and served as a special agent in Seattle and Tacoma. After growing bored with his agency assignments, he returned to New Orleans to practice law. He served as an assistant district attorney from 1954 to 1958.

In 1961, Garrison decided to run for district attorney on a platform openly hostile to then-New Orleans Mayor Victor Schiro. To the surprise of many, he was elected without any major political backing. He was 43 years old and had been district attorney for less than two years when Kennedy was killed. "I was an old fashioned patriot," he writes in *On the Trail of the Assassins* (Sheridan Square Press, NY), "a product of my family, my military experience, and my years in the legal profession. I could not imagine then that the government would ever deceive the citizens of this country."

A few hours after the assassination, Lee Harvey Oswald was arrested. Two days later, while in Dallas police custody, Oswald was murdered by nightclub-owner Jack Ruby. Garrison learned that Oswald was from New Orleans, and arranged a Sunday afternoon meeting with his staff. With such an important case, it was their responsibility to investigate Oswald's local connections.

Within days, they learned that Oswald had recently been seen in the company of one David Ferrie, a fervent anti-Communist and freelance pilot linked to the Bay of Pigs invasion. Evidence placed Ferrie in Texas on the day of the assassination. Also on that day, a friend of Ferrie's named Guy Banister had pistol-whipped Jack Martin during an argument. Martin confided to friends that Banister and Ferrie were somehow involved in the assassination. Garrison had Ferrie picked up for questioning, and turned him over to the local FBI, who immediately released him. Within a few months, the Warren Commission released its report stating that Oswald was a "lone nut" murdered by a misguided patriot who wanted to spare Jackie Kennedy the ordeal of testifying in court. Like most Americans, Garrison accepted this conclusion.

Three years later, in the fall of '66, Garrison was happily married with three children and content with his job, when a chance conversation with Senator Russell Long changed his views on the Warren Commission forever.

"Those fellows on the Warren Commission were dead wrong," said Long. "There's no way in the world that one man could have shot up Jack Kennedy that way."

Intrigued, Garrison went back to his office and ordered the complete 26-volume report. "The mass of information was disorganized and confused," writes Garrison. "Worst of all, the conclusions in the report seemed to be based on an appallingly selective reading of the evidence, ignoring credible testimony from literally dozens of witnesses."

Garrison was equally disturbed by the background of the men chosen by President Johnson to serve on the commission. Why, for example, was Allen Dulles, a man fired by Kennedy, on the panel? A master spy during WWII, Dulles had supervised the penetration of the Abwehr (Hitler's military intelligence agency) and the subsequent incorporation of many of its undercover agents into the CIA. He was powerful, well-connected and had been Director of the CIA for eight years. Certainly, he was no friend to John Kennedy. Serving with Dulles were Representative Gerald Ford, a man described by *Newsweek* as "the CIA's best friend in Congress"; John McCloy, former assistant secretary of war and Commissioner for Occupied Germany; and Senator Richard Russell, chairman of the powerful Senate Armed Services Committee. Russell's home state of Georgia was filled with military bases and government contracts. The balance of power on the commission was clearly in the hands of the military and the CIA. The entire "investigation" was supervised by J. Edgar Hoover, who openly detested the Kennedy brothers.

Another interesting link also turned up: The mayor of Dallas was Earle Cabell, brother of the General Charles Cabell JFK had earlier fired from the CIA. Earle Cabell was in a position to control many important details involved in the case, including the Dallas police force.

Based on these general suspicions, Garrison launched a highly secret investigation around Lee Harvey Oswald's links to David Ferrie and Guy Banister. Unfortunately, Banister had died nine months after the assassination. An alcoholic and rabid right-wing fanatic, Banister had been a star agent for the FBI and a former Naval Intelligence operative. He was a member of the John Birch Society, the Minutemen, and publisher of a racist newsletter. His office at 544 Camp Street was a well-known meeting place for anti-Castro Cubans.

Ferrie's background was even more bizarre. A former senior pilot for Eastern Airlines, Ferrie had been the head of the New Orleans Civil Air Patrol, an organization Oswald had joined as a teenager. Ferrie suffered from alopecia, an ailment that left him hairless. He wore bright red wigs and painted eyebrows. Ferrie had founded his own religion and kept hundreds of experimental rats in his house. He reportedly had flown dozens of solo missions for the CIA in Cuba and Latin America, and had links to Carlos Marcello, head of the Mob in Louisiana. Like Banister, he was extremely right wing. "I want to train killers," Ferrie had written to the commander of the US 1st Air Force. "There is nothing I would enjoy better than blowing the hell out of every damn Russian, Communist, Red or what-have-you."

On the day of the assassination, Dean Andrews, a New Orleans attorney, had been asked to fly to Dallas to represent Oswald. When asked by the Warren Commission who had hired him, Andrews had replied Clay Bertrand. Bertrand, Garrison discovered, was a pseudonym used by Clay Shaw, director of the International Trade Mart. Shaw, a darling of New Orleans high society, was also well-connected in international high-finance circles. He was also an associate of Banister and Ferrie. Like many others connected with the assassination, Shaw was a former Army Intelligence operative. The case against Shaw was highly circumstantial, but Garrison did have an eyewitness willing to testify that Shaw had met with Lee Harvey Oswald just prior to the assassination.

Just as Garrison was marshalling his case, some strange events took place. On February 17, 1967, the New Orleans *States-Item* published a story on Garrison's secret probe, indicating that he had already spent over $8,000 of taxpayers' money investigating the Kennedy

CANNABIS ACTION NETWORK

BY STEVE BLOOM

Men dominated the marijuana movement until CAN came along. Meet Hemp Tour activists Debby Goldsberry, Maria Farrow, Sarah Johnson and Monica Pratt.

HT: There's a conscious effort to do something as women somewhat excluded from men, at least in leadership roles?

DG: It didn't start out as that, but as we got further into the movement we came up against all sorts of discrimination. The marijuana movement seems to be dominated by older men, and these older men seem to want to have a certain amount of control over what goes on in the movement.

HT: What's CAN's stand on legalization in general?

DG: What we're trying to do is first educate people about marijuana, open that door and plant a seed—that's what we call it, planting seeds. We're breaking those people into the idea of marijuana, of hemp, of what the government's doing. By starting off talking about marijuana, you can move onto something bigger, which is a total change in the policy of the United States. That would include legalizing a lot of the hard drugs, because the big problem is the black market. The way to beat the drug problem is to educate people about what's really going on. For example, we know from government information that there is really no harm in smoking marijuana except for inhaling hot smoke and little particles of ash into your lungs.

MP: But if you use a water bong there are virtually no harmful effects.

DG: A vaporizer in every home. That's our first creed.

Interview, #186, February 1991

That's all, Folks!

OLD HYPOCRITE SINCE 1937

DOUG BEEKMAN

LAST DAYS OF THE DRUG BIZARRE

BY JON GETTMAN

At a White House ceremony on November 8, 1990, William Bennett resigned as Director of the Office of National Drug Control Policy (ONDCP). As President Bush offered supportive smiles and accolades about being "on the road to victory," knowledgeable observers described the real reason for Bennett's sudden departure: "He's tired and worn out. He's been shouting at this problem and not really doing anything to solve it." Bored and frustrated with the job, Bennett decided to shove it.

Though some praised Bennett for keeping the drug issue on the front pages, he had deteriorated into something of a joke. Kevin Zeese, vice president of the Drug Policy Foundation, ridiculed Bennett at September's NORML conference for attributing drug use to Satan's influence and predicted that Bennett would soon resign because the Administration was fed up with the Drug Bizarre's histrionics.

HighWitness News, #186, February 1991

RICHARD STRATTON

Before marijuana was around everyone was into drinking. You got drunk on the weekends and got into fights and automobile accidents. But when marijuana came along it really changed everything. I think it saved a lot of lives, because guys got into a lot less trouble.

When I got to Arizona, I started going to Mexico and getting real good pot. Then I went to Europe; and after that Morocco, Lebanon and Afghanistan. A lot of those original centerfolds were mine—like the Afghani oil and the Afghani hash. I think we sent some Nepalese temple balls.

I knew Tom [Forçade] from the old Yippie days, and in addition, I was real close to some of the original editors. I used to contribute all kinds of different things.

Interview by Judy McGuire, #187, March 1991

assassination. Soon thereafter, Garrison received an unusually strong letter of support from a Denver oil businessman named John Miller, hinting that Miller wanted to offer financial support to the investigation. When Miller arrived in New Orleans, he met with Garrison and one of his assistants.

"You're too big for this job," said Miller. "I suggest you accept an appointment to the bench in federal district court, and move into a job worthy of your talents."

"And what would I have to do to get this judgeship?" asked Garrison.

"Stop your investigation," replied Miller calmly.

Garrison asked Miller to leave his office.

"Well, they offered you the carrot and you turned it down," said his assistant. "You know what's coming next, don't you?"

Suddenly, reporters from all over the country descended on New Orleans, including the *Washington Post*'s George Lardner, Jr. At midnight on February 22, 1967, Lardner claims to have conducted a four-hour interview with Ferrie. The following morning Ferrie was found dead. Two unsigned, typed suicide notes were found. The letters made reference to a "messianic district attorney."

Three days later the coroner announced that Ferrie had died of natural causes and placed the time of death well before the end of Lardner's supposed marathon interview. Lardner's complicity in the affair would never be called into question, while his highly influential articles in the *Washington Post* branded Garrison's investigation a "fraud." It was just the beginning of a long series of disruptive attacks in the media, and the first in a long series of bodies connected with the case that would mysteriously turn up dead.

With Ferrie gone, Garrison had only one suspect left. He rushed his case to court, arresting Clay Shaw.

Ellen Ray, a documentary filmmaker from New York, came to New Orleans to film the story. (She is now the director of the Institute for Media Analysis.) "People were getting killed left and right," she recalls. "Garrison would subpoena a witness and two days later the witness would be killed by a parked car. I thought Garrison was a great American patriot. But things got a little too heavy when I started getting strange phone calls from men with Cuban accents." After several death threats, Ray became so terrified that instead of making a documentary on the trial, she fled the country.

Attorney General Ramsey Clark, a close friend of President Lyndon Johnson, announced from Washington that the federal government had already investigated and exonerated Clay Shaw. "Needless to say," writes Garrison, "this did not exactly make me look like District Attorney of the Year."

Meanwhile, all sorts of backpedalling was going on at the Justice Department. If Shaw had been investigated, why wasn't his name in the Warren Commission Report? "The attorney general has since determined that this was erroneous," said a spokesman for Clark. "Nothing arose indicating a need to investigate Mr. Shaw."

Realizing he was in a political minefield, Garrison presented his case as cautiously as possible. A grand jury was convened that included Jay C. Albarado. "On March 14, three criminal-court judges heard Garrison's case in a preliminary hearing to determine if there was sufficient evidence against Shaw to hold him for trial," Albarado recently wrote in a letter to the New Orleans *Times-Picayune*. "What did they conclude? That there was sufficient evidence. Garrison then presented his evidence to a 12-member grand jury. We ruled there was sufficient evidence to bring Shaw to trial. Were we duped by Garrison? I think not."

Thanks to all the unwanted publicity, Garrison's staff had swollen with volunteers eager to work on the case. The 6'6" Garrison, now dubbed the "Jolly Green Giant," had already become a hero to the many citizens and researchers who had serious doubts about the Warren Commission. Unfortunately, a few of these eager volunteers were later exposed as government informers. Shortly before the case went to trial, one of the infiltrators xeroxed all of Garrison's files and turned them over to Shaw's defense team.

On September 4, 1967, Chief Justice Earl Warren announced that Garrison's case was worthless. The *New York Post* characterized the investigation as "a morbid frolic." *Newsweek* reported that the conspiracy was "a plot of Garrison's own making." *Life* magazine published the first of many reports linking Garrison with the Mafia. (Richard Billings, an editor at *Life*, had been one of the first journalists to gain access to Garrison's inner circle, under the guise of "wanting to help" the investigation.) Walter Sheridan, a former Naval Intelligence operative and NBC investigator, appeared in New Orleans with a film crew. Their purpose? An exposé titled *The Case of Jim Garrison*, which was broadcast in June '67. "It required only a few minutes to see that NBC had classified the case as criminal and had appointed itself as the prosecutor," writes Garrison.

Puzzled by the intensity of NBC's attack, Garrison went to the library and did some research on the company. He learned the network was a subsidiary of RCA, a bulwark of the military-industrial complex whose defense contracts had increased by more than a billion dollars from 1960 to 1967. Its chairman, retired General David Sarnoff, was a well-known proponent of the Cold War.

"Some long-cherished illusions about the great free press in our country underwent a painful reappraisal during this period," writes Garrison.

Clay Shaw was brought to trial on January 29, 1969. It took less than one month for Garrison to present his case.

Demonstrating a cover-up was the easy part. Although the overwhelming majority of eyewitnesses in Dealey Plaza testified that the fatal shot came not from the Texas School Book Depository—where Oswald worked—but from a grassy knoll overlooking the plaza, the FBI had encouraged many witnesses to alter their testimony to fit the "lone nut" theory. Those that didn't were simply ignored by the commission. The ballistic evidence was flawed and obviously tampered with. Even though the FBI had received several warnings of the assassination, they had ignored them. Security for the President was strangely lax. Although Oswald's killer, Jack Ruby, had ties to the CIA and Mafia, this evidence had been suppressed. Ruby was never allowed to testify before the commission, and when interviewed in a Texas jail by Chief Justice Warren and Gerald Ford, he told them: "I would like to request that I go to Washington.... I want to tell the truth and I can't tell it here.... Gentlemen, my life is in danger." Ruby never made it to Washington. He remained in jail and died mysteriously before Garrison could call him as a witness.

Even more disturbing was the treatment given the deceased President's corpse. Under Texas law, an autopsy should have been performed by a civilian pathologist in Dallas. Instead, the body was removed at gunpoint by the Secret Service and flown to a naval hospital in Maryland, where an incomplete autopsy was performed under the

THE DOPE ON THE POPE

BY CHRIS FLASH

The storefront office of "We Deliver," a marijuana messenger service run by Mickey Cesar, New York's so-called "Pope of Dope," was raided by the NYPD, Manhattan South Narcotics Squad, on November 13....

Police claimed that We Deliver was taking in $40,000 a day, that they had seized seven pounds of pot, and that the Pope had a luxurious mansion in New Jersey he'd purchased with the profits from the delivery service. The Pope countered that the service took in about $15,000/day before expenses, that there were four pounds of pot in the office and that the mansion was inherited by his sister from their father.

Cesar had been making quite a spectacle of himself. First he and his delivery service were featured on the PBS series *The Nineties*; then he promoted his toll-free pot-purchase telephone number (1-800-WANT-POT) on Howard Stern's top-rated morning radio show; and finally, he marched in New York's Halloween Parade in papal regalia that sported a giant marijuana leaf, passing out free joints and handbills that advertised his service.

HighWitness News, #188, April 1991

PROHIBITION IN ALASKA

Alaskans voted 81,857 to 67,231 to recriminalize marijuana use and possession on this past Election Day, November 6. But Proposition 2 didn't pass without a battle from Freedom Fighters and Alaskans for Privacy. The following report was filed by Terry Mitchell, Mission Focalizer of the Freedom Fighters' "Operation Keep Free."

Though we lost, the two-to-one mandate sought by our opponents was warded off. Now the issue can go back to court where it originated in 1975—when Alaska's Supreme Court ruled unanimously that marijuana was such a relatively non-dangerous substance that it was no business of the state if adults wanted to possess it in private. We're convinced the court will once again rule in favor of privacy.

The day after Election Day, we assembled at 11:30 in our permit area downtown. We warned Alaskans of the coming jump-out squads, night vision equipped helicopters peering into homes, barbed-wire fences around schools, boot camps—all the signs of fascism in the name of the Drug War. We burned a Nazi flag and chanted, "No mandate for a police state!"

HighWitness News, #185, January 1985

EDDY ENGELSMAN

TEUN VOETEN

BY TEUN VOETEN
Engelsman runs the Netherlands' Department of Alcohol, Drugs and Tobacco, a branch of the Ministry of Welfare, Health and Cultural Affairs. He is one of the most influential strategists behind Dutch drug policies.

EE: First, let me make one thing clear—drugs, even soft drugs, are not legal in the Netherlands. The same holds for alcohol and tobacco, which are regulated by certain laws, for instance, alcohol licenses for bars and a minimal drinking age. But within the boundaries of prohibition, we try to act as humanely as possible. From a medical point of view, we don't like people to use drugs. But we know that whatever we do, people will take drugs, so we favor a pragmatic and realistic approach.

HT: How is the drug problem approached in the Netherlands?

EE: First, we see it basically as a health problem. That is why drug policy, together with alcohol and tobacco, primarily comes under the Ministry of Health, and not the Justice Department. Criminal law is only used to reduce the supply of drugs, not to punish and criminalize users. In other countries, drugs are considered an outrageous evil, resulting in a discussion that becomes very mixed up with emotional and irrational arguments.
Interview, #189, May 1991

LATE PLANTING

BY ED ROSENTHAL
The solution growers have discovered [to growing short plants] is to start late in the season. The plants will grow for only a short time before the long nights and short days force them to begin flowering. They will ripen at about the same time as plants of the same variety which were in the ground earlier and have grown much larger....

Although large gardens with large plants of yesteryear are things of the past for the most part, plants *are* being grown outdoors—either small individual plants or in small groups. They are not as impressive to look at in the field, but the buds are the same high quality as the ones from the larger plants. Besides, with only one stem, they are easier to manicure.
#189, May 1991

---

supervision of unnamed admirals and generals. The notes from this "autopsy" were quickly burned. Bullet holes were never tracked, the brain was not dissected, and organs were not removed. The autopsy was a botched and tainted affair, performed under military supervision. (The medical aspects of the case were so weird, they would later form the basis for a best-selling book on the assassination, *Best Evidence*, by David S. Lifton [Macmillan, New York].)

The most important and lasting piece of evidence unveiled by Garrison was an 8mm film of the assassination taken by Abraham Zapruder, a film that only three members of the Warren Commission had seen, probably because it cast a long shadow of doubt across their conclusions. A good analysis of the film can be found in *Cover-Up*, by J. Gary Shaw with Larry R. Harris (PO Box 722, Cleburne, TX 76031):

Had the Zapruder film of the JFK assassination been shown on national televison Friday evening, November 22, 1963, the Oswald/lone assassin fabrication would have been unacceptable to a vast majority of Americans.... The car proceeds down Elm and briefly disappears behind a sign. When it emerges the President has obviously been shot.... Governor Connally turns completely to his right, looking into the back seat; he begins to turn back when his body stiffens on impact of a bullet. Very shortly after Connally is hit, the President's head explodes in a shower of blood and brain matter—he is slammed violently backward at a speed estimated at 80-100 feet per second.

Although Time, Inc. could have made a small fortune distributing this film around the world, they instead secured the rights from Zapruder for $225,000, then held a few private screenings before locking the film in a vault. It was shown to one newsman, Dan Rather, who then described it on national television. Rather asserted that Kennedy's head went "forward with considerable force" after the fatal head shot (a statement that would have supported a hit from behind, from the direction of the School Book Depository). Several months later, Rather was promoted to White House correspondent by CBS. As if to buttress this fabrication, the FBI reversed the order of the frames when printing them in the Warren Report. When researchers later drew this reversal to the FBI's attention and demanded an explanation, Hoover attributed the switch to a "printing error."

Although Garrison proved his conspiracy, the jury was not convinced of Clay Shaw's role in it. He was released after only two hours of deliberation.

The end of the Clay Shaw trial was just the beginning of a long nightmare for Garrison. On June 30, 1971, he was arrested by federal agents on corruption charges. Two years later, the case came to trial at the height of Garrison's reelection campaign. Although he won the case, he lost the election by 2,000 votes. However, The Jolly Green Giant remains widely respected in his home state, and has recently been elected to his second term on the second highest court in Louisiana.

In 1967, the machinations of the CIA were unknown to most Americans. Today, thankfully, many brave men have left their comfortable careers in the agency and spoken out against CIA-sponsored terror around the world. One of these is Victor Marchetti, who was executive assistant to Director Richard Helms, and then coauthored *The CIA and the Cult of Intelligence* with John D. Marks. In 1975 Marchetti confirmed that Clay Shaw and David Ferrie had been

CIA operatives, and that the agency had secretly worked for Shaw's defense.

Over the years, many high-ranking officials have come forward to support Garrison's theory. "The big story in the Kennedy assassination is the cover-up," says retired Colonel L. Fletcher Prouty, Chief of Special Operations for the Joint Chiefs of Staff until 1964. Prouty was on assignment in New Zealand on the day of the assassination. After carrying a New Zealand newspaper article back to Washington, he checked the time of Oswald's arrest against the hour the paper had been printed and, with great horror, realized Oswald's bio had gone out on the international newswire before Oswald had been arrested by the Dallas police. Prouty has since become one of the most persuasive and persistent critics of the Warren Commission. His book, *The Secret Team: The CIA and Its Allies in Control of the United States and the World*, is a frightening portrayal of the hidden rulers of America.

On March 6, 1975, the Zapruder film made its national-television debut on ABC's *Goodnight America*. As a result of this long-delayed national screening, enough public pressure was put on Congress to reopen the case. Unfortunately, this reinvestigation became as carefully manipulated as the Warren Commission, eventually falling under the control of Professor G. Robert Blakey, a man with close ties to the CIA. As could be expected, Blakey led the investigation away from the CIA and toward the Mob. Blakey's conclusion was that President Kennedy was killed as a result of a conspiracy and that organized crime had the means, method and motive. "The Garrison investigation was a fraud," said Blakey. Richard Billings, the former *Life* editor, was a prominent member of Blakey's staff.

Recently, however, a number of highly detailed books on the assassination have appeared, most of which support Garrison's thesis rather than Blakey's. The best of these include *Conspiracy* by Anthony Summers (Paragon House, New York), *Crossfire* by Jim Marrs (Carroll & Graf, Inc., New York) and *High Treason* by Robert Groden and Harrison Livingstone (Berkley, New York).

"Could the Mafia have whisked Kennedy's body past the Texas authorities and got it aboard Air Force One?" writes Garrison. "Could the Mafia have placed in charge of the President's autopsy an army general who was not a physician? Could the Mafia have arranged for President Kennedy's brain to disappear from the National Archives?"

Today, we know the CIA frequently hired Mafia assassins to carry out contracts. Undoubtedly some of these men were involved in the assassination and cover-up. Shortly before his disappearance, Teamster boss Jimmy Hoffa said: "Jim Garrison's a smart man. Anybody who thinks he's a kook is a kook himself." Was Hoffa silenced because he knew too much about the plot? Just before their scheduled appearances before the House investigation, Johnny Roselli and Sam Giancana were brutally murdered in gangland fashion. Was this a message to other Mob figures who had fragmentary information on the case?

In July, 1988, *The Nation* published an FBI memorandum from Hoover dated November 29, 1963. Obtained through the Freedom of Information Act, the memo implicated "George Bush of the CIA" in the Kennedy assassination cover-up. Although President Bush denies any contact with the CIA prior to his being named director in 1976, it is reasonable to assume that Zapata, the oil company Bush founded in 1960, was a CIA front.

Former President Richard Nixon is also implicated in the cover-up. Nixon was in Dallas the day before the assassination, and his greatest

JUDI BARI

DAVID J. CROSS

During the summer of '90, Earth First!'s Judi Bari organized Redwood Summer in northern California—three months of civil disobedience aimed at stopping the logging of old-growth redwoods.... A pipe bomb was set off in her car, nearly killing Judi and fellow activist Darryl Cherney.

"I'm a single mother of two children who was the primary spokesperson for this nonviolent movement. I had nothing whatsoever to gain by being associated with bombs in any way, shape or form. They claim that I was carrying a bomb in order to blow up my car and gain sympathy for the movement. However, this bomb was way under the front seat. They said it was in the back seat and then later admitted that it wasn't. It was an antipersonnel bomb. It wasn't a bomb to blow up a car....

"Why did they do it? Well, the man who is in charge of the FBI in San Francisco is a man named Richard Held. He was involved in sabotaging the Black Panthers in Los Angeles. He was also involved in the assassinations of the American Indian Movement (AIM), where they again used vigilantes just like they did here. This is the man who is in charge of our case."
Interview by J.S. Zer, #190, June 1991

KEN AND BARBRA JENKS

BY JOHN HATHAWAY

Ken and Barbra Jenks—a Panama City Beach, Florida couple battling AIDS—received their first supply of legal medical marijuana on February 22. It was the third time the government has supplied pot for AIDS patients.

Arrested for cultivating and possessing marijuana on March 29, 1990, the Jenkses' lawyer, John Daniel, argued medical necessity during a one-day trial in July. They lost, but were leniently sentenced to one year of unsupervised probation and 500 hours of community service spent caring for and comforting each other.

TEACH (Therapeutic & Ecological Applications of Cannabis Hemp) assisted in the researching of this article. TEACH has drawn up a petition that asks "our government to immediately end federal and state prohibition of herbal and medical use of cannabis sativa." For copies, call (904) 763-6812. To contact ACT (Alliance for Cannabis Therapeutics) and MARS (Marijuana-AIDS Research Service) call: (202) 483-8595.
HighWitness News, #191, June 1991

MOUNTAIN GIRL

BY SANDY TROY

While she's probably best known for being Jerry Garcia's wife, MG was in fact one of the original Merry Pranksters and a close associate of Ken Kesey—definitely a pioneering woman of the counterculture.

ST: Why don't you tell me how you got involved with Ken Kesey?

MG: I moved to Palo Alto in '63, and met Neal Cassady and the Pranksters in '64. We had this idea to give away LSD free to people at events that we were going to set up. It grew out of a party idea—a Saturday-night party. Every Saturday night you have a colossal party, and you invite anybody and everybody you can think of to invite and turn them all on and have a good time and show weird movies, light shows or anything we could think of at the time to do.

ST: How did you meet Jerry?

MG: I met Jerry at the Acid Tests, and that's where we got to know each other. We spent time doing that together. Those guys were really game. The more they did it, the more they got into it, and the more they would play. We tried to do an Acid Test without them and it didn't work. It wasn't the same without the band.

From Prankster to American Beauty, #190, June 1991

JELLO BIAFRA

BY JUDY MCGUIRE

Best known for being the singer of the notorious '80s San Francisco hardcore band, the Dead Kennedys, Jello Biafra leapt into the public eye after a painting/poster included in his band's *Frankenchrist* album was deemed obscene. The following is an excerpt from a performance rant he did at New York University which will be released as an album called *I Blow Minds for a Living.*

"We *need* fuel. We *need* paper, and it's almost gone. Where are we going to get more? The answer for centuries has been right under our nose—GROW MORE POT. If we're serious about saving the Earth and saving the ozone, we should start right now.

"Before the 20th century, the marijuana plant provided almost all the world's clothing, textiles and rope. According to none other than the US Department of Agriculture, you can make four times as much paper from an acre of marijuana/hemp plants as you can from an acre of trees."

Jello Biafra Says: Grow More Pot, #192, August 1991

fear during the early days of Watergate was that the "Bay of Pigs thing" would be uncovered. According to H. R. Haldeman in *The Ends of Power,* "Bay of Pigs" was Nixon's code phrase for the Kennedy assassination.

As liaison between the CIA and the Pentagon during the Bay of Pigs, Fletcher Prouty was put in charge of ordering supplies for the invasion. "The CIA had code-named the invasion 'Zapata,' " recalls Prouty. "Two boats landed on the shores of Cuba. One was named Houston, the other Barbara. They were Navy ships that had been repainted with new names. I have no idea where the new names came from."

At the time Bush was living in Houston. His oil company was called Zapata, and his wife's name was Barbara.

If Garrison's investigation was not a fraud, it's reasonable to assume that high-placed individuals in the conspiracy would either be dead or would have obtained considerable power in the last 28 years. According to an article in the March 4 issue of *U.S. News & World Report,* Nixon and Bush have remained close associates. "Nixon is in contact with Bush or his senior staff every month," writes Kenneth Walsh. "Nixon also speaks regularly on the phone with [National Security Advisor] Brent Scowcroft...and Chief of Staff John Sununu."

Earlier this year Len Colodny and Robert Gettlin published *Silent Coup,* a well-documented analysis of the real forces behind the Watergate scandal. According to the authors, Nixon fell prey to a military coup after refusing to work with the Pentagon. They claim the famous Deep Throat was, in fact, General Alexander Haig.

In the meantime, a well-orchestrated disinformation campaign against Oliver Stone's movie has predictably appeared, long before Stone could even begin editing his film. Longtime Kennedy researchers were not surprised to find the charge led by George Lardner, Jr., of the *Washington Post,* the last man to see David Ferrie alive.

"Oliver Stone is chasing fiction," wrote Lardner in the May 19 edition of the *Post.* "Garrison's investigation was a fraud." Later in the article, he adds: "There was no abrupt change in Vietnam policy after JFK's death."

"That is one of the most preposterous things I've ever heard," says Zachary Sklar, editor of *On the Trail of the Assassins,* and coscreenwriter with Stone on *JFK.* "Kennedy was trying to get out of Vietnam, and Johnson led us into a war in which 58,000 Americans died. Lardner's article is a travesty."

"I wouldn't give Lardner the time of day," adds Gary Shaw. "I think he's bought and paid for."

Mark Lane, author of *Rush to Judgment,* one of the first books critical of the Warren Commission, agrees. "The CIA is bringing out the spooks who pose as journalists," says Lane. "The amazing thing about the Lardner piece is he's reviewing the film months before it's even completed."

Time magazine also slammed the film long before its release. "Garrison is considered somewhere near the far-out fringe of conspiracy theories," writes Richard Zoglin, a film critic who admits to knowing "very little" about the assassination. (For the 25th anniversary of the assassination back in '88, *Time* ran a cover story titled "Who Was the Real Target?" Inside was an excerpt from *The Great Expectations of John Connally* by James Reston, a curious book that argued Oswald really meant to kill *Connally* and only hit JFK by mistake. Someday this book may be viewed as a textbook example of CIA-sponsored

146

disinformation.)

Time, Inc., it will be remembered, is the same company that hid the Zapruder film for five years. When HIGH TIMES requested slides from the film to accompany this article, the current copyright holder sent us a three-page contract to sign. It included a prohibition against "any reference...that the Zapruder film was ever owned by Time, Inc...."

We decided not to run the photos rather than assist Time, Inc. in their continuing cover-up of the real facts behind John F. Kennedy's assassination.

In the next few months, the American people will be bombarded with information about the Kennedy assassination. Most of it will be critical of Stone and Garrison. It's important to understand that much of this criticism will be written by intelligence assets working for the CIA. Although the Cold War is supposed to be over, the CIA budget is at an all-time high; $30 billion of taxpayers' money buys a lot of propaganda.

How extensive is the CIA's infiltration of the national media? I called former agent Ralph McGehee, author of *Deadly Deceits*, who has compiled a computer database on everything published about the agency. "In 1977, Carl Bernstein wrote an article in *Rolling Stone* that named over 400 journalists uncovered by the Church Committee who were working for the CIA," says McGehee. If anything, their numbers have only increased in the last 12 years.

When will the subversion of the national media end? When the American people demand it. Unfortunately, the public has not flexed any muscle in this country since they ended the war in Vietnam. If you want to help bring justice in this case, there's plenty you can do: 1) Assist the Assassinations Archives in Washington in their quest to obtain the documentation on the Kennedy case that remains sealed to the public. For more information call Jim Lesar at (202) 393-1917. 2) Subscribe to *Covert Action Information Bulletin*, a national newsletter on covert CIA activities. For more information call (202) 331-9763. If you want more detailed information on the CIA, McGehee's database can be purchased for $99. For more information call him at (703) 437-8487. 3) Write your representatives in Congress. Tell them you want a law passed prohibiting journalists from working for the CIA. Although such a bill has been proposed many times, it never makes its way of committee.

Finally, stop accepting everything you hear on TV and read in the newspapers. Buy books on the assassination and cover-up and educate yourself. Only in this way can we keep hope alive that one day America will be the sweet land of liberty her founders intended.

THE BALLAD OF GRANDMA MARIJUANA

by Steve Bloom

A roomful of eyes focus on the elderly couple that has just been called to the podium. They applaud loudly for Mae and Arnold Nutt, recipients of the Drug Policy Foundation's Robert C. Randall Award for Achievement in the Field of Citizen Action. Both short and somewhat

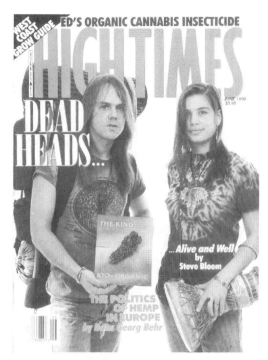

DEADHEADS

BY STEVE BLOOM

While we waited through the traffic jam on the way into the Centre's parking lot, dozens of Deadheads straggled on the side of the road or in between the lines of cars. This procession had only one thing on its mind: tickets. Some carried elaborately designed placards while others simply placed their index fingers quietly in the air. The meaning was simple: I need *one* ticket. The Dead have a song called "I Need a Miracle," a title that has been transmogrified into what Deadheads call the "miracle ticket...."

Ticketless, we planned to spend the day and night in the lot, hanging with the 'heads. Music blared from various car stereos and people banged conga drums and other percussion instruments. Waif-like girls walked around barefoot, selling slices of organic banana bread; guys hovered over coolers hawking beer. The party had just begun.

As concert-time approached, "miracle ticket" desperation escalated into a frenzy. Most people simply wagged their forefinger, while others stopped and asked if you had an extra. I didn't see any scalping.

The sun was setting as the concert began. Shrouded in darkness, the scene took on an ethereal quality. The wall-to-wall vendors on the back lot looked like a Turkish bazaar. Dust kicked up, dogs skipped along, drums beat, sufis danced....

We headed for the hill, where sweaty drummers pounded out a tribal beat. People nestled in the grass with balloons. Everyone appeared to be tripping. But there was one thing missing: Where was the "kind bud" I had heard so much about?
Deadheads: Fighting for the Right to Party, #178, June 1990

MAKING SINSE OF THE '90S

"There are some things people should do if they want to avoid detection—for instance, covering their tracks. Many outdoor growers unwittingly leave telltale signs of their activity. These might include leaving tools laying around, creating a trail to their patch from constant visiting, attracting attention by crossing private property or leaving watering hoses out in view. Much care must be taken to hide all traces of activity. If possible, hoses should be buried underground." —MEL FRANK

"As I always say, if you want to avoid detection, don't charge it. Pay cash. Also, don't order equipment through the mail. People using the United Parcel Service found out too late that UPS handed over all their records to the DEA. Since you can't trust UPS, mail order is out.

But it is a good idea to support your local merchants. They want your business, and, in most cases, have more to lose than gain by snitching." —THE BUSH DOCTOR

"There are different ways to get seeds. You could go to current seed companies, but these are either rip-offs or government traps. In some cases they offer sterile seeds and in others they never deliver. This leaves growers with other options: domestically-grown seeds or illegally smuggled seeds from Holland.

Seed production in Holland continues, since domestic use there remains strong. Understandably, Dutch companies don't want to risk exporting to the States. But if US laws change...?" —ED ROSENTHAL
Post-Green Merchant Growing,
edited by Nate Eaton, #197, January 1992

stout, the Nutts look like clay bookends as they listen to a brief speech by Kevin Zeese, the DPF's vice president.

The banquet audience, seated around dinner tables in Washington DC's Mayflower Hotel, learns that virtually 11 years ago the Nutts lost their oldest child, Keith, to cancer. It was their second such tragedy. In 1967, the Nutts' second-born, Dana, died of Ewings Sarcoma. He never reached his 10th birthday.

Zeese explains how the Nutts—and Mae in particular—had since become leaders in the fight to legalize marijuana for medical use. Dubbed "Grandma Marijuana" by the local Michigan press, Nutt had discovered, during Keith's last days, that cannabis was an effective, even miraculous, cure for the horrendous nausea caused by chemotherapy. When Keith smoked pot, he could eat and participate in family activities. Unfortunately, marijuana couldn't save Keith's life, but at least it helped make it more bearable as his time ran out.

Zeese hands them their award—a plaque and a $10,000 check—and then moves aside. The applauding audience rises to a standing ovation. It's a wonderful moment.

Red-faced and teary-eyed, both attempt to speak, but words will not come out. Mae makes a valiant second attempt. Again, her voice breaks. Overwhelmed, the Nutts return to their table. The banquet continues, but the high point has already been reached.

That's what happens when you invite Grandma Marijuana to Washington.

Five months later, back home in Beaverton, Michigan, the Nutts are beaming about the new car that's sitting in their garage. "First, we put the money in the bank, and then we thought about it," Mae says. "We had a car that had.... "

"A hundred-and-ten-thousand miles on it," Arnold adds.

"In our financial condition," Mae continues, "we decided the chances of us being able to buy a new car were nil or none, so we started shopping and bought the car."

Did they consider purchasing $10,000 worth of marijuana, which could have been clandestinely distributed to cancer patients?

"I thought of that," Mae cheerfully admits, "but as conservative as I am, I thought, 'That's the sure way to go to jail.' I have never been in jail and I have no desire to."

How conservative Mae Nutt and her husband of 38 years are depends on your definition of the word. A lifelong Democrat, Mae is quick to criticize George Bush. "We have to have somebody who cares about people. Our government spends millions for bombs, while people who are starving to death are just ignored—they don't even exist. It's tragic and it's getting worse."

When Mae speaks of her conservatism, she's really referring to years of government brainwashing that, among other things, made her ignorant about marijuana. "People like us who grew up in the '30s and the '40s were so programmed against marijuana," she explains, describing the effect of reefer madness. "[We were told that] we would go mad and tear off our clothes and run naked through the streets, or who knows what? In our generation, if the government told us something we believed it. I have to admit when our kids were teenagers we weren't even going to *discuss* it. It's not easy for people our age. It took the illness of a child to make us open our minds."

The Nutts' transformation began in 1978, when they received a call from Keith, who was 22 at the time and living in Columbus, Ohio.

Keith's news was their worst nightmare: He had testicular cancer. In April, one testicle was removed. A subsequent operation left him minus a large number of lymph nodes between his pelvic and breast bones. Keith returned home to central Michigan, where the disease stayed in remission until just after the new year. In January, he had his remaining testicle taken out. To stop the rampant spreading of cancer throughout his body, Keith was given a highly-toxic form of chemotherapy called Cisplatin.

What this all has to do with marijuana we now know. Some 13 years later, a survey of oncologists (cancer doctors) conducted by Harvard researchers Richard Doblin and Mark A.R. Kleiman revealed that "more than 44% of the respondents report recommending the [illegal] use of marijuana for the control of emesis [vomiting] to at least one cancer chemotherapy patient.... Almost half [48%] would prescribe marijuana to some of their patients if it were legal," the survey's authors wrote in May.

The first Mae Nutt ever heard about pot's antiemetic properties was in a newspaper story in 1979. "I read about somebody smoking marijuana for nausea from cancer," she recalls. "I mentioned it to Keith. 'Did you know this?' He said, 'Yes.' They were smoking it in Columbus. 'Why didn't you say something?' I asked. He said, 'You made it abundantly clear that this was not acceptable.' He hadn't started chemo [in Columbus], so he didn't smoke there, but the rest of the people had. He knew that it worked."

Described as extremely bright and independent ("he would do his own thing"), musical ("he could play any instrument he touched") and a rock- and mountain-climbing enthusiast ("he loved Colorado"), Keith never graduated from college. "He didn't really know what he wanted to do," Arnold says.

Finishing school was perhaps the furthest thing from Keith's mind when he began taking injections of Cisplatin in February, 1979. The side effects from the drug were devastating. Despite the use of such prescribed antiemetics as Compazine, Keith still vomited violently for eight to 10 hours after each chemo treatment. When he had nothing left to throw up, Keith would just retch and convulse. By April, he had lost 30 pounds.

"I don't have a problem with the chemotherapy," Mae says. I've seen it work. I work with cancer patients all the time. I see enough of them survive that if it were me I think I would try the chemo. It's a poison and it destroys healthy cells as well as malignant cells, but I have seen it work. When they give chemo, there's hope."

With his parents' consent, Keith began smoking to offset his rapid debilitation. "When he first smoked, I had to leave the room," she notes. "But then I thought, 'My God, I saw them poke him full of needles and him having seizures from too many drugs in the hospital. What am I doing?'"

Laid up in Midland Hospital, Keith puffed pot before his chemo treatments. "If we're going to do something, we're going to tell you— we're not going to play games," Mae says, explaining the family's decision to "go public." "We simply told the doctors and the nurses that he was smoking. Never did we hide or pretend that he wasn't, and no one had a problem with it."

Then Mae phoned up the nearby *Bay City Times* and spilled the story to the press. That's how "Grandma Marijuana" was born.

"When we went public, marijuana rained out of the sky," Mae drifts back fondly.

WHAT WOULD YOU PUT ON THE COVER?

BY JOHN HOLMSTROM

Editor-in-chief Steven Hager has installed a democratic method for deciding what should go on the cover of HIGH TIMES. Once a month, the staff gathers for a vote. First, there's a friendly discussion, then a vote is taken. That's followed by another discussion. If there's a serious disagreement over what should go on the cover, we fight it out until one idea wins.

For instance, Judy McGuire chose a nude photograph of Allen Ginsberg as one cover possibility, while Steve Hager picked an eerie picture of a red road for the peyote article, and I thought Lennie Mace, the ballpoint-pen artist, would do a fine spaced-out pic for "Pot on the Moon."

The art staff put together three cover mock-ups. I opened the discussion by pointing out how great Lennie's drawing came out, and how it's perfect for a HIGH TIMES cover. As usual, Steve Bloom disagreed with me. "Allen Ginsberg is a legend!" he barked. "He's a celebrity!" "He's an important countercultural icon," Judy shot back, "and deserves to be on the cover." The art staff—John Dinsdale, Brian Spaeth and Frank Max—were holding out for the red road. "It's aesthetically pleasing," they insisted.

"If we put Ginsberg naked on the cover it'll sell! Look what happened when *Vanity Fair* put Demi Moore on their cover!" "No one wants to look at Allen Ginsberg buck naked." "OK, then, what if we put a pot leaf over Ginsberg's private parts?"

Nate Eaton, our editorial assistant, was firmly against the moon cover. "No one's gonna believe it." *Page Six, #198, February 1992*

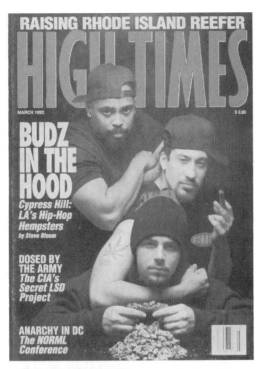

CYPRESS HILL

BY STEVE BLOOM

Cypress Hill's self-titled debut on Ruffhouse/Columbia contains more marijuana references than a classic Peter Tosh or Bob Marley album.

"A lot of rap groups try to stay back and don't talk about it," says Muggs, the white guy in the group. "They all get high. We know 'em, we hang out with 'em."

"We did it because nobody else will," B-Real explains.

"In all our demos, we rhymed about gettin' high," Sen Dog adds. "It's just something that comes natural to us."

#199, March 1992

CANNABIS CUP '91

BY LOU STATHIS

Several months before the scheduled trip, it looked like, very possibly, there wouldn't even *be* any Cup this year. Then Managing Editor Judy McGuire decided to change the focus of the competition from the manufacturing to the retail end. That is, turn things into a pothead version of barhopping—a coffeeshop crawl, if you will. This way, instead of judging high-sci designer pot that may well never make to the average street smoker, we'd be sampling the very same things HIGH TIMES readers would encounter on an Amsterdam vacation....

Judging was tight, and ultimately the winner, by a 3-2 vote margin, was determined to be Free City's Sample #3.

One Week in Amsterdam..., #197, January 1992

"In the mailbox, on the porch.... " Arnold chimes in.

"I had a priest bring me an attaché case [full of pot]," Mae goes on. "He said he liked it, but didn't think he should use it. I wrote him a check. Keith had a fit. He said, 'Mother, you don't pay for marijuana with a check!' "

The chemotherapy Keith was receiving may have given him and his parents hope, but that was about all it did. He smoked to dull the nausea and spur his appetite, but the cancer marched on. "He was full of cancer, his liver, the whole thing," Mae says. Informed by doctors that he had a less-than-30% chance of living, Keith began contemplating suicide. "Keith was his own man, and I could not say to him, 'This is what you're going to do.' But I did say, 'I would rather you didn't do this.' " In the next breath, however, Mae admits, "I would have, without any hesitation whatsoever, given him sleeping pills."

By October, the end was near. "Keith was in the hospital, and it was like he knew this was his last trip to the hospital because he'd been in and out many times," Mae explains. "He said, 'Mother, I don't want to stay alone. I want somebody to stay with me all the time.' So I said okay. I never promised my children anything I didn't fully intend to do. After making that promise I was having a difficult time figuring out how it was going to happen, because Mark [Keith's younger brother] and Arnold were both working. Then he said, 'Mother, I'd like to see David.' David was a friend of Keith's that he'd gone to school with since first grade. When David moved to Columbus, Keith went down there and they shared an apartment. Keith discovered he had cancer when he was living with David. I said, 'I can't get David. He's on a ship off the tip of South America exploring for oil.' A day later, he said, 'Mother, I want to see Jim.' Jim was a very close friend. I said, 'I can't get Jim. He's backpacking out in Yellowstone.'

"Keith had been raised in church, but as he grew older he became an agnostic. That was okay with me. You can't make anybody believe anything they don't want to believe. About three days later I got a phone call, and it was David; he was in Detroit! The company he worked for had come back to shore and given him a plane ticket home. He didn't know Keith was back in the hospital. He called from Detroit and asked if we could pick him up. And about a day later, Jim called. He had called home and found out from his folks that Keith was back in the hospital; he flew home right away. So these two young men spent nights with Keith and I spent days.

"You know what Keith said the night before he died? 'Mother, there is a God.' "

Keith Nutt died early in the morning of October 22, 1979.

Grandma Marijuana had begun her crusade to legalize the medical use of cannabis in the months before her son's death. Her public stance quickly came to the attention of Michigan lawmakers, who convened hearings in both branches of the state legislature. The Nutts testified about Keith's positive experience with marijuana before the Michigan State Senate Judiciary Committee and the House Committee on Public Health. On October 10, 1979, the Michigan House unanimously voted in favor of making marijuana available to patients suffering from "life- or sense-threatening" diseases like cancer, glaucoma and multiple sclerosis. Five days later, the Senate followed suit. The day Keith passed away, Act No. 125 of the Public Acts of 1979 ("The Michigan Controlled Substances Therapeutic Research Program") was signed into law by Lieutenant Governor James Brickley. (The Senate subsequently adopted "a resolution of tribute offered as a memorial for Keith Nutt.")

Meanwhile, Mae began operating what she called the "Green Cross" out of their modest home off the beaten path in Beaverton, 40 miles north of Saginaw. "We had a lot [of pot]," she says. "Once Keith was gone, there was no way I could throw it away. So I simply made it available. "People heard about us and came to us. One woman asked me to get in touch with a friend of hers—married, had a couple of children—who had migraine headaches all her life. I gave her a nice-sized amount. A year later, she calls me. Her friend hadn't had a headache since."

Months passed, and the Michigan medical-marijuana program still couldn't get any pot (blame the feds for that). As a result, the Nutt house became the drop-off point for pot, which Mae illegally distributed to medical patients. Weren't they harassed by the police? "Never," Mae says emphatically. "I think it was partly because we were open and honest. There was this woman in a community not too far from here who began making [pot] brownies for a friend who had cancer. The friend's husband was a policeman. I went to their house to deliver some marijuana and he told me, 'If you ever run out I might be able to help you out.' "

Mae realized that, for certain cancers (primarily, lung), smoking marijuana was not the optimum way to absorb the herb's healing powers, so she started baking marijuana into brownies and shipping them off to patients. Even more radical was her decision to make pot suppositories out of marijuana butter she cooked up puna-style. "I got some empty capsules—the pharmacists would say, 'Don't tell me about it, just take them and go'—and, with a hypodermic syringe, filled them with the butter."

Wasn't Grandma going a little too far now, playing doctor with the suppositories? "I talked to people, to physicians, to nurses—everybody agreed, what do we have to lose? I knew what I was doing was not going to hurt anyone, and it could very possibly ease the discomfort. I had no problem with it."

What she did have a problem with, however, was the fact that both the brownies and suppositories were not controlled amounts and didn't absorb into the body as readily as smoke. "The smoke gets into the system quicker," Mae says, "and is more easily controlled."

Her comments predated the marijuana versus Marinol (synthetic THC) debate by several years. While marijuana remains a Schedule I(d) "hallucinogenic substance" under the Controlled Substances Act of 1970 (translation: it can't be prescribed), tetrahydrocannabinol has since been switched from Schedule I(d) to the Schedule II prescription list (alongside opium, morphine, methadone, cocaine and amphetamine). "I've talked to patients who have used Marinol and its terrible," Mae says. "They're up and down and up and down. They're not happy with the high. It doesn't make a lot of sense."

According to the 1991 Harvard survey, "Oncologists believe smoked marijuana to be roughly as safe as legally-available or synthetic THC [Marinol] and somewhat more effective.... Oncologists may prefer smoked marijuana over oral THC for several reasons. The bioavailability of THC absorbed through the lungs has been shown to be more reliable than that of THC absorbed through the gastrointestinal tract; smoking offers patients the opportunity to self-titrate dosages [determine the strength] in order to realize therapeutic levels with a minimum of side effects; and there are active agents in the crude marijuana which are absent from the pure synthetic THC."

CHEF RA FOR PRESIDENT

The United States is a sick and ailing nation in search of a leader. But who can expose the secret government, abolish the CIA, and put an end to petrochemical pollution? After searching the list of potential candidates, the editors of HIGH TIMES have come to the conclusion there is only one person who can save our country in 1992: The Great Chef Ra! The Platform: 1. Plant hemp throughout the land for paper, fuel and fiber. 2. Give every American a job, a home, an education and free health care. 3. Sell American-grown sinsemilla to the Japanese. 4. Abolish income tax for the poor and middle classes. 5. Bust anyone who pollutes our Mother Earth. 6. Let the Rainbow Family run the Department of the Interior, and let Native Americans run the National Parks. 7. Let our sisters have the ERA, abortion rights, free day care, and let them help run the country. 8. Put an end to gender warfare with men agreeing to do dishes and cooking. 9. Let gays and other subcultures live in peace. 10. Tax all drugs that kill: alcohol, tobacco, heroin, crack.
#200, April 1992

RA FOR PREZ!

First came Pot on the Moon. And now, Chef RA for president. I don't know the man personally, and I'm sure he's one hell of a man, but here we are trying to get recognized as a serious movement, and here he is dressed as Uncle Sam waving the peace sign. Who's his VP, Wavy Gravy?
Get Real
Alameda, CA

Letters, #205, September 1992

JOHN LENNON

BY BILL WEINBERG

So it certainly did not escape the FBI's notice when, shortly after the Ann Arbor rally, John Sinclair visited Lennon and Ono at Bank Street. There, in a brainstorming session with Yippie leaders, they decided to take the idea of rock concert/political rally on the road—with the ultimate destination being that summer's Republican National Convention in San Diego, where Richard Nixon was expected to be nominated for a second term. Lennon would be the star who would draw thousands of kids to San Diego to protest Nixon and the war in Indochina....

By then John and Yoko had applied for citizenship. A February FBI report on Lennon's citizenship application was stamped COPY TO CIA. That same month, a CIA report (one of four Central Intelligence Agency documents that have been released to [John] Wiener) noted that Lennon had paid for activist Rennie Davis to attend the World Assembly for Peace & Independence of the Peoples of Indochina, held in Paris that month.

John Lennon: The Radical Years, #201, May 1992

WHEN TO HARVEST

BY MEL FRANK

Resin glands are barely visible to the naked eye, so use a magnifying lens. Examine the glands that coat the female flowers on your most mature plant. if those glands haven't developed long stalks, then potency is still increasing. If many glands are brown or missing, then the peak has passed and potency is decreasing.

#206, October 1992

Be that as it may, the Nutts continued their campaign to spread the good word about marijuana. In 1986, when hearings were being organized by the DEA to consider rescheduling marijuana, Mae and Arnold received a call from Robert Randall, head of the Alliance for Cannabis Therapeutics (a fledgling organization dedicated to promoting the medical uses of marijuana) and, more importantly, the first person to receive legal pot from the federal government. Together with NORML, he asked Mae to testify before the DEA's chief administrative law judge, Francis L. Young. She agreed.

So in January, 1988, Mae, 66, and Arnold, 68, made their first trip to the nation's capital. The hearings, which had begun in November in New Orleans, were now taking place in the US Court of Claims Building, Court 10, Room 309, Judge Young presiding.

On January 5, the most unlikely of marijuana advocates—silver-haired, red-cheeked, bespectacled Mae Nutt—took the stand. Back in May, she had written and filed her affidavit with the state of Michigan. Now had come the time to tell Washington everything she knew about marijuana as a medication for cancer, glaucoma and MS patients. In great detail, Mae spun her story—about Keith's smoking, her pot giveaways ("we had a booming clinic"), the suppositories and brownies and the dormant state of Michigan's Marijuana Therapeutic Research Program.

With a dramatic flourish, Grandma Marijuana concluded: "Michigan and more than 30 other states have legislatively recognized marijuana's medical utility. Hundreds of physicians throughout the country are telling their patients to smoke marijuana. Thousands, if not tens of thousands, of patients with glaucoma, cancer, MS and other disorders are gaining relief from smoking marijuana. As a parent, I once had to confront a stark choice—obey the law and let my son suffer, or break the law and provide my son with genuine relief from chemotherapeutically induced misery. I chose to help my son. Faced with the same choice again, my husband and I would help our son again. We are confident any parents confronting such circumstances would make the same decision."

Eight months later, Judge Young sided with Mae Nutt and the many other witnesses who came forth to testify in favor of medical marijuana. Calling marijuana, in its natural form, "one of the safest therapeutically active substances known to man," Judge Young recommended changing its status from Schedule I to Schedule II. In particular, he ruled that marijuana had medical applications in at least three areas: to treat MS, hyperparathyroidism, and nausea suffered by some cancer patients as a result of chemotherapy. He was not convinced of marijuana's usefulness in treating glaucoma.

"The evidence in this record clearly shows that marijuana has been accepted as capable of relieving the distress of great numbers of very ill people and doing so with safety under medical supervision," Judge Young wrote in his 69-page ruling. "It would be unreasonable, arbitrary and capricious for [the] DEA to continue to stand between those sufferers and the benefits of this substance in light of the evidence in this record."

To the surprise of few familiar with this then-16-year-old legal battle royale between promarijuana forces and the DEA, the agency's administrator at the time, John Lawn, promptly overruled Judge Young's decision.

"I understand when those hearings first started they thought the judge would have a decision almost immediately," Mae points out. "He didn't. It took him quite a while. He really considered his decision. He's a brilliant, brilliant man who cared and listened, yet they acted as if he was a simpleton."

For the third time, the case was appealed, and for the third time—this past April—it was remanded back to the DEA for further consideration. "I don't think I've got that many more years left, and I've got to get my goal—which is to make it legal for medicine," says an outraged Mae Nutt.

"I think putting people in jail for smoking it is ridiculous, but I think that letting people suffer when something so simple will help alleviate such horrible pain and misery is ludicrous. It's absolutely insane!"

Mae Nutt gets phone calls and letters, lots of them. They subside sometimes, then pick up again after she's been profiled by another newspaper or magazine, filmed by another TV crew. In March 1991, *The CBS Evening News* devoted three minutes to Grandma Marijuana. The segment also featured Bill Sebastian, a 60-year-old glaucoma sufferer the Nutts know well, toking up as Mae looked on approvingly—truly an amazing image. Pot's come a long way, baby.

Though she no longer gives cannabis away (today's hefty prices have ground the donations to a halt), Mae busily spends her time working with cancer patients at Midland Hospital and fielding the many queries that arrive in the mail or over the phone. "The calls and letters I get are heartbreaking," she says. "On one letter, the handwriting was like a five-year-old's. As I read it, I learned that he had had his right arm amputated. His last words were, 'I'm in pain twenty-four hours a day.'

"The longer I live I'm more amazed at the different things I hear about marijuana. The other day I was told about a man who has emphysema. I would think with emphysema or lung problems the last thing you would ever want to do is smoke anything. And yet he insisted he smokes [pot], and that he coughs up secretions from his lungs and then he's able to breathe better.

"There's this one man who suffers terrific itching. He's in the Army and they're going to amputate his arm because he's had gangrene. Somehow or other he doesn't have his arm amputated and he goes out to a party, smokes pot and the itching stops. There's another one about a man [Irvin Rosenfeld] who has bone spurs on his joints. When he walks, his muscles and tissues shred on these bone spurs, and he ends up bleeding internally. He found when he smokes marijuana it relaxes the muscles in the tendons so they don't shred. He's one of the ones who gets [pot] legally.

"I got a call the other day from a sixty-five-year-old lady from Atlanta. She's blind in one eye, has glaucoma and is looking for [pot]. In a Southern accent she says, 'Child, I smoked it about forty years ago in a carny—if I can save my sight, I'll smoke it now.' I heard from a young mother in Texas who's paralyzed. She said her brother was getting her one [pot] cigarette every two weeks! I asked, 'What does that do?' She said it helps her that one day. 'I can do my housework, I can play with my children and I can enjoy life. The other days I'm taking prescription drugs and I'm a zombie.' "

"Most of these people who call can't afford it," Arnold explains.

"Some of them have the money, but a lot of them are looking for someplace to get it," Mae clarifies. "This man in Beaverton with glaucoma, Bill Sebastian, gets maybe a couple of ounces a month. He took pain pills, sleeping pills, tranquilizers and eye drops. He had to sign himself into a rehab center and get dried out. When he can get marijuana he doesn't need any of it. He says it makes all the difference."

"If the guy that's using it says it works, you've got to believe him," Arnold says.

"Each time I hear of another illness that is helped by this drug, plant, herb, whatever, my mind is blown away," Mae adds. "There's no hard and

TERENCE MCKENNA

KATHLEEN CARR

"The time travel question is more interesting. Possibly the world is experiencing a compression of technological novelty that is going to lead to developments that are very much like what we would imagine time travel to be. We may be closing in on the ability to transmit information forward into the future, and to create an informational domain of communication between various points in time. How this will be done is difficult to imagine, but things like fractal mathematics, superconductivity, and nanotechnology offer new and novel approaches to the realization of these old dreams. We shouldn't assume time travel is impossible simply because it hasn't been done. There's plenty of latitude in the laws of quantum physics to allow for moving information through time in various ways."
Interview by David Jay Brown & Rebecca McClen, #200, April 1992

NINA GRABOI

BY REBECCA MCCLEN & ANNE SPILLING
Born in Vienna, Austria, [Nina Graboi] was a refugee from Nazi Europe and came to America in 1940 at the age of 21. She lived the life of a society hostess in an exclusive Long Island community, but gave it up for a very different lifestyle when she became enmeshed in the counterculture of the '60s.
NG: Psychedelics allow you to view the world with new eyes in new ways. They are very dangerous because they are going to make people less willing to swallow a lot of stuff that the politicians hand out to them and which the general society believes in. I believe that subconsciously that is the reason for the War on Drugs.
HT: Fear of something new?
NG: Yes. Something new is coming into the world through the mind-expanding substances, and that's frightening to the establishment. However, psychedelics of one kind or another were used in the Eleusinian mysteries of Greece, and they are a part of the Native American tradition. It's an ancient tradition, and I'm not sure that the animals don't do it too. There's a man named Ron Siegel who claims that the need to change one's consciousness is part of not only the human genetic heritage but also of all animals.
Interview, #202, June 1992

FRANK MAX

DOWN WITH THE FARM

BY NATE EATON

George Washington had five farms on his estate, Mount Vernon, where he grew cannabis hemp and "other crops." Thanks to a $1.75-million private grant, one of his farms will be reactivated—and on it will grow wheat, corn and "other crops." According to the Mount Vernon Ladies' Association, development is underway, but no word yet on whether hemp will be included for historical accuracy.

Quick Flashes, #202, June 1992

DENNIS PERON

BY PETER GORMAN

On January 27, 1990, Dennis Peron was at home in San Francisco caring for his partner Jonathan West, who was suffering from AIDS. Shortly before midnight, 10 narcotics police in street clothes appeared at the door with a search warrant. They ordered Peron and West to lie on the kitchen floor while they ransacked the house looking for pot. Two policemen remained in the kitchen. One of them put a foot on West's neck. "Know what AIDS means?" he asked. "Asshole in deep shit."

The search turned up four ounces of Humboldt Green and nothing else. Despite the fact that neither scales nor packaging equipment were found, Peron was arrested for possession with intent to sell.

"They had a report I had marijuana," says Peron bitterly. "Well, I did. It was medicine for Jonathan."

Dennis Peron: The Man Who Gave Away Pot, #202, June 1992

fast evidence, but it seems to be a trend that AIDS patients who smoke marijuana are living longer than AIDS patients who don't. Hopefully, out of AIDS, which is a terrible, terrible tragedy, the medical profession will find out how important marijuana is.

"I had a phone call after the TV show from a group of young men that were part of an organization—one's anorectic, another has a nerve problem and somebody else has insomnia. He said, 'Do you want me to send you some?' I said, 'No.' He said, 'You don't have a problem?' I said, 'I have a lot of them, but I don't think I have one that marijuana could help.'"

Mae smiles and giggles at her answer. Does Grandma Marijuana smoke? "I've never even been slightly tempted," she answers firmly. "I have to assume that part of that old training in the back of my mind is still there."

Getting back to her "problems," Mae says she has high cholesterol and high blood pressure. "I had a doctor give me three different pills for high cholesterol. The same physician gave me something for high blood pressure. The blood pressure medication takes potassium out of your system, so he gave me four potassium tablets a day. Then the drug I was taking for high cholesterol was giving me diarrhea, so he writes another prescription. I said, 'What's that for?' He said, 'It'll make you constipated.' I left that physician. Enough is enough is enough! I switched physicians and now I'm down to one pill a day."

The point here is that the pharmaceutical companies have come to control the medical industry with their chemical cures for whatever ails us. "Why are we selling these drugs? Because somebody's making a lot of money," Mae says rhetorically. "Why are we not making marijuana legal? Because nobody can make a lot of money off of it. It has to be some humongous research project, with some vast pharmaceutical company behind it. They're just not willing to say, 'Let's try it.'"

And so the suffering goes on. Despite countless reports of marijuana's incredible healing properties, cannabis continues to be demonized by the government and those who have special interests in keeping it prohibited. But that doesn't stop the Mae and Arnold Nutts of the world from speaking out, from telling their side of the story.

Two final tales offer a rare sort of uplift. Can marijuana actually save lives? Mae Nutt thinks so. "A man called me the other day and said his son has leukemia. He had refused to take the treatment until a friend got him stoned on marijuana. What they didn't know then is that he needed marijuana to keep the nausea down. He took the treatment and survived. He's a man in his thirties today. Because of marijuana, he survived.

"The other one was a small child out west. She was taking chemo and was so emaciated and couldn't eat that the family simply had to stop her treatment. There was nothing left to give treatment to. They started giving her marijuana brownies to eat; that built up her body so that she could continue her treatment. The story I read is that she went around the hospital riding a tricycle, while all the other children were either in their beds, or if they were up walking were carrying around buckets to vomit in. The other parents were saying to the parents of the child that was so happy and having so much fun, 'What are you doing that we aren't?' One of the things the government says is that this drug makes people euphoric. What in the hell is wrong with being euphoric if you're dying of cancer?

"To the best of my knowledge," Grandma Marijuana says with a lovely twinkle in her eye and a sweet smile from rosy cheek to rosy cheek, "that child is still alive."

HEMPSEED: NATURE'S PERFECT FOOD

by Lynn Osburn

In May 1991, as the California Hemp Initiative was fully underway, Jack Herer did a guest spot on a radio talk show in Los Angeles. One listener was a Ph.D. biochemist from UCLA. Dr. Roberta Hamilton got in touch with Jack and arranged for a meeting to tell him about the nutritional value of the oils in hempseed. Jack asked Judy, my wife, and me to attend. We joined him at Dr. Hamilton's house near UCLA.

Dr. Hamilton, a talkative and intelligent woman in her sixties, invited us into her library. Jack was excited and wasted no time getting into the subject.

"What's so nutritious about the oils, the hempseed oil? You said they're essential?" he asked.

"Yes, linoleic and linolenic acids. They're essential. Life requires them. GLA, linoleic and linolenic acids, EPA, sunshine and protein high in phosphorus are all part of the battery of life. They assist the prostaglandins that... "

Jack interrupted, "Whoa, wait a minute, what's this other stuff? Is any of it in hemp?"

Dr. Hamilton looked at Judy and me and said, "You're his editors. Do you know anything about these oils?"

"GLA is gamma linolenic acid, and EPA is eicosapentaenoic acid, I think, but it's been awhile. And don't the prostaglandins have something to do with immunity?" Most of what I knew had come from reading research about life extension.

"Good. You know what I'm talking about. You can fill in the others later," she said. "It's where Pritikin went wrong. He limited the oils in his patients' diets. He didn't know the oils were essential.

"These essential fatty acids are responsible for our immune response. In the old country the peasants ate hemp butter. They were more resistant to disease than the nobility. The higher classes wouldn't eat hemp porridge because the poor ate it. To them hemp was low-class food."

She discussed many interesting bits of biochemistry from the nutritional viewpoint and nutrition's relevance to disease. But Jack wanted more simplification. He was concentrating on the CHI political campaign and needed a short statement he could use in speeches and for the press.

"Dr. Hamilton—Roberta—could you give me one line summing up the essential fatty acids in hemp that I could quote you on?"

"Yes. Hemp is the highest of any plant in essential fatty acids." She went on to point out that hempseed oil is 55% linoleic acid and 25% linolenic acid. Only flax oil has more linolenic acid at 58%, but hempseed oil is the highest in total essential fatty acids at 80% of total oil volume. And hempseed oil is among the lowest in saturated fats at 8% of total oil volume.

I explained to her how important it was for our campaign to have documentation on the claims we made about hemp. She took a book down from her library shelf and said, "This book has in it most everything we've talked about today. You should get a copy." The book was *Fats and Oils: The Complete Guide to Fats and Oils in Health and Nutrition*, by Udo

ALAN BRADY'S HEMPSCREAM ICE CREAM RECIPE

BY LYNN OSBURN

Wash hemp seeds several times until thoroughly clean. Then soak hemp seeds in water overnight until they sprout. (Sterile, imported hempseed will absorb water until the swollen embryo cracks the shell into two halves, but the embryo will not turn green and grow like alfalfa or bean sprouts.) Separate the hulls from the sprouts using a vegetable juicer. Take the hempseed sprout puree and add sweetener. Place in ice cream maker and churn until desired consistency is obtained.

The amount of water left in the de-hulled sprouts influences the final consistency of the hempscream. Plus, operator skill is needed to fine-tune the juicer to get satisfactory separation of the embryos from the hulls.

High Vibes, #218, October 1993

HIP-HOP HEMPFEST

BY CHEF RA

To kick off the Chef RA political campaign, we needed a gala event. The HIGH TIMES posse decided I should come to New York and participate in a huge party with the rap group Cypress Hill. I love rap music and Cypress Hill is one of the hottest groups around. They also love to smoke JAH HERB. Unfortunately, what happened was a cataclysmic culture clash.

The HIGH TIMES crew was in panic mode. The deejay skipped out, the stage manager could not be found. Only Hempty Hemp, the emcee, seemed calm and collected. "Don't worry, RA," he assured me. "I'm going to wing it."

The crowd began to boo and throw things. The situation got worse when David Peel, Aron "Pie-man" Kaye and the Lower East Side band took the stage to sing "Marijuana."

Before I could make it out the back door, Steve Hager grabbed me. "I'm going up on stage to introduce you, RA," he said. "Let's go!"

David Peel and crew launched into "Hail to the Chef!" and we paraded up to the stage. The crowd was so stunned by my black dreadlock ass ranting about the state of the nation that they actually calmed down and listened. I began feeling positive about getting through to the hip-hop nation despite the hippy/hip-hop culture clash. I was almost ready to depart, feeling like I'd salvaged my kick-off party when David Peel broke into a rendition of "Chef RA for President," causing the crowd to start booing again.

Psychedelic Kitchen, #202, June 1992

JOHN TRUDELL

COURTESY RYKODISC

"My DNA needs THC, OK? These things are not to be confused, because they weren't confused in the beginning, when we were young in the sixties. The reality of it is the tribal peoples of the world have always used it in one form or another. If it was where they were at, they didn't shy away from it. They understood the value of it. The problem with youth and marijuana is that people don't really understand that it's a medicine. They abuse it and then this fucks them up a little bit. It's a nice high, a nice escape. I think if people understand that it's a medicine and use it as they would medicine, then I think, yes it's not harmful for people.

"I come from a culture that is deeply rooted in the whole idea and reality of the continuation of life. And I'm dealing with another culture whose perception is a reality of death."
Interview by Steve Bloom, #204, August 1992

ALFRED W. McCOY

Could the CIA be responsible for the majority of the heroin that's plaguing our streets? Alfred McCoy thinks so. The author of *The Politics of Heroin: CIA Complicity in the Global Drug Trade* (Lawrence Hill Books, Brooklyn, NY), McCoy faced death threats, income tax audits, phone taps and other forms of harassment while writing the first edition of his book titled *The Politics of Heroin in Southeast Asia* in 1972.

AM: There's one rather large question that nobody is asking about BCCI. It's a Pakistani bank, it booms during the '80s, in exactly the same period Pakistan emerges as the world's largest heroin center. We know the Pakistan military officers involved in the drug trade had their accounts with BCCI. There's a three-way relationship that really cries out, screams, demands, a congressional investigation.

The relationship between BCCI and the CIA operations in Afghanistan and Pakistan; how much money was the CIA moving through these accounts? Secondly, the relationship between the Pakistan military connected with the operation and BCCI. Thirdly, the relationship between the booming heroin trade of Pakistan and BCCI.
Interview by Paul DeRienzo, #205, September 1992

Erasmus, a Ph.D. nutritionist from Canada.

The next day I called Dr. Erasmus to order a copy of his book. When I told him we were very much interested in hempseed essential oil content, he became curious.

"Well, that is marijuana, you know." He wondered why I was so interested in hemp.

"Hempseed is legal here in the United States. We can still buy it legally," I replied. "We're trying to get hemp back into the California economy, but first we have to legalize marijuana. I'm a proponent for an initiative here to change the law so we can get hemp back."

He had a good laugh and wished me luck. Then he related remembrances his parents had told of the hemp fields in Russia and the delicious hempseed butter they used to make, "Their hemp butter puts our peanut butter to shame for nutritional value."

CHI failed to make the ballot. Jack had promised the volunteer petitioners an Extravaganja—win or lose. Jack sponsored, and Judy and I hosted, the four day celebration during the full moon in June. The cannabis drought was so extreme that one CHI patriot proclaimed this to be a "Smokeless Extravaganja."

There may not have been any ganga, but there was plenty of hempseed food. Carol Miller of the Sonoma Civil Rights Action Project (SCRAP) and other hempseed nutrition enthusiasts brought their stone mills. Alan Brady, exuding a feeling of health and vitality affecting anyone near him introduced many to the spiritual aspects of Zen seed grinding. His smile was contagious.

SCRAP had catered the first ever hempseed banquet at the San Francisco Earth Day Hemp Expo in April 1991. That was my first exposure to hempseed cookery. The meal was unique, but some diners had difficulty accepting the texture and taste of the Nutty Hempseed and Walnut Loaf. I found it to be satisfying, with a flavor that grew on you. My banquet favorite was the Chocolate Almond Hempseed Torte. The hempseed banquet left me with a sense of good health that lasted well into the next day—and I don't mean intoxication. Hempseed won't get you high, but the feeling of good health is an exalted state that few people in modern society experience anymore.

When the Extravaganja was over and the last of the CHI patriots had gone, we finally had time to sit back and relax a bit. I noticed how supple my skin had become. The chronic dry spot on my scalp had disappeared. After four days and nights of near nonstop hosting duties I should have been exhausted, but I felt quite content and contemplative. And since the birth of our youngest daughter, Judy had been experiencing painful breast swelling just prior to her menstrual period. Now for the first time in years there was no painful swelling. We had been eating loads of hempseed foods for the last four days. And we both remembered well the feeling of good health we had experienced after the hemp banquet back in April.

Brady had given us his surplus hempseed date and raisin bars. We continued to eat them and ordered fifty pounds of legally imported, sterile, Chinese hempseed from a national distributor. We believed it was the oil in hempseed that was responsible for our feelings of good health.

Fats and Oils was finally delivered to my mailbox a week after the Extravaganja. The book was so compelling I couldn't put it down. The oils in hempseed had noticeably improved our health and sense of well-being. And as it turns out, the secret of life-giving health in those oils is the fulcrum of a shameful and deadly conspiracy perpetrated by the other oil companies—the big time vegetable oil refiners—the food oil companies (FOCs).

We have to look back to the turn of the century to learn what happened.

American society was rapidly changing as more people departed rural-agricultural communities to become dwellers in densely populated and fast-paced cities. Getting large quantities of perishable foods to people in metropolitan areas was a difficult task. Spoilage and food poisoning occured regularly. The advent of refrigeration solved many of the problems.

Food manufacturers sought alternatives to the traditional ways of small scale production on farms and ranches. Vegetable oil production was no exception. The hydrogenation process was patented in 1903, and Procter & Gamble marketed the first commercial vegetable oil shortening, Crisco, in 1911. Since then butter use has fallen to one-fifth of its 1910 consumption level, while margarine use has increased by a factor of nine. Vegetable fat consumption increased by more than 300% and animal fat intake went down slightly. Overall, total fat consumption increased by 35% from 1910 to 1980. Fifty-seven percent of this increase is from refined and hydrogenated vegetable fats and oils. Dairy products account for 7% and 31% is from meat, poultry and fish.

During that period, the cancer rate climbed from one person out of every 30 to one in five. The death rate from cardiovascular disease (CVD) was one in several at the turn of the century. It is now the leading killer in Western civilization. One out of two Americans will die from CVD.

We eat a little less animal fat than our grandparents did. And we've been taught that it is healthier for us to eat vegetable oils. Our consumption of salad and cooking oils has increased 1200%. So why have cancer and CVD become our worst epidemics?

Vegetable oil production used to be a small scale industry even though seed oil crops were cheap and easy to grow. Because these raw oils spoil rapidly, batches were made weekly, often in home kitchens and sold locally while still fresh. This cottage industry employed many independent homesteaders throughout the country providing stability in local economies—until large companies applied chemical engineering principles to food production. Then food technology was born. And the giant food oil refining industry came into being.

They didn't know it at the time, but refining the vegetable oils to retard spoilage changed the electro-chemical activity of the oils. The seed crops readily available to the FOCs contained high percentages of unsaturated fatty acids, now called mono- and polyunsaturates. Decades would pass before nutrition scientists discovered that we can't live without two polyunsaturated oils in our diet. Cis-linoleic acid (LA) and cis-alpha-linolenic acid (LNA) are the two essential fatty acids (EFAs) indispensible to human nutrition.

LA and LNA quickly become rancid when exposed to light and air. Then the oils smell and taste bad so no one wants to eat them. That's good because the rancid oil is full of toxic compounds dangerous to health and highly reactive oxidation breakdown products called free radicals. Free radical chain reactions in the body is a persuasive theory used to explain the biochemistry of degenerative disease and of aging in general.

The oil makers overcame the problem of rancidity by heating the oils to very high temperatures. That changed cis-LA to trans-LA and cis-LNA to trans-LNA. The FOCs weren't able to tell the difference, because the chemical analysis necessary to make that determination had yet to be developed. But they refrained from using seeds with the highest percentage of EFAs (especially LNA) like hemp and flax because they spoiled the fastest. LNA breaks down five times faster than LA, so flax and hempseed oils, while being the most nutritious vegetable oils, are at the same time the most susceptible to toxic rancidity upon exposure to light

LEONARD PELTIER

"The American Indian Movement brought life out of the Indian people, taught them to be proud of who they were. Indian people were joining us in masses. But of course we were nearly crushed. So we have to go back to some area, some thing, that can make our people proud of themselves again. We have to go back to something like that. I hope it's not armed conflict—I don't want to see any more armed confrontations, but we've got to do something to give them some hope."
Interview by Peter Gorman, #206, October 1992

SMART DRUGS

BY DAVID JAY BROWN
Dr. Vincent Forshan, a California-based plastic surgeon who prescribes smart drugs claims, "I have a patient who is over eighty years old. When he came to me, he couldn't count to ten without losing his place. On piracetam and other smart drugs he can easily count to ten, forwards and backwards. He's improving tremendously." Hollywood writer and director Jeff Mandel, who has been on a regiment of smart drugs for about a decade says that, "I recently wrote twenty episodes of the television show *Super Force*, and at the same time I was working on a feature-length screenplay, and I never burned out."
According to *Nightline*, there are an estimated 100,000 people in the US taking smart drugs.
On Curing Stupidity...And the FDA's War on Smart Drugs, #205, September 1992

GEORGE BUSH

BY BILL WEINBERG

Bush rode out Contragate by exploiting political connections. In 1987, Reagan was forced to appoint a panel to probe the scandal. The so-called Tower Commission was led by ex-Senator John Tower, one of Bush's oldest political allies. Another leader was Brent Scowcroft, who had served as NSC chief in the Ford administration when Bush was CIA chief. Only one member, Ed Muskie, was not linked to Bush.

The Tower Commission focused narrowly on the one 1985 arms shipment to Iran which netted the Contra kickback and had been a bribe for the release of hostages taken in Lebanon the previous year. The Commission did not examine the allegedly humongous earlier shipments, which Barbara Honegger claims were vastly in excess of the $30 million 1985 deal. Nor did it probe allegations that the shipments were bribes for the release of the original embassy hostages.

George Bush: The Superspy, Drug-Dealing President, #207, November 1992

DICK COWAN

Businessman Dick Cowan was elected to succeed Greg Porter as the new National Director of NORML at the Spring meeting of the NORML board of directors. Cowan, from Fort Worth, TX, will officially take over the post on October 1.

Born in 1940, Cowan graduated from Yale in 1962 with a degree in economics. While at Yale, he was President of the Young Republicans Club, but shortly thereafter his political views evolved and he became a Libertarian.

HighWitness News by Peter Gorman, #207, November 1992

and air.

The FOCs could have overcome the problem of rancidity without making trans-fatty acids by simply cold pressing the oils into small airtight opaque bottles, but that was too expensive. Plus it is not possible to make vegetable fats like Crisco without hydrogenation in high heat. Their main goal was to make and market uniform stabilized vegetable fats and oils that undercut prices for food products made from animal fats. Mass production, volume storage and long shelf life were the major elements in the FOC battle plan. Their incredible success built the mega food oil industry of today.

Go into any supermarket and you will find shelves fully stocked with clear bottles of colorless oils. Light shines right through them causing free radical chain reactions to happen a thousand times faster than on exposure to air. But only the EFAs that weren't turned into trans-LA or trans-LNA after refining are affected.

Cheap generic vegetable oils look quite the same as the more expensive oils with polyunsaturated written in large print on the labels. Bottles of canola, corn, peanut, safflower and soy oils seem to offer the consumer a good seletion of different vegetable oils to choose from, but the only variation they offer is in the percentage of trans-polyunsaturates, toxic compounds and free radicals each contains. And that depends on the amount of EFA in the seed oil and what percentage of the EFA was changed from the cis- to the trans-shape during refining. Manufacturers are not required to give the percentage of trans-polyunsaturates in their oils or shortenings. And they do not have to account for the toxic polymers and free radicals either.

Today FOCs are enjoying the good press health journals give to polyunsaturated oils. But nutrition science has determined the bodily needs for cis-polyunsaturates—not the trans-polyunsaturates. So the FOCs have applied their formidable economic power lobbying to make sure trans-fatty acids are treated the same as cis-fatty acids when nutritional guidelines are determined.

One pioneer nutrition scientist in Germany, Dr. Johanna Budwig, has proposed that trans-fatty acids are at the heart of cancerous tumor growth. Dr. Budwig developed new techniques to accurately identify the different fatty components in a mix of biological material. She systematically analyzed thousands of blood samples from sick and healthy people. Blood samples from people suffering from cancer, diabetes and some liver diseases consistently lacked the EFA cis-linoleic acid and substances which combine with LA: phosphatides, vital to cell membranes, and fatty acid carrying albumin, a type of blood lipoprotein. The blood lipoproteins containing LA plus sulphur-rich proteins were gone. In their place Dr. Budwig found a sickly yellow-green protein substance.

She reasoned that if cancer is a deficiency disease involving a lack of EFA then feeding patients a diet high in EFAs should alleviate some of their problems. When she fed flax oil high in LNA and LA along with sulfur-rich skim milk protein to cancer patients whom traditional cancer therapy had failed the yellow-green pigment slowly disappeared; tumors receded and patients recuperated. It took about three months and during this time symptoms of diabetes and liver disease also disappeared.

Dr. Budwig has used her oil-protein combination therapy to successfully treat cancers of the brain, breast, liver, lymph and stomach; leukemia; melanoma; CVD; diabetes; acne and other skin conditions; weak vision and hearing; dry skin; menstrual problems like cramps and breast pain; glandular atrophy; fatty liver; gall stones; pancreas malfunction; kidney degeneration; immune deficiency; low vitality and many other ailments including arthritic conditions.

Dr. Budwig ran afoul of the FOCs when she discovered that fatty substances in soft tumors contained polymerized fats of marine animal origin. These polymers are formed when highly unsaturated fish and whale oils are heated to very high temperatures. She knew these oils were used to make margarine, a partially hydrogenated fat that cannot be made without high temperatures.

The director of the institute where she worked had financial interests in margarine. He held patents on its manufacture including the hydrogenation processes that produced the toxic polymers she had found in tumors. He was afraid her discoveries would ruin margarine sales. He offered her money and ownership of a drugstore to keep her quiet. Dr. Budwig refused to be bribed, and in her official capacity made public statements warning people of the possible health hazards from consuming margarine.

Access to her laboratory was cut off. She was prevented from using research facilities at other institutes, and she could not get any more of her papers published in the fat research journals. This was astonishing because she had worked in collaboration with several hospitals, plus she held a high government post. It was her official responsibility to monitor the effects of drugs and processed foods on health.

Dr. Budwig courageously fulfilled her public duty in the face of FOC opposition and threats to her career. She left the government position in 1953 and opened the clinic where she has successfully treated cancer patients by nutritional therapy. Because this great woman was blackballed by FOC greed, EFA research has been slowed for over 30 years. Current investigations are merely following in her footsteps.

Cardiovascular disease and cancer are the greatest killers in modern society because we have become obese and malnourished. It's an insane paradox that most of the foods offered in the commercial marketplace ultimately fatten us up while our strength and vitality slowly shrivel and wane.

We eat too much junk food loaded with empty calories from starch, sugar, saturated animal fat and refined vegetable fat. Few would defend the nutritional value of junk foods. They're simply convenient.

A great deal of the foods we eat come from ingredients conveniently available at the supermarket. You can buy wheat flour by the five-pound sack. It's refined and bleached white. That means the protein, vitamins and fiber have been refined out of the grain; the starch remains. The human body is built with protein, not starch. It can't make disease-fighting antibodies with starch. In fact, you can live without starch or any other carbohydrates including sugar. Excess carbohydrates your body can't burn outright or store as glycogen in the liver are converted into sticky fats that can clog up your arteries. But sugar is delicious and a sweet tooth is fun to feed. If you're health conscious and concerned about what you eat, you have to look long and hard or go somewhere else to find any stone-ground whole-grain flour on the supermarket shelf.

You will have to go on a crusade not unlike the quest for the Holy Grail if you want to find food oils rich in cispolyunsaturated fatty acids. Food oil companies don't make cold pressed raw vegetable oils because the cis-fatty acids—the EFAs—they contain are too unstable. Our bodies utilize that very instability—that sensitivity to light and oxygen—to enable the energy of life to flow through each of us. The high percentage of trans-polyunsaturated fatty acids in refined vegetable oils dampen the flow-of-life energy through our bodies, causing short circuits and brown-outs that eventually manifest as one or more of the degenerative symptoms of

BRETT KIMBERLIN

What convict claimed, during the 1988 presidential campaign, that he was Dan Quayle's former pot dealer? Is Brett Kimberlin a common criminal or is he the man who knew too much?

HT: How well did you get to know the future Vice President during that time?
BK: Fairly well. I didn't go places with him. It was business. He would call me at home and say he wanted to get together. I knew what that meant. I'd usually drive right down the street, or sometimes he'd say he's coming off the Interstate and I'd meet him at a hotel parking lot or some place like that.
HT: Did you get high with him?
BK: Just one time. That was the first time I ever met him—at IU [Indiana University] down in Bloomington. I went to a fraternity house to meet another guy and Danny happened to be there. One of the things that was strange about Danny was he had short hair. When I first met him, he kept pressing me for marijuana. I thought he was a narc.
HT: But you decided to do business with him?
BK: Yeah. It was business after that. As time went on, he became a connoisseur. One time I sold him some shake. He was disappointed. He said, "I'll pay you more for buds."
Interview by Steve Bloom, #207, November 1992

JOE PIPE

ANDRE GROSSMANN

BY NATE EATON
A lover of marijuana throughout his life, Joe Pipe attended technical schools for about six years and he almost got his bachelor's degree studying aerospace engineering. His advanced technical expertise has, no doubt, helped him develop his pipe-making skills. Even in high school, he sought maximum stealth technology in his pipes.

"In '68, I would take a clicking pen, strip the guts out of it, put in a screen at one end and pack in a little herb, then put in another screen to hold the herb in place," he said. "I could sit and toke in class. With a pen in my mouth, no one would get suspicious."
The Legendary Joe Pipe, #207, November 1992

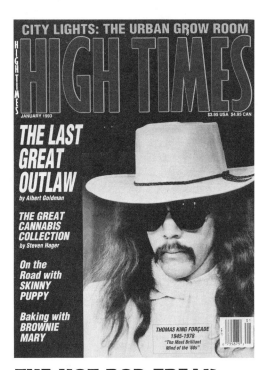

CITY LIGHTS: THE URBAN GROW ROOM

HIGH TIMES

JANUARY 1993

$3.95 USA $4.95 CAN

THE LAST GREAT OUTLAW
by Albert Goldman

THE GREAT CANNABIS COLLECTION
by Steven Hager

On the Road with SKINNY PUPPY

Baking with BROWNIE MARY

THOMAS KING FORÇADE
1945-1978
"The Most Brilliant Mind of the '60s"

THE HOT ROD FREAK

BY THERESE COE

I met Tom Forçade in Salt Lake City in '65 when he was Junior Goodson, the writing and business administration major and hot rod freak. His pad was lined with hulking black auto engine parts in various states of custom greasiness. The black '40s buggy he drove sported fat racing tires, a blast-furnace engine, and the rear-end was four feet off the ground. This was before acid, before grass, and before "Junior's" indications of genius and wit.

Without compunction, my old man and I jumped into the front seat when he suggested showing off the wheels of his custom-built....

Junior had the short floored for a few minutes when he hit the twisting drop—no brakes in sight. The demonic balls!—to start shimmying the steering wheel violently as we twisted downward full-tilt. That souped-up short rocked all over three lanes while my heart rocked up to the roof and my eyes zipped the speedometer and the white grip of his hands on the wheel. We thought he hit Out of Control, but Junior never let up on the accelerator. That was his idea of a fix—he nearly killed us all.

The Bonneville Salt Flats, where all the land speed records are set, stretched hundreds of miles west. It was Junior's fave pave. He'd take us out to the Utah-Nevada border with the single out-of-state license plate removed from the back so the Nevada state smokeys could get real close. He'd get them to siren him down for speeding, and then floor it the whole hundred miles back to Utah, and never miss, even if he had to cross that last dry-gulch with two wheels up over the cement bridge siding.

That was Tom.

#209, January 1993

cardiovascular disease and cancer.

When I contacted Procter & Gamble to ask about the nutritional value and chemical content of the food oils and shortenings they manufacture, my call was immediately transferred to product nutrition information. However, the spokesperson was unable to answer any questions about the essential fatty acid content of their food oil products. Instead she offered to send me the free Procter & Gamble official product nutrition brochure.

Procter & Gamble's "Helpful Guide to Understanding Dietary Fats" says polyunsaturated fats are "Fatty acids with two or more double bonds, such as the essential fatty acids linoleic and alpha-linolenic acids. Previous studies showed that polyunsaturates can have the beneficial effect of lowering serum cholesterol. Recent studies suggest that moderation in consumption of polyunsaturates is desirable."

Procter & Gamble recognizes that LA and LNA are essential fatty acids, yet they make no distinction between EFAs and trans-polyunsaturates in their fats and oils products. Instead they divide fat and oil content into three categories: polyunsaturated, monounsaturated and saturated. They downplay the issue by suggesting moderation. Of course, common sense says moderation is desirable when consuming any food. But trans-fatty acids are not food; they're artificially-altered unnatural vegetable fats and oils.

Like the tobacco companies, the FOC nutrition think tanks are very guarded when it comes to questions about the health value of their products.

I contacted the FDA to see if the government could shed some light on the nutritional value of vegetable oils. John Wallingford from the FDA's clinical nutrition division said the FDA has established no minimum daily requirements for LA and LNA. When I asked if the FDA considered LA and LNA to be essential to human nutrition, he replied by stating the FDA does not take a position on whether one type of food is essential to the diet, but prefers to consider nutritional value from the standpoint of a balanced diet.

"Is the FDA aware of the electro-chemical difference between the cis- and trans- forms of LA and LNA?"

"Yes," he answered, and went on to say FDA clinical nutrition scientists had completed extensive analysis of the European research papers on fatty acid value to human health.

"And what did they find?"

"The results were inconclusive."

Dr. Budwig's clinical reports and research papers are published in German. Europeans are way ahead of the US in realizing that bigger is not always better. They're turning away from the unnatural trans-polyunsaturates refined by the FOCs. The flax oil cottage industry in Europe is making a big comeback using the old cold press methods that make fresh, unrefined, nutritious oils. This trend is slow in coming to the US because most of the European studies haven't been published in English. Our ignorance is fading now, and the FOCs are worried after seeing European trends in food oil consumption change, adversely affecting refined oil sales.

The energy of life is in the whole seed. And we should eat more whole seeds to insure we get enough essential amino acids and essential fatty acids, to build strong bodies and immune systems, and to maintain vitality and health. You can get the most of both by adding hempseed to your diet.

The amino acids in hempseed are complete and easy to digest. The EFAs in hempseed are in the optimum ratio for human nutrition, two-and-one-half parts LA to one part LNA. Hempseed can abundantly supply the human body with these essential nutrients. And the seed's outer shell safely protects the vital oils and vitamins within from spoilage. It's a perfect food in a perfectly edible container.

Ground hempseed has a taste similar to peanut butter only more delicate. And even more wholesome foods are being created from it by the new George Washington Carvers of hempseed, who like the original, work quietly out of the way getting no respect from conventional wisdom.

EPILOGUE: Alan Brady was arrested on September 6, 1991, after he took a large shipment of legal, sterilized, Chinese hempseed to a Hollister seed company to be cleaned. The bulk hempseed contained small stems, pebbles and debris that had to be removed before Brady could make the popular snacks he sells in the Santa Cruz community.

The Hollister company called the local sheriff after Brady dropped off the hempseed. When Brady returned to pick up his cleaned hempseed, a narco-spy in company clothing propositioned him, "Can you get me some buds?" Brady said no and drove home. The narco-cops, using Department of Justice test standards, claimed the hempseed was marijuana. They got a search warrant and staked out Brady's house for six hours, then burst in on him at midnight and dragged him off to jail after they found personal-use quantities of hashish, marijuana and magic mushrooms. Alan Brady was never charged with possessing the hempseed. It was found to be legal after all. And just as a picture is worth more than a thousand words, Brady's hempseed snacks had more to say to the people of Santa Cruz than government wanted them to hear.

For more information on hempseed nutrition:
Hemp Seed Cookbook, SCRAP, PO Box 510, Cazadero, CA 94521, (707) 847-3642, $2.25.
Fats and Oils: The Complete Guide to Fats and Oils in Health and Nutrition, Alive Books, PO Box 80055, Burnaby BC, Canada V5H 3X5, $20.

RODGER BELKNAP
by Gern Klausman

In March, 1990, Steven Hager was busy planning the first annual Freedom Fighters convention, to be held during the Ann Arbor Hash Bash on April 1. The previous year, the HIGH TIMES staff had traveled to Michigan aboard a psychedelic bus. Sadly, the old wreck had been put out to scrap. How could there be a solid and right-on marijuana protest without a hippie school bus? It was unthinkable.

To solve this dilemma, 10 medals were offered in the Let Freedom Ring newsletter for anyone willing to provide a school bus. (It was also announced that whoever had the most medals at the end of that year would get a free ride to the Cannabis Cup in Amsterdam, the most exalted of cannabis-connoisseur adventures.) I happened to be lingering in Hager's office the day a man named Rodger called. Responding to the notice, he wanted to send the Freedom Fighters $5,000 to buy a school bus.

"What do you think?" Hager asked me. "He must be a narc. Who else would send us five grand?"

Hager called back the next day and told the voice on the phone he "should get the bus himself and bring it on down to Michigan."

Three weeks later, I met Rodger in the parking lot of Ann Arbor's Red Roof Inn. Bearded and bespectacled, seated behind the wheel of the purplest '67 International Harvester school bus I'd ever beheld, the man

RODGER BELKNAP

The Freedom Fighters held a Rainbow-style encampment in a local park. Rodger Belknap, a Freedom Fighter focalizer from West Virginia, brought the Purple Bus, along with an enormous 28-foot tepee designed by Earthworks of Ridgeway, Colorado. The first council in the lodge easily held 87 people. During the night more than a dozen people slept inside. Linda Noel, focalizer for the Freedom Fighter newsletter, helped run a 24-hour free kitchen.

No major points of consensus were discussed during the two main councils held at Madison. Don Fiedler expressed doubts about the Freedom Fighter trip to Alaska, which prompted Chef Ra to ask, "You mean the Freedom Fighters are perceived as the lunatic fringe of the movement?"
Freedom Fighters March in Madison by Steven Hager, #185, January 1991

ANDRE GROSSMANN

RICK DOBLIN

"Virtually everyone will either get cancer or will have a loved one get cancer. Marijuana can help them. MDMA can help them. Everyone wonders about religious questions. Psychedelics can help them. We need to talk a language that our opponents can hear and we also need to band together and stand up for what we believe. I urge people to consider joining MAPS as well as other organizations that are willing to stand up to the government's campaign of repression." To join MAPS and receive their newsletter, send $30 (tax-deductible) to:

MAPS
23-A Shaler Lane
Cambridge, MA 02138
Interview by Thomas Lyttle, #208, December 1992

THE LONE REEFER

BY MARK BARNET

HT: How did you get started in the hemp legalization movement?

LR: I got started 19 years ago, when I was 16 years old and I had a gun pointed at my head because I was smokin' reefer. That was in Pennsylvania. I was arrested and strip-searched down to my underwear. Ever since then I've been doing everything I can.

HT: When did you become the Lone Reefer?

LR: In 1976, I rented a billboard and put "Legalize Marijuana" on it. They couldn't handle the "M" word locally and a lot of rednecks splashed paint all over it. My name was printed in the newspaper and I figured that since I was going to do all I could for legalization, I should change my name. The Lone Reefer is a symbolic representative for the 50,000 Americans imprisoned for pot, and the 350,000 that will get arrested this year. I'm their voice, since most of these people can't be heard. Nobody should be subjected to guns pointed at their heads or imprisonment for marijuana. Individual freedom and choice is my motivation, as well as restoring our original heritage of using hemp for all its good purposes.

HighWitness News, #187, March 1991

RODGER'S STATEMENT

During general council of the Freedom Fighters in Ann Arbor, MI, last April, Rodger Belknap was elected Freedom Fighter of the Year. This honor included the right to attend the Cannabis Cup as a judge. Unfortunately, after arriving in Amsterdam, Rodger quickly came to the conclusion that the restrictions placed on this year's contest were so severe that they "seriously infringed upon the integrity of the Cannabis Cup." In previous years, the contest had included what many believed were the finest examples of cannabis in Europe. This year, because only five entries were submitted (from four different coffeeshops), the quality was much lower. "I didn't even finish the buds they gave me," says Rodger. "It was yawn dope. Three of the five entries tasted like mayonnaise. The strains were obviously grown for bulk commercial considerations, not for quality buds. Because I was able to find better and more potent varieties, not only at other coffeeshops, but from other growers in Holland who were not allowed to [or refused to] participate in the contest, I voluntarily withdrew from the event."

Judge's Statement: Rodger Belknap, #197, January 1992

from the Appalachian Mountains greeted me with empowering warmth. "Well, hello there," he smiled. "Would you care for some cannabis? It's very high quality." Before I could suspiciously say, "Umm...sure, I guess so," I held a Belknap Bomber in my hand—a jay sized more like a submarine than a joint. Sitting next to Rodger was Ahbleza, his dog and constant companion.

"This is Crow's Foot," he explained. "My own strain. It's something special." One long look at him, a short glance into his humane eyes, an ample puff on that savory spliff and I knew: This man was no DEA agent, that was certain. He was too damned real.

Later that weekend, in a wide-open field with unmarked police cars parked nearby, Rodger delivered an impassioned address to a huge crowd of enthusiastic new Freedom Fighters. He was elected to head their West Virginia chapter. "I was honored and I intended to do some real work," Rodger reminisces today.

Rodger began by placing full-page advertisements in his local newspaper proclaiming the many attributes of hemp. Every week a new ad was inserted into *The Braxton Citizens' News* detailing a different aspect of hemp. Always at the bottom of each ad was Rodger's name and address. The ads generated plenty of controversy, with folks writing the newspaper to complain about "drug propaganda," but publisher Eddie Givens did not censor the information, quoting the First Amendment of the US Constitution in his editorial reply. He said as long as the claims made in the advertisements were true, he had no reason to block them. Eventually, Rodger had to scale back his media plan when parents complained that the ads were turning up in local schools. Rodger agreed to run the pages only when school was not in session. Instead, he ran pages with headings like "Just Say No to Censorship."

Possibly the most recognized and appreciated gift Belknap made to the fledgling Freedom Fighters was his contribution of a permanent meeting place. Taking inspiration from the Native American tradition of making decisions by group consensus, the Freedom Fighters had been making policy in councils.

"Basically, anyone can participate in a Freedom Fighter council," Hager explains. "Anyone who is present at the council is a Freedom Fighter and council member. Everyone gets a chance to speak and be heard. All decisions must be made by unanimous vote." This ultra-democratic system has given an effective platform to all who want it, and moderation in council decisions has been the norm. Usually these assemblies were held in motel rooms, but this transience didn't give the councils the atmosphere of solidity and importance that many wanted. The problem had been casually mentioned to Belknap. Taking the Native American inspiration a step further, Rodger donated a historically accurate reproduction of an American council tipi, holding upwards of 100 people.

The tipi made its first surprise appearance at the fall Harvest Festival in Madison, Wisconsin in 1990. "At the second raising of the tipi in Ocala, Florida, in January 1991, there was a great spirituality in the event," Hager remembers. The tipi would become a permanent fixture at all major Freedom Fighter actions.

HIGH TIMES: How did you come to the hemp movement?

Rodger Belknap: I guess it came about when I learned of Operation Green Merchant and Gatewood Galbraith's campaign for governor of Kentucky. On the one hand there was this completely fascist police operation going on, creating a lot of fear and suffering for decent people, and on the other, here finally was an honest politician trying to change things. It inspired me to do something. I also understood how much cannabis had helped me medicinally and how much it could help others. Probably the biggest motivator for me was the knowledge I learned from HIGH TIMES when it changed its format to include the facts about hemp. I'd always known that most of the things the government says about cannabis are lies, but all this exciting stuff about hemp was news to me.

Later, Rodger purchased and sent out close to 50 copies of Jack Herer's *The Emperor Wears No Clothes*, the now famous compendium of hard-hitting hemp facts. The books went to judges, magistrates, police officers and many others in his hometown region. He organized and proctored several hemp-awareness seminars right in Sutton, West Virginia. Such cannabis luminaries as Jack Herer, Elvy Musikka, Thom Harris, Cliff Barrows and the Cannabis Action Network made appearances. Musikka, a well-known political dynamo among the few legal recipients of government cannabis, calls Belknap "the most powerful crusader for truth" she has worked with during her many years as a marijuana activist.

Rodger's intended use of a National Guard armory for one of his Cannabis Awareness Seminars was met with harsh resistance by the army, who decided to withdraw his already confirmed reservation for the space when they learned of the seminar's content. Rodger contacted the ACLU. Not only did the army back down, but they paid him $5,600 in a settlement which he promptly donated to the West Virginia ACLU. *USA Today* carried a report of the affair, making Rodger's presence on the national stage loom larger. Rodger was drawing a lot of attention to himself, some of it unwelcome.

Already, the Drug Enforcement Administration had his name from their ongoing Operation Green Merchant, a systematic program of surveillance and asset seizure aimed at the indoor agriculture industry. Belknap's name was discovered on shipping records confiscated from Superior Growers Supply, a gardening store located in Michigan and Hamilton Technology Corp., based in California. He had ordered approximately $1,000 worth of hydroponic trays and high-intensity lights. In May of 1990, the DEA handed an accumulated list of purchasers living in West Virginia to Trooper Charles "Chuck" Jackson of the West Virginia State Police. The DEA told Jackson that Rodger was the largest purchaser of "marijuana-growing equipment" in West Virginia. Based on this information, Jackson subpoenaed Belknap's power-consumption records and discovered that his electricity usage had risen after he ordered the growing supplies.

HT: How did marijuana help you?

RB: Well, I've had a history of some pretty serious substance abuse. The kind of abuse that was affecting my life—making my life negative and destructive. For some time I was doing heroin, Dilaudid, Mandrax, whatever, and constantly mixing things. For me, it was a subconsciously acceptable form of suicide. I was slowly killing myself: '76 to '87 was the worst of it. I began drinking way too much in '77, about a fifth of Lord Calvert a day. The overall mix of alcohol and pharmaceuticals was bad, but usually I would take things separately, though during the same period. For example, I'd take some Dilaudid (a synthetic heroin substitute) in the morning and when I'd come down from that I would drink. There was no sense in spoiling a good high, which alcohol would do. I've been straight since '87, when I started smoking cannabis exclusively. In '87 it had been 21 years since I'd had

CHAIM ELI JEHU

Quiet and unassuming, Chaim Eli Jehu does the work of five Freedom Fighters every time he stops by HIGH TIMES and volunteers his services and time. Chaim traveled hundreds of miles last year with his fiancée, Joanne, attending hemp rallies in Ann Arbor and Madison from his native New York. While he awaits this year's Hash Bash, Chaim has been painstakingly transferring the Freedom Fighter mailing list from one computer system to another here at HT. So, when you receive your next copy of *Let Freedom Ring*, (the official newsletter of the Freedom Fighters of America), think of Chaim Eli Jehu. He's the reason why it reached your mailbox.
HighWitness News by Steve Bloom, #200, April 1992

LINDA NOEL

Linda Noel is a founding member of the Freedom Fighters. Launched by HIGH TIMES in March '89, the Freedom Fighters attempted to put more drama and excitement into the cannabis protest movement. They began staging rallies, wearing tricorn hats, carrying Betsy Ross flags and spreading the good word about hemp. Today, they supervise the only national letter-writing campaign in the movement. The most important function of the group, however, is the publication of *Let Freedom Ring*, an open forum for the cannabis movement. Linda has been sole editor of the newsletter for two years.
HighWitness News by Mark Barnet, #199, March 1992

THE SOUL ASSASSINS

Lucy Knight (vocals), Abbey Lavine (vocal s), Brian Spaeth (bass), Flick Ford (vocals), Kimona 117 (vocals), Steven Hager (rhythm guitar). Not shown: Bob Brandel (lead guitar) and Dave Rodway (drums).

HOW TO PRESERVE POT POTENCY

HIGH TIMES

50 YEARS OF LSD

INTERVIEWS WITH:
ALBERT HOFMANN
TIMOTHY LEARY
KEN KESEY
ALLEN GINSBERG
AND MORE!

RAVE NEW WORLD
DAWN OF THE TECHNO-HIPPIE

MAY 1993

RAVE NEW WORLD

BY BRIJITTE WEST & STEVEN HAGER

Welcome to the techno-future, a celestial tribal powwow populated by toon town caricatures flying high on designer drugs.

Every weekend, in every major city in the US, thousands of people are gathering together, dropping MDMA (and other psychedelics) and dancing until dawn. The setting is not a nightclub or disco, but an abandoned warehouse, empty lot, or makeshift party space. There is no door policy or official dress code. Even so, most of the androgynous crowd wears baggy, black-and-white striped jerseys and pants. Hats are popular, especially large, oversized ones and long, Dr. Seuss-style ski caps. The bar has no alcohol, only mineral water and "smart drinks" (juice cocktails laced with brain-enhancing amino acids). This is not a concert. There is no performance here, just a thumping bass line, flashing laser light show, and 3,000 sweaty bodies doing the happy trance. Who are these people and why is their scene growing faster than a mad hacker's computer virus?

"I lived with a born-again Christian family for four months and I learned the fear of that mind-set," explains David Prince, editor of *Reactor*, a rave-scene magazine published in Chicago. "Then I went to some of these super-big mega-raves and what I found was that the born-agains' fears are not unfounded. Their world is over. A culture that is based on a set of rules that is so repressive to natural human urges is dead. Christian ideals are very beautiful, peace, love, unity, respect. But the biggest crime to evolution was the pushing down of paganism. I think we are starting to recover from that now, and rave is a small part of that."

#213, May 1993

a straight summer.

Belknap graduated from Gassaway High School in 1966 and filed for conscientious objector status as the war in Vietnam was getting hot. His request was denied so he enrolled in Glenville State College where he played football until he was kicked off the team for refusing to get a haircut. "I was cruisin' in my new '67 Chevelle at that time—just cruisin' and groovin'." Rodger transferred to Morris Harvey College in Charleston, WV, in his sophomore year. "In my third year I switched schools again and went to Salem College. I got a '64 Corvette and I was having fun!" The year was 1969 and Rodger found himself subject to the draft again. "My lottery number was 340-something and they only drafted up to 120 that year so I escaped the war. My parents bought me a new '70 'Vette for graduation and then I got married. My life gradually transformed from something beautiful into five ugly years of being married."

Sometime in the late afternoon of August 27, 1990, while relaxing at home, Rodger heard a noise. Stepping out onto his porch, he saw a police helicopter swooping around the rear of his property. "Yeah, I knew something was up then," he says. After taking what later turned out to be illegible photographs of nine alleged "marijuana plants" growing outside his house, the craft landed right smack in front of Rodger's porch. The pilot brought the chopper to a precarious perch on a steep incline and three state cops climbed out running up to a bewildered Rodger Belknap. "I live a very peaceful life up here on my hill, and you can imagine what a shock it was to have this incredible noise and commotion. Many of the beautiful hummingbirds I've befriended and fed for years were scared away. They never came back after that."

They didn't have a warrant but they had a helicopter, guns and badges, so Rodger let the agents into his home. While Trooper Chuck Jackson went to get the warrant, two cops stayed behind to make sure Rodger didn't tamper with any "evidence." "This is my home and I'll appreciate it if you show me the same respect you'd have me show you in yours," Rodger calmly and cooperatively told the officers.

True to his beliefs, Rodger spent the anxious time with the plant hunters educating them on the extensive attributes of cannabis. They had already read the copies of *The Emperor Wears No Clothes* which Belknap had mailed to these very officers some time before, so they had a good idea where Rodger was coming from. "I reviewed in detail that hemp was the fastest-growing biomass on Earth, that it can be used for paper, oil, cellulose-based commodities and everything else I could rattle off. We also sat together and watched *Hemp for Victory*, the US Government film on hemp production during World War II." Then he picked up a three-inch roach of Crow's Foot and sparked it up. "I don't mean to be disrespectful," he stated, "but I'm in my own home, I've not been found guilty of any crime and I should be allowed to do as I please here." One of the officers laughingly remarked that "he's smoking that stuff again." An air of mutual regard existed, and there was no animosity exchanged between Belknap and the police officers. Rodger smoked marijuana the entire time the police guarded him. "It's my medicine," he told them, "and I'm entitled to it."

HT: What happened in '76?

RB: That was when my wife Jan walked in on me with a needle in my arm, and it was just too much for her. She and I started dating in '65 and we got married in '71. In 1975 she became unexpectedly pregnant, and that was what triggered my really heavy substance use. I just wasn't ready to be a father then. At that time I was a social worker at Weston State Hospital near my home in West Virginia. I'd worked there for over five years at that point. I was assigned to the Crisis Intervention Unit. We had a twelve-bed ward with no locked doors. We worked with drug addicts, alcoholics, people with various emotional and mental problems. Our recidivism rate of 9.7 percent was a remarkably low figure. I was happy and productive there, but that all changed when my own substance problem became uncontrollable for me. Now my ex-wife is married to a heart surgeon. We have a daughter together, Lorelie Ariel, whom I haven't seen since she was a year old. I've always kept my problem away from her so she can lead her own life, you know. My little girl is seventeen now. It's one of my biggest regrets that I have missed seeing her grow up.

Later that evening, after police obtained their warrant and the ransacking of Rodger's home began in earnest, Steve Hager and HIGH TIMES photographer Andre Grossmann happened to be trekking up the winding forest road that leads to Rodger's house. They were coming to talk to Rodger about an upcoming hemp event. As they drove around the final bend they ran into a startling sight: Several police cars squatted around with their lights flashing and cops were hauling boxes out of the house. "We were stopped and told that Rodger was being arrested for cultivation of marijuana," Hager remembers. "They told us to leave, which we did, but as we were traveling down the hill we decided to go back, figuring Rodger might need our help."

When Hager and Grossmann returned they had their IDs run through the police computer, and immediately they were tagged as HIGH TIMES employees. These two showing up at this time was quite a coincidence, especially to the police. Trooper Jackson, who was in charge of the plant-eradication operation, was all smiles and eager to cooperate. It turned out that Jackson is an avid HIGH TIMES reader and he was happy to permit "one photograph" to be taken of the entire event, "as long as you don't refer to me as a fascist pig."

"Jackson was very high on the idea of appearing in HIGH TIMES," Hager told me. "He wasn't hostile at all. We weren't searched. He really enjoyed himself." Lighting equipment, reservoirs and several Europonic growing trays were spread out on the lawn. Fifty-six marijuana plants were allegedly growing in the trays. Beside the trays Belknap's Camaro could be seen sporting the West Virginia license plate "HEMP IV."

HT: How did you end up with cannabis?

RB: My first drug experience was alcohol, of course, when I was around thirteen. I first smoked cannabis when I was nineteen. Later, in 1968, I started tripping on mescaline, psilocybin and pure LSD-25. My drug use was productive then, not like when I started taking heroin and pharmaceuticals and drinking alcohol heavily. In the fall of '69 I began skin-popping heroin occasionally. I developed an IV habit in '76 when I was running heroin and dilaudid. This is when my life began to deteriorate after ten enlightening years of predominantly psychedelic use. After overdosing several times I was committed to St. Allban's Hospital in Virginia. When I got out I got into pharmaceuticals like carbitals, demerols, preludins, 'ludes, etc. In '87 I made a decision that I wanted to turn my life around, to heal myself. I didn't like what I'd become. I was a drunk, a drug addict, and I was letting everyone down. I'd disappointed my friends, my family, everyone really. Somewhere in the back of my mind, I'd always remembered that cannabis had many medically documented attributes that I thought might help. From my own experience I also knew that cannabis sure wasn't dangerous. So

HIGHWITNESS NEWS

MALCOLM MACKINNON

Starting this month Bill Weinberg and Peter Gorman will be editing the HighWitness News section.

Can you imagine trying to cover a beat that includes the worldwide operations of the DEA, medical marijuana, the hemp movement, Operation Green Merchant, as well as the 400,000 annual arrests for cannabis violations? Because our resources are so small, we rely on your help and assistance. So send Bill and Peter your newspaper clips, rally reports, HighWitness Views, and let them know if a local story in your area has national significance.

Page Six by Steven Hager, #201, May 1992

BOGART AND BUDHEAD

SUCK

~SUCK

FRANK MAX

THIS SUCKS, HEH, HEH!!!

BROWNIE MARY

On July 21, Brownie Mary Rathbun, who bakes marijuana brownies for San Francisco AIDS patients, was arrested by the DEA and local authorities in Sonoma County, CA, while at the home of a friend. At the time of her arrest she was folding just under a kilo of pot into her brownie batter. Rathbun, a longtime advocate of medical marijuana, was charged with felony possession of marijuana and released on $5,000 bail.

Brownie Mary Rathbun, who has been distributing her brownies for free for nearly 10 years—and who also works as a volunteer at San Francisco's General Hospital in Ward 86, the AIDS ward—earned her nickname when she was arrested in 1981 for selling her magic brownies to an undercover San Francisco policeman.

HighWitness News by Peter Gorman, #208, December 1992

HERBS AND PAGANISM

BY MARY FORSELL

Before Christianity, polytheism was the religion of choice throughout Europe and the British Isles. To these country people, all forces of nature were divine. Pantheons of gods and goddesses symbolized the natural energy that ran through every river, stone, tree and flower. The earth provided everything necessary for living contentedly, including a vast array of scented green medicines with mysterious curative powers—known today as herbs. These medicines were so revered that they were a part of religious ceremonies, usually held in the open air at river sources, in forests and other sacred places.
#218, October 1993

THMQ ANALYSIS

BY POPE WEASEL

Prices for the herb have been remarkably steady for some time now. It's really getting a bit boring, actually. High-quality domestics can still be had for $280-$400 per ounce, while decent imports can sometimes be found for $150 per ounce. That still seems like a lot for dried flowers though, doesn't it? Five dollars an ounce would be more realistic, but that won't be for awhile yet. The upcoming '93 season will be historically critical for the industry. Will there be no drought again because of massive importation? Will the domestic crop become larger due to a relaxed political climate? I'm hoping, as I always do, for a drop in prices as availability of high-quality imports remains stable.
Trans-High Market Quotations, #214, June 1993

that's when I threw out all the pharmaceuticals, all the powders and the alcohol, and stuck with cannabis. It's worked. I've been clean, healthy and productive ever since.

Eventually his house was thoroughly searched. The police confiscated growing equipment, a typewriter and a 9mm Beretta. And then they piled into their cars and departed. Belknap, Hager and Grossmann were left stunned. It was two in the morning. Belknap wasn't arrested, only told by Trooper Jackson: "We're deciding what to do with you. You'll be hearing from us." Rodger looked off at the retreating motorcade of police cars. He knew his life was going to become very difficult, that the bureaucratic wheels of law enforcement had begun their grind through his freedom. He had expected this day, planned for it, even invited it: "I knew this day was coming, but when that helicopter landed I felt fear like I'd never known before. It was me in my little home against the guns, police and laws of prohibition. I felt very alone."

Rodger never had any doubts about growing cannabis or the obvious risks involved for an outlaw farmer, particularly an outspoken marijuana activist. Not wanting to participate in the criminal activities of the black market and requiring top quality, he had decided to raise his own. "When I first heard about Operation Green Merchant, the DEA assault on indoor horticulturalists, I knew I was on some of the shipping records they had illegally seized. The reports about it in HIGH TIMES provided me with plenty of time to close down, but I didn't. I was growing because I felt it was the right thing to do and that it shouldn't be against the law to do so. Cannabis provided me with a functional, productive and totally nonviolent lifestyle. It's the most legitimate medicine I've ever taken. I could have bowed down to the forces of oppression, but I had to be honest with myself and my morals. So in defiance of Green Merchant I opted to expand my growing to a new area in my house. I called it the O.G.M. Room."

The bust weighed heavily upon Rodger's mind when he boarded an Air Pakistan flight to Amsterdam almost exactly one year to the day later. He was still free on $1,000 bond with his case yet to come to trial. The Braxton County prosecutor was maneuvering to put Belknap's case in federal rather than state court; it was evident the authorities felt they wouldn't get a conviction or even an indictment in a local proceeding. (Rodger's low bail may have been some indication of that.) Two days before the jet took off, Rodger received a notice by mail informing him that a Grand Jury True Bill had been issued against him and that a federal indictment would shortly follow. But the Cannabis Cup was about to begin and Rodger still had enough enthusiasm for this, the now less-tantalizing but still meaningful reward for his struggles.

"Judging the Cannabis Cup was a real dream come true for me," he recalls. "Being in Holland, where I could live as a law-abiding citizen without fear of the police, was a beautiful thing." Rodger told me several times while we toured the Dutch capital that he was tempted to simply stay there as a political refugee. Ultimately that was not his choice. He saw himself as an American, one who belonged at home. He was confident he would be given a fair trial by his peers. He still had great faith in American justice.

"Today I don't have to look left and right to make sure there aren't any cops watching me smoke dried flowers. I'm free, I'm in a free country." I sadly watched a tear roll down his ruddy cheek.

On February 17, 1992 Rodger was back in Elkins, West Virginia to begin his trial the next day. His charge: manufacturing marijuana, a controlled substance. Present were Steve Hager, Andre Grossmann, Eric Sterling of the Drug Policy Foundation, Elvy Musikka, noted Freedom Fighters Thom Harris, Joe Yaron, Mike Cox and others. Spirits were high among everyone, especially Belknap, who was confident that he would be acquitted by an "honest and intelligent jury of [his] peers." Motivated by Gatewood Galbraith's campaign in Kentucky, Belknap had also just announced his candidacy for Governor of West Virginia on a hemp-legalization platform, declaring, "This is a way for me to regain control of my life."

On the the first day of Rodger's trial, a trio of Freedom Fighters led by HIGH TIMES columnist Pope Weasel distributed pamphlets on jury-nullification rights to everyone entering the courthouse. They also plastered the flyers on every parked car for a two-block radius around the courthouse. The following day, an unusual conversation was entered into the trial record. Judge Robert Maxwell called both counsels to his bench.

"I have been advised that...this pamphlet, which is six pages, was placed on the windshields of the cars around the parking area of the courthouse.... It appears to be a publication that is typical to the political philosophy of those who are expressing revolutionary-type thoughts with regard to modifying the existing systems of courts and laws.... Now, whether some of the defendant's friends may have done this or not, I don't know.... Now, I'm not saying that [this is] positive or negative, you know, but I certainly think it is their right to try to change within the system."

The judge then asked Belknap's attorneys, "If you could in a diplomatic sort of way talk to your people, you know, I would appreciate it."

"It is the government's information that the fellow sitting in the last row was observed putting these on the windows. We are still looking into it," said prosecutor Tom Mucklow.

Mucklow (who later proclaimed during the trial "I don't want to appear in HIGH TIMES magazine") pointed out Freedom Fighter Mike Cox as the most likely culprit. Actually, Mike had nothing to do with the fliers, although he was the most conspicuous counterculture type in the room.

The primary strategy of Rodger's defense team was to assert that a medical necessity existed for Belknap's cannabis use, compelling him to grow marijuana in order to acquire his otherwise unobtainable medicine. Charles Shields and Patrick Wilson were the court appointees representing Belknap, who has since become disappointed with them. "They left a huge amount of information out of the trial. They never even provided testimony to confirm that I was, in fact, an alcoholic and a substance abuser. None of my medical records were ever mentioned. Nothing definitive was entered into the record about my behavior while an alcoholic and how all that had changed once I switched to cannabis exclusively. I got as much justice as I could afford," Belknap says today. In addition, the many pertinent court decisions establishing the unconstitutionality of the DEA's seizure of agricultural store records were never brought up.

Among those rallying to Belknap's defense was Dr. John Morgan of New York City. Formerly the Director of the Department of Pharmacology at the Sophie Davis School of Bio-Medical Education in Manhattan, Dr. Morgan brought an impressive resume to the case. He also acted as Belknap's personal physician at the time. There is much medical evidence to support Rodger's medical-defense claim. It is

PAUL KRASSNER

"When I used to think of Richard Nixon, the first thing I'd remember is how he *forgot* that he was in Dallas the day John F. Kennedy was shot. Moreover, when a reporter asked him what his reaction was to the murder of Lee Harvey Oswald, he replied, 'Two rights don't make a wrong...I mean....' But it was too late. Nixon was the personification of a Freudian Slip.

"On the Watergate tapes, only six days after the break-in, he was discussing the possibility of getting a million dollars hush money for E. Howard Hunt. Nixon said, 'It would make the CIA look bad. It's going to make Hunt look bad, and it is likely to blow the whole Bay of Pigs thing, which we think would be very unfortunate.' Years later, his chief of staff, H.R. Haldeman, wrote in his book *Ends of Power*, that the 'Bay of Pigs' was slang used by Nixon to refer to the 1963 Kennedy assassination."
HighWitness Views, #218, October 1993

ALBERT HOFMANN

HT: When people like Leary began to popularize LSD, what were your feelings?
AH: I was quite astonished, because the very deep effects of LSD are not at all just pleasurable. There is always a confrontation with our deepest ego. So I was quite astonished by this development. I wondered what happened. And I thought that it would be very dangerous when it began to get on the streets in the United States.

It turned out that my fear was well-founded because so many people were not conscious enough to use it well. They did not have the respect which the Indians in Mexico had. The Indians believe you should only take the mushrooms if you have prepared by praying and fasting and so forth, because the mushrooms bring you in contact with the Gods. And if you are not prepared they believe it can make you crazy or even kill you. That's their belief based on thousands of years of experience....

If we learn to use [LSD] with respect and under the right conditions, the beneficial effects would be enormous.
Interview by Peter Gorman, #213, May 1993

IBOGAINE

BY PETER GORMAN

In 1962, Howard Lotsof, a 19-year-old junkie from the Bronx, New York, ingested a little-known West African psychoactive substance called ibogaine. The trip was a startling hallucinatory voyage. More startling than the trip, however, was the drug's residual effect: When he came down he no longer had any desire to shoot heroin.

HT: How important could it be to have ibogaine on the market?

HL: In most cases when the patient wakes up they no longer want to use drugs. We're talking about an effective treatment for chemical dependency that would provide the majority of people who want to stop using drugs the ability to do so. If we were talking about the treatment of cancer and I had a drug that could keep cancer in remission for six months at a time, it would be hailed as the greatest success in the world. And here we have a nontoxic procedure that can do that for chemical dependency. To say that the cancer patient deserves life for six months at a time, but that the addict doesn't, is irresponsible, unethical and immoral.

Interview, #219, November 1993

THE HOPI PROPHECY

BY MALCOLM MACKINNON

Near the village of Oraibi, Arizona, a 10-foot slab of rock has stood for the ages, carved with jagged lines and stick figures of people. The origin of the petroglyph on Prophecy Rock is unknown, but for the Hopi Indians of Arizona, the stone etchings represent a key element in the Hopi prophecy.

Oraibi is the oldest continuously inhabited settlement in the United States—its existence can be traced back to 1050 AD.

The path of the white man—one of invention, cleverness and greed—was seen by the ancient interpreters of the petroglyph, but it is the zigzag line at the path's end which has always spoken ominously to the Hopi. It signifies *koyaanisqatsi*, a time when these people, who will have lost sight of their original purpose, will become extremely dangerous. For the Hopi, that zigzag line symbolizes our current global strife and signifies that the final stage of world purification is occurring now.

Traditionalists believe that the Spirit Being *Massau* offered the Hopi sacred stone tablets which portrayed the manner in which they were to make spiritual migrations to find their promised land and how to live their lives when they arrived.

#221, January 1994

universally acknowledged by scholars that marijuana has been in use for millennia for a variety of ills, including drug addiction; its efficacy in suppressing the cravings of alcoholics also has wide support in modern medical circles.

As far back as 1942, Allentuck and Bowman published a report in the *American Journal of Psychiatry*, which detailed their research on drug addicts, primarily those using opiates. They found that for controlling their subjects' addictions, "The results, in general suggest that the marihuana substitution method of treatment is superior." Even earlier, in the November 1891 edition of the *St. Louis Medical and Surgical Journal*, Dr. J.B. Mattison described marijuana as a "remarkable" treatment for drug and alcohol dependence. Again, in 1971, the *American Journal of Psychiatry* published a paper detailing Dr. J. Schyer's experiments showing cannabis to be a "most effective treatment" for the control of alcoholism. The literature supporting the use of marijuana in the treatment of drug and alcohol addiction is expansive, including too many published reports to list here.

With stacks of documents and his own personal expertise to support his belief that Rodger was medicating himself with marijuana, Dr. Morgan was Belknap's star witness. The general mood in the hotel where the activists and press assembled was that Rodger would soon go free.

The trial essentially revolved around the prosecution's assertions regarding the uncompromising fact of the law, that marijuana is illegal and that's all the jury needs to know. It was constantly stated that it mattered not one whit whether or not Belknap was taking cannabis as a medicine. Rodger's electric bills were waved around like a flag to justify the investigation leading up to his arrest. Strange non-logic often prevailed, as when Trooper Jackson stated that not only had Rodger ordered a lot of electrical agricultural equipment through the mail, which justified peering into his power bills, but that after Rodger received the equipment, his electric bill went up. Somehow this obviously demonstrated he was growing marijuana. I waited for someone to ask Belknap if his electric bill would have gone *down* had he been growing, say, tulips. But no one did.

Belknap's attorneys presented a loose and disjointed amalgamation of evidence attempting to substantiate their claim of medical necessity. There was also a feeble effort to suggest that what had been confiscated during the raid was not marijuana at all but drugless fiber hemp. The confiscated crop had apparently "disappeared" from the police evidence facility before all of it was tested. (The explanation given by Trooper R.R. Reed was that it had "probably rotted away.")

Dr. Morgan was unflappable. Mucklow attempted to portray him as unqualified, an outrageous charge considering the doctor's long and distinguished career. Dr. Morgan detailed the long history of marijuana's efficacy in medicine and his own opinion that it was indeed saving Rodger from a life of drug addiction and alcoholism. The prosecutor's response was that "you can get anyone to say anything about anything if you look hard enough, can't you?" Dr. Morgan provided the most erudite and credible testimony during the case.

Elvy Musikka eloquently testified regarding her legal use of marijuana for glaucoma. Larry Hutcheson, Belknap's mental-health counselor at the Summit Center in Braxton County, appeared. Hutcheson threw a wild card into the proceedings when he introspectively offered testimony about his own past marijuana use to the prosecuting attorney. A decorated marine officer as well as a professional counselor, he sided with Dr. Morgan in claiming that Rodger's cannabis use was definitely what kept him healthy and alcohol-free.

During breaks, friends of Belknap mingled with the arresting officers outside the courtroom. I asked Trooper Jackson if he thought Rodger should go to jail. "No," he quickly replied. I asked him if he felt bad that Rodger might soon go to prison for staying at home and bothering no one. "If I paid attention to the personal realities and feelings of everyone I arrested, I wouldn't be able to do my job," he said thoughtfully. "The law is the law whether it's right or wrong, and it's my job to enforce it. What else can I do?"

The majority of the court statements regarded what was confiscated, how, by whom and how Rodger had a background of hemp activism. HIGH TIMES magazine was displayed and railed against. Rodger's history in the hemp movement was detailed and always described mockingly by prosecutor Mucklow. In the end, Belknap's entire case rested on whether or not the jury would buy the medical-defense strategy. Unfortunately, contained in the final instructions given by the court to the jury was no mention of their power to find Belknap not guilty based on this notion.

In fact, in the last five minutes of the third and final day of the case, Judge Maxwell said, "You [Attorney Shields] may be accurate on the medical-necessity defense...but I think your problem is, you're about twenty years ahead of time." The judge's opinion went uncontested by Belknap's lawyers. With his remark, the possibility of acquittal seemed very dim.

It took the jury less than 30 minutes to find Rodger guilty. As the verdict was read I saw Rodger slump just a little as he turned around and looked me straight in the eye. At that moment a line was drawn from my first meeting with him on the purple bus, through all of our experiences together, to this day—the day that would see him headed for prison for being an honest man who rose up to embrace his ideals, and who spoke loudly of what he knew was right and just.

HT: Now you're in prison.

RB: Now I'm in prison. I knew what I was doing all along. I knew I was getting a lot of attention and that it would probably catch up with me. I was so tired of sneaking around. It was time to stand up and be counted, to test the democratic system and see just how far free speech goes in this country. There was never any legitimate reason to investigate me. The records the DEA had on me showed nothing. They showed I ordered equipment to grow plants, any plants. My electric bill showed nothing, but it was enough to get the air cavalry on me to have my rights violated. Obviously I am a political prisoner now. That offers some comfort, but I'm in a cage, man, I'm in a cage.

Postscript

At Belknap's sentencing hearing on May 27, 1992, Judge Maxwell said that although he could think of several creative alternative sentences for Belknap, the Federal Sentencing Guidelines compelled him to sentence Rodger, "with great reluctance," to 33 to 41 months in prison. Today Rodger remains in the Federal Correctional Institute in Morgantown, West Virginia. Those wishing to contact him may write Rodger Belknap, #02062-087, F C I-Morgantown, Randolph Unit, PO Box 1000, Morgantown, WV 26505. Much needed donations for Rodger to use the prison canteen may be sent via US postal money order only. Be sure to include his ID number on any correspondence.

HASH BASH '93

BY C.J. DAVEY

Authorities were unable once again this year to stifle free expression and make Ann Arbor's annual Hash Bash go up in smoke.

More than 4,000 people braved freezing temperatures and flurries of snow April 3 to gather on the Diag at the University of Michigan and celebrate the 22nd annual freedom festival, which in recent years has become an important networking occasion for the national marijuana movement.

The Freedom Fighters and NORML met at a local tavern for the traditional post-Bash Council. A struggle that had been brewing for some time over the direction of the movement finally came to a head as the Council voted to place control of the Freedom Fighter newsletter and mailing list in the hands of NORML.

The Green Panthers, perhaps the most radical wing of the legalization movement, vocally opposed the idea, charging that NORML is out of touch with the grass-roots activists represented by the Freedom Fighters. In the end, though, most of the assembled activists agreed the move was for the best. NORML's new national director, Dick Cowan, was optimistic that there would be progress in bringing the groups together.

HighWitness News, #215, August 1993

THE REAL REASON HEMP IS ILLEGAL

BY RICHARD COWAN
NORML NATIONAL DIRECTOR

Hemp is illegal not because of what others are doing but rather because of what the cannabis community is *not* doing. There are almost certainly more pot smokers than there are blacks or gays in America. Consider the progress that these groups have made against brutal police oppression. Consider how little we have made. I know all the reasons (read: *excuses* we have for being underlings) but let me offer you a little analysis and then tell you what we at NORML are doing about it.

Let me emphasize that I am not fantasizing about millions of us rising up. We don't need an uprising, just a conventional political organization doing the same thing that everyone else does. And we don't need millions or even hundreds of thousands, just tens of thousands.

HighWitness Views, #221, January 1994

ORGANIZATIONS DEDICATED TO PERSONAL FREEDOM, SOCIAL CHANGE AND DRUG LAW REFORM

REGIONAL AND NATIONAL GROUPS

**Alliance for Cannabis
Therapeutics and Marijuana-
AIDS Research**
PO Box 21210
Kalorama Station
Washington, DC 20009
(202) 483-8595

**American Anti-Prohibition
League**
3125 Southeast Belmont St.
Portland, OR 97214
(503) 235-4524

American Civil Liberties Union
132 W. 43rd St.
New York, NY 10036
(212) 944-9800

**Americans Against
Marijuana Prohibition**
PO Box 2062
Westminster, MD 21158
(410) 857-6484
FAX: (410) 346-7968

AZ4NORML
PO Box 50434
Phoenix, AZ 85076
(602) 491-1139

Birmingham CAN
PO Box 253
Bessemer, AL 35020

**Business Alliance For
Commerce In Hemp (BACH)**
PO Box 71093
Los Angeles, CA 90071-0093
(310) 288-4152

California NORML
2215-R Market St. #278
San Francisco, CA 94114
(415) 563-5858

Cannabis Action Network
4428 South Carrollton
New Orleans, LA 70119
(504) 482-4094

**Clergy for Enlightened Drug
Policy**
St. Luke's Methodist Church
Wisconsin Ave. and Calvert St. NW
Washington, DC 20016

Colorado NORML
137 West Country Line Road #500
Littleton, CO 80126
(303) 470-1100

Drug Policy Foundation (DPF)
4455 Connecticut Ave. NW
Suite B-500
Washington, DC 20008-2302
(202) 537-5005

**Emergency Coalition for
Medical Cannabis**
1001 Connecticut Ave. NW
Suite B-500
Washington, DC 20036

Florida NORML
800 W. Oakland Pk. Blvd.
Suite #102
Wilton Manors, FL 33311
(305) 763-1900

Future of Freedom Foundation
PO Box 9752
Denver, CO 80209

Green Panthers!
PO Box 9845
Washington, DC 20016
(202) 363-0068

**Help End Marijuana
Prohibition (HEMP)**
Box 42, Student Organization
Southeast Missouri State
University
1 University Plaza
Cape Girardeau, MO 63701

Hemp Advocates
PO Box 10176
South Bend, IN 46680

**Hemp Environmental
Activists**
PO Box 4935
East Lansing, MI 48826
(517) 371-HEMP

Houston NORML
PO Box 1952
Bellaire, TX 77402

Institute for HEMP
PO Box 65130
St. Paul, MN 55165
(612) 222-2628

Maine Vocals
PO Box 189
Anson, ME 04911

**Massachusetts Cannabis
Reform Coalition (MASS CAN)**
One Homestead Rd.
Marblehead, MA 01945
(617) 944-CANN

**Multidisciplinary Association
for Psychedelic Studies, Inc.
(MAPS)**
1801 Tippah Avenue
Charlotte, NC 28205
(704) 358-9830

**National Drug
Strategy Network**
2000 L St. NW, Ste. 702
Washington, DC 20036
(202) 835-9075

Northcoast Ohio NORML
PO Box 771154
Cleveland, OH 44107-0049
(216) 521-WEED

North Idaho TEACH
PO Box 155
Sagle, ID 83860
(208) 265-5096

**Northwest Hemp
Foundation**
333 S.W. Park Avenue
Portland, OR 97205
(800) 595-HEMP

Ohio NORML
PO Box 36
New Plymouth, OH 45654
(614) 385-4167

**Therapeutic & Ecological
Applications of
Cannabis Hemp
(TEACH)**
PO Box 1297
Youngstown, FL 32466

Texas NORML
PO Box 13549
Austin, TX 78711
(512) 441-4099

**U-Mass at Amherst
Cannabis Reform
Coalition**
S.A.O. Mailbox #2
Student Union Building
UMass Amherst, MA 01003

**United Marijuana
Smokers of Michigan
(UMSOM)**
11280 McKinley
Taylor, MI 48180

University of MN NORML
CMU 235
300 Washington Ave. SE
Minneapolis, MN 55455

**Vermont Civil
Coalition Against
Prohibition**
63 George St.
Burlington, VT 05401
(802) 864-7107

Vermonters For Pot Peace
PO Box 237
Underhill, VT 05489

Vermont Grassroots Party
PO Box 537
Waitsfield, VT 05673
(802) 496-2387

Vermont Vocals
RFD 1 Box 148
Newport, VT 05855

Virginia BACH
Route 1, Box 2142
Crewe, VA 23930
(804) 645-1038

**Washington Citizens for
Drug Policy Reform**
PO Box 1614
Renton, WA 98057
(206) 227-4164

INTERNATIONAL GROUPS

**A & G Hanf und FuB
Forschungsprojekt zur
Hanfkutur**
c/o Nachtschatten-Verlag
Ritterquai 2-4
4502 Solothurm
Schweiz

Flinders NORML
c/o Clubs and Societies
Association Inc.
Flinders University
BEDFORD PARKS AUSTRALIA
5042

**H. A. N. F. e.V.
(Hanf als Nutzpflanze fördern
eingetragener Verein)**
c/o Hodge, SchloBstr. 33
BRD-14059 Berlin
Tel: 030-342-95-26

Hemp UK
Middleway Workshops
Summertown
Oxford 0X2 7LG,
UK
Tel: 0865-311-151

**International
Anti-Prohibitionist League**
PO Box 6128
University of Montreal
Criminology Dept.
Montreal, Quebec H3C 3S7
CANADA

Legalise Cannabis Campaign
BM Box 2455
London WC1N 3XX
UK

Museo della Civita Contadina
Via S. Maria 35
400 10 Bentivoglio
Italia
Tel: 891-050

**Verein Schweizer Hanf Freunde
(Association of Hemp Friends)**
Postfach 323
9004 St. Gallen
PC 90-18025-5
SWITZERLAND

PART 6
MEDICAL MARIJUANA

DUE IN LARGE PART TO THE GROWING AIDS CRISIS, THE FIGHT FOR
MEDICAL MARIJUANA HAS BECOME THE MOST IMPORTANT ISSUE IN
THE BATTLE FOR LEGALIZATION.

MARIJUANA & HEALTH

BY PETER GORMAN

Although cannabis has been subjected to endless study and clinical analysis, very little can be stated categorically as to its effect on health. The scientific literature is confusing and contradictory, and the marijuana issue polarizes emotions, making moralists of scientists. Since every researcher is aware that his or her work is going to be used somehow by someone in the case for legalizing or not legalizing public consumption, personal and political bias seems to filter through the work.

Marijuana and its compounds are not simple drugs. What shows up theoretically doesn't always appear in the lab; what appears in the lab doesn't always appear in clinical practice. Being a psychotropic, its effects can vary widely from user to user. Perhaps it confounds science because it is a psychotropic. Spiritual aids are rarely classifiable.

In a time when designer cocktails can blow you into deep space with a single dose, and crack makes instant addicts of nearly everyone who smokes it, the issues of marijuana and its significance to health seem trivial. But here at HIGH TIMES, where pot is still king, we thought you should be appraised of developments in the field.

First things first: Nobody's found web-footed babies, tiny testes, atrophied brains, shrunken limbs or 44Ds in the average pot-smoking male's contribution to conception.

But that doesn't mean perpetual intoxication has the green light.

#147, November 1987

ELVY MUSIKKA

ANDRE GROSSMANN

In a triumphant decision for medical marijuana advocates, a Broward County (Florida) Circuit Court Judge ruled on August 15 that Elvy Musikka, a 43-year-old Hollywood FL resident and glaucoma sufferer, had a medical need for marijuana that far outweighed the law's need to prosecute her.

Ms. Musikka was arrested last March 4 on charges of felony possession and cultivation of three cannabis plants (approx. 300 grams), which she willingly showed to tipped-off police with the words, "I need to save my sight."

HighWitness News by Lou Stathis, #159, November 1988

THE BATTLE FOR MEDICAL MARIJUANA

by Peter Gorman

In September, 1972, Robert Randall, an aspiring speech writer from Washington, DC, was diagnosed with glaucoma—a degenerative eye disease and the leading cause of blindness in the US—and placed on the standard medical treatment. Unfortunately, he developed tolerances to drug therapy and his sight, which already suffered from massive damage to both eyes, continued to degenerate. By early 1974 he was approaching maximum allowable doses. His disease was out of control.

But in the fall of 1973, Randall, a former marijuana user who hadn't smoked since his diagnosis, smoked two joints someone had given him before going to bed one night. "When I got done," he says, "I looked at a streetlight outside my window and noticed there were no tri-colored halos like I usually saw when the pressure in my eyes built up." After six months of experimentation, he'd incorporated marijuana into his medical care—without telling his doctor. For the first time his disease began to come under control.

Randall began growing his own marijuana to insure a supply, and was arrested in August 1975. Shortly after his arrest he discovered that both NIDA and the Food and Drug Administration (FDA) not only had information on the use of marijuana in the treatment of glaucoma, but that NIDA grew marijuana for research on a farm at the University of Mississippi at Hattiesburg.

In December 1975, Randall underwent a 13-day controlled experiment at UCLA under the direction of Dr. Robert Hepler, to test the efficacy of marijuana in glaucoma therapy. The study concluded that left on conventional therapy, Randall would either go blind or be forced into risky surgery.

The conclusions of a second set of tests, conducted at the Wilmer Eye Institute at Johns Hopkins University in March 1976—during which he was given the highest doses of the most effective drugs used in glaucoma therapy but no marijuana—were that Randall was a candidate for immediate surgery.

Following that test, and using the conclusions of both, in May 1976 Randall petitioned the Drug Enforcement Administration (DEA) for immediate access to medical marijuana. In November 1976, NIDA, FDA and DEA jointly agreed to provide it through Dr. John Merritt at Howard University in Washington, DC. The same test conclusions were later used in court as a "defense of medical necessity" in Randall's criminal case. All charges against him were dismissed on November 24, 1976.

The federal government continued to supply Randall with medical marijuana until January 1978—when his supply was abruptly cut off following his refusal to stop speaking publicly about his medication. Randall launched a suit to reacquire legal medical marijuana in May of that year. The Federal government agreed to an out-of-court settlement and the Compassionate IND program was born.

This established a precedent by which patients, through their doctors, could be provided access to a drug prior to its approval for marketing. Randall has been receiving 300 marijuana cigarettes per month ever since as part of his medical therapy, and with the exception of the short period in early 1978 when his supply was interrupted, his glaucoma has remained stable. Though his sight is limited, he has not gone blind.

Kenny and Barbra Jenks of Florida's Panama City made a similar discovery concerning the efficacy of marijuana after they contracted AIDS through a tainted blood supply. Kenny, a hemophiliac, found he was ill when his wife Barbra came down with pneumocystis, a form of pneumonia often found in AIDS patients, in December 1988. Both tested positive for AIDS and began AZT therapy.

One month from the time she entered the hospital, Barbra had lost 40 pounds, one-third of her body weight. Kenny didn't begin to lose weight until the AZT therapy began, but by the end of that same month he had lost 10 pounds.

"It was impossible to eat," he explained shortly before his death from the disease in July 1993. "And when we did, the nausea brought on by the AZT could last several hours."

Doctors at the Bay Medical Center in Florida prescribed six different medications for the nausea, but none worked. "Then we started going to an AIDS support group in Bay County, where someone told us he used pot and it took his nausea away," said Kenny.

Though the Jenks were nonsmokers—he'd tried it a few times during high school, Barbra never had—they felt they had nothing to lose. Barbra, who has also since died, once said that the first time Kenny smoked, "he went into the refrigerator and ate everything in sight. That's when I decided to try it as well." During the following year she regained 35 pounds. Kenny described marijuana as effective enough to stop nausea even in the middle of a bout. "Just a few puffs and the nausea goes away."

Like Randall, they too began to grow it to provide themselves with a supply, and like Randall, they were arrested. The Jenks pleaded innocent on the grounds of medical necessity—but their defense was barred by the judge. They were convicted of marijuana possession, cultivation and possession of drug paraphernalia. Judge Clinton E. Foster, recognizing their bind, sentenced them to one year's probation and 500 hours of community service, "to be served loving and caring for each other."

In June, 1990, their doctor applied for Compassionate IND access to marijuana, and eight months later, on February 22, 1991, the Jenks received their first shipment of legal marijuana. Later that same year the Florida Court of Appeals overturned their conviction. The decision was upheld in Florida Supreme Court, establishing the defense of medical necessity in that state.

To Robert Randall, marijuana is a medicine, not a recreational drug. Randall says emphatically that he would be blind without it, and several studies confirm this. Kenny Jenks used to say that Barbra would not have made it through the first Spring following her pneumocystis without it, and credited it with prolonging his life as well.

They are not alone. Across the country marijuana is being illegally used by thousands of afflicted people who claim it is not only safer but more effective than prescriptive medicine in treating the symptoms of numerous disorders.

MEDICAL POT ON HOLD

The Drug Enforcement Administration is currently standing in the way of one of the biggest breakthroughs regarding marijuana legalization. Though the DEA's chief administrative law judge Francis Young recommended in September that pot be legalized for treatment of multiple scierosis and nausea suffered by cancer patients undergoing chemotherapy, the DEA issued a 75-page document in November recounting the standard government exceptions to medical marijuana usage. A finding by the DEA's Administrator John Lawn is expected sometime this year.

At issue is changing marijuana's status from a Schedule I drug (heroin, PCP, LSD) to a Schedule II drug "so that it can be employed in treatment by physicians in proper cases," Judge Young concluded.

"The case is an overwhelmingly powerful one," says NORML's lawyer Kevin Zeese. "Unless you have a closed mind and ignore the inescapable evidence, you can't help but reach this conclusion."

The 16-year-old case will be reviewed by Lawn, who Zeese expects will agree with the DEA's exceptions. The next step would be for NORML to file suit with the Court of Appeals. "We're looking at at least another two years," Zeese estimates.

HighWitness News by Steve Bloom, #162, February 1989

RICK MORRIS

Millions of marijuana smokers have experienced "the munchies." But for Rick Morris, a cancer patient in Staffordsville, Kentucky, pot before dinner has become a matter of life and death.

After two years of radiation therapy and chemotherapy for brain tumors, lung and liver cancer, Morris, 32, says pot is the only thing that turns on his appetite. Not only have the therapies destroyed his salivary glands and hypothalamus—the part of the brain that controls eating—but Morris suffers from constant nausea.

Morris's fight is not only against cancer. He's also battling the law. While two glaucoma patients in the US are currently smoking pot with the Federal government's permission, Morris is the first cancer patient to be arrested and live long enough to challenge his state's marijuana classification in court. He was tried last year in Eastern Kentucky US District Court after being charged with misdemeanor possession of 7 1/2 ounces. Fined just $1, the case was widely heralded as a victory for Morris.

HighWitness News by J.W. Spector, #164, April 1989

THC AND THE BRAIN

Those of us who have tried marijuana know the high. But what does marijuana actually do to the body? What are the actual physiological effects that create the "high?" Recent research has been making great progress towards answering these questions.

Long studied for its analgesic or painkilling properties, marijuana has 421 molecular compounds, but only one main psychoactive compound—delta-9-tetrahydrocannabinol—better known as THC.

Cannabinoids affect the central nervous system, specifically the brain. Cannabinoid molecules and their effects on the brain and body have been extensively studied by Dr. Allyn Howlett, a pharmacology professor at St. Louis University Medical School. In the fall of 1988, Dr. Howlett and her group had a breakthrough. They located receptor sites on cell membranes that were coded for a major cannabinoid molecule.

#172, December 1989

LINDA PARKER

In the small town of Camp Verde, Arizona, just 60 miles north of Phoenix, Linda Parker, a middle-aged, terminally ill woman and her 18-year old daughter were quietly sleeping in their mobile home when they were abruptly awakened by the sound of several officers from the Narcotics Task Force kicking in their front door.

Parker, who suffers nausea and spasms from an intestine stapling operation she had 15 years ago, had been using marijuana to treat her ailments. After trying several different prescription drugs, Parker found that marijuana best alleviated her physical problems. Parker contends that marijuana, used in conjunction with her own self-healing techniques, has allowed her to live way beyond her projected life expectancy.

The Narcotics Task Force goons threw Parker to the floor, pointed guns and spit in her face, and held her down while they ransacked the mobile home and trashed her greenhouse. Desperately trying to appeal to some shred of humanity within the three officers who held her down, she exclaimed, "I'm terminally ill, what about my rights?" The officers replied mockingly, "We're at war—you have no rights."

HighWitness News by Mitch Stillman, #175, March 1990

Chris Woiderski of Tampa is a paraplegic who uses marijuana to control his muscle spasms—which "can be as simple as one of my feet tapping, or I can have them to where I'll be sitting in a chair and I'll suddenly go rigid as a board." Paralyzed from the chest down by a shooting accident in 1989, Woiderski began to experience severe muscle spasms shortly afterward. To combat the spasms, he was placed on Baclofen, Valium and Darvon, and within 10 months of the accident was taking 480 prescriptive pills per month.

But the therapy provided Woiderski little relief, and the medications' side effects were intolerable. He was in a continual drugged state which left him incapacitated. He suffered weight loss, insomnia, severe headaches and developed a problem with his left kidney that now requires surgery.

But while undergoing treatment at the Tampa VA hospital, several paralyzed patients told Woiderski they used marijuana to control their muscle spasms. "I'd smoked occasionally, but never since the accident," he says, "and I was skeptical. So I investigated at the local university's medical library and found several papers dealing with marijuana's success with spasms. So I tried it."

He discovered that half-a-joint in the morning before his first transfer from his bed to the wheelchair controls his spasms for about six hours. Another half-a-joint during the afternoon controls them for the remainder of the day, and a whole joint before bed "lets me sleep without being tossed around all night." Since then, Woiderski has stopped all prescriptive medication, returned to college, and helped organize Paralyzed Americans for Legal Medical Marijuana (PALM).

On November 16, 1990, Woiderski's neurologist—who wishes to remain anonymous—applied for Compassionate IND access to marijuana. He was approved on February 16, 1991, but has never received a shipment. HHS started to phase out the Compassionate IND in June 1991, suspending all shipments to 28 recent approvals. On March 4, 1992, the program was officially shut down for all but those 13 persons who were already receiving the government pot. The only official comment made at the time of the program's suspension came from James Mason, MD, director of PHS. "If it's perceived that the Public Health Service is going around giving marijuana to folks, there would be a perception that this stuff can't be so bad," Mason told the *Washington Post* on June 22, 1991. "It gives a bad signal."

Others in the Bush administration disagreed. Shortly before Mason made his comments, Herbert D. Kleber, the deputy national drug control policy director at the Drug Czar's office, was "touting the program on national television as a 'compassionate' option that was available to seriously ill patients," according to the *Washington Post* report. On January 31, 1992, the *Los Angeles Times* reported that Ingrid Kolb, acting deputy director of the Office of Demand Reduction, another post under the Drug Czardom, "said that dozens of patients who would have been eligible for the drug 'are suffering from great pain—many are dying.'" She recommended that marijuana be given immediately to patients approved for it.

The decision to shut down the Compassionate IND program has placed thousands of medical marijuana users in the position of having to either continue to secure their marijuana illegally or forego the therapy altogether. "I resent being criminalized because the medicine I use for an incurable disease has arbitrarily been made illegal," says Connie Tillman, an award-winning cable-access talk show host, the mother of two and a muscular sclerosis sufferer who says marijuana markedly decreases her muscle spasms. Others, like Fred Cole, agree. Cole, a fishing guide from Washington state, uses marijuana for back spasms resulting from a logging injury and has spent time in jail for growing marijuana for personal medicinal use.

Before the IND was shut down, the government had implicitly acknowledged marijuana's utility in treatment of glaucoma, chemotherapy nausea, chronic pain, the AIDS wasting syndrome and spasm disorders. But studies and anecdotal evidence also suggest it is beneficial in treating arthritis, anorexia, head injuries, epilepsy, migraines, PMS, sickle cell anemia and stress disorders.

But if marijuana is so effective in the symptomatic treatment of these ailments, why is it illegal as a medicine? And why was the Compassionate IND program shut down?

In brief, marijuana had been popular in a variety of tinctures until the Marijuana Tax Act of 1937 made prescriptive use of the plant obsolete. The 1937 Act was opposed by the American Medical Association's lobbyist, Dr. William C. Woodward, but the medical industry ultimately acquiesced to the new order. There were few protests when the 1970 Federal Controlled Substances Act placed marijuana in the Schedule 1 category, meaning it had no recognized medical value or applications, and could not be used even for experimental purposes.

Shortly after the Compassionate IND was shut down, Rayford Kytle, a PHS spokesman, was quoted in the April 1, 1992 *Journal of the National Cancer Institute* as saying that the program was closed because the "National Institute of Health believes there are better and safer treatments than smoked marijuana for controlling chemotherapy-induced nausea, relieving eye pressure caused by glaucoma and stimulating the appetites of patients with HIV-wasting syndrome." Kytle added that NIH scientists believe the presence of carcinogens in marijuana smoke pose a significant health hazard to AIDS and chemotherapy patients, whose immune systems are impaired. "There was concern that NIDA's supply could not keep pace with the increasing demand," said Kytle.

Both Kytle and PHS chief James Mason made it clear that dronabinol—a synthetic derivative of marijuana, marketed under the name Marinol—would continue to be available for chemotherapy-related nausea.

While there have been no reliable reports of marijuana smokers who do not also smoke cigarettes developing either emphysema or lung cancer, studies indicate that heavy cannabis smoking does produce some respiratory system damage. If an alternate method of delivery could be devised—an aerosol spray or vaporization are frequently touted possibilities—that damage could be eliminated. But current US laws banning the production of drug paraphernalia prevent experimentation with these methods. Until new delivery systems are available, however, proponents feel that the potential benefits of smoked marijuana outweigh the dangers. They point to more than 2,000 years of historical medicinal marijuana use worldwide with no long-term negative effects.

Many doctors feel similarly. In a 1990 study conducted by researchers Richard Doblin and Dr. Mark Kleiman, a random, anonymous sampling of 2,430 cancer specialists from the American Society for Clinical Oncology showed 48% of the respondents answering that they would prescribe marijuana if it were available, and 44% admitted they had already recommended illegal marijuana use to at least one patient.

GORDON HANSON

JACKIE LORENTZ/COURTESY GRAND FORK HERALD

BY MARY LYNN MATHRE
On the morning of July 27, 1989, 51-year-old Gordon Hanson of Lake of the Woods, Minnesota, was busted for growing 120 marijuana plants. Five armed law officers, including a border patrolman, a highway patrolman, the local sheriff and two deputies, broke down his front door to make the arrest. Handcuffing Hanson and his son to kitchen chairs, they proceeded upstairs where his wife awoke with a rifle aimed at her head. Hanson's daughters, who live nearby, were on their way over to go blueberry picking with their mother, but were not permitted on the property while the drug bust was in progress. They looked on in horror as their father and brother were taken way in handcuffs.

Since he was 18, Hanson has suffered from epilepsy—also known as convulsive disorder or seizure disorder. About one in every 250 people have epilepsy—roughly one million Americans. Epileptic seizures are caused by uncontrolled electrical discharges in the brain.

Treatment for epilepsy generally requires one or more types of medication prescribed by a physician. Under a physician's care, Hanson was put on various combinations of drugs to control his seizures, including Dilantin, Mysoline and phenobarbitol. For a time, he was taking 11 pills a day. His seizures decreased in frequency, but Hanson complained the medications made him "feel groggy, lose my ambition, be temperamental and not able to communicate well."

After Hanson's physician and marriage counselor concluded that the medications were responsible for his complaints, he was prescribed Valium and Tranxene. They didn't help. Finally, it was suggested that he try marijuana. A non-smoker, Hanson began reading about pot's medicinal qualities. After about six months of research, he started using marijuana in 1973. Pot made Hanson feel better. In the ten years prior to his bust, the grand mal seizures disappeared and he experienced only four to five petit mal seizures a year.

Hanson has suffered an alarming number of petit mal seizures (85) since he stopped smoking pot. Hanson says, "I don't think I've done anything wrong...if I could use marijuana, I could return to work."
NORMLizer, #183, November 1990

DEA REJECTS MEDICAL MARIJUANA

BY JON GETTMAN

The legal effort to allow medicinal prescription of marijuana suffered a setback March 18, when Drug Enforcement Administration Chief Robert Bonner issued his final ruling on the Medical Marijuana Petition. Bonner called his decision "a final rule concluding the plant material marijuana has no currently accepted medical use." The DEA hopes this will be the end of medical marijuana litigation.

But Kevin Zeese, attorney for the Drug Policy Foundation, says that medical marijuana advocates are discussing various responses to the DEA ruling, including continued litigation.

Administrative Law Judge Francis Young recommended in September 1988 that DEA make marijuana available as medicine. DEA rejected Young's ruling in December 1989. In April 1991 the US Court of Appeals ordered a reconsideration of DEA's decision, rejecting the original ruling on the grounds that the standards used by DEA were impossible to meet. For example, in order to qualify was having "accepted medical use," the substance must have widespread availability in the medical community. This is, of course, impossible for drugs such as marijuana which are subject to legal prohibition.

Bonner complained that, "beyond doubt, the claims that marijuana is medicine are false, dangerous and cruel. Sick men, women and children can be fooled by these claims and experiment with the drug. Instead of being helped, they risk serious side effects...It is a cruel hoax to offer false hope to desperately ill people."

Yet AIDS, cancer, glaucoma, multiple sclerosis and chronic pain patients who have discovered medicinal benefits from marijuana feel that it is cruel to deny them medicine.

HighWitness News, #203, July 1992

DANA BEAL

Dana Beal, lifelong marijuana crusader and veteran of the Yippies, is free after a close brush with a lengthy prison term. This is especially significant because Beal had been busted while delivering medical marijuana to AIDS sufferers, and the judge's decision not to impose the long sentence was based on the undisputed morality of Beal's actions.

Beal was busted at New York's LaGuardia airport while on his way to a Boston meeting of Treament on Demand, a group of Massachusetts African-American drug treatment professionals, where he was to give an address on Ibogaine, the African herbal addiction-interrupter he is promoting. But in his suitcase were two pounds of marijuana intended for distribution to Boston-area AIDS sufferers.

HighWitness News by Bill Weinberg and Peter Gorman, #214, June 1993

Kytle's concern over marijuana's effects on the immune system also appears to be unfounded. While early studies did indicate that exposure to large amounts of cannabinoids produced alterations in the immune function of animals and cells, human studies do not confirm any correlation between marijuana use and impairment of the immune function.

Kytle's third reason for the program's closure, concern that federal supply would not keep pace with increasing demand might be a reason for producing a larger supply—but doesn't warrant additional comment.

As for Marinol, it is a synthetic derivative of cannabis which contains only one of the active constituents of marijuana, delta-9-tetrahydrocannabinol, or THC. While some users find relief through this pill form of THC, many complain that it doesn't work as well as marijuana, that it takes longer to begin working, and that they prefer the dosage control they have when smoking marijuana to the lack of control they have with the pill. The National Cancer Institute agreed in a 1992 factsheet titled *Marijuana for Chemotherapy-Induced Nausea and Vomiting*: "Research has shown that the active ingredient THC is more readily and quickly absorbed from marijuana smoke than from an oral preparation of the substance."

Medical marijuana proponents maintain that those suffering diseases for which there are no acceptable medical alternatives should have their choice of therapy in the hands of physicians rather than the DEA, which controls the Controlled Substances schedule.

Despite the Public Health Service's refusal to restore the Compassionate IND program, there is increasing evidence of a change in the public's view of marijuana as medicine. Proposition P, a medical marijuana measure, was put on the ballot in San Francisco in 1991. It passed with an overwhelming 80% of the vote. And in 1992, in considerably more conservative Santa Cruz County, a similar ballot initiative gained 77% of the vote. Since then, dozens of similar initiatives and propositions have been passed nationally. Additionally, 35 states have endorsed the use of medical marijuana—although none of them are actually distributing cannabis at this time because the federal agencies which control the supply will not provide it. (During the early '80s, state programs in California, Georgia, Michigan, New Mexico, New York and Tennessee provided a total of nearly 800 patients with medical marijuana supplied by the National Institute of Drug Abuse, but Federal bureaucratic interference and expense led to their closing.)

This change in the perception of marijuana as medicine is rooted in a decision by the DEA's own Administrative Law Judge Francis L. Young, who ruled in the case of *Alliance for Cannabis Therapeutics, et al, vs. US Drug Enforcement Administration*, in the matter of *Marijuana Medical Rescheduling Petition*. In his September 1988 determination, Judge Young said: "One must reasonably conclude that there is accepted safety for use of marijuana under medical supervision. To conclude otherwise...would be unreasonable, arbitrary and capricious...."

On the question of whether marijuana as a whole plant, as opposed to synthetic derivatives such as Marinol, should be used, Judge Young said: "The cannabis plant considered as a whole has a currently accepted medical use in treatment in the United States...and it may lawfully be transferred from Schedule I to Schedule II." The rescheduling would have legalized medical marijuana. But the DEA, under the direction of John C. Lawn, refused to act on Judge Young's decision.

One of the consequences of the DEA's refusal to reschedule marijuana was that many physicians who accept marijuana's therapeutic value began to publicly call for the right to prescribe it. On March 17, 1992, the 450-member House of Delegates of the California Medical Association voted to adopt a resolution sponsored by Berkeley psychiatrist Dr. Todd Mikuriya which, while opposing the recreational use of marijuana, stated that "the therapeutic use of cannabinoids...may be appropriate for certain conditions." More recently, the House of Delegates for the American Medical Student Association, at their 1993 Miami Conference, unanimously endorsed marijuana's rescheduling. And this past August 26, California became the fourth state to pass a resolution urging the White House and Congress to make marijuana prescriptively available.

These changes in public awareness of medical marijuana have been reflected in court decisions as well. The Jenks conviction, as previously noted, was overturned. And in October 1993, a jury acquitted 39-year-old AIDS-sufferer Sam Skipper of two counts of felony marijuana cultivation despite his admission that the more than 20 plants found in his California home were his. It was the first such acquittal in US history.

Additionally, the courts have recently taken a more lenient view of care-givers—those who provide marijuana to seriously ill patients. "Brownie" Mary Rathbun, a 70-year-old from San Francisco, was arrested in July 1992, when she was caught folding two pounds of marijuana into her brownie mix for free distribution to AIDS sufferers. She faced a five-year sentence on felony charges. But all charges against her were dismissed when the local District Attorney refused to prosecute. And when Oregon care-giver Sharon Place, arrested in May 1990 for growing 64 plants for free distribution to cancer, MS and AIDS patients, was convicted of manufacture and possession of marijuana, she faced 18 months—but the judge gave her only two years probation and 80 hours community service.

Whether any of these developments will hasten a rescheduling of marijuana to allow for its prescriptive use is unknown. But there is considerable optimism among medicinal marijuana advocates that the election of Bill Clinton will bring a change in federal policy. Clinton's appointment of Dr. Joycelyn Elders—who favors medical marijuana use under certain conditions—as Surgeon General is a hopeful signal. Secretary of Health Donna Shalala's order to the PHS to look into the Compassionate IND program may also bode well.

But if the decision is made to reopen the program, both Clinton and Shalala will not only have to face political heat from those who applauded the closure of the program. They'll also have to contend with the bureaucratic question of how to provide medical marijuana to new applicants. This is a problem the PHS never had to contend with, as Compassionate IND access to marijuana was never given to more than 15 people at one time. But with awareness of marijuana's benefits spreading rapidly through the AIDS, cancer, MS and paraplegic communities, it is conceivable that tens, and perhaps hundreds of thousands of people will ask their doctors to apply for the program. Providing the amount of marijuana necessary to meet those needs would require a major effort.

One short-term solution to the problem would be to have the DEA provide confiscated marijuana to the PHS for distribution, after it has been heated to eliminate potentially harmful bacteria or mold. For the

KENNY JENKS

BY ROBERT RANDALL
Some people see my good friend Kenny's life as unvarnished tragedy. Born with hemophilia, Kenny contracted AIDS from a tainted blood transfusion, then unknowingly passed the disease to his wife, Barbra. Helpless, he watched Barbra die an agonizing death. Having lived this horror, Kenny himself died of AIDS on July 19th. He was 31 years old.

Kenny Jenks was not a fragile, button-down man. While coming of age he hunted, trapped game and fished. He sold pelts, herded cattle, hiked the desert, worked on old cars and ran off with the girl he loved. As a grown man he cleaned bars, worked in convenience stores, sold hot dogs on the beach, installed fire alarms. a regular guy living a regular life on Florida's redneck Riviera.

Then came AIDS. And then came jail.

When I met Kenny he was a lonely, frightened guy. His world had imploded. He was dying. His wife was dying. And just arrested, he was facing 15 years in prison. The state of Florida, having nothing better to do with taxpayers' money, wanted to incarcerate Kenny and Barbra Jenks for smoking marijuana to ease the debilitating nausea, vomiting and rapid weight loss caused by advanced HIV infection.

In private, Kenny called Washington's drug warriors "practicing, professional jerks." In public he was much more candid. "The DEA is killing people with AIDS. That's wrong!"

He didn't much like being pushed around by government types who wanted to regulate his life and manage his death. Kenny asked questions that caused other Americans to think. Which is why the pointy-headed bureaucrats came to hate him.

Kenny and Barbra faced fear together, fought an unjust law, and won. Kenny and Barbra Jenks made legal and medical history when the Florida Supreme Court eventually ruled their use of marijuana was not criminal but an act of "medical necessity." Their victory gave courage, comfort and hope to millions of Americans weary of oppressive prohibitions and the petty, pension-pandering authoritarians who enforce them.

When Barbra died I asked Kenny if he wanted to stop. "Robert, I can't stop. I'm the last AIDS patient in America with legal marijuana. People with AIDS are still starving. I have to speak out. Besides, Barbra would have a fit if I didn't."

HighWitness News, #219, November 1993

ROBERT C. RANDALL

ANDRE GROSSMANN

BY PETER GORMAN

In 1971, Robert C. Randall was diagnosed as having glaucoma, a degenerative disease of the eyes which, if untreated (or treated with traditional medicines), leads to blindess. Two years later he made the discovery that smoking marijuana temporarily alleviated the symptoms of the disease.

He began a series of experiments with marijuana—used in conjunction with his regular medicinal regimen—which proved to his satisfaction that marijuana indeed aided his condition.

To ensure a supply of what had become a medical necessity, he began to grow his own. Unfortunately, a neighbor reported him to the police while he was away on vacation in 1975, and he returned home to discover his house in disarray, a search warrant on the table, and a request to turn himself in for arrest.

Thus began a two-year fight to acquire legal, government-provided marijuana—a fight Randall won in 1977, when he became the first person in the USA to receive medical marijuana.

Over the past 16 years, Randall has published four books on marijuana and medicine, founded the Alliance for Cannabis Therapeutics, and started both the MARS and PALM programs, which are designed to make sure that legal medical marijuana is available to all who need it.

Interview by Peter Gorman, #194, October 1991

long run, the government could simply plant enough to supply citizen needs until licensed private marijuana farms could be established. An alternate to those solutions would be to allow those who need medical marijuana to grow their own, or designate someone to grow it for them.

All of those solutions are political minefields: providing confiscated cannabis raises the question of quality control, since the cannabis would vary widely in potency. Using confiscated marijuana would also lead to the moral quandary of a government encouraging illegal marijuana production to ensure an adequate supply for medicine while imprisoning those who would be the suppliers. And it will be difficult to convince diehard opponents of medical marijuana to back government planting of thousands of acres of cannabis. Licensing private marijuana farms would also bring political heat. And allowing people to grow their own for medical purposes would terrify the police agencies.

But the bureaucratic concerns involved in making marijuana medically available to those who are suffering are only a distraction from the real issue. The question is not *how* we will solve the problem, but whether the administration is willing to make the effort to solve it. And if so, when?

It remains to be seen in which direction the administration will turn.

NOTE: Readers wanting the annotations and bibliography for this article are asked to send a self-addressed 9" x 12" envelope with two 29-cent stamps to: HIGH TIMES, 235 Park Ave. So., 5th Fl., New York, NY 10003, Attention: Peter Gorman.

PART 7
ROCK FOR POT

IN 1993, ROCK AND RAP STARS MOVED TO THE FOREFRONT
OF THE LEGALIZATION MOVEMENT.

BOB MARLEY

ARTHUR GERSON/COURTESY ISLAND

HT: Have you seen HIGH TIMES magazine?
BM: Hard Times? Ooo-ee! Ooo-eee! HIGH TIMES! Dis supposed to 'ave de bes' high in de worl'. HIGH TIMES, only de bes'.
HT: Some Thai weed?
[Pause.] **Do you think herb will be legalized?**
BM: I don't know if dis government will, but I know Christ's government will.
HT: What about the Jamaican government?
BM: It's kinda legalized already.
HT: What's lamb's bread?
BM: De ability what de herb 'ave ya call lamb's bread. Dat is when ya really get good herb.
HT: Do you find it hard to get good herb?
BM: Me fin' it hard to get in England.
HT: In England, they always mix it with tobacco. It's really foul.
BM: Yeah, man. It's time to let de people get good herbs an' smoke. Government's a joke. All dey wan' is ya smoke cigarettes and cigar. Some cigar wickeder than herb. Yeah, man, ya can't smoke cigar. Smoke herb.
This Man Is Seeing God, #13, September 1976

JERRY GARCIA

KEN FRIEDMAN

HT: Have you been to the rainforest?
JG: I've been to a couple of them, the Yucatan down in Mexico, and Hawaii. It's definitely not friendly to humans—you're covered with bugs in a matter of seconds—everything else eats you. It's weird as hell, but it's an amazing place. From an aesthetic point of view, the world should leave it alone just for that. Just so there is such a place.

The rainforest problem seems so remote. We started hearing the bad news about this 20 years ago. They said, "We gotta do something about the rainforest. They're burning it down—they're tearing it up even as we talk." Now, here it is 20 years later, and sure enough, the rainforests are almost gone now. Fifty years—they'll all be gone. That's it. Fifty years is not a long time anymore. That's in the life span of my kids.
Interview by Legs McNeil, #162, February 1989

FLYIN' HIGH WITH THE BLACK CROWES
by Steve Bloom

Chris Robinson is mad as hell and isn't gonna take it anymore. That's why I'm sitting in Robinson's spacious living room in Atlanta, GA listening to the Black Crowes' skinny-ass lead singer hold court about pot. "You're gonna tell me puttin' up a nuclear plant in my neighborhood is good for me, but I'm not allowed to smoke weed?"

HIGH TIMES caught the buzz on the Black Crowes last year. First we heard the group brought out a table full of hemp products at a club in Kentucky while they were on tour. One thing led to another and an interview was set up. Then it was canceled. With the hype building for the release of the Crowes' latest album, *Southern Harmony and Musical Companion* (it hit the stores in May), we heard from their record company once more. My instructions were simply to show up in Atlanta and expect to spend the afternoon "hangin' out with Chris."

So here I am at Chris' crib, drinking a Red Star, smokin' a Southern spliff and checking out Robinson's pro-pot rap. Free's "Alright Now" blares in the background. Two bulldog pups wrestle on the floor as Ed Hawrysch (pronounced "harsh"), the band's keyboard player, twists up another.

"Sometimes it's dry for weeks—you can*not* get any weed," Chris complains. "You tell me it's ever been dry to get fuckin' cocaine? They'll catch you with a bag of cocaine and let you go. They'll catch you with a roach and throw you in jail."

Fortunately, it's not dry today. Puff, puff. The joint travels around the room. We all chase the smoke with chugs on our Red Stripes.

"When you get high, you see things from another angle," Chris says, his laid-back Georgia drawl rising up a notch. "Why would a manipulative government want you to see any angle but the one they're giving you? It's fucking obvious!"

The Black Crowes are on a mission. Today, they're coming out of the pot closet. In the past, Robinson slam-dunked corporate sponsorship of rock (this got them kicked off Miller's ZZ Top tour in March '91) and challenged the use of backup tapes by such major-league acts as Aerosmith, Heart and Robert Plant (the Crowes toured with them all). Simply put, they're determined to take back rock'n'roll from the poseurs and give it a booster shot of nonconformity. "How about just a few good things?" Chris asks. "Real things, real emotions. Not just writing songs because you're gonna get blown at the gig."

Surely such opportunities were available to the band during their long march to the top of the charts in 1990 (Robinson didn't elaborate). Right about then I was one of those people singing along to Robinson's white-boy cover of Otis Redding's "Hard to Handle" ("Hey little baby, lemme light your candle/'Cause mama I'm *so* hard to handle now, yes I am."). A tight package of classic rock and blue-eyed soul, the Black Crowes' debut album *Shake Your Money Maker* made the band rich and famous.

"*Shake Your Money Maker* was really like letting the steam off a pot that's boiling," Chris offers. "That pot was boiling for a couple of years. I think this record [*Southern Harmony*] might be the step in the right direction to something different. Maybe it'll open up a few new doors."

Slamming open the door of the cannabis closet is a new step for the Black Crowes—a door of perception, so to speak. "There's a lot of people into the Black Crowes who've just never probably put two and two together," Chris says. "They just haven't thought of it. Everyone in this band smokes weed." To prove the point, Robinson personally made sure this interview happened. And, in April, the Crowes performed for free at the Atlanta Pot Festival, sponsored by Georgia NORML.

The Black Crowes consist of the Robinson brothers—Chris and his younger guitar-playing brother Rich—bassist Johnny Colt, drummer Steve Gorman, the recently-recruited lead guitarist Marc Ford (formerly with Burning Tree, he replaced Jeff Cease) and Hawrysch, who is the band's unofficial sixth member.

Chris, Hawrysch and Colt are the Crowes' hardcore stoners. Throughout the afternoon Chris and Ed pepper me with questions you'd only ask a HIGH TIMES writer/editor. Ed rolls the fatties and Chris loads up the bong hits. Between weed (apparently the preferred Southern terminology for pot) and beer, we're pleasantly high, chatting like old friends as the day's soundtrack (courtesy of Chris) segues into the chunky New Orleans funk of the Meters.

"When I was young," says Chris, who is 25, "I always listened to groups like Parliament-Funkadelic, Sly & the Family Stone and BT Express." These days, Chris can't get enough of Leon Russell, Humble Pie and *Fresh* by Sly ("we play it at least once a day"). Prince's *Diamonds and Pearls* and Lenny Kravitz's *Mama Said* are the only contemporary discs in his current rotation.

Alternative music turns Chris off ("I just don't like English alternative rock"), and he labels Georgia's favorite rock'n'roll sons, R.E.M., "adult-contemporary," adding with a smirk: "We're not very concerned with being mellow." However, Chris admits that R.E.M. "has always been a great influence, [because] they always did what they wanted to do, regardless of what the record companies and people said—at least that was the illusion."

Actually, there's quite a rivalry between the Black Crowes and the denizens of the Atlanta scene, where R.E.M. and sundry other bands started out. (Athens, the infamous college town and home of the University of Georgia, is about an hour northeast of Atlanta.) "The people that didn't like 'em before," says Ed, an objective outsider from Detroit, "hate 'em even worse now." The Crowes' retro look and sound just don't jibe with the alternative sensibility that put Georgia back on the musical map in recent years. The result is that they've been rather brutally ignored in their home state.

"I just think people in Atlanta fail to see the big picture," Chris says. "The big picture to us wasn't selling out the local rock club—that's only six-hundred people. The big picture for us was trying to be the best band we could be, not having limitations and not letting local music scenes or national music scenes, record labels, money, fame—whatever—that was gonna come down the turnpike really stray us from what we really dug."

Locals remember the Black Crowes in their original incarnation as Mr. Crowe's Garden (named after a children's story). One resident of Atlanta's hip Little Five Points community, where Chris moved when he was 18, described Mr. Crowe's Garden as nothing more than a Monkees cover band. Again, Chris explains:

JIMI HENDRIX

BY JOHN HOLMSTROM
There is no disputing that the death of Jimi Hendrix resulted from complications due to a heavy dose of prescription sleeping pills and alcohol. But he didn't die from a drug overdose. He was not an out-of-control dope fiend or junkie. And anyone who would use his death as a warning to stay away from drugs should warn people against the other things that killed Jimi—the stresses of dealing with the music industry, the craziness of being on the road and, especially, the dangers of involving oneself in radical, or even unpopular, political movements.

COINTELPRO was out to do more than prevent a Communist menace from taking over the United States, or keep the Black Power movement from burning down cities. COINTELPRO was out to obliterate and ruin the reputations of people involved in the antiwar movement, the civil rights movement and the rock revolution. Whenever Jimi Hendrix's death is blamed on drugs, it accomplishes the goals of the FBI's program. It not only slanders Jimi's personal and professional reputation, but the entire rock revolution in the '60s.
Who Killed Jimi Hendrix?, #181, September 1990

BOB DYLAN

BY LARRY JAFFEE
Dylan has said in interviews that he can't remember who turned him on to pot the first time. All he knows is that weed was plentiful in the Minneapolis bohemia, coffeehouse scene that he frequented circa 1960.

According to Eric Von Schmidt, an early '60s contemporary of Dylans's in the Cambridge, MA folk scene, when he, Dylan and singing pal Richard Farina usually got together, "a lot of pot was smoked." A few years later, Von Schmidt remembers being backstage with Dylan at a Joan Baez concert, smoking their brains out: "All of a sudden Joan calls Dylan out to the stage, and he sings what seemed like a hundred verses of 'A Hard Rain's Gonna Fall.' I couldn't believe how this guy could remember all the verses. I was amazed by his ability to function."

In a 1963 *Playboy* interview with Nat Hentoff, Dylan explained what opium, hash and pot meant to him. "Now those things aren't drugs; they just bend your mind a little. I think everybody's mind should be bent once in a while."
Bringing It All Back to Dylan, #210, February 1993

ROCKERS FOR POT

Chris Barron (Spin Doctors): The whole premise of marijuana being illegal is utterly ridiculous and pretty transparent. Basically, it seems to me that marijuana, being an herb that cannot be patented, is just not lucrative compared to patented chemicals, which make billions upon billions of dollars.

Dave Abbruzzese (Pearl Jam): Some of the guys smoke once or twice a month just to take the edge off and have a good time. For others, it's an everyday, after-the-show, enjoy-the-rest-of-the-day thing. As a band, I think everyone would say, "Pot definitely has its place."

Mike Bordin (Faith No More): I happen to enjoy a smoke every now and again. I don't use it in conjunction with acid, speed, coke, alcohol, tobacco or heroin. Pot and hash are what I enjoy. I like how I feel after I take two or three hits off of a fucking bud.
Rockers for Pot by Steve Bloom, #212, April 1993

DAVID PEEL

Before punk there was David Peel, screaming cogent political harangues and songs of frustrated youth over simple guitar chords and pulsating drumbeats. Lyrics like "Up against the wall, motherfucker" (pre-Jefferson Airplane) and "I like marijuana/ You like marijuana too" on *Have a Marijuana* became the rallying cries for an entire generation.
Culture Hero by Harry Wasserman, #28, December 1977.

REDMAN

TIM CARTER/COURTESY RAL

BY GREG CASSEUS
It's time to roll another blunt. Redman takes the opportunity now to compare Phillies and White Owls. "Some people don't use Phillies. Muthafuckas is usin' White Owl for the simple fact that it is a thicker flavor, but it's nastier because it's thicker. It burns real slow. Real slow."

Redman carefully lights the brown bomber. "A lot of people have a problem with lighting a blunt! That's one of the hardest things about the whole shit 'cause, see, muthafuckas think it's a cigarette. They just put it in their mouth and light it. That's why they always get a canoe."

Redman kicks back as the smoke fills the room. "I treat my music as an individual, you know, as a person, a human life," he says in a burst of thought. "You gotta puff weed to get really deep like that."
Rolling With Redman, #211, March 1993

"We were always a rock band. It just wasn't ever as heavy. It was definitely more country-oriented, quirky. The difference [between Mr. Crowe's Garden and the Black Crowes] is like the first time you masturbated in your room and when you had a girlfriend for a year and you started making it happen."

It started happening for the Black Crowes when the Robinson brothers began writing their own songs. After high school, Chris did two short stints in college before quitting school for good. This disappointed his mother, Nancy, who thought Chris was destined to become a teacher and perhaps even write the Great American Novel. Chris tried his hand at songwriting instead.

Chris and Rich grew up in a musical family. Their dad, Stan Robinson, had a solo hit in 1958 with "Boom-a-Dip-Dip," toured with Phil Ochs and was once a member of the folk group, the Appalachians. He met Nancy, also a singer, at a hootenanny in 1965. Stan, however, didn't encourage his sons to become professional musicians. "It's such a hard-ass life," he told *People*. "But once it became apparent they were good at it, we supported them."

About his cool parents, Chris raves: "I love my parents. Any topic was open for conversation. There was nothing taboo."

As a teenager, Chris was into basketball and black music. An anonymous classmate from high school recalls that Chris knew the words to every rap song, liked the group Cameo, regularly sang the "Soooooooul Train" theme song and wallpapered his room with basketball posters. The more I learn about Chris Robinson, the more I realize he's a funky white boy with a heart of soul.

In fact, the original name for *Southern Harmony and Musical Companion* was *Souled Out*. As we listen to it together (it's the first time I've heard it), I find myself moved by its audacity—the songs are catchy in a Top-40 way but are all six to eight minutes long (or so they seem). He promises the singles won't be edited down for radio consumption, which I find hard to believe. Chris' hellfire vocals, the double-lead guitar work and extended jams give *Southern Harmony* plenty of kick and muscle. "No compromise" appears to be the message behind this second Black Crowes album.

Southern Harmony was made in whirlwind style. "We got home, took a week off, then got together one weekend and wrote half the record—lyrics, arrangements—all of it, basically. Got together the next weekend and wrote the rest of it. Went in the studio about a month later, cut it in eight days. Went to LA and mixed it in a night."

This stands in stark contrast to the two months it took to create *Shake Your Money Maker*, which has been on the *Billboard* 200 album chart for two years running (it was No. 98 as of April 4). It's platinum three times over (upwards of 3.5 million copies sold). Chris credits avid support from rock radio and MTV and their heavy touring schedule for the album's prolonged success.

"I don't know why they embraced us," Chris says as he cues up Humble Pie's *Live at the Filmore*. "They could've made it easier on themselves and picked someone else, because, you know, we never pull punches—we tell the truth. If ya ask me, I tell ya."

OK, so what does he think of the Grateful Dead? "I went to my first Dead show [at the Omni] last week. I always dug them for what they stood for and I've always been a Jerry Garcia fan, but I was never into them. Then I got *Workingman's Dead* and checked out the show. That was the most fun I had in a long time. Just trippin' around everywhere. I had the best time."

Hmmm, "trippin' around".... Does he take a lot of acid? "I've done it, but it's sort of [too] chemical [for] me. I like to stay with things that come out of the earth."

What about Ecstasy? "That's such a middle-of-the-road, half-assed drug. I have no room for it. I really don't dig it."

Mushrooms? "Ate a lot of them yesterday. Got really fucked up. Went up on my roof with a bottle of wine, talked about John Coltrane and hung out forever. It was beautiful. The problem with mushrooms is you can conquer the high pretty quick. Where do you go from there?"

"Yeah," Ed jumps in, "is there anything new and organic that we haven't tried yet?"

I suggest some psychedelic jungle concoctions, but remind them that ayahuasca and nu-nu have yet to be bottled and marketed for North American consumption. They're more than content to talk about weed, their favorite organic intoxicant. "We did three-hundred-fifty shows, smoked every night," Chris boasts, "and never got busted." Not even in Moscow, where the Black Crowes joined Metallica and AC/DC for a "Monsters of Rock" extravaganza last year.

"We smoked weed there," he says. "It wasn't very good."

"It was hemp," Ed adds. "It was like smoking rope."

"The excitement in the whole thing was sitting in this tent in Moscow smoking a joint," Chris reports, "with sixty-thousand police and Army troops outside! We didn't know what was going on. They were beating the shit out of anyone who gave them a look. I got kicked. It was heavy."

The Black Crowes manage to secure pot wherever they go. In England, they sampled a variety called Durban Poison that Ed says is "worth going over just to try it." And Amsterdam, the connoisseur-bud capital of the Western world, has virtually become the band's home away from home.

"Pot's nothing to be taboo about, man," Chris says. "It's part of pop culture. In the eighties, it was sorta passé. People who were wrapped up in money saw weed as a frivolous extravagance. It's really old-fashioned. It goes way, way back. I'm really into how it's interwoven into cultures—Afghani culture, Moroccan culture. I'd really, really like to go to Morocco."

Predictably, Kashmir is also on Chris' wish-list of exotic drug meccas to visit. I'm sure he'll get there. But first he has a new album to hustle and another round of touring to do (the Black Crowes' "High as the Moon" tour gets underway in July). "People put so much on you," Chris says as he sucks down another bong hit. "Maybe if we're still around to check out after four or five records, it might be easier to see what the Black Crowes mean to everyone. I'd like to think we represent something that's not in abundance—like a real, live, breathing, rock'n'fuckin'roll band."

And now the Black Crowes also represent the ongoing movement of people all over the world working to legalize marijuana. "If we could only get in the Hemp 100," Chris laughs, "we'd be happy."

SEBASTIAN BACH

WILLIAM HAMES

Bas and his beautiful wife, Maria, visited HIGH TIMES after the Australian finale of Skid Row's 15-month world tour in February. He is an informed advocate of hemp legalization, and an avid reader of HIGH TIMES. "Hey, do you have an extra copy of *Cooking With Cannabis?*" he asked within moments of their arrival. "I want to give one to my friend, Axl Rose.

"I wouldn't tell someone to smoke pot or not to—I'm just telling you how I live. That's why I'm saying it. This is the biggest hypocrisy of all: If Bill Clinton smoked pot, they should go and take his house away. 'Hey, Bill, we're coming over and we're taking the house, Chelsea's cat and Hillary's wardrobe. Why? Because you smoked pot. So you didn't inhale—we'll teach you while we're there.'"

Candy Buds, Hash Coffee & Rock'n'Roll by Brijitte West, #215, July 1993

ZIGGY MARLEY

RUEDI HOFMANN/COURTESY VIRGIN RECORDS

The younger Marleys certainly have quite a reputation to live up to. In the '70s and up until his death in 1981, Bob Marley brought reggae to the masses. Preaching peace and love, Marley's Wailers (Peter Tosh, Bunny Wailer) were Jamaica's Beatles—the island's original reggae royalty espousing Rastafarian notions of spirituality through conscious music and healing herbs.

In 1978, Bob Marley named an album and song for the herb he so admired. "Got to have *kaya* now," Marley sang over and over. Herb songs are a staple of the Melody Makers' albums as well, from 1989's "Urb-an Music" to 1991's "Herbs an' Spices" to the current "African Herbsman," named after the 1970 Bob Marley album.

"'Urb-an Music' is ganja music," Ziggy says. "When we play music, we smoke herbs. So it's herbal music, ya know?"

Manchild in the Promised Land by Steve Bloom, #221, January 1994

INDEX